German-Jewish History
in Modern Times

VOLUME 1
Tradition and Enlightenment
1600–1780

German-Jewish History in Modern Times

VOLUME 1

Tradition and Enlightenment
1600–1780

VOLUME 2

Emancipation and Acculturation
1780–1871

VOLUME 3

Integration in Dispute
1871–1918

VOLUME 4

Renewal and Destruction
1918–1945

Advisory Committee
Jacob Katz, Jürgen Kocka, Werner E. Mosse, Jehuda Reinharz, Reinhard Rürup,
Ismar Schorsch, Fritz Stern, Yosef Hayim Yerushalmi

Coordinator
Fred Grubel

German-Jewish History in Modern Times

Edited by Michael A. Meyer

MICHAEL BRENNER, ASSISTANT EDITOR

VOLUME 1
*Tradition and Enlightenment
1600–1780*

MORDECHAI BREUER • MICHAEL GRAETZ

Translated by William Templer

A Project of the Leo Baeck Institute

Columbia University Press

NEW YORK

Columbia University Press
Publishers Since 1893
New York   Chichester, West Sussex
Copyright © 1996 Leo Baeck Institute

Library of Congress Cataloging-in-Publication Data

Deutsch-jüdische Geschichte in der Neuzeit. English.
    German-Jewish history in modern times / edited by Michael A. Meyer
and Michael Brenner, assistant editor.
        p.   cm.
    "A project of the Leo Baeck Institute."
    Includes bibliographical references and index.
    Contents: v. 1. Tradition and enlightenment : 1600 –1780 /
Mordechai Breuer, Michael Graetz; translated by William Templer.
    ISBN 0-231-07472-7
    1. Jews—Germany—History. 2. Judaism—Germany—History.
3. Haskalah—Germany—History. 4. Germany—Ethnic relations.
5. Germany—Ethnic relations. I. Meyer, Michael A. II. Brenner,
Michael. III. Breuer, Mordechai, 1918–   . IV. Graetz, Michael.
V. Title.
DS135.G32B48   1996
943'.004924—dc20   96-13900
                                                                     CIP

Printed in the United States of America
c 10 9 8 7 6 5 4 3 2 1
p 10 9 8 7 6 5 4 3 2 1

Contents

Preface to the Series

Shortly after the Leo Baeck Institute was established forty years ago, the second chairman of the board, Dr. Siegfried Moses, declared its "final aim" to be the production of a comprehensive history of German Jewry. Optimistically, he anticipated that such a history might be entrusted to a group of historians within four or five years. In fact, it has taken more than a generation to attain his goal, and still these volumes make no claim to finality. The institute, through its centers in Jerusalem, London, and New York and its Working Committee in Germany, continues its scholarly enterprise, even as historians of German Jewry, ever more widely represented in universities and research institutions, unearth new sources and gain fresh insights. Yet it has become increasingly apparent that the rapidly growing scholarly literature in the field requires an encompassing, synthetic work that reflects the current state of research and, at the same time, seeks to integrate it into an easily readable narrative.

As early as 1972 Professor Jacob Toury of Tel Aviv University attempted to launch a "Collective History of the Jews in Germany" that would draw upon the research of the preceding two decades and aim at "a new view of the development of forms of Jewish life in Germany." His ambitious project, which was to include the entire span of Jewish history in Germany, foresaw nine volumes and more than thirty contributors. However, it could not be carried out at that time. Fourteen years later, at a meeting of the board of directors of the Leo Baeck Institute in New York, the late Professor Lucy Dawidowicz proposed the composition of a similar collective work, and the process was set in motion that led to the current set of four volumes focusing more broadly upon Jews in German-speaking Central Europe and concentrating on the period since 1600.

Three meetings among advisers and contributors, held in Jerusalem, New York, and Berlin, were devoted to discussing the issues arising from the project. The often lively deliberations gradually arrived at a conceptual framework for these volumes, which were intended from the start to be a cooperative venture.

On certain issues we readily agreed. Despite the overwhelming reality of the Holocaust, which brought the history we relate here to a tragic close, we were intent on not viewing that history through its lens. We did not want hindsight to prejudice our analysis of earlier hopes. Yet we also decided not to minimize the role that antisemitism has played throughout the history of Jewish life in German lands. We had to recognize that a leitmotif of our narrative would be the trajectory from emancipation to exclusion and destruction.

We were also in agreement that German-Jewish history constitutes a phase both in the history of the Jews and in the history of the Germans. We have therefore tried to portray it from both of these perspectives. The bonds of German Jewry to Jews elsewhere, although weakened at times and overlaid with ambivalence, were never entirely severed and experienced periods of reinforcement. The ties of German Jews to Germany grew more firm for much of the period discussed here as emancipation and acculturation went forward, only to come apart at its end. In the beginning of our narrative Jews stand clearly separate from their non-Jewish environment: their cultural history is mostly contained within their own tradition. Then, beginning markedly in the eighteenth century, their history becomes one of integration into the German milieu, both culturally and politically. Much of their history becomes an account of their relations with the world around them.

We have differed somewhat on the extent to which our narrative should emphasize the inner Jewish life persisting in religious and cultural forms that were adapted in various ways to modern circumstances. Should our focus be on the Jewish community—its religious, ideological, and cultural expressions—or rather on individual Jews who became important for their roles in German history, although they were often far removed from identifying themselves as Jews? We have concluded that both require attention. The inner history of German Jewry deserves to be brought to greater awareness, yet the extraordinary role that Jews played in German culture needs elaboration and explanation as well. So we have sought to strike a balance between the two. Among Jews who achieved prominence, we have especially turned attention to the nature of their Jewish identity, noting its residue even among those who left Judaism but continued to be widely regarded as Jews.

In our deliberations we agreed on eight subject areas that would require treatment in each volume: demography, political and legal status, socioeconomic structure, relations between Jews and non-Jews, family life, the Jewish community, Jewish religion and culture, and Jewish participation in the general society. In some form each of the volumes addresses these areas. We have also sought to give due attention to topics hitherto neglected, especially to the role of Jewish women and to the rural Jews, who, for most of our period, made up the great majority of German Jewry.

Geography and periodization proved to be difficult problems. Whereas at the beginning of our narrative German-speaking Jews are contained within the Holy Roman Empire, during the nineteenth century their history becomes more differentiable according to the states in which they live. We were thus, for a time, uncertain whether to limit our account, at least following 1871, to the boundaries of the Second Reich. In the end, we decided to formulate our task broadly. We have consistently included the German-speaking portions of the Habsburg Empire, especially for those developments that cut across political borders: movements like antisemitism and Zionism and the participation of Jews in German culture.

Although arguments can be made for beginning our account with the end of the Thiry Years War in 1648 or with the settlement of fifty Jewish families, expelled from Vienna, in the Margravate Brandenburg in 1671, our principal narrative starts at the dawn of the seventeenth century. It was at this time that significant demographic and political processes that would gradually reshape Jewish life from medieval to modern were initially set in motion. A substantial prologue provides the background for these developments. Volume 1 ends with the year 1780, the eve of the lengthy process of Jewish emancipation, which plays a central role in volume 2. It should be noted, however, that the chronological boundaries between volumes are not absolute. The Jewish Enlightenment, which began around the middle of the eighteenth century, did not end in 1780. We have therefore included its later stages, as well, in volume 1 and begun the cultural history of German Jewry in the next volume with the developments that followed in the wake of that Enlightenment but were no longer an integral part of it. Similarly, in other volumes we have not held strictly to chronological boundaries where the logic of the presentation demanded making connections across them.

We have imagined a broad readership, composed of educators and general readers as well as fellow historians of Germany and of the Jews. We have kept notes to a minimum, using them mainly to identify primary sources used in the text. The bibliographical essay in each volume is intended to offer the reader an annotated survey of significant secondary literature, mostly of recent vintage, that readers may want to consult in further pursuing a particular topic. We have not attempted to produce a comprehensive bibliography.

Finally, in our meetings we decided that, although ours was a cooperative venture, each author should be able to speak in his or her own voice without any attempt by the editor to create a uniform tone. The result has been a degree of variation both in approach and in style, but, we hope, a harmonic presentation. Despite all our analytic awareness, we have sought to tell a coherent story that holds the reader's attention.

As general editor, I wish to thank those who have assisted in the conceptualization and execution of this project. Due to the mediation of Ernst Cramer, I was able at an early stage to meet with Wolfram Mitte of the Propyläen Verlag in Berlin, who gave me valuable advice. Professor Henry Feingold, who edited the five-volume *Jewish People in America*, also let me profit from his experience. The members of the advisory committee for the project, whose names are listed in the front matter, have all been of assistance, providing counsel and reading individual chapters. Among them I would like to single out for special appreciation Professors Jacob Katz and Reinhard Rürup. Not only have they each read and commented upon many manuscript pages, they have participated actively in the entire course of the project and have been a great source of strength to me in my editorial work. I am also pleased to express appreciation, in the name of the authors, to the following individuals who, in addition to fellow contributors and advisers, have each read at least one chapter of one of the volumes, and in some cases considerably more: Aryeh Segall, Amos Funkenstein, Jacob Toury, Jeffrey Sammons, Erik Lindner, Werner T. Angress, Marion Kaplan, Guy Stern, Yehoyakim Cochavi, Michael Brocke, and Joseph Walk. Thanks go also to Ann Millin, who conscientiously performed a variety of editorial and technical tasks.

We have been fortunate that our project received encouragement from prominent personalities and institutions in Germany. Due in large measure to the efforts of our coordinator, Dr. Fred Grubel, who has guided the project from the beginning, we were able to obtain funding, first in the form of a seed grant from the Deutsche Bank, where our cause was championed enthusiastically by the late Hermann J. Abs, then more substantially from the Stiftung Volkswagenwerk and the Bundesministerium für Forschung und Technologie of the German government. A small supplementary grant was also received from the Memorial Foundation for Jewish Culture and Gerald Meyer generously donated his legal counsel.

I owe the profoundest debt of gratitude to Dr. Michael Brenner, who since 1993 has served as my coworker for virtually every element of the project. In addition, he undertook primary responsibility for assembling the illustrations, arranging for the maps (drawn by John Hollingsworth of Indiana University), and compiling the chronologies. Our editors at Columbia University Press, Kate Wittenberg and Susan Pensak, have made this project their special concern, giving it an extraordinary measure of their attention.

In introducing one of his major scholarly works in 1845, the founder of the scholarly study of Jews and Judaism, Leopold Zunz, wrote that he wished his work would have "not just reference readers but reading readers." So too we who have produced this history hope for readers who will immerse themselves in these volumes and succeed in drawing from them a richly variegated and enduring image of German-Jewish history in modern times.

Michael A. Meyer
The First Day of the Hebrew Month of Av 5755
July 28, 1995

Tradition and Enlightenment
1600–1780

Introduction

Historiography and historical analysis are meaningful only within the framework of some form of historical periodization. Yet it remains difficult, if not impossible, to pinpoint an era's termini by reference to a specific generation, let alone decade. The division of history into centuries is an artificial operation, a construct not suggested by the contours of history itself but meant to achieve a better, clearer understanding of the course of events.

In the realm of Jewish history in Central Europe (Hebr. *Ashkenaz*), the earliest mention of Jews and of documents with a Jewish content marks the beginning of the Jewish Middle Ages. A more complex question is how to determine their endpoint. Many scholars have grappled with the specific character and temporal delimitation of the Jewish medieval period. They have also questioned the value of conventional categories of periodization: just how valid and useful are the concepts of Middle Ages, early modern period, and modern times customarily employed in general historiography when applied to Jewish history? The nineteenth-century Jewish historian Heinrich Graetz commented that Jewish history had no Middle Ages in the more pejorative sense, that is, no "dark ages" intervening between antiquity and the modern period. Later research has repeatedly addressed the question, though without arriving at a consensus.[1]

In contrast with Spanish Jewry, the Jews in Germany generally avoided engaging in the general scientific disciplines of the age—apparently because they felt repelled by the Christian theological character of many contemporary fields of learning—yet there is no justification to the contention that the Ashkenazi Middle Ages were characterized by cultural retrogression. The study of Torah flourished, and Jewish scholarship today still refers to the masterworks produced by the sages of that era.

In other respects as well, the Ashkenazi Middle Ages were a time of growth and upsurge. Within an astonishingly short span, Ashkenazi Jewry—which up to the beginning of the eleventh century was an insignificant peripheral part of the Jewish world—became an important and influential Jewish center. It developed a special character, manifested in three principal spheres. First and foremost was its particular communal organization, the corporate kehilla: these structures evolved at an early point, in a form and to a degree previously unparalleled. This development was probably rooted in the specific interplay between Jewish settlement and the Christian town. Closely associated with the emergence of the community was the evolution of a corpus of Ashkenazi traditions and customs that stamped this Jewry with a distinctive religious-cultural character. Third, there was the heroism of kiddush hashem (the sanctification of God by martyrdom in religious persecutions); it imbued the Jewry of Ashkenaz with the consciousness of occupying a certain pre-eminent position within the Diaspora.

In the present analysis the seventeenth century marks the beginning of the early modern period in the Jewish communities of the German-speaking cultural orbit, although no rigid periodization is intended. At the close of the sixteenth century numerous signs pointed to the dawn of a new era, particularly in political and demographic terms. As we approach the seventeenth century, a debate similar to the controversy among major scholars on the "lachrymose conception" of medieval Jewish history loses its relevancy, if only because Jewish suffering had diminished and was no longer as central a factor in Jewish existence as in the past, despite the abiding animosity toward Jews that remained endemic in Christian society.[2] Positive developments in Jewish political and economic life and in the structure of Jewish settlements justify postulating a turning point, a historiographic caesura. At a somewhat later juncture, though long before the beginning of the movement for emancipation, various changes also took place in Jewish internal affairs. Although the seventeenth century witnessed a number of expulsions, that is of no greater significance than the fact that even in the age of liberalism there were setbacks, reactions, and reversals—the general trend is unmistakable.

The source materials on internal Jewish history in German-speaking Europe are meager: strictly speaking, Ashkenazi medieval historiography was limited to martyrology. Aside from legendary reports on the immigration of Jewish families from Italy to Germany, virtually the only authentic historical accounts available are the chronicles of the tragic events at the time of the Crusades. Ashkenazi Jews internalized the long succession of sanguinary experiences in various ways, but were little disposed to creating a historical record. Nonetheless, their agony is given eloquent expression in the religious poetry of the time, a body of hundreds of individual poems. The rich literature on minhagim (traditions and customs) is also justifiably regarded as a text genre in the service of collective Jewish remembrance.[3] The large number of halachic (religious-legal) decisions, the rabbinic responsa (*she'elot u-teshuvot*) by numerous medieval and several early modern scholars contain historically significant data and commentary.

To be sure, utilizing such legal source materials to gain historical knowledge is problematic. In particular, researchers are often confronted with the question of generalization, namely the extent to which it is warranted to derive more general conclusions on the basis of the unique, one-time situation that was the occasion for the specific legal decision. It is not even always clear how the events presented to the rabbi for a halachic decision should be interpreted or what their historical significance is.

Non-Jewish materials are far more abundant than Jewish historical sources. That is due principally to the fact that a large proportion of the medieval and early modern texts and documents written by Jews in the German-speaking lands were destroyed during persecutions. By contrast, thousands of official documents with references to Jewish matters have been preserved in the relevant archives. The closer we come to the age of Enlightenment, the more ample is the documentary source material. By its nature, such official documentation consists principally of laws and ordinances for regulating Jewish affairs and concerns enacted by the empire, the princes, and the cities. Examining these sources, one is often struck by the differences among official directives and by various contradictions, especially between the formal ordinances and their practical implementation. At one and the same time, Jews were both persecuted and tolerated within German-speaking Europe: they were encouraged to settle in one place and expelled from another; they were accepted as traders but also driven from their homes and communities; their scriptures were deemed holy, but their Talmud was vilified. All this led again and again to contradictory declarations and actions with regard to the Jews.

With the rise of the absolutist principalities from the early seventeenth century on, this inconsistency in the state's approach to dealing with the Jews became especially patent. There can be no doubt that the ascendancy of the absolutist princes and their petty states provided impetus for a number of positive changes in Jewish existence in the modern period as contrasted with the late medieval era. Phenomena such as the emergence of the court Jews (*Hofjuden*)—an elite often able, by virtue of their special status and functions, to benefit the lot of their brethren—and the *Landjudenschaften*, regional corporate autonomous bodies in which Jews scattered over hundreds of small towns and villages banded together in an officially recognized framework, warrant detailed examination. Against the background of such changes for the better, it seems all the more conspicuous that the authorities obstinately continued to pursue practices designed to hound and harass Jews collectively as a minority.

A contradiction of a different sort was evident in Jewish intellectual life in this era. Under the impact of the changes alluded to, among which the influx of numerous scholars fleeing from Poland-Lithuania was of paramount importance, intellectual life was reinvigorated and flourished anew. This was reflected not only in the many yeshivot (Talmud academies, sing. yeshiva) and printing presses established at the time but also in the mounting interest in the general secular disciplines. A new intellectual open-mindedness was perceptible, both in the content of what was studied and the writing of books. However, as absolutism evolved as a form of political rule, sovereigns interfered more and more in Jewish internal life, especially in the work of the rabbinical courts. The restriction of their jurisdiction limited the application of Jewish law, removing significant areas of public life and the economy from its authority. The result was that certain sections of Jewish law were no longer actively applied. This process had already commenced in medieval times but became far more pronounced in the age of absolutism and later on in the era of emancipation.

It is important to bear in mind that the shift to the Enlightenment and to modernity among Jews in the German-speaking lands was not as sudden a phenomenon as is sometimes supposed. Diverse paths already taken in economic and literary activity in the seventeenth and early eighteenth century converged in that century's last quarter, pointing toward a nascent change in consciousness. This shift in perspective and outlook increasingly transformed Jewish self-understanding: from a form of existence rooted in Judaism, oriented to its values, developing from within its traditional mold, to one centered on cosmopolitan European civilization and later focused on *Deutschtum*, the world of German culture and mores. Yet down to the end of the eighteenth century the circle of those who were conscious of this shift and fervently espoused it was minuscule. And, even well into the nineteenth century, they constituted only a fraction of German-speaking Jewry. During the entire period examined in this first volume the preponderant majority of Jews were still guided by Jewish tradition and religious law.

Prologue
The Jewish Middle Ages

With the exception of Italy, Jews had resided longer in the German-speaking lands than in any other areas of Europe. In Germany, as well as Spain and elsewhere, there were reports about the great antiquity of Jewish settlements; purportedly, these had already been in existence at the time of the Second Temple. However, such accounts were solely the product of a tendency to legitimate the presence of Jews in these parts. The earliest Jewish settlements in Germany are attested for late antiquity (321 and 331 C.E. in Cologne, possibly also in Trier). Although sources from the subsequent centuries of the Germanic migrations and the early medieval period make no mention of these settlements, continuity cannot be ruled out. Clear documentary evidence for continuous Jewish settlement in Germany exists from the early days of the Carolingian Empire (800) to the destruction of German Jewry in the twentieth century, though Jews were often compelled to move from place to place. This settlement provided the basis for the development in Central Europe of a Jewish tradition and culture marked by a distinctive character. From approximately the end of the eleventh century on, the term *Ashkenaz* was in common currency to designate the Jewish communities located specifically in northwestern and central Europe. In the early modern period, as a result of the expulsion of the Jews from many German towns and territories, the term was extended to encompass a number of northern Italian settlements and all communities in Eastern Europe.

1   Epistle of Emperor Constantine to the Cologne magistrates
containing the earliest mention of Jewish settlement in Germany, 321 C.E.

1. The Beginnings of Jewish Settlement

The early Jewish settlements in Germany constituted the first Diaspora
outside the sphere of ancient Jewish settlement in the lands along the
Mediterranean. In the eighth and ninth centuries Jews were among the
first merchants who traded in goods between the Rhineland and Bohemia,
active as far afield as Poland and the regions further east. There is no
unanimous view regarding the origin of these settlers on the Rhine and
the Danube. In all likelihood, a portion migrated from Italy, others from
France. Their migration into the area did not assume larger proportions
until the tenth century, possibly in connection with the coming of the
Kalonymos family, headed by Rabbi Moses b. Kalonymos (c. 870–940),
from Lucca in northern Italy to Mainz.

Down to the late eleventh century communities generally crystallized
around the nucleus of several eminent families of large-scale merchants
and scholars and were established in the political and economic centers
along the waterways of the Rhine (Cologne, Bonn, Mainz, Worms,
Speyer), Moselle (Trier, Metz), Main, Neckar, Danube (Regensburg), Elbe
(Magdeburg), and Saale (Merseburg, Halle) as well as in Prague and a
number of other localities. Jews also participated in the colonization of the
German East. In contrast with the overwhelmingly rural Christian population, Jews generally remained in urban areas, gravitating almost exclusively to episcopal cities. It may have been easier in such ecclesiastically

ruled towns to grant them a special status, since the clergy there already formed an autonomous corporate body.

The economic activities engaged in by the Jews determined where they chose to live—generally in the center of cities situated on trade routes, where the proximity of the fortress, the church, and town hall provided them protection. In Cologne, for example, the town hall in the eleventh century was located *inter judaeos* (i.e., among the Jews). Separate Jewish quarters did not spring up until later, but residence patterns remained mixed: Jews also lived outside those areas, and Christian townspeople often resided in the predominantly Jewish quarter, interspersed among the Jews. Topographic designations such as *Judensteige* (Jews' stairs), *Judenhalde* (Jews' slope), and *Judenacker* (Jews' field) point to the formation of special streets and sections for Jews in the towns.

In comparison with the large Jewish centers in the Orient, Africa, and Spain, the communities in Germany were all comparatively small. Even in the High Middle Ages and the late medieval period, a large community seldom boasted more than a thousand inhabitants. The intimacy that marked the communities was a major factor contributing to the special character of Ashkenazi Jewry. In the two hundred years before the First Crusade (1096–1099) the Jewish population in Christian Europe increased six- to eightfold—a development due in large measure to immigration, though also to proselytizing. At the close of the tenth century the Jewish population in Germany numbered between five and ten thousand persons; on the eve of the First Crusade, it is believed there were some twenty to twenty-five thousand Jews living there. The significance of this group for all of Jewry—a total population usually estimated at between 1 and 1.5 million, a figure more or less constant throughout the Middle Ages—far outweighed its numerical strength.

2. Church, State, and Economy

In the Middle Ages, and later, relations between Europe's Jews and their environment were largely determined by their distinctive religious character. In Jewish eyes, their dispersion was more than an onerous fate forced upon them by economic and political conditions and had a deeper religious meaning. The Diaspora signified expiation for past sins; at the same time, it represented a task and challenge, namely, to proclaim God's truth in the world and to embody it as a living testimony. It was written in the Talmud: "The Lord, praised be His Name, has only dispersed Israel

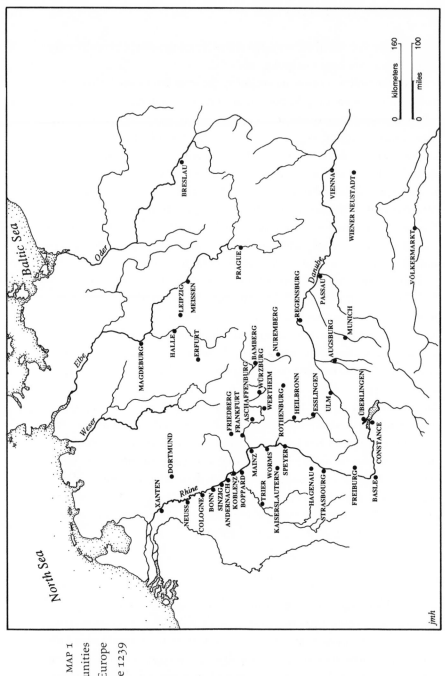

MAP 1
Jewish Communities
in Central Europe
Before 1239

North Sea

Baltic Sea

Oder

Elbe

Weser

Rhine

Danube

XANTEN
NEUSS
COLOGNE
BONN
SINZIG
ANDERNACH
KOBLENZ
BOPPARD
TRIER
KAISERSLAUTERN
MAINZ
WORMS
SPEYER
HAGENAU
STRASBOURG
FREIBURG
BASLE
CONSTANCE
ÜBERLINGEN
DORTMUND
MAGDEBURG
HALLE
ERFURT
LEIPZIG
MEISSEN
BRESLAU
PRAGUE
FRIEDBERG
FRANKFURT
ASCHAFFENBURG
BAMBERG
WÜRZBURG
WERTHEIM
NUREMBERG
ROTHENBURG
HEILBRONN
ESSLINGEN
ULM
REGENSBURG
PASSAU
AUGSBURG
MUNICH
VÖLKERMARKT
WIENER NEUSTADT
VIENNA

kilometers   0   160
miles   0   100

jmh

to dwell amongst the peoples so that proselytes might join them."[1] Jewish monotheism ventured out into a world that was just beginning to slowly abandon its heathen ways, a process accompanied by much bloodshed—nor was that renunciation of heathenism, from a Jewish perspective, complete and total. The Jews regarded themselves as pioneers of the pure faith in God, blazing the trail for its recognition in the world. At the same time, Judaism did not share the exclusivism of the Church: it did not claim to be the sole source of salvation (*extra ecclesiam nulla salus*). Instead, Ashkenazi and Sephardi (Spanish and Portuguese) scholars adhered to the ancient rabbinic principle: "The pious of all nations have a portion in the world to come."[2]

For its part, Christianity had appropriated the "Old Testament" from the Jews but viewed the Hebrew Bible as evidence corroborating its own doctrines. The Jews roundly repudiated the validity of this claim, like that of other essential dogmas of Christian teaching. Thus, the Church repeatedly found it necessary to vilify the Jews and exclude them as an alien group. However, in accordance with Church doctrine, unlike heathens and Muslims, the Jews were to be granted toleration—albeit no more than that. The Augustinian thesis stated that the Jewish people was destined to suffer yet should not be eradicated, since its existence in misery was tangible proof of the truth of Christianity. Jews and Christians both condemned apostasy, forbade mixed marriage, and claimed the right to convert those of other faiths. In practice, however, under threat of severe penalties by the Church and secular authorities, open Jewish missionary activity declined.

As a result of the social segregation engendered by dietary and Sabbath laws, Jews distanced themselves from Christians, though that process was less an expression of animosity toward the non-Jewish environment than a manifestation of the desire among Jews to preserve their traditional special character and the purity of their own religious spirit. For its part, the Church also called more and more vigorously for a strict separation between Christians and Jews. From the beginning of the seventh century, under Pope Gregory I, the Church had prohibited Jews from keeping Christian slaves, servants, and wet nurses. While allowing them the basic right to exist, it demanded the curtailment of other rights, restricted Jewish public worship, and hindered the construction of synagogues. The Church forbade its members from dining with Jews or consulting Jewish physicians. In addition, it impressed upon the secular authorities the importance of excluding Jews from appointment to public office.

Yet despite all antagonisms and differences, the two religions retained much in common. Both counterposed monotheism to paganism. An especially deep bond was their shared and profound fear of God, the belief in reward and divine retribution, salvation and the hereafter, as well as certain ethical principles derived from the Jewish Bible. Given this shared ground, Ashkenazi Jewry was also able over time, consciously or unconsciously, to absorb various elements from Christian culture.

From the old Roman Empire Charlemagne (768–814) and his successors adopted not only its claim to state power but also the Christian religion as a basis for governance. Only with the aid of Christianity and the Church was it possible to rule over the large expanses of the Frankish empire, and later the German Empire, and to infuse it with a certain cultural unity. Right from the start, this political frame excluded the Jews. Moreover, the principle of "personal law" prevailing in the Germanic polities, according to which each member of a tribe was born into his tribe's legal system, was not extended to the Jews. Rather, as immigrant and itinerant merchants, they came under the law for aliens, though there too they constituted an exception. Originally, the Jews were not made subject to a unified body of legislation but were only granted certain privileges, bestowed upon individuals and their relatives. As a result of such charters of protection, the Jew—who was not a member of a social class and not subservient to any local or regional power—came under the immediate protection of the sovereign yet, simultaneously, was also subject to his absolute dominion.

The alien status of the Jews as outsiders was consolidated by the feudal system, which reserved no place for them. In feudalism the vassal's pledge of loyalty on the enfeoffment of land had the form of a Christian oath, thus making it more difficult for Jews to own land. The fact that the Jews nonetheless managed to acquire land in some regions is only further evidence of the frequent contradiction that existed between theory and practice in their treatment. Since it was impossible for Jews to swear a Christian oath, special legislation was ultimately enacted. For trials between Jews and Christians, the so-called Jewry Oath (*Judeneid, more judaico*) was introduced, a practice probably already familiar in the Byzantine Empire. It combined Germanic-Christian and Talmudic law on oaths in order to guarantee the reliability of the sworn oath. The Jewry Oath was required of

Jews far down into the modern period. Such oaths often assumed reprehensible forms and constituted a peculiar mixture of state "Jewry Law" (*Judenrecht*) and "Jewish law" (*jüdisches Recht*, Mosaic-rabbinic law). In adjudicating internal Jewish cases Charlemagne accorded the Jews extensive autonomy on the basis of Jewish traditional law.

However, Charlemagne also enacted special laws circumscribing Jewish economic activity. Thus he prohibited Jews from dealing in wine or grain, minting coins, or taking Church property in pawn. By contrast, his son Louis the Pious granted some Jews extremely advantageous privileges. He even issued a prohibition on baptizing the slaves of Jews without their consent and appointed Jewish officials (*magistri judaeorum*) to supervise and protect Jewish merchants. In all probability these merchants were purveyors to the court, an assumption strengthened by the fact that there are detailed reports about the utilization of Jews in the service of the imperial court.

In the early medieval period the Jews differed from most Christians in three areas: their energetic economic activity, effective communal organization, and relatively high levels of education. Thus, the term "dark early Middle Ages" in German historiography has as little applicability for the Jewish medieval period as for the Byzantine Empire. The lifestyle of the Jewish merchants was marked by opulence. In any case, the many famine years of the tenth and eleventh centuries left no echo in the sources. By virtue of their experience in commerce and superior knowledge of commodities, markets and monetary transactions, their versatility in languages and the dispersion of their coreligionists across several continents, the Jews occupied a preeminent position in international trade, a field of commerce where Greeks, Syrians, Egyptians, Frisians, Vikings, and Normans were also active. Typical are reports about a Jewish merchant who traveled frequently to the Holy Land, where he gathered up precious and rare goods to bring back to the West, or accounts about Muslims and Jews who journeyed to Prague, returning with flour, lead, and animal skins.

The role played by Jews in global trade at the time was so central that in many writs of privilege and ordinances, formulae such as *judaei et ceteri mercatores* (Jews and other merchants) were common. The responsa of the Babylonian academies mention a broad array of commodities dealt with by Jewish traders active in international east-west commerce: expensive clothes, gold, pearls, silk, pepper, grains, and animals—in the main, luxury items of various kinds. As we know from other sources, Jews were also involved in the slave trade. At the time of the rise of the Arab empire and the resulting rupture in trade relations, Jewish international traders played a major role as intermediaries between Christian Europe and the Muslim East. This may help explain the relatively favorable attitude of the Carolingian emperors toward the Jews. The Jewish settlements in the Rhineland, on the Danube, and in Prague were way stations on a key over-land trade route.

Most Jewish landowners had their fields worked by non-Jewish ten-ants. It is probable that the prohibitions on employing Christian slaves acted as a further lever to drive Jews from land ownership. Thus they attempted at an early juncture to gain access to internal trade, and the Jews were also the first to deal in money. Nonetheless, in over three hun-dred rabbinic responsa before 1096, Jews whose main source of income was moneylending are rarely mentioned.

As reports increase about Jewish settlements, there are more and more references to a worsening of their situation. A council convened in Mainz at the end of the ninth century resolved that the killing of a heathen or Jew motivated by hatred was homicide; yet that resolution only under-scores the fact that it was by no means self-evident for such an act to be judged as murder. Although there was as yet no attempt to restrict Jewish rights, there was serious discussion in Church circles about whether it was desirable—indeed even possible—for Jews and Christians to live together. In 937–939 Pope Leo VII wrote to the archbishop of Mainz that, should attempts to convert the Jews fail, expulsion was preferable to forced bap-tism. The eschatological expectations associated with the millennium aggravated religious antagonisms. There were a number of persecutions between 1008 and 1012, including one in Mainz, probably triggered by the news from Jerusalem that the Arabs, at the supposed instigation of the Jews, had destroyed the Church of the Holy Sepulcher. When a high Church dignitary converted to Judaism, Henry II decreed the expulsion in 1012 of all Jews from Mainz who refused to be baptized. Although they were permitted to return to the city the following year, this event left deep scars on Jewish consciousness. Conversions to Christianity multi-plied, even in the families of the most respected rabbis. Among those who underwent baptism, perhaps by force, there were also several sons of the greatest Jewish scholar of the time, Rabbenu Gershom b. Judah of Mainz, and of his contemporary, Rabbi Simon, the latter praised for his contributions to the Jewish communities and their welfare.

In the eleventh century the religious atmosphere became increasingly more tense. The growing emphasis on the martyrdom of Christ in Christian religiosity and the depiction of his sufferings, which became ever more drastic in pointing a finger at the Jews, soon had disastrous consequences for the Jewish population. Christianity consolidated its position in Western Europe as never before, establishing many new monasteries and monastic orders. A call for the religious reform of the monasteries reverberated from Cluny in Burgundy across Europe. The influence of the "militant" church on the people was enormous; its tendency to sacralize the world became ever clearer.

This same period was marked by the beginning of the rise of the urban burgher class. New social and political forces intent on gaining greater power now arose, a development that would have a major impact on Jewish life. In the last quarter of the eleventh century tensions appeared between those who had previously been partners in power, namely, the emperor, the Church, and the nobility. The prolonged struggle over investiture (1075–1122), with all its associated events and the lengthy stay of the emperor in Italy, generated a crisis atmosphere in Germany. This led to a weakening of the power both of the emperor and local authorities and a decline in general security. When a large conflagration broke out in the Mainz Jewish quarter in 1084, many Mainz Jews, fearful of the Christian townspeople, fled to Speyer, establishing a Jewish community there for the first time.

The new political situation and its differential impact in individual towns may help to explain why—precisely at that time and on the eve of the catastrophe of the First Crusade—Emperor Henry IV (1056–1106) issued highly advantageous charters of rights to the Jews in Speyer (1084, mediated by the local bishop Rüdiger [Huozmann]) and Worms (1090). The Jews were exempted from certain taxes and their religious and legal autonomy was largely reconfirmed. In Speyer a wall was constructed around the Jewish community for its own protection. In Worms the Jews were granted the "right of receivership" in the case of stolen items: stolen goods purchased in good faith had to be returned to their rightful owner, but only if the purchase price was reimbursed. In his introduction the bishop even declared that he was bringing the Jews to Speyer in the conviction that they would "enhance a thousandfold the glory of our city."[3] It is also possible to understand Henry IV's attitude toward the Jews at the time of the First Crusade in the light of general political considerations then motivating him. Among these was his claim to sovereignty and the desire to restrict the authority of his adversaries as well as his sense of obligation to preserve peace and security in the country. The privileges granted the Jews attest to their often documented tendency to rely as much as possible on a central authority for their protection.

3. Early Ashkenazi Culture and Community

In its beginnings Ashkenazi culture lay totally in the shadow of the old cultural centers in the Orient and Italy. From them the Jewish communities in Ashkenaz adopted the spiritual and intellectual legacy of late Jewish antiquity: the Bible and its Aramaic translation, the oral tradition set down in the Mishnah and Gemara (the two components of the Talmud), the homiletic treasure of the midrashim, the first compendia of the religious law, the prayers and religious poetry. Down to the middle of the eleventh century the traditions of the Land of Israel in prayer, ritual, and custom had a significant influence among certain prominent families. As late as 960 Jews in the Rhineland consulted the "scholars of the Land of Israel" on questions of jurisprudence and asked them for verification as well of the rumor that the Messiah had come. Later on the importance attached to Babylonian tradition grew. The intellectual elements brought from Italy by the Kalonymos family remained a powerful force that found its special expression in religious poetry and mysticism. The links with Italy, as well as the contacts with the Frankish West, help to explain the occurrence of Romance names such as Leontin and Perigoros as well as borrowings from Latin in the Ashkenazi dialect, such as *oren* ("pray," from *orare*) and *klamen* ("make a complaint," from *clamare*).

Despite these strong bonds to the various lands of origin, the Jewish settlements in Germany developed substantial intellectual independence. Notwithstanding the recognition granted the authority of the foreign academies, the predominant tendency was a powerful impulse to engage in independent investigation and exegesis of the halachic sources. As a result of this orientation and the pressure of external conditions, a new body of religious custom came into being. It displayed many innovations, deviating at times from norms grounded in the Babylonian Talmud. A strong sense of attachment to the special local or regional tradition of religious practice remained a characteristic feature of the Ashkenazi communities, even after the Babylonian Talmud became the principal focus of study among their scholars. *Minhag Yisrael—Torah*, "Ancient custom has the binding force of sacred law," was a familiar apothegm.

The Jewish communities did not come into being in response to external compulsion. Rather, these kehillot formed as a result of their own, internal impetus, probably even before the genesis of the urban Christian communities. Without a structured community, a freely developing life anchored in Judaism was inconceivable. The solidarity of all members of the Jewish people, their mutual responsibility for the observance of religious law, daily public worship, the spread of Talmud study, an autonomous judicial system, the establishment and maintenance of a whole series of ritual and social institutions, without which a Jewish community would forfeit its special character—all these made the formation of a communal structure an existential necessity. Of course, there had always been a substantial number of Jewish families living in isolation or in minute groups in small or even the tiniest localities. Yet that was only feasible if a community located in relative proximity could provide them with the services they were lacking. There was only one external factor, albeit very powerful, shaping the formation of communities—namely, the duty to pay taxes. As a rule, the authorities made the kehilla collectively responsible for the total amount of taxes due, leaving its distribution among the members up to the community. With time, the collection of tax payments became one of the most important, though most difficult, functions of the community.

A community administration developed at an early juncture, consisting of the *tuve ha-ir* (town notables, *boni viri*), with the parnas (leader) at its head and the shammash (caretaker) as a paid official. For a long period there was no official rabbinate in Germany. The community also achieved, early on, an astonishing degree of authority and administrative competence. It had the power to impose a ban on any new settler and could thus prevent undesirable newcomers from taking up residence in the community (*ḥerem ha-yishuv*). Originally, this prerogative had been a means to prevent economic competition, but it was later motivated by professed concern for maintaining the high level of morality in the community. Thus, already at an early point, the interest of the authorities in limiting the number of Jews settling in a locality coincided on occasion with a similar desire among the local Jewish residents. The *ma'arufyah* (right to clientele) was also an institutionalized practice for the benefit of the old established residents. It guaranteed the monopoly enjoyed by individual merchants in their commercial relations with certain Christian customers, generally princes, knights, and monasteries. The origin of the expression is probably Arabic and attests to the fact that Jews had introduced various trading customs and practices from the Orient. Traditionally, Jews had always regarded the laws of the country as valid and binding on them (dina de-malkhuta dina, i.e., the law of the land is law [for us]), but only to the extent that the Jews enjoyed equality before the law with the rest of the population.

The early Ashkenazi scholars attempted to legitimate and consolidate the authority and competency of the communities. There was no supreme Jewish authority, such as the exilarch in Mesopotamia or the heads of the two central academies (geonim, sing. gaon, "great scholar") there, and each community persevered in watching over its own independence. The scholars bestowed the status of a competent higher court (bet din hashuv) on the community elders, to whose ranks they also belonged, and interpreted the duty of each individual to recognize and submit to its authority as a biblical injunction. The scholars themselves took part in community administration. Invested with extensive competencies, the communities issued statutes and ordinances (takanot) binding on all Jews in the locality. Even transient Jews just passing through, against whom a complaint had been brought by a local resident, could be prosecuted before the local rabbinical court (herem bet din). In coming to a decision the legal principle initially operative was one of unanimity. Later on it was supplanted by the majority principle, although at first on the basis of a qualitative majority, i.e., a majority of the elders and respected persons in the community. In urgent cases any individual community member had the right to interrupt prayer in synagogue until he received redress, thus putting pressure on the elders and the court to assist him in gaining his rights (ikuv ha-tefilah or ikuv ha-keri'ah, hindrance of prayer or recitation)—for example, when a court, threatened by an influential defendant, wished to avoid handing down a judgment in favor of the plaintiff.

The last-mentioned legal means, colloquially known as klamen, points up the fact that violations of the law in small communities were quite common. In actuality, the earliest cases that have come down in written form deal with breach of the peace and violence, denunciation and perjury, as well as the refusal to obey valid regulations. Rabbinical courts in the eleventh century had to grapple with such serious offenses as forcible dispossession of land, denial of the competency of a court, or even refusal to accept the authority of the community administration. It is possible that at least some of these phenomena were connected with the rise of prosperous merchants able to take advantage of their connections and influence.

Since there was no professional rabbinate and the Talmudic scholars earned their living by some other occupation, no dividing line existed between "clergy" and laymen. All local male Jewish residents were expected to take part in study and in economic and community life, which was quite feasible in the small number of early Ashkenazi communities. This interlinkage of study and economic activity among Ashkenazi Jews bolstered their sense of being an important branch of Jewry and the custodians of a distinctive tradition—one in which the translation of teachings into practical everyday life played a major role. Another factor was that they were led by pious scholars who, independent of the leaders of the Babylonian academies regarded as authoritative in the Jewish world of that era, struck off to some extent on their own paths, enriching rabbinic literature with outstanding contributions.

A substantial number of scholars, whose names are known and some of whom left rabbinic writings or liturgical poetic compositions, were active in the eleventh century in the Rhineland. Among these the greatest was Gershom b. Judah (950/960–1028), who was always referred to by the title *rabbenu* (our master), and was distinguished by the rare honorific addition *me'or ha-golah* (light of the exile). Views differ as to where he was born, but there is no doubt that he lived most of his life as a student and scholar in Mainz, where he died. Gershom b. Judah was the towering figure who transformed Mainz into the spiritual-intellectual center of Judaism in Germany at that time. He trained numerous pupils, some of whom headed the yeshiva in Worms, an academy so renowned that Solomon b. Isaac (Rashi, 1040–1105) from Troyes in France, the later famed Bible and Talmud commentator, spent many of his years as a student there.

Rabbenu Gershom wrote a commentary on the Talmud, left a large number of responsa, and composed religious poems (selihot and piyyutim) that were incorporated into Ashkenazi liturgy and also took a firm and decisive hand in managing communal affairs. He issued (or at least was later credited with) numerous takanot dealing with public and private life that subsequently gained general validity. The most famous ordinances, most probably due to his own initiative, dealt with the prohibition of polygamy and of divorce forced upon a woman against her will. Although polygamy was not widespread even earlier, these ordinances attest to the social advancement of women in the Jewish com-

צור
חוינבלזכר
ר׳ גרשום בר
מאור

2   Memorial stone for Rabbenu Gershom (ca. 960–1028) in Mainz,
from the twelfth century

munity—even if one assumes a certain influence here from the Christian milieu. Women ran the household in the frequent absence of their husbands away on business and often played a key role in economic life.

Liturgical poetry was of major importance for the intellectual and spiritual life of Jews in the German-speaking lands. This medium was the expressive vehicle for all their thoughts and sentiments, and was of central significance for the life of the community. Rabbi Simeon bar Isaac (the "Great"), an older contemporary of Rabbenu Gershom in Mainz, was an eminent author of such piyyutim. They frequently give voice to the sufferings caused by persecution and have remained a part of Ashkenazi liturgy down to the present.

In the genre of piyyutim the Jews communed with God, asking for forgiveness and redemption; rising up in indignation against hatred and persecution, they appealed to divine justice. The poems also contained didactic elements; in part, they were intended as a catalog of the religious regulations for the Sabbath and festivals. Their poetic form had been decisively influenced by Palestinian and Italian poetry. Down to the fifteenth century there was hardly a Jewish scholar in Germany who did not compose liturgical pieces, and many of the most respected scholars officiated in leading public prayer. For them it was an honor to enrich the liturgy and to convey the affliction and anguish of their era to coming generations.

4. The First Crusade and Subsequent Developments

During the course of the eleventh century there was a rise in the number of Christian pilgrims from the German-speaking lands to the Holy Land. In 1064–1065 a group of seven to ten thousand of the faithful journeyed there on pilgrimage. In his proclamation of the First Crusade (1096), Pope Urban II (1088–1099) thus seized on ideas and movements already popular among the broader population. The path taken by the crusaders from France to the Holy Land followed the major trade routes, passing through a number of Jewish centers. The Jews were the first to be victimized by crusader violence against the "infidels." "We depart to wage war against the enemies of God, while here in our very midst dwell the archenemies and murderers of our Redeemer."[4] Fired by this slogan, the crusaders stormed in to attack the Jews, who had tragically pinned messianic hopes on the fateful year 1096. The chain of excesses had already erupted in northern France, yet the Jews in Mainz still felt they were in no danger. Their response to warnings from France reflected that sense of false security: "We are fearful for your safety. As for ourselves, we have no need to worry."[5]

In actual fact, however, it was in Mainz and the Rhineland where the truly horrendous scenes of carnage would take place. Jews there were taken by surprise, yet ready to face death. Their tormenters were all the more reckless since Pope Urban II had absolved the crusaders in advance of their sins. Confronted with the alternative of baptism or death, many Jews chose martyrdom. Despite the unqualified condemnation of suicide in Jewish law, they preferred to die at their own hands rather than be murdered by the Christians. Their hatred of an enemy who showed no mercy was mingled with religious ecstasy. Thus the places of their sacrifice became sites of kiddush hashem—sanctification of God by martyrdom. Those condemned to death united in spirit with the long line of heroes in Jewish martyrology that dated from the period of the Maccabees and the destruction of the Second Temple. The most horrible scenes were the immolation of the children and women, performed as a holy act, as Abraham had once been prepared to bind and sacrifice his son Isaac. In terms of strict religious tenets, such a deed was unforgivable, though justified here by the certainty that survivors had no option and would be compelled to undergo baptism. Precisely because the crusaders were concerned about the religious beliefs of the Jews, not their lives, fathers and husbands chose to sacrifice themselves, their children, and their women—in the name of and for the sake of faith.

The Church itself was not responsible for the slaughter, and in quite a few cases Jews found refuge with clergymen. Yet the Church did virtually nothing to put a stop to the persecutions. The sole cleric who took resolute and successful action to save the Jews of his city was Bishop Johann of Speyer. Though the townspeople generally did not take part in the excesses, they stood idly by, hardly raising a finger to protect the Jews in their city. Jews often tried to defend themselves with weapons, yet, greatly outnumbered, were nowhere able to repulse their attackers. The Hebrew chronicler Solomon b. Simon, whose report contains many striking similarities to the Christian chronicles, emphasizes in this connection that the Jewish warriors had been weakened by much fasting. For those who opted to save their lives by undergoing a feigned conversion, the chronicler has praise for their determination to return to Judaism as soon as possible.

Although German Jewry in the Rhineland was not completely annihilated, there were many victims—some 5,000 persons lost their lives, about a quarter of the Jewish population. The greatest devastation was in Mainz (between 1,100 and 1,300 killed) and Worms, the centers of rabbinic learning and of the old established families. There and elsewhere numerous manuscripts were destroyed. The disappearance of an entire generation of scholars and the irretrievable loss of a large proportion of early Ashkenazi writings meant that this persecution, known in Jewish annals as the *gezerot tatnu* (i.e., the massacres of 4856/1096), marked a profound caesura in the history of Ashkenazi Jewry. The rupture of 1096 was apparently one of the reasons why the early representatives of Ashkenazi learning had so little influence on the work of later generations. These tragic and violent events had a lasting impact on the self-understanding of Ashkenazi Jewry, how it reacted in times of persecution, its traditions and customs.

During the onslaught of the crusade, Henry IV continued his Jewry policy as supreme protective patron of the Jews. At the request of Jewish community leaders, he had written at an early point to rulers in the areas along the route—and most particularly to Godfrey of Bouillon, field commander of the crusaders—requesting that they protect the Jews. In 1097 the emperor permitted Jews baptized by force to return to their Jewish faith. One year later he ordered a court investigation into the whereabouts of goods stolen from Jews in Mainz, to which he laid claim as protective patron. In 1103 he promulgated the first Land Peace (*Landfriede*). This was a royal proclamation of general pacification, prohibiting feuding and violations of the public peace, which became subject to heavy penalty, and placing the Jews and other groups in need of it under special protection.

The events of the First Crusade point up the gaping divergence between the policies of the Church and the crown regarding Jews on the one hand and the fanaticism of the masses and the monks on the other. The Jews had their first bitter lesson in the vicissitudes of protection: namely, that in times of crisis the protective shield of the authorities was preferable to that of their Christian neighbors but that the possession of privileges was no sufficient guarantee against an enraged mob on the rampage. In Germany the fate of Jewry had become entangled to an unparalleled degree with the swirl of general political events. Among the reasons the movement for the hegemony of the Church championed by

Pope Gregory VII viewed Henry IV as an enemy was his Jewry policy, that is, his decision to grant the Jews rights that the Church adamantly rejected. Thus the question of rule over the Jews, both in its material and symbolic sense, remained a focus of intense dispute among the secular and spiritual powers.

For almost two centuries the movement of the Crusades continued. Each successive wave, especially in the years 1146, 1189, 1204, and 1217, visited renewed agony and bloodshed upon the Jews, claiming further victims. The act of self-immolation to escape baptism and apostasy thus became a general phenomenon. It was so widespread that, as a scholar noted, "even the worthless among us sacrifice themselves for the sake of kiddush hashem, and hardly one in a thousand turns apostate."[6] The suffering, sorrow, and yearning for deliverance left distinct traces in liturgy and custom. Long lists of those murdered were read publicly from memorial books on certain Sabbath days and festivals, additional fast days were held, annual weeks of mourning were instituted in remembrance of the dead, lamentations were recited in the synagogue. From that time on the communities were called "holy communities," a designation that probably also meant "communities of the holy," that is, those who had sanctified the name of God by their ultimate sacrifice.

The events of the First Crusade left a lasting imprint on the relation of the surrounding Christian world to the Jews in its midst. The psychological impact of the fact that the Jews were, for all practical purposes, defenseless was profound. For the first time the great mass of the Christian population became aware that a minority resided among them that was highly vulnerable and whose property, despite official protection by the authorities, could be plundered with little resistance. Moreover, the burgeoning of urban centers and the general growth in their population (from eight to fifteen million by the end of the thirteenth century) had, to be sure, led to a concomitant increase in the Jewish settlements, yet was accompanied by a deterioration in their overall economic situation. The Jews were pushed out of foreign commerce into local small trade and finally displaced into pawnbroking.

During the twelfth and thirteenth centuries the greatest single influence on Christian-Jewish relations were the religious changes within the Church. Under the impact of the Cluniac reform movement and the newly established mendicant orders of the Franciscans and Dominicans, popular animosity toward the Jews intensified. Throughout Europe disputations were held between Jewish and Christian scholars, with the Jewish disputant always forced onto the defensive, a reprobate in the dock, so to speak, on mock trial for his sins. It was not a question of persuading those of another faith but rather an attempt to force them to embrace, under threat, the dominant religion. In the twelfth century the

3 *Ecclesia* and *Synagoga* on the Bamberg Cathedral
(ca. 1230–1240)

4A, 4B   Scenes from a contemporary woodcut showing the purported
acquisition of a host and its desecration by Jews in Passau, 1470

number of demeaning pictorial representations of Jews and Judaism in
church buildings begins to mount. One popular motif was the contrast
between the triumphant *ecclesia* and the blind, humbled *synagoga* with
broken staff, fallen crown, and blindfolded eyes. In numerous depictions
of the crucifixion scene the Jews—in medieval dress, with crooked nose
and malicious mien—were branded as the murderers of God. Jews now
stood counterposed to Christian society not as individuals but as a collective. The Jew was thus transformed into a stereotype, his figure dehu-
manized and demonized. Characterized as a recalcitrant rejecter of God,
he now became the incarnation of the devil, capable of any vicious,
underhanded, and murderous deed. Jews lived in the lengthening
shadow of cathedrals on whose walls they were portrayed as murderers
and monsters.

It was a short step from the visual demonization of the Jews by the
Church to the fabrication of allegations among the broader population.

The charge of ritual murder was raised for the first time in the twelfth century, alleging that Jews murdered Christian children and used their blood for ritual purposes. Charges of "blood libel" were initially widespread especially in England and France; however, their number soon soared in Germany, far exceeding similar accusations elsewhere. The libel of Host desecration was analogous: it asserted that Jews stole and then desecrated the Christian eucharistic bread. The piercing of the Host, which represented the body of Jesus, was supposed to symbolize the Jews' ever repeated attempt to murder God. These allegations multiplied and spread with increasing ferocity during the course of the thirteenth century, even though popes and emperors sought to make clear that such calumnies were baseless, founded on fantasy, lies, and perjury.

A typical incident was the case of blood libel in Fulda in 1235. A grain mill burned down and, in their parents' absence, the children of the miller and his wife had perished in the flames. Several crusaders happened to be in Fulda at the time, and they bruited the rumor that the Jews were to blame for the fire and deaths. In the ensuing violence thirty-two Jewish men and women were killed; all Jews in the Holy Roman Empire were placed under suspicion of committing ritual murder. The Hohenstaufen emperor Frederick II (1212–1250), who espoused liberal religious views, ordered a thorough investigation of the charges. The inquiry was conducted by a large number of princes, clergymen, and baptized Jews and resulted in the acquittal of the Jews.

Frederick II appended this verdict to a writ of privileges that extended the protection of the Worms charter of Henry IV to all Jews in Germany (1236). Here, for the first time, Frederick declared the Jews "serfs of our chamber" (*servi camerae nostri*), thus adopting the concept of perpetual Jewish serfdom (*perpetua servitus iudaeorum*) from the Church, a doctrine enunciated by Pope Innocent III in 1205 and formally incorporated into canonical law in 1234 by Gregory IX. In the second half of the thirteenth century the leading scholastic philosopher, Thomas Aquinas, formulated this notion of vassalage in the following words: "Since the Jews . . . have fallen into eternal serfdom for their sins, sovereigns have the right to strip them of their possessions, leaving them only with the barest necessities for life."[7] In the Fourth Lateran Council (1215), Innocent passed a number of resolutions whose aim was to isolate and humiliate the Jews. Among these was the obligation of distinctive dress. In practice, this meant wearing a yellow ring or a similar badge on the chest, or the pointed "Jew's hat."

While the special fiscal relations of the Jews with the imperial treasury had been mentioned in documents even before the Fourth Lateran Council, the concept of chamber serfdom was new. Instead of an ecclesiastical-theological justification based on canonical law, the secular *Sachsenspiegel* (a catalogue of legal customs and rules compiled in the first third of the thirteenth century and the most important book of law in German Middle Ages) noted that the Jewish historian Josephus Flavius was reportedly granted the privilege of protection for the Jews by the Roman emperor Vespasian as a reward for having cured his son of the gout. This explanation served to justify the political claim of the emperor, locked in a power struggle with the pope, to the "prerogative over the Jews" (*Judenregal*) and its associated revenues. By 1275 chamber serfdom (*Kammerknechtschaft*) was already a full-fledged legal institution. Thus the contemporaneous *Schwabenspiegel* (the major South German medieval collection of customary law) reports that Titus sold the captured Jews to the imperial treasury in Rome as servants in bondage; since that time they had been vassals of the empire under the protection of the Roman emperor. The *Schwabenspiegel* contains numerous prohibitions and regulations also found in the resolutions of the Lateran Council.

An important circumstance accompanying the introduction of chamber serfdom was the prohibition against Jews bearing arms (a restriction whose effect was to make Jews equal in this regard to clerics and women). Formerly—for example, in Worms—Jews had at times even been forcibly mobilized to help defend the city. This prohibition on carrying arms diminished their legal and social status. Indeed, the introduction of chamber serfdom was a step backward: it accelerated the process of civil deprivation, stripping Jews of their rights and restricting their freedom of movement. On the basis of chamber serfdom, Jews were compelled to pay their taxes to the imperial treasury. In 1241, for the first time, the tax listings of the German cities document a regular imperial tax levied on Jews. Thus there was a kind of "nationalization of the Jews," a device by which the state appropriated their economic power. According to one estimate, Jews in the thirteenth century accounted for some 13 percent of the revenue of the Empire and 20 percent of the imperial taxes collected from the cities. Theoretically, chamber serfdom entailed intolerance on the one hand, protection and care on the other. The Jewry policy of Frederick II

5 Monk and Jew armed on horseback. From the
Wolfenbüttel *Sachsenspiegel*

had less to do with tolerance than with the needs of realpolitik. While employing Jews in Sicily in enterprises important to the state, he removed them from all offices in Vienna in 1237, "because they are condemned to eternal servitude."[8] By contrast, in 1244 Duke Frederick of Austria issued what was to become one of the most liberal Jewry laws of the entire medieval period. It granted the Jews equal rights in trading with specific products, expressly forbade forced baptism, and permitted Jews extensive autonomy in managing their internal affairs. This so-called Fridericianum became the model for numerous charters of rights in Bohemia, Silesia, Hungary, and Poland.

The institution of chamber serfdom gave the king the option of selling the Judenregal to territorial rulers. In view of the growing power of territorial and urban rulers vis-à-vis the empire, this took on ever increasing importance. Emperor Frederick II initiated the practice; in 1298 King Albert I (1298–1308) presented the archbishop of Cologne, in gratitude for his support in the election, various revenues and offices, including Jewry protection (*Judenschutz*) in his city of Dortmund. But after the proclamation of chamber serfdom, Jews were no longer mentioned in the Landfriede legislation as a protected category. In practice, "Jewry protection" was now hardly more than a pretext for their ruthless exploitation.

Nonetheless, the number of Jewish settlements rose sharply, from some fifty in the middle of the twelfth century to approximately one thousand over the course of two hundred years, though a number of such settlements were minute, consisting only of a few persons. There was a discernible shift eastward, out from the Rhineland, particularly into Hesse, Franconia, and Austria. The increase in Jewish settlements was the result of the establishment of new towns as part of the process of developing the country and the growing independence of the towns, which offered the Jews a certain modicum of security. Although they were excluded from the guilds, and thus from the artisan trades and large areas of commerce, the towns provided them, at least temporarily, with a field for economic activity largely free from competition, restricted principally to moneylending and pawnbroking.

Moneylending by Jews reached its high point in Germany in the thirteenth and fourteenth centuries. The flourishing of the cities under the Hohenstaufen emperors, the constant insecurity that bedeviled currency transactions, the unreliable system of coinage, and the lack of ready cash made a widespread system of credit an absolute necessity. The Church had repeatedly forbidden Christians to engage in moneylending for profit, under the threat of severe penalty. Finally, in the thirteenth century, the prohibition on interest became a postulate of ecclesiastical economic theory as formulated by Thomas Aquinas, who regarded all manner of commerce as despicable. From that juncture on, Jews were increasingly invited to settle as moneylenders. As an incentive, they were granted a remission of taxes for the first year, and, in some cases, for several years running. Jews performed the function of moneylenders in a broad array of localities: not just in the cities, but in many market centers with small and even tiny Jewish communities, they lent money (against securities deposited in pledge) to noblemen, clerics, and wealthy farmers from the surrounding countryside. This economic activity provided them a relatively secure income, so that few suffered hardship, despite the many taxes and difficulties, and the number of impoverished Jews remained comparatively small. However, the displacement of the Jews into the despised field of

6   Peasant and Jewish moneylender at his abacus. Woodcut (1531)

moneylending also generated mounting anti-Jewish sentiment in the population. "Jewish usury" became a popular theme in Christian-Jewish polemics. In particular, the Jews were accused of preferring crosses, goblets, vestments, and Christian books as security against loans and of demanding inordinately high interest. Since the depositing of security was often a kind of disguised purchase, Jews were accused of prohibited trafficking in used goods, especially clothing.

The term *judaize* became synonymous with "dealing in money," first mentioned in this sense in writings by Bernard of Clairvaux. Yet the Jews were by no means alone in lending money for interest. The Lombards had established a reputation in the field throughout Europe, and monasteries, churches, chapters, and religious orders were among the most respected moneylenders. The older prohibitions on usury enunciated by the Church were addressed almost exclusively to the clergy, since they administered substantial charities from the pious and were often in a favorable position to undertake large-scale financial transactions. The Christian moneylenders, especially the Lombards, charged the same interest rates as the Jews, frequently even higher. Moreover, the interest Jews were permitted to take was set down in law—not in order to prevent excesses but, quite the contrary: it assured that Jews would accumulate large sums that could later be extracted from them in the form of taxes, because "[the Jews in the Middle Ages] were used like sponges, first left to soak until full, and then squeezed empty."[9] Those who controlled the institution of "Jewry protection"—the kings and princes—regarded them as their agents, sources they could make use of at will to replenish their own coffers. In many instances individual Jews or even entire communities were locked up in order to extort money from them. A remarkable fact deserves mention in this connection: the assets of a convert (and there were always converts) were confiscated, since, as a Christian, he was no longer permitted to engage in pawnbroking, and even in such a case the state wished to make good for anticipated loss. People distrusted the newcomer to Christianity, assumed he maintained secret contacts with former coreligionists, and approached him with a slew of suspicions.

Nonetheless, the inclusion of Jews in the economic life of the town and countryside also intensified social contacts between Jews and Christians, a fact confirmed by the repeated church prohibitions against common meals. There was even a certain degree of cultural convergence. If the

7   Süsskind of Trimberg.
From the Great Heidelberg Minnesang Manuscript

minnesinger Süsskind of Trimberg (thirteenth century) was indeed a Jew
(which has not been definitively established), he was symptomatic of this
development. Trimberg, depicted with a yellow Jew's hat in the Heidelberg Manesse manuscript of the early fourteenth century, noted in one of
his songs that he had abandoned courtly poetry; he would now grow a
long beard and live according to age-old Jewish custom: wrapped in a long
coat, walking humbly.

The background of the anonymous author of the poem "Dukus
Horant" is, like Süsskind's, unexplained. This manuscript, dating from the
year 1382 and discovered in Cairo at the beginning of the present century,
is noteworthy principally because it is the oldest extant medieval German
poem written in Hebrew characters, composed in a pure Middle High
German, and closely connected with the German heroic poetry of the
period. Although it has not been definitely determined that the author of
the "Dukas Horant" was a Jew, the manuscript was doubtlessly intended
for a Jewish readership and thus attests to the influence of Middle High
German literary creativity on the Jewish population.

5. Flowering of Ashkenazi Intellectual and Communal Life

Already a short time after the First Crusade the Jewish communities had
recovered and were pulsating with fresh life. The synagogues were at the

8   Jews praying. From *Maḥzor Lipsiae* (13th c.)

heart of the community, and great value was placed on their proper embellishment. The community gathered twice a day for prayer. In order to call the faithful to prayer, a *Schulklopfer* (synagogue door knocker) made the rounds from house to house in the early dawn to wake the sleeping for worship; afternoon and evening prayers were held one immediately following the other. Yet the functions of the synagogue were not limited to worship and study (the combination of the two led to the designation *Schul* [school] for synagogue in Judeo-German)—all important community and family events took place there. The rabbinical court and the other community bodies met either in the synagogue or in one of its side rooms. It was the venue for the annual elections to the lay community board, the place for weddings and circumcisions.

As a rule, the elementary school was located in the synagogue building. Hardly a religious duty was more rigorously observed than the requirement to attend school from an early age, though only in the case

9 Teacher and pupil (late 14th c.)

of males. The celebration of the first day of school had its honored place among the sacred traditions of Jewish festivals:

> It is the custom of our fathers to commence with the education of the small children at the festival Shavuot, since that is when our Torah was given us. On this day the boys, wrapped in a coat, are brought at dawn from their house to the synagogue or the rabbi's house. They are placed on the lap of the rabbi, who begins to teach them. Then a slate is brought on which the Hebrew letters are written, first letter to last as well as in reverse order. The slate also contains the words: "Moses has given us the Torah," "May the Torah be my main occupation," and "God called to Moses." The rabbi reads each letter of the alphabet and the child repeats it. He also repeats "May the Torah" and "God called." After that the slate is covered with a bit of honey and the child proceeds to lick the honey from the letters.[11]

The relative isolation of Ashkenazi Jewry from the large Jewish centers in the Orient now yielded to a perceptibly greater awareness of those communities. Characteristic of such increased contacts was the global trip of Petahyah from Regensburg in 1175. Departing from Prague, he journeyed through Poland and the Crimea to Baghdad and Susa, returning to Germany via Palestine and Greece. His travel descriptions provide a vivid impression of the rich diversity of Jewish life at the end of the twelfth century.

Torah study also resumed in the twelfth century. The old academies awakened to renewed life and new centers sprang up. While in France the flourishing of the yeshivot coincided with the founding of the first universities there, the yeshivot in Germany predated the universities by several generations. In the major Rhenish communities of Speyer, Worms, and Mainz (known by their Hebrew acronym SHUM) Talmud study was in full bloom, and scholars and community representatives gathered there on a number of occasions to discuss topical questions and pass resolutions. Other important communities arose once again in Cologne, Bonn, Würzburg, Regensburg, Vienna, and Prague. The interpretation of the Talmud following the method of the tosafists (from Hebr. *tosafot*, "additions") spread throughout Germany simultaneously with its taking root in France, or perhaps even earlier. Using this method, the text and the halachic statements of almost all tractates of the Talmud were reinvestigated and compared; contradictions were reconciled. In its essence the

Talmud consists of an endless series of discussions, all based on a strict logic. This "dialectical" method was continued by the tosafists in a direct line. In addition, scholarship concentrated on pragmatic interpretation and codification of religious law and the accommodation of custom with Talmudic legal prescriptions, a tendency that would continue to characterize Ashkenazi Torah studies even in later centuries.

The extensive restriction of Jews to moneylending helped facilitate a vigorous development of Torah study. An often quoted saying attributed to Rabbi Shalom of Wiener Neustadt reflects the way moneylending was viewed in circles of the intellectual elite: "The fact that the Torah is more followed in Ashkenaz than in other countries is because interest is extracted from non-Jews, and there is no need for any [other] occupation. Consequently, we have the time and leisure to study the Torah."[12]

Hardly two generations after the catastrophe of 1096, advanced education among Jews was flourishing once again. It is worth recalling that that catastrophe coincided roughly with the end of the Babylonian gaonate (i.e., the prime of Jewish self-administration and the Babylonian academies under the direction of the geonim from the seventh to the eleventh centuries). However, advanced education in its meaning here was limited almost exclusively to the interpretation and application of Talmudic law, as fostered by the autonomy of the Jewish administration of justice. Religious philosophy and the secular sciences, still completely integrated within the framework of Christian scholastic doctrine in Europe (in contrast, for example, with the Islamic cultural world), found no entry into the Ashkenazi academies; in Islamic Spain they were an integral part of Jewish culture.

For both teachers and pupils the intensive study of the Talmud, its analysis at times overly pointed, replaced systematic research in other fields. There was little interest in speculative theology or allegorical biblical exegesis. Characteristic of the naive faith and unschooled love of God that were accorded great religious value are the following lines by the celebrated Rabbi Meir of Rothenburg (c. 1215–1293): "And I ask not / And I brood not— / You are [God] / And there is none except for you."[13] There was a predilection at the time to delve into the legendary worlds of the Agada; in the thirteenth century the Frankfurt rabbi Shimon Hadarshan had created a special compendium for this, *Yalkut Shimoni*. From the Agada, it was but a short path to mysticism.

Jewish mysticism came to Germany with the first settlers from Italy. It was first formulated by the disciples of Judah b. Samuel he-Ḥasid, "the

Pious" of Regensburg (c. 1150–1217), among whom Eleazar b. Judah of Worms (c. 1165–1230) was the most significant. German-Jewish mysticism was marked by ecstasy and theosophy and never attained the philosophical profundity of its Spanish equivalent. Angelology played an important role, as did the world of dreams, which even had an impact on halachic decisions. Leanings toward mysticism were especially pronounced in the circle of the Ḥaside Ashkenaz (pious men of Germany), whose origins date back to the period preceding the Crusades. They were neither a sect that might have led to a split in Judaism, nor a clearly defined movement. Rather, they constituted a circle of individuals with a strong family interconnection whose traditions and writings exercised a profound influence on popular religiosity over many centuries. Their mystical literature is prodigious, in part preserved only in manuscript form. Especially well-known is the *Sefer Ḥasidim* (The Book of the Pious), reputedly authored by Judah the Pious, and the halachic book *Sefer ha-Roke'aḥ* by Eleazar of Worms.

This circle around Judah the Pious contrasted to a certain degree with the customary talmudism of the time, especially in its French tosafistic form that, nonetheless, it practiced as well. It called above all else for selfless, ethical behavior, heightened to the point of asceticism, extending beyond the norms of Torah law. This also involved altered attitudes toward the surrounding Christian world: the circle stressed that in dealing both with Christians and Jews, similar moral criteria should be adhered to. This was all the more remarkable a position since Jews at that time often felt a profound disgust for Christianity, vividly recalling the atrocities perpetrated against them in its name. They awaited God's retribution in the messianic age and some performed symbolic acts of revenge, such as spitting before Christian images of saints. However, this view did not prevent a partial communality of faith and thought with their Christian neighbors. Thus there are several parallels between religious conceptions espoused by various orders of monks established at this time, especially the Franciscans, and the traditions of the Ḥaside Ashkenaz handed down in the *Sefer Ḥasidim*. This is manifest, for example, in the special importance attached by both to asceticism and martyrdom, their belief in spirits, their general social criticism and ethical codification. The *Ḥaside Ashkenaz* and the mendicant orders shared the conviction that it was necessary to take greater burdens upon themselves over and beyond the generally valid religious laws and precepts.

The affirmation in the *Sefer Ḥasidim* of a popular piety not always in accord with the norms prevailing in learned circles is reflected in the following example typical of the book:

> If you come into a region in which there are ignorant persons, and there is peace there, and satisfaction, and none is harmed, but people do not study the Torah, then know this: [the reason is] that there is no scholar among them or anyone else who might rebuke them. For someone who sins out of ignorance is not like one who sins intentionally. Or [the reason is] that they practice charity or that love abounds among them.[14]

At about the same time a rabbinic authority whose impact extended far beyond the boundaries of the country appeared in Ashkenazi Jewry, Rabbi Meir b. Baruch of Rothenburg (Maharam, c. 1215–1293). He was a disciple of Rabbi Isaac b. Moses of Vienna (c. 1180–c. 1250), the latter born in Bohemia and the author of one of the first great halachic works written in Germany, *Or zaru'a* (Sown Light), in four volumes. Many sources seem to indicate that Rabbi Meir was appointed imperial rabbi (chief rabbi for the empire). He left numerous writings, principally dealing with Halacha (over one thousand responsa and tosafist commentaries on several tractates of the Talmud) as well as religious poetic works. Rabbi Meir had a decisive influence on the codification of Ashkenazi custom; he took pains to maintain the peace in the Jewish communities and preserve their unity. He struggled against social injustices that had appeared in the communities and recommended that breaches of discipline be prevented, if necessary by calling on the authorities for assistance.

It was Meir of Rothenburg who successfully pressed for the adoption of the earlier mentioned majority principle in the communities: election results and resolutions were now valid on the basis of a simple majority vote, without any special voting privileges for the scholars and community elders. The apportionment of taxes among individual community members often sowed the seeds of contention, as did the duty of ransoming prisoners. In these and similar questions he called on the community to maintain solidarity. A large number of eminent disciples spread his teachings in Germany and abroad. Among these were Rabbi Asher b. Yeḥiel (c. 1250–1327), who was very active in Spain after fleeing from Germany, Rabbi Mordechai b. Hillel (d. 1298), author of the most widely used codification of the Talmud in Ashkenaz, and Rabbi Meir ha-Kohen, the first Ashkenazi scholar who wrote addenda to the *Mishneh Torah* of Maimonides, the *Hagahot maimuniyot* (Notes on

Maimonides), which related the legal decisions of the Spanish scholar to Ashkenazi practice.

As excavations in Cologne and elsewhere indicate, the Jewish quarters in the large communities attained their most extensive medieval proportions during this century, at times justifying the appellation of a veritable "city within a city." Some synagogues were constructed in a Gothic architectural style resembling that of Christian churches, such as the Regensburg synagogue built in 1220. Characteristic for Ashkenaz, most synagogues had a separate section for women. This so-called *Frauenschul* was completely separated from the men's hall by a partition, the only connection being a small round opening. Thus, most of the women were unable to see the men and likewise could not be seen by them; the women could hear only faintly what was spoken and sung in the synagogue service. Consequently, a "prayer leader" was often present; she sat at the partition window, repeating and singing the prayers to the women. Other structures included the ritual bath (mikveh), the public bathhouse, the infirmary, and the "dance hall" for weddings. The oldest extant illumi-

10 Worms synagogue (12th c.),
with a separate section for women (*left*) from the thirteenth century

nated manuscripts also stem from this period, such as the two-volume Worms maḥzor (festival prayer book) from the year 1272.

6. Deterioration of the Legal Situation, Persecutions, and Expulsions

While the intellectual and community life of the Jews grew more vigorous, their political situation deteriorated over the second half of the thirteenth century. The disorder and numerous infractions of law during the stormy years of the Interregnum (1254–1273) and the tensions and struggles in the cities between the patriciate and the guilds also contributed to the worsening political climate. Moreover, there was a new attitude in the Church toward Judaism. Increasingly, the critique of Jewish texts played a role in Christian anti-Jewish polemics. While Christians had previously paid little attention to the Talmud, it was now viewed as a source for erroneous Jewish interpretations of the Bible. In particular, Christian itinerant preachers, such as the Franciscan Berthold of Regensburg, denounced the Talmud as a heretical work, claiming that all Jews had become heretics.

A rabbi wrote at this time that it had become "mortally dangerous" to live in Germany; each petty ruler was a king, and none could be told what to do.[15] At many points in his responsa Rabbi Meir bluntly calls the exorbitant taxes and duties increasingly being demanded and extorted "robbery." When Jews began to flee from Germany, Emperor Rudolf I (1273–1291) issued a prohibition on leaving the country, thus restricting their freedom of movement for the first time. In 1286 Rabbi Meir himself, apparently on his way to the Holy Land, was taken into custody at a border crossing in Tyrol, along with many others, and held prisoner until his death. Under Rudolf I the concept of chamber serfdom forfeited much of its previous mutuality and was reduced solely to its fiscal importance for the crown.

In 1298 a wave of appalling massacres swept through Germany, engulfing several large and numerous small communities, including Würzburg, Nuremberg, Bamberg, Rothenburg, and Heilbronn. The political, social, economic, and religious turmoil of this period contributed significantly to the scope of these tragic events. Contemporary chronicles link the fate of the Jews with the charge of Host desecration raised repeatedly by the common people. The local clergy played an important role in this. Yet it can be shown that the charges of Host desecration were spread post hoc in a bid to justify crimes whose true motive was simple greed for loot or the destruction of promissory notes held by Jews. Moreover, the Christians could often profit from a new source of revenue: the sites where the Host ostensibly pierced by the Jews had been stored frequently became favored places of pilgrimage for centuries thereafter, attracting the devout from all corners of the empire.

The Host libel was also the basis for the wave of persecution that erupted in 1298, associated in historical memory with the name of its leader, Rintfleisch. Similar bloody excesses were repeated several times in the first half of the fourteenth century, for example, during the great European famine of 1315–1317 and especially in the 1330s, when lawless bands of farmers—called *Judenschläger* (Jew bashers) and led by "King Armleder"—attacked the Jews in many parts of southern Germany and Austria, including Styria. Here and there the towns attempted to protect their Jewish inhabitants. But the word abroad was that Germany had become a "land of disaster" for the Jews.[16]

Based on the institution of chamber serfdom, a theory gradually developed that later was to have very grave consequences: it contended that the Jews were vassals who belonged completely to the emperor, who might do

11   Jews before Emperor Henry VII in the year 1312

with them as he pleased. This was the formulation of Louis the Bavarian (1314–1347) when he released the Burggraf of Nuremberg from his large debts to the Jews in 1343. Louis was not the first emperor to cancel debts owed to Jews and take compensation from the debtors for his services, yet he was the first monarch to implement this measure systematically. The previous year he had for the first time imposed a high poll tax on the Jews, which was later called the *güldener Opferpfennig* (lit. "golden sacrificial penny"). This annual tax, the sum of one gulden, which was demanded of every Jewish male aged twelve and above possessing assets of more than twenty guldens, was not just an important source of revenue for the coffers of the treasury. It also served as a constant reminder of the direct dependence of the Jews on the crown. All these persecutions and discriminatory measures demonstrated to the population that it was quite possible to encroach upon Jewish life and property with impunity.

After Louis's death a situation tantamount to civil war developed in the empire as several pretenders struggled among themselves for the imperial crown. The cleverest, most pragmatic, and unerring among them, Charles of Luxembourg (Charles IV, 1346–1378), prevailed by means of political agreements and unscrupulous promises of money. Yet, before he could achieve his purpose, a horrible plague swept across Europe, the Black Death. In the years 1348–1350 between one-quarter

12 Martyrdom of the Jews at the time of the Black Death, from a contemporary source

and one-third of the entire population of Europe fell victim to its ravages. Already in earlier epidemics the Jews had been suspected of poisoning the wells. In 1267 councils in Breslau and Vienna had enjoined Christians from purchasing food from Jews, since there were suspicions it might be poisoned. The Black Plague now became a terrible disaster for the Jews in Germany. They were everywhere accused of having contaminated the wells, and the mere rumor of the appearance of the plague in a locality was enough to unleash a violent wave of persecution. The fact that Jewish communities were likewise devastated by the disease, and that it also raged in areas where there were no Jews far and wide, had no influence on the libel.

In many towns the massacres, spreading from France across Switzerland to Germany, Austria, and Eastern Europe, were part of an uprising against the patriciate. The flagellant movement, whose adherents believed they could avert divine retribution by self-laceration and ecstatic public displays, whipped the crowd up into a frenzy and thus also played its role in the butchery of the plague years. In many localities it was not only Jews who were accused of polluting the wells: clergymen, the sick, noblemen, the crippled, aliens, and beggars were all suspected of foul play—in short, any who happened to be hated or under the blot of social stigma. However, the Jews, universally rejected by society, were singled out in particular as the evildoers responsible for the Black Death. Already in September 1348 Jews on the shores of Lake Geneva confessed under torture to having poisoned the wells. The tortured Jews were forced to state that the aim of their conspiracy was to rule the world, that they had suffered long enough as servants and now wished to be masters.

Meanwhile, Charles IV, initially counterposed to Louis the Bavarian as rival monarch (*Gegenkönig*), required huge sums of money to assure his election to the throne (July 1346) and his later coronation (November 1346). Jews were to serve him as a convenient means to this end. He turned the Jews into chattel, a negotiable commodity, selling his claim to their taxation. In his own hereditary lands, such as Luxembourg and Bohemia, Charles IV took relatively successful energetic measures to protect Jews from their persecutors. Yet in return for a high fee he concluded agreements with numerous cities in Germany stipulating that should any Jews be killed the townspeople were assured of immunity.

In some large cities the burghers tried to save the Jews. Their efforts proved successful in Regensburg, for example, where the mayor, the town council, and 254 prominent citizens banded together in 1349 to defend the

Jews. In other localities, such as Frankfurt am Main, the townspeople initially took defensive precautions, financed in large part by the Jews, and fought against the flagellants. Yet, a short time later, they participated in a bloodbath against the Jews and in plundering their houses. In many places the Jews put up forceful resistance, because unlike the persecution that accompanied the First Crusade the Jews now were rarely given the option of baptism. Even baptized Jews were persecuted. Thus a contemporary chronicle comments: "The cash they possessed . . . was also the poison that killed the Jews."[17] When all measures of defense appeared to be pointless, the Jews often set fire to their houses and burned themselves in their synagogue.

At least three hundred communities were destroyed during this period and the localities affected vowed never again to allow Jews to settle there. Yet, after only a short time, the cities, one by one, began to readmit Jews, all their resolutions to the contrary notwithstanding. The main reason for this haste was the urgent need for their renewed financial exploitation. The cities had incurred enormous debts as a result of purchasing the remaining possessions and assets of murdered or expelled Jews from the emperor or princes. Now as before the princes continued to be dependent on tax revenues from the Jews. Moreover, the cities were in urgent need of Jewish capital to rebuild their plague-devastated economies. Insofar as they were unable to emigrate, the survivors of the Jewish communities, largely widows and orphans, returned to the cities.

As Jews were permitted once again to take up residence in the towns, a new phase began in their political history in Germany: usually they were accepted only on an individual basis and only for a specified limited period. This impermanence gave rise to a process of internal migration, in whose course the center of gravity of Jewish settlement shifted from the west to central Germany and the eastern regions of Central Europe, where the new arrivals anticipated better conditions. There are only a small number of localities where Jews were resident before the plague for which it has been possible to establish their continuous presence as an organized community after the period of the Black Death persecutions. In over half the towns and villages where Jews resided during the late Middle Ages, there was only sporadic, or even temporary, settlement by one to two Jewish families; just twenty-four settlements boasted twenty families or more. Specific houses or sections were assigned to those returning, sometimes in more remote and poorer residential areas than before. Previously, they had enjoyed various civil rights that were not connected with political prerogatives: Jews had the privilege of permanent residence, could purchase property, and lived integrated among the other townspeople. Now their social and civil status sank to that of a barely tolerated marginal group, virtually stripped of all rights and privileges.

After readmitting them, the cities pursued a thoroughly independent Jewry policy—a sure sign of their bolstered political position within the empire. However, the relation of the emperor to the Jews did not undergo any fundamental change; formally, they remained his *Kammerknechte*, serfs of the royal chamber. Although his power over Jewry had been reduced because of the augmented influence of the cities, he demanded one-half of the taxes Jews were obliged to pay to the cities. In return for a large sum King Wenceslas (1378–1400) issued a moratorium in 1385 and again in 1390 cancelling the debts of all who had borrowed money from Jews, underscoring in this way the fact that he was still the supreme "protective patron" of the Jews. However, this action led to such chaos in the system of credit that Wenceslas and his successor, Rupert of the Palatinate (1400–1410), had to promise they would never again decree a moratorium on debts. And for that promise they also exacted a high price. In addition, Wenceslas and his successors imposed special one-time payments levied on exceptional occasions, such as coronations, the Hussite Wars, and the Constance and Basel Councils.

Throughout the entire late Middle Ages Jewish taxes constituted the largest single segment of revenues flowing into the coffers of the imperial treasury. They were so indispensable that when Dortmund Jews refused to pay the güldener Opferpfennig the city was placed under an imperial ban and only released after the Jews had paid the required levy. Tax burdens became more and more intolerable. Special levies were added on top of the regular payments; at the same time, moneylending entailed ever greater difficulties. The constant threat of a possible moratorium on debts increased the risks in lending and thus pushed up the rate of interest. That, in turn, intensified the hatred for the Jews among the general population—a vicious circle from which there was no egress. More and more Christians in the towns became moneylenders, displacing the Jews, who now had to be content with providing small loans against pawned security to burghers, craftsmen, and farmers. This, in turn, exacerbated the animosity toward Jews among the burghers, partially because the sale of pawned goods by Jews was in competition with small trade. However, above all else, Jew hatred was fanned by the constant anti-Jewish agitation propagated by the Church and its itinerant preachers.

The wars against the Hussites (1419–1436) played a significant role in this rise in anti-Jewish sentiment; waged in bloody campaigns in Bohemia, the wars affected large areas in Germany. Even though in many localities the Jews suffered hardships as a result of the conflict, they were accused of a share in the responsibility for the spread of the Hussite heresy. Meanwhile, the attitude of the Church toward the Jews became yet more hostile in the wake of the councils held at Constance (1414–1418) and Basel (1431–1449). Their alleged ties with the Hussites were an occasion for the terrible persecution of Jews in Vienna in 1420–1421 (the Vienna gezerah), where the charge of Host desecration also played a role. Vienna was then known among Jews as the "city of blood," Austria "the land of blood." A further manifestation of the rankling animosity toward Jews, on the rise in the fifteenth century and nourished by the Church, was the increased display of loathsome, degrad-

13   *Judensau* (Jewish sow) on the Wittenberg Town Church (14th–15th c.)

ing images of Jews on sacred buildings, such as the *Judensau* (Jewish sow) on the town church in Wittenberg in the fourteenth/fifteenth century (in other towns, such images had already appeared in the thirteenth century) and the religious or secular plays regularly performed in open squares or large cathedrals before gigantic audiences. In many localities passion plays enjoyed special popularity. These dramas depicted the Jews as the cruel tormenters of Jesus, murderers of God in league with Satan. Such morality plays, which did not shy away from presenting even the most brutal scenes, had their established place in the round of life of the medieval city. They often lasted for several days, attracting huge crowds and captivating the towns where they were performed.

In 1434 the Basel Council resolved that Jews should be compelled to attend and listen to missionary sermons. When the pope dispatched the Franciscan monk John of Capistrano to speak out against the Hussites, this fanatically anti-Jewish itinerant preacher agitated so successfully against the Jews, inflaming the masses, that hundreds of them were murdered or expelled, as in Breslau in 1453. Known as the "scourge of the Jews," he was later canonized by the Church. The dynamism of hatred for the Jews also made itself felt in the higher ranks of the clergy, as reflected in the thought and action of cardinal Nicholas of Cusa (1401–1464). Nicholas, who was honored by Ernst Cassirer with the epithet "first modern thinker," wrote in *De pace fidei* that he firmly believed in peace among all religions in the world, since each one mirrored a facet of divine truth; the only religion he expressly excluded was Judaism. Even before that Nicholas had pushed through a resolution at the Bamberg Synod in 1451 calling for the strict observance of the regulations of the Fourth Lateran Council and a prohibition on Jewish moneylending. Although Pope Nicholas V, under pressure from the emperor, later rescinded the clauses affecting economic life of this so-called decree on the Jews, it still had a powerful popular impact.

That same emperor, Frederick III of Habsburg (1440–1493), was concerned to protect the Jews in other ways as well; indeed, his detractors dubbed him *rex judaeorum*. Officially, nonetheless, he gave chamber serfdom a radical definition that aptly characterized the contemporary attitude prevalent toward the Jews: every Roman emperor "is entitled, by virtue of ancient custom, either to burn the Jews or to pardon them in return for a third of their fortune."[18] At that time charges of blood libel were again on the rise. Incited by the sermons of the Franciscan Bernadino da Feltre, townspeople in Trent accused Jews who had immigrated from German-speaking Central Europe in 1475 of the murder of a Christian boy, Simon of Trent, whose dead body had been found next to the house of the senior member of the Jewish communal board. Fifteen Jews were executed, the others expelled. One year later, a Christian confessed to the murder of the boy. Despite this confession, the local clergy unleashed a fierce propaganda campaign; chronicles and pictures of the alleged ritual murder of Simon of Trent were spread across Germany. The pope beatified the child, and the religious ceremony in Trent connected with the legend of ritual murder became an annual event, not discontinued until 1965. Since one of the accused Jews had, during his forced "confession" under torture, implicated several Regensburg Jews as accomplices, the bishop of Regensburg had them arrested and tortured. Shortly before, all assets belonging to the Jews of Regensburg had been confiscated under the impact of the hate sermons of the Dominican Peter Schwarz (Nigri). Only as a result of forceful intervention by the emperor was it possible to prevent a further tragedy. Yet he demanded ten thousand guldens from the Jewish community, for the granting of his protection, and a fine of eight thousand guldens from the city, with permission

14 German Jew with his chests for valuables plundered by
looters (ca. 1450)

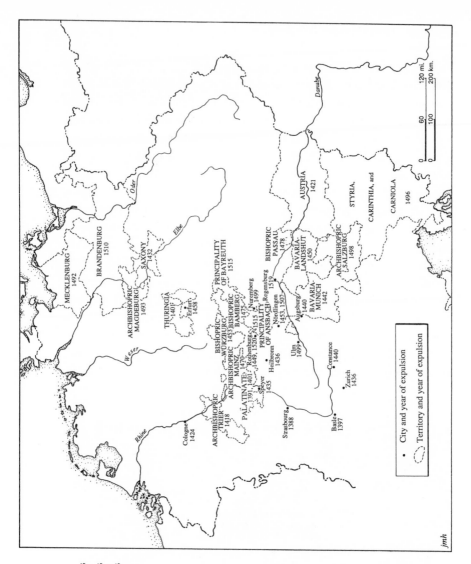

MAP 2   Expulsions of Jews from German Cities and Territories

MECKLENBURG
1492

BRANDENBURG
1510

SAXONY
1432

ARCHBISHOPRIC
MAGDEBURG
1493

THURINGIA
1401
Erfurt
1458

PRINCIPALITY
OF BAYREUTH
1515

BISHOPRIC
WÜRZBURG
1453 BISHOPRIC
BAMBERG
1475

ARCHBISHOPRIC
MAINZ
Nuremberg
Rothenburg
1449, 1520, 1515
1391, 1401 PRINCIPALITY
OF ANSBACH
1499

Regensburg
1453, 1507
Nördlingen
1436

BISHOPRIC
PASSAU
1478

BAVARIA-
LANDSHUT
1450

BAVARIA-
MUNICH
1442

AUSTRIA
1421

STYRIA,
CARINTHIA, and
CARNIOLA
1496

ARCHBISHOPRIC
SALZBURG
1498

PALATINATE
Speyer
1435

Heilbronn
1436

Augsburg
1440

Ulm
1499

Constance
1440

Zürich
1436

ARCHBISHOPRIC
TRIER
1418

Cologne
1424

Strasbourg
1388

Basle
1397

• City and year of expulsion

⬡ Territory and year of expulsion

Rhine

Weser

Elbe

Oder

Danube

0   60   120 mi.
0   100   200 km.

jmh

to levy this sum on the Jews as well. Not until 1480, when the impoverished community finally succeeded in paying off these levies, were the imprisoned Jews let go.

Thus the situation of the Jews in the fifteenth century was precarious: they lived in constant insecurity, and the necessity for sudden flight was persistently on their minds. One of the greatest rabbinic authorities of the time, Rabbi Jacob b. Moses Halevi Moellin (Maharil, 1360–1427), ruled that in times of danger it was permissible to carry coins on the Sabbath, an act otherwise prohibited.[19] His confrere Rabbi Israel Isserlin wrote, "Nowadays we are unsettled, constantly on the move, and hardly have fixed places of residence."[20]

The onerous burden of taxation prompted many Jews to flee Germany. Initially, they migrated in the main to northern Italy; in the course of the fifteenth century the stream of emigrants to Lithuania and Poland swelled, later on increasing to the Ottoman Empire as well. Yet the most important change within German Jewry was due to internal migration. The lower middle class and guilds had become a political force in the cities and were in fierce economic competition with the Jews. Thus pressure mounted in the towns to expel the Jews. However, lengthy and tedious negotiations with the emperor and the territorial rulers were required on any such drastic move. To justify their position, the cities mustered various arguments—religious, economic, social, political, and the issue of internal security. Finally, almost all larger cities and many of the largest territories proceeded to expel their Jewish inhabitants. Yet these expulsions differed from town to town and were not radically executed everywhere. Due to the territorial disunity of the Reich, it was impossible to launch a unified operation against the Jews similar to the measures implemented in England, France, and Spain. There was no uniform legislation for Jews valid throughout the entire empire, and each territory had its special features. The expelled Jews often took refuge in minor territories belonging to counts or knights of the empire situated in the suburbs (of towns) or in the nearest village. They also were granted limited permits to visit cities located nearby. This opened the door for Jews to establish themselves in trade between the city and the countryside. Thus the Judenregal claimed by the cities forfeited its relevance almost everywhere, and the Jews returned to the jurisdiction of the respective territorial rulers.

The only urban Jewish communities that did not suffer the upheaval of expulsion in the fifteenth century were in Frankfurt am Main, Worms, and Friedberg. There and elsewhere the Jews were forced into a cramped and more or less closed quarter, a ghetto in an unfavorable location or on the outskirts of the town. The first Jews ordered into such a separate quarter were the community in Frankfurt am Main in 1462; the city granted them a form of collective protection, the so-called *Judenstättigkeit*. Developments in the towns were overshadowed by the displacement of the Jews into the countryside and their dispersion throughout hundreds of villages. In such rural localities there was generally only a very small number of Jews living together. Without the protection of the city, but also free from the fear of violence by urban

15 Illustration showing the exodus of the Jews from Egypt against the
background of a medieval German city, which may allude to a
contemporary expulsion

mobs, these *Landjuden* were dependent on the goodwill of major or minor potentates. For centuries to come rural Jews would form the core of German Jewry and determine its character. Without constant contact with the intellectual and social dynamism of the cities, German Jews in the countryside clung for many generations to their distinctive traditions and character.

7. Internal Jewish Life in the Late Middle Ages

Deepening poverty among the Jews also made itself felt in the internal affairs of the communities. Data on Jewish intellectual life in the fourteenth century is more sparse than in the preceding and subsequent centuries, due in all probability to the terrible fires and devastation of the plague period, which destroyed large numbers of manuscripts and documents. Doubtless, Torah study was on the decline as a consequence of the incessant persecutions; as in intellectual life in Christian Europe, this deterioration was made more acute by the ravages of the Black Death. Nonetheless, rabbinic literature can boast outstanding figures, even from this period, such as Rabbi Moses of Zürich, author of the *Zürich Semak* (glosses on the collection of precepts by Isaac of Corbeil, the *Sefer mitsvot katan* [Small Book of Precepts], acronymed SEMAK), and Rabbi Alexander Süsslin Hakohen. The latter was active in Erfurt and Frankfurt am Main, and authored the collection of glosses *Agudah* on various tractates of the Talmud. A number of Jewish scholars from Ashkenaz spent several years studying and teaching in the Holy Land in the second half of the fourteenth century, some choosing to remain there. Toward the close of that century the Talmud academies in Germany, Austria, and Bohemia began to thrive once again. A large number of scholars were active in the communities there, including personalities such as the Maharil in Mainz, Rabbi Jacob b. Judah Weil (d. before 1456) in Augsburg and Erfurt, and Rabbi Israel Isserlein (c. 1390–c. 1460), active in Maribor (Marburg in southern Styria) and Wiener Neustadt. These and several other rabbis earned renown by their collections of responsa.

The recording of Ashkenazi customs was initiated at a time when the codification of everyday life and custom was a widespread practice in the Christian cities as well. The literature of minhagim, which imbued Jewish religious culture of the fifteenth century in Germany with its special intellectual character, was a major factor in stabilizing Ashkenazi tradition and played a central role even later in the general codification of

Halacha in the sixteenth century. Maharil had a significant part in this. In his eyes custom had paramount importance in everyday life, in the community, and in ritual law; he reputedly was the rabbi who established Ashkenazi synagogue song and provided it with a permanent niche in liturgy. Maharil was a leading rabbi in his community but never placed the stringent demands on it that he exacted from himself. As a teacher, he had a paternal concern for the many pupils of his Mainz yeshiva. These were virtues that also distinguished the younger Rabbi Israel Isserlein. Maharil's common touch and warmth enshrined him in the memory of succeeding generations.

At the periphery of this main current of intellectual life—which, despite certain novel features, did not differ much in essence from the traditions previously typical of Ashkenazi Jewry—a new philosophical school arose into prominence. Along with Talmud study, it grappled for the first time with the basic questions of religion and faith. Its most important representative was Rabbi Yomtov Lipmann Mühlhausen (Thuringia, later Prague, d. 1421). His major work, *Sefer ha-nitsaḥon* (Book of Disputation, or of Triumph), in which he examines the challenges posed by Christianity and philosophy, was later to attract the interest of a whole series of Christian humanists and Hebraists. In addition, a kabbalistic current also emerged; among these scholars the works of Rabbi Seligmann Bing (from Bingen and Oppenheim) are especially outstanding. Thus, a certain intellectual open-mindedness began to make itself felt in the fifteenth century, a receptivity that would later bear more abundant fruit.

At this time, the Western Yiddish ("Judeo-German") vernacular acquired a new importance as well. This was undoubtedly bound up with the decline in the knowledge of Hebrew and Hebrew literature. Halachic rules, such as those dealing with ritual slaughter, appeared in Western Yiddish, and rabbinical court proceedings were increasingly conducted and recorded in this language. Simultaneously, a Western Yiddish literature developed, consisting of paraphrasings of sections of the Bible, such as the Book of Esther, and pious tales. Segments of the liturgy also appeared in Western Yiddish translation; songs were composed in the idiom, and, set to popular German folk melodies, were sung at festive celebrations. Much more common than before was the use of Western Yiddish first names, such as Meisterlein, Seligmann, and Süsslein.

There were substantial changes in community life as well. Even earlier, communities had chosen a rabbi to be responsible for all religious affairs and questions; now this tendency toward the formation of a professional rabbinate became perceptibly stronger. It was promoted by a new practice among heads of Talmud academies to bestow a formal, certified ordination on their advanced students, the *semikhah*. It may well be that the destruction of virtually an entire generation of scholars had made the creation of an official rabbinate a necessity, but other causal factors were also involved. The impoverishment in the Jewish population no longer permitted the luxury of part-time rabbis—that is, persons active in other professions who discharged rabbinical functions on the side and in an honorary capacity. The young scholars were dependent on the office of rabbi for their livelihood, either by the receipt of a fixed salary or from remuneration for religious services. This development did little to enhance the status of the rabbinical calling. One consequence of the institutionalized rabbinate was that the personal skills and ability of the rabbi

16   Learned discussion among German Jews ca. 1460

now carried less weight. "The ordained are many," complained Israel Isserlein, "the knowledgeable but few."[21]

A key factor underlying the formation of the professional rabbinate was also the inclination on the part of the territorial rulers, increasingly manifest since the end of the fourteenth century, to interfere in rabbinical affairs and, more generally, in community self-governance. Increasingly, they attempted to restrict community autonomy. Rabbis, community elders, and non-Jewish *Judenrichter* (judges presiding over a mixed Jewish-Christian court) were appointed more and more frequently by the state authorities. Aside from the general drift toward depriving Jews of their rights and the mounting aspirations on the part of the territorial rulers for enhanced power, this development was largely motivated by the desire for lucre: to exploit the Jews financially, now more ruthlessly than before. Only the rabbis had the power of imposing a ban; by this means rulers were able to coerce the payment of taxes and fines. That, in turn, was one of the causes underlying the fact that complaints were voiced more frequently in the fifteenth century than before about rabbis who had placed community members under a ban and imposed fines on them.

This phenomenon was closely linked with the manifold and diverse social crises buffeting the communities. Analogous to the situation in Christian society, new circles of laity appeared and attempted to seize control of the reins of communal leadership. Even earlier, there had been lay leaders, parnasim, who, although not rabbis, occasionally appropriated the title "Jews' bishop." But now a stratum of community leaders emerged in many localities—men who, because of the circumstances of the time, had learned but little Torah. Lay law courts, which heard civil cases, were formed. As the gap between rabbis and laymen widened, tensions were also generated that at times led to noisy clashes and even defamations and physical violence.

Likewise, among the rabbis themselves, there were disputes over spheres of competency and intense rivalries. Such controversy weakened the standing and respect they enjoyed, sometimes leading to confrontations in the yeshivot, where students opposed their mentors. This was compounded by disagreements over novel and excessively pointed methods of Talmud exegesis (pilpul, *ḥiluk*), named in part after the communities in whose yeshivot they were cultivated ("Regensburger," "Nürnberger," etc.).

Along with the intellectual polarization between scholars and laymen, there arose a new, previously unknown socioeconomic polarization between rich and poor—an emerging divide in an Ashkenazi society that had been largely homogeneous until then. While the majority of community members found it ever more difficult to earn a living, a thin stratum grew increasingly wealthy. This new affluent class cultivated good connections with the authorities and influential burghers and exploited these to its advantage, often to the detriment of the wider community. In addition, the rising frequency of divorce reflected a certain loosening of family bonds. Some rabbis, such as Seligmann Bing, tried to restore discipline in the communities by a uniform and authoritative interpretation of the old takanot, thus strengthening religious practice more generally. But these efforts ran up against stiff opposition from rabbis and community leaders and ultimately proved abortive. Rabbi Moses Mintz, a disciple of Isserlein, characterized his contemporaries as "a generation that judges its judges," yet even he rejected Rabbi Seligmann's plan.[22]

Nonetheless, despite all the perils and oppression from without and the disharmony within, everyday Jewish life often continued to reflect a positive outlook and a healthy interest in mundane affairs. The minhagim of Maharil indicate a sense of enjoyment of life's pleasures, a worldly fondness for pomp and ceremony, such as at weddings. Music was an essential component of marriage celebrations and other festivities. Jews exchanged their views on news and "politics" from the wider world outside. Often, at festive occasions and entertainments, there was also contact with Christians. In contemporary responsa, for example, there are references to Jews among the crowds of spectators at horse races. Thus, even in an age fraught with tense relations, Jews and Gentiles were not totally separate.[23]

8. Humanism and Reformation

The dawn of a new era, a time when many turned away quite consciously from the medieval world, initially did not produce any essential change in attitudes toward the Jews. For the humanists the words of Erasmus of Rotterdam summed up the prevailing stance: "If it is Christian to hate the Jews, then are we not all Christians to excess?"[24] And in this attitude Erasmus led the way for his associates. The prince-bishop of Trent, for example, who had helped stage the indictment of the Jews of his city for ritual murder, boasted an excellent humanistic education and was on friendly terms with many leading humanists. As a member

הגדה הפסח

Ritus et celebratio phase iu

deo₂/cum oꝛationibus eo₂/ꝫ benedictionibus menſe
ad littera interpꝛtatis/cum omi obſeruatione vti ſoliti
ſūt ſuū paſca extra terra ꝑmiſſionis ſine eſu agni paſca
lis celebꝛare ꝑer egregiū ꝺoctorem. Ꞇhoma murner
ex hebꝛeo in latinū tꝛaducta eloquium

17 The seder evening of the Passover festival in a Latin Haggadah
from the year 1512

of the Nuremberg magistrate, the celebrated humanist Willibald Pirck-heimer shared responsibility for the expulsion of the Jews from his city. And in 1497 a traveler from France reported that in Germany the most staid burghers soon became agitated if talk turned to the Jews and their usury. It is remarkable that these very same humanists were intrigued by the great antiquity of the Jewish settlements in Germany and Austria and the numerous legends that had been spun around them. Under the impact of Erasmus's rallying cry, *ad fontes* ("[back] to the sources") and the newly awakened interest in Greek and Latin, they also delved into the cultural traditions of Judaism. Thus, the Basel Council in 1434 passed a resolution calling for the introduction of Hebrew language instruction at the universities—though this move was based less on a serious academic interest in the Jews than on the linguistic needs of anti-Jewish polemics.

There were only a few Christian Hebraists who came out in support of more humane treatment for the Jews; preeminent among these was Johannes Reuchlin (1455–1522). Reuchlin was no friend of the Jews either, but in his capacity as a legal scholar, and out of a deep commitment to law and justice, he was to a certain extent an advocate of their interests. In his writings he berated the Jews in the traditional manner, castigating them for their blindness and obstinacy. But he had appreciative words for his Hebrew teacher, Jacob b. Yeḥiel Loans from Mantua, the court physician of Frederick III and the first Jew to be knighted by an emperor of the Holy Roman Empire. In Rome Reuchlin studied Hebrew with the eminent biblical exegete Obadiah Sforno. Pico della Mirandola instructed him in Kabbala, implanting in him the conviction that the Kabbala furnished proof of the divinity of Christian teachings. His Hebraism had deep religious roots, since he believed he could hear the very voice of God reverberating in the sounds of the Hebrew language.[25] Reuchlin regretted the expulsion of the Jews from Spain and their persecution in Germany—though principally because of his scholarly concern for the preservation of the Hebrew language and the furtherance of biblical research.

Reuchlin spoke out publicly in his condemnation of the confiscation of all the Hebrew books belonging to the Jewish communities in Frankfurt am Main, Worms, and several other cities. This operation had been initiated by the converted Jew Johannes Pfefferkorn (1469–1522/23), who ventilated his hatred against his former coreligionists by publishing denunciatory pamphlets in Cologne from 1507 to 1509 with the aid of his Dominican brother monks. In these diatribes his principal target was rabbinic literature, and he asserted that the Jews would convert—when their books were taken away from them. As a direct consequence Emperor Maximilian I (1493–1519) ordered all books belonging to Jews confiscated. The elector of Mainz protested against this action. With the agreement of the emperor, he gathered expert opinions on the matter from several universities and scholars, including Reuchlin, who was the only one to condemn Pfefferkorn's actions. Reuchlin championed the claim of the Jews to basic civil rights involving protection of property, protection from bodily harm, and freedom of religion. Consequently, he protested against the arbitrary confiscation of their books, recommending the burning of only those books that contained demonstrable blasphemies.

The Dominicans disagreed, and the two parties expressed their clashing views in a series of leaflets. Reuchlin was denounced as a friend of the Jews and suspicions of heresy were raised against him. In 1513–1514 he was indicted in Mainz and Rome. The controversy dragged on until 1520, when Pope Leo X finally condemned Reuchlin's pamphlet against Pfefferkorn together with Luther's writings. The so-called Reuchlin affair was not a conflict pitching humanists against scholastics, as Ulrich von Hutten had contended in his *Epistolae obscurorum virorum* (Letters of Obscure Men, 1515–1517), since there were also humanists among Reuchlin's enemies. Even Erasmus believed it was better to destroy the Old Testament than to allow the peace of the world to be disturbed because of the books of the Jews. The danger Reuchlin exposed himself to by his position makes it understandable that other outstanding Hebraists, such as his pupil Sebastian Münster (1489–1552), wished, by demonstrative hatred for the Jews, to dispel doubts about any judaizing tendencies. Another pupil of Reuchlin, the Nuremberg reformer Andreas Osiander (1498–1552), was one of the very few scholars who defended the Jews against unjustified accusations. Sometime after 1529 he published a refutation, albeit anonymous, of the charge of ritual murder.

Despite these isolated tractates in defense of the Jews, the anti-Jewish mood was now more fierce and virulent than ever. The art of printing facilitated the broad dissemination of hate literature in the form of leaflets and pamphlets. Between 1492 and 1519 the Jews were expelled from Mecklenburg, Brandenburg, Württemberg, Carinthia, Styria, and Salzburg as well as the cities of Magdeburg, Halle, Nuremberg, Colmar, Oberehnheim,

Regensburg, and Rothenburg on the Tauber. In the years 1515 and 1516 there was a serious effort to banish them throughout the Rhine-Main area and even to dislodge the Jews in toto from the entire Holy Roman Empire. However, these designs foundered on the rocks of the conflicting interests of the emperor, the local rulers, and the estates. In 1510 in Berlin thirty-six Jewish martyrs from the Margravate Brandenburg were burned at the stake because of alleged desecration of the Host, although the bishop had been informed in time that the allegations were baseless. A similar incident occurred in 1529 in Pösing near Pressburg (Bratislava). In the meantime the Peasants' War (1525) erupted in all its fury, engulfing southwestern Germany; its impact on the Jews was devastating. They were blamed for the distress of the peasants and craftsmen, yet that did not prevent Erasmus from accusing the Jews of complicity in the peasants' revolt, because of their supposed bitter hatred for Christianity.

In this charged situation two personalities now came to the aid of Jews in the German-speaking lands, protecting them from worse: Rabbi Joseph b. Gershon of Rosheim in Alsace (also called Joselman or Josel of Rosheim, c. 1478–1554) and Charles V, holy Roman emperor from 1519 to 1558. Joselman was a scholar who also served as a judge at the Jewish court. He championed Jewish causes in Alsace early on; in 1510 he was elected one of the lay leaders of the Jews in his district. From this juncture there was hardly an expulsion or persecution in the area between the Rhine, Main, and Danube in which Josel of Rosheim was not actively involved in trying to save his coreligionists. His ceaseless activity on behalf of the Jewish communities is amply attested by official documents and his own records. He was able to obtain letters of protection and charters of rights in a number of audiences with Charles V that usually took place on the occasion of the emperor's presence at sessions of the Reichstag (imperial diet). In the Peasants' War, by means of astute negotiations with the rebels, Josel was successful in representing both Jewish interests and those of the cities as well. In 1551 he negotiated with the dukes of Bavaria and Württemberg to permit the transit of expelled Jews through their territories. It was the first and, for a long period, the only time that all Jewish communities in Germany were represented at negotiations with imperial and territorial princes by a single unified leadership.

Over this entire period the policies of the empire and the territories were dominated by the schism generated in the wake of Martin Luther's teachings and his call for Church reformation. With political sagacity and diplomacy, Josel was able to exploit this situation to help ease the burdens on the Jews. Politically, he remained loyal to the emperor and his agenda to preserve a Catholic unity of faith in the empire—if only because Jews had to clear themselves of the suspicion that they bore complicity in the spread of the Reformation. His shrewd understanding of realpolitik became evident at the Reichstag in

18   Josel of Rosheim. From a contemporary anti-Jewish leaflet

Regensburg in 1532, when he received the news that Solomon Molcho was on his way to the city. Molcho, a Marrano (descendant of forcibly baptized Sephardi Jews) who had returned to Judaism, was the charismatic founder of a self-styled messianic movement. Josel left Regensburg immediately in order to avoid creating the impression that he was in some way involved in Molcho's subversive mission.

Josel would soon experience personally just how much caution he had to exercise as a Jewish statesman. In 1535 he was fined by the Imperial Supreme Court because he had referred to himself in a petition to that court as "Regierer der gemeinen Jüdischheit" ("ruler of common Jewry"). However, the title was nothing more than a German rendering of the Hebrew appellation customarily given by the communities to him and other lay leaders: *parnas u-manhig*. In the case of Josel, it had a special justification, since he was active as a leader and adviser in communities throughout the empire, as in Prague, for example, where he arbitrated a serious controversy between local factions. At the Reichstag in Augsburg in 1530, he presented takanot that had been passed at a meeting of the heads of communities he had chaired; these regulations were aimed in particular at putting an end to abuses in commerce and other dealings with the Christian population. Inter alia, they contained restrictions on moneylending and pawnbroking as well as the obligation on the part of the community elders to assist Christian plaintiffs in gaining their rights in cases brought against Jews. Joselman also requested in his petitions that Jews be freed from the "heavy yoke" of moneylending.

Though Josel was not a "humanist," he borrowed certain elements from the humanists of his time. His petitions repeatedly underscored the intrinsic value of the human being and the equality of all, Jews and non-Jews. His free and confident demeanor also reflected something of the zeitgeist. Josel's writings attest to his political acumen and profound religiosity. He was the ideal embodiment of the shtadlan, the advocate and intermediary for Jewish interests, and this to an extent probably not attained by anyone else. Joselman was also preeminent as a debater in religious disputations. At the 1530 Augsburg Reichstag, upon the order of the emperor and in his presence, he engaged in a disputation with the apostate Antonius Margarita. Margarita, who came from a prominent rabbinical family, had published a defamatory tract against the Jews entitled *Der gantz Jüdisch glaub* (The Jewish Faith in Its Entirety). Joselman emerged victorious from the disputation, and Margarita was expelled

Der gantz Jüdisch glaub

mit sampt ainer gründtlichen vnd war-
hafften anzaygunge/ Aller Satzungen /Ceremonien/
Geßetten/haymliche vnd offentliche Gebreüch /deren sich bye
Juden halten/durch das gantz Jar/Mit schönen vnd ge-
gründten Argumenten wyder jren Glaußen. Durch
Anthonium Margaritham hebrayschen Leser
der Lößlichen Statt Augspurg /beschri-
ben vnd an tag gegeben.

M. D. XXX.

19   Title page of Antonius Margarita, *Der gantz Jüdisch glaub*

from the city. When the landgrave in Hesse wished to compel the Jewish communities there to listen to sermons by Protestant clergymen, Josel sent them "words of consolation," advising how they could confront and respond to the attacks by Christian theologians.

The Jewry policies of Emperor Charles V were in keeping with his general tendency to renew the old imperial traditions. On the occasion of his coronation and later, he confirmed the "long-standing rights and privileges" of the Jews, such as the charter of Frederick II from the thirteenth century that subordinated the Jews directly to the emperor via the concept of Kammerknechtschaft. At the Augsburg Reichstag in 1530, the emperor was persuaded by Josel that the persistent rumor to the effect that the Jews were assisting the Turks in their advance into Europe was baseless, and he reaffirmed their rights. The louder the voices of animosity toward the Jews resounded in the Protestant camp, the more Charles championed the rights of the Jews—albeit in return for substantial compensation. The Speyer charter of privileges (1544) was the most favorable ever granted the Jews in the empire. In particular, it promised protection of their synagogues and forbade expulsions and blood libels. Outside their place of residence Jews were excused from the obligation of displaying a distinctive badge. In addition, they received permission to charge higher interest rates than the Christians in recognition of the special economic restrictions imposed upon them. Although the emperor and his successors lacked the power to implement this charter everywhere in the empire, it held out a new possibility for Jewish existence in Germany—one that could not have been hoped for in this form even a short time earlier.

The reign of Charles V was indeed a turning point for the Jews, since the Holy Roman Empire of the German Nation had entered a significant phase on its way to becoming a state ruled by constitutional law. The general administration of justice was subject to ever more extensive control. The rulers, who increasingly were advised by legal experts, gradually came to view the Jews in a different light: not as individuals bereft of all rights, who should be at the mercy of the arbitrary will of their fellow men, but as human beings with a basic right to toleration, though no more than that. Josel conducted a tedious suit against the city of Colmar in Alsace, which had illegally expelled its Jews and was refusing to allow them to return. Though the suit proved unsuccessful, the fact that these and other similar proceedings could even take place marked a fundamentally new legal stance on the part of the state toward the Jews. There was gradual recognition of a new legal status for Jews, based in increasing measure on the Jewry regulations (*Judenordnungen*) that had been enacted by territorial princes from the beginning of the sixteenth century. These regulations spelled out in exact terms many of the rights accorded the Jews and the duties incumbent on them. On the basis of these laws Jews were able to turn to the Imperial Supreme Court, at times even successfully. In no case was this path of redress denied them.

Seen against this backdrop, Martin Luther's attitude toward the Jews appears anachronistic. Soon after his first emergence onto the public scene, he published a pamphlet *Das Jhesus Christus eyn geborner Jude sey* (That Jesus Christ Was Born a Jew, 1523). The tract caused such a sensation that within a short span it went through nine printings and appeared in two Latin translations. On the one hand, the work was meant as an attack against the Roman Catholic Church; on the other, its intent was missionary, attempting to persuade the Jews to convert to the true faith, i.e., the new reformed church. The impression possibly left by certain sections of the tract—namely, that Luther was propagating a humane and just treatment of the Jews on their behalf—was doubtlessly unintended. For Luther the question of Judaism and the Jews was part of Christian theology, a component of missionizing. His expectations that the Jews would recognize the truth of his "pure" Christianity—spontaneously and in large numbers—thus lending his reform efforts a stamp of legitimation, met with bitter disappointment.

In 1538 Luther initiated the series of his unabashedly anti-Jewish writings with the pamphlet *Wider die Sabbather* (Against the Sabbatarians), in which he accused the Jews of blame for the upsurge in heretical Christian sects, such as the Anabaptists and the judaizing groups in Moravia, who practiced circumcision and sanctified the Sabbath instead of Sunday. This was followed over the next decade by other writings and sermons, saturated with virulent hatred of the Jews, though it should be borne in mind that the discourse of the time was generally brusque and brutal. Luther went from theology to its practical implementation. In his *Von den Juden und iren Lügen* (Of the Jews and Their Falsehoods, 1543) he rejected the idea of extirpating the Jews but called for burning down their synagogues and homes, confiscating their books, forbidding their rabbis to teach, and imposing severe restrictions on their freedom of

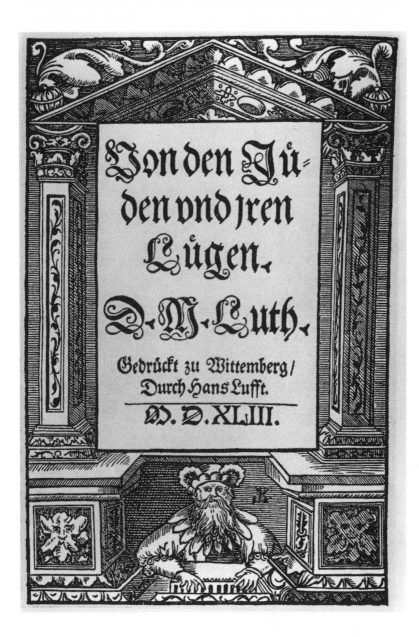

Von den Jüden vnd jren Lügen.

D. M. Luth.

Gedruckt zu Wittemberg /
Durch Hans Lufft.

M. D. XLIII.

20 Title page of one of Luther's anti-Jewish tracts

movement. Instead of engaging in usury, they should be compelled to perform the most strenuous and humiliating menial labor.

In contrast with these statements, Luther had stressed in his earlier 1523 pamphlet that, under pressure from the Roman Catholic Church, "Jews had been dealt with as though they were dogs, not humans." Did he change his views on the Jews so radically between 1523 and 1543? Opinions on this are divided. It is, however, clear that his fundamental theological position regarding the Jews had not changed: since rejecting Jesus, the Jews were irretrievably lost and had forfeited all chance of redemption. In his eyes their refusal to embrace the "true," reformed Christian church was the final confirmation of their irredeemable depravity. Consequently, he had, "in good conscience," to "despair of them."[26] This despair, then, led to his change of attitude.

It is true that Luther's vitriolic attacks against the Jews were not much cruder in tone than his railings against the papacy and Catholic clergy. As Luther aged, his general intolerance and irascibility increased. Perhaps the threat of the Turks and the widespread suspicion that Jews were prepared to betray Christians to them played a certain role. In any event, Luther and his movement had a decisive impact on the fate of the Jews in Germany, at least in the Protestant areas. Down to the Enlightenment and often even beyond, the lingering influence of Luther impeded the evolvement of an unprejudiced relation to the Jews. Over several centuries his writings, statements, and public activity provided more fuel for the old stereotypic views and allegations.

Luther's anti-Jewish writings soon made their influence felt in the realm of politics. In 1537 the elector John Frederick of Saxony, Luther's patron, denied Jews the right to settle in his principality and even to transit through the state. Two years later, the landgrave Philip "the Magnanimous" of Hesse issued a Judenordnung that became the paradigm for all later such codes in Hesse down to shortly before the emancipation of the Jews. Among other things, it enjoined them from building new synagogues, introduced compulsory missionizing sermons, and imposed a variety of economic restrictions that made it difficult for Jews to earn a livelihood. The driving force behind these laws was the Protestant theologian Martin Bucer (1491–1551), a close associate of Luther, whose "advice" to the landgrave had been far more drastic, including a prohibition on the Talmud.

Only a small number of the great Protestant reformers were less malevolent in their statements on the Jews. Philip Melanchthon

(1497–1560), a pupil and great-nephew of Reuchlin, spoke out against the blood libel, and the humanist reformer Wolfgang Capito (1478–1541) repeatedly championed Jewish interests. It must also be stressed that the Reformation and the totally new situation to which it gave birth also had some favorable impact on the Jews. The interdenominational struggle among Christians served to divert public attention. From now on Jews were not the sole religious minority; they shared their demand for tolerance with multiple other groups and sects. In addition, the growing esteem for the Hebrew Bible generated a positive interest in Judaism among reformed Christians. Nonetheless, the anti-Jewish mood of the Lutheran Reformation remained an abiding feature.

Despite the severe anti-Jewish legislation promulgated by Pope Paul IV in his papal bull *Cum nimis absurdum* (1555), the living conditions of Jews in Catholic areas were sometimes better than in Protestant regions. In his *Judenbüchlein* (Booklet on the Jews, 1541), Johannes Eck (1486–1543), Luther's Catholic adversary, had expressed an animosity toward the Jews similar to that of Luther. However, in contrast with the reformer, he insisted that they should not be dispossessed, expelled, or forced to perform debasing menial labor. Eck argued that there should be no interference in their laws and customs.

The Religious Peace of Augsburg (1555), which stipulated that subjects were to follow the confession of their territorial prince (*cuius regio, eius religio*), an important principle of Luther's religious politics, was potentially fraught with enormous peril for the Jews. Nonetheless, in most of the German states, this principle was not consistently implemented. The Catholic Restoration, promoted especially by the newly established Jesuit order and its institutions, strengthened the power of the Habsburg emperors, thus indirectly reinforcing the protection of the Jews from arbitrary will. The favorable policy of Charles V regarding the Jews was most effective in Alsace, the seat of the Habsburg government in its western territories (*Vorderösterreich*), where, in 1548, the emperor ordered the Alsatian cities of Rosheim and Türckheim to protect their Jewish inhabitants. Some expulsions did take place in Bohemia and Moravia, especially in Prague, under the pretext that the Jews maintained secret contacts with the Turks—yet these were temporary measures, taken under pressure from the townspeople. In 1577 Emperor Rudolf II (1576–1612) promised the Jews of Bohemia never to expel them again. Despite this relative improvement, the situation of German Jewry continued to appear particularly precarious from the perspective of contem-

21A, 21B   Traditional dress of the Jews of Worms
(with yellow ring) in the sixteenth century. The money bag indicates
dealings in cash; the garlic (Hebr. *shum*) alludes to their residence in the
SHUM communities of Speyer, Worms, and Mainz.

porary observers outside Germany. Thus Polish Jews wrote that there was
far greater hatred for Jews in Germany than in other lands.[27]

9. The Jewish Community in the Sixteenth Century

The intellectual and social life of the Jews in German-speaking Europe
in the sixteenth century shows signs of a departure from medieval
thought patterns, in many respects heralding the advent of a new era.
The Jewish community duly registered the fact that numerous Christian
scholars were studying Hebrew language and literature with Jewish

teachers. The resulting personal relations between Jews and Christians had been extremely rare in earlier periods. Josel of Rosheim was a friend of the reformer Wolfgang Capito and even attended some of his sermons. When Luther's anti-Jewish writings were published, Josel's knowledge of the Christian world of scholarship enabled him to state that Luther's demands for tyranny and violence against the Jews were unprecedented: never had any scholar called for such drastic measures.[28] Since, according to Jewish religious law, the imparting of Jewish knowledge to non-Jews was indeed quite questionable,[29] it is possible to assume there was at least an expectation in contemporary Jewish scholarly circles that intellectual contacts might result in a lessening of religious-political tensions.

When Luther then began to propagate a form of Christianity that, at least on the surface, seemed to be more in keeping with Jewish religious conceptions, and initially published a pamphlet that was "well-disposed" toward them, the Jews were absolutely convinced that these events were portentous and harbored messianic significance. Counterposed to Luther's hope of the mass conversion of the Jews was their own expectation that the rapprochement initially intimated by the Reformation would lead to the prophesied recognition of Judaism throughout the world. Though the Jews were disappointed by the publication of Luther's anti-Jewish tractates, these messianic hopes continued to glimmer. After all, did not any reasonable person have to recognize that the truth of Judaism had preserved the continuity and unity of the Jewish people over the ages, while the Christians by contrast were quick to change their creed? They had splintered into diverse factions and fought one against the other, embroiled in bloody internecine religious wars.[30]

Already at the beginning of the sixteenth century, an age rich in messianic stirrings in Judaism, there had also been great excitement among the German Jews when Asher Lemmlein was celebrated in Istria as the prophesied Messiah (1500–1502). Linked with messianic currents was a distinct tendency toward Kabbala. About the middle of the century, Rabbi Naphtali Herz Treves was active as a cantor in the synagogue in Frankfurt am Main. His kabbalistic interpretation of the prayer book, *Dikduk tefilah* (The Precise Interpretation of Prayer, 1560), reflects a rise in such tendencies. Ashkenazi intellectual life, previously oriented almost exclusively in terms of rabbinic Judaism, now surged in other directions as well. Elijah Levita (1468/69–1549), who hailed from Neustadt near Nuremberg, made a name for himself in Italy as a Hebraist and could count well-known Christian humanists among his closest friends. Levita authored a great many linguistic works, publishing numerous volumes between 1540 and 1544 in Isny, including several important first publications in Western Yiddish. Josel of Rosheim wrote compendia on ethics, based in part on Spanish-Jewish moral philosophy.

Meanwhile, Hebrew printing had also established itself in the German-speaking cultural orbit, and Jews from Germany contributed to the spread of Hebrew printing abroad. In 1512 a Hebrew press was opened in Prague, and Hebrew printing was also begun in other German cities, initially promoted by the Hebraic interests of Christian humanists. The Basel edition of the Talmud (1578–1581) served as the model for many later printings in Germany and beyond. Among Jews, as among other groups, printing also promoted popular writings. Western Yiddish literature flourished, not just in the German-speaking lands but also in communities of Jewish emigrants from Germany in Italy and Poland. Aside from its functions of edification and moral instruction, it was also a source of diversion and amusement, as evidenced by the Western Yiddish versions of German heroic legends.

The preeminent rabbinical figure in the empire was Rabbi Judah b. Bezalel (c. 1525–1609), titled Maharal and popularly known as "the eminent Rabbi Löw." From a Worms family, he had studied in Poland and served as Moravian chief rabbi in Nikolsburg (Mikulov). After 1573, except for brief intervals, he lived and taught in Prague. Maharal was the first Ashkenazi scholar who not only enriched rabbinic literature but also systematically recorded his conception of Jewish religious philosophy and ethics in a series of publications. Versed in medieval Jewish philosophy and Kabbala, he remained quite independent in his thinking. His influence on his contemporaries and subsequent Jewish thought, extending down into the modern period, was enormous. Maharal's combination of philosophy and mysticism points to a certain kinship with other Renaissance thinkers. Thus, for example, in his *Be'er ha-golah* (The Well of Exile), his rationalistic view of numerous Talmudic legends deviates substantially from conceptions customary in Ashkenaz and is molded by his fundamentally scientific approach to natural events. Traces of Renaissance thinking can also be found in the social criticism contained in his writings. He was an outspoken critic of the pedagogical method common in Ashkenaz to introduce young boys to the Talmud before they were fully conversant with the Bible. Maharal accused the Talmudic academies of exaggerated concentration on pilpulistic interpretations, an exegesis that reflected sharp wit and a thirst for fame—but not a love for the truth. His theory of exile and redemption and the place of the Jews among the nations had a fruitful impact on later Jewish thinkers. In its own way, the folk legend that attributes the creation of a golem, an artificial human being, to Judah b. Bezalel attests to the status and respect accorded him.

Maharal's thinking fell on fertile ground in Prague, where there had been an open-minded scholarly tradition since the fourteenth century. The learned talmudist Abraham Horovitz (c. 1550–1615), trained in philosophy, had publicly protested in youthful fervor against the rabbi of Posen, who in a sermon had denounced Maimonides' philosophy as heretical. Maharal was surrounded by a large circle of like-minded followers and disciples. Rabbi Mordechai Jaffe (c. 1535–1612), a native of Prague, served there at various times as the head of a yeshiva and chief judge. Along with his immense learning in Talmud, he had acquired knowledge of Jewish philosophy and Kabbala in Poland and Italy, as reflected in several of his numerous works. Like Maharal, he inveighed against the one-sided method of pilpul. Rabbi Yomtov Lipmann Heller (1579–1654), from Wallerstein in the principality of Ansbach, a disciple of Maharal and a member of the Prague rabbinate, wrote a commentary on the Mishnah, the written codification of the oral law, under the influence of his mentor. It was widely read and is evidence of the enormous breadth of his general knowledge.

David Gans (1541–1613), from Westphalia, became famous in Prague as an author of chronographic and astronomical works. His Jewish and world chronicle, *Tsemaḥ David* (Scion of David, 1592), for which he made extensive use of German chronicles, betrays in many respects the impact of the humanistic spirit of the age. Maharal's older brother, Ḥayim b. Bezalel (ca. 1520–1588), rabbi in Friedberg, also deserves mention. Among other works, he authored a Hebrew grammar, venturing into an area previously neglected by Ashkenazi Jewry. A large number of philosophical and general scholarly works were published at this time by the Hebrew presses in Prague. This open-mindedness within the circle of Jewish scholars in Prague is probably connected with the fact that Emperor Rudolf II had made Prague his residence, turning it into a cosmopolitan city characterized by extensive religious tolerance, a spirit from which the Jews also profited. The community of the Prague *Judenstadt* represented the Jews of the empire at the imperial court.

This vigorous intellectual life in Prague contrasted with a pronounced decline in Torah study in most other parts of German-speaking Europe. With the expulsion of almost all of the old large communities most of the academies and rabbinical courts also vanished, and the few rabbis of great repute bemoaned the "intellectual vacuum" dominant in the small village communities.[31] The structural changes in the internal administration of the communities, which in the fifteenth century were still accompanied by powerful convulsions, were an established fact a century later. In small communities the lay leaders were now in complete control. In the Jewry regulations drawn up by Josel of Rosheim (1530), they were mentioned as the repositories of authority, the men invested with the power to punish and impose bans within the community. This tended to increase the traditional independence of the communities from each other, a trend reinforced in 1542 by a gathering of rabbis and community leaders meeting in Worms that resolved to strengthen the exclusive judicial authority of a local community over all its members.

Such assemblies of rabbis and community lay leaders were held frequently but generally had only a regional character. The strengthening of local rule in the various territories and the traditional particularism of Ashkenazi Jewry made it difficult to bring all communities in the empire together in a single organization. The appointment of so-called imperial rabbis (*Reichsrabbiner*) did nothing to alter this fact. There is documentary evidence for this institution, in which the imperial treasury had a particular fiscal interest, for the fifteenth and sixteenth centuries, until it lapsed with the death of the last imperial rabbi, Rabbi Jacob b. Ḥayim, in Worms about 1574. In the meanwhile, the Jewish communities had recognized the competency of the Frankfurt rabbinical court and its learned assessors (*bene yeshiva*) for all of Germany in practical terms, although not formally. Serious conflicts in the communities were a quite common occurrence. Thus, for example, a vehement dispute erupted in Prague regarding the election of the lay leadership. The wrangle finally prompted the emperor to arrange for a new electoral procedure, worked out by the rabbis of three other large communities and aimed at curbing oligarchical tendencies in the community.

10. End of an Era and New Beginnings

One of the decisive changes in the Jewish population during the sixteenth century was its rapid growth. Already in the first half of the century figures for the two largest communities in the empire soared at a previously unprecedented rate. In the Prague ghetto the number of Jews doubled over the span of two decades, from 600 in 1522 to 1,200 in 1541. In the ghetto in Frankfurt am Main the population rose from 250 in 1520 to 900 in 1569. In Breslau there was a ban on Jews moving to the city, yet there were increasing instances where the town council admitted Jews temporarily as visitors to the trade fair, and later on other occasions as well. New Jewish settlements were also established in a number of localities. In part, this was at the initiative of the territorial rulers, as in the ecclesiastical territories under the control of the bishop of Hildesheim and the archbishop of Cologne—though not within the two cities proper. In Vienna a Jewish community gradually began to form once again during the sixteenth century. Jews were also readmitted in Mainz (1583) and Metz (1564–1567). A Jewish community was reestablished in Metz only after the territory of the bishopric—until then part of the Upper Rhenish Imperial District—had become French territory in 1592. Nonetheless, this important community continued to belong for a considerable time to the cultural ambit of the German communities.

Already in the sixteenth century the strengthening of territorial rule led to entrusting Jews with certain tasks involving the provisioning of the royal court and the securing of the state budget. One of the first such court factors (*Hoffaktoren*, contractors and suppliers)—though not yet a court Jew in the full sense of this term—was Michel von Derenburg, who maintained business connections with several German princes and functioned as court factor of the elector Joachim II of Brandenburg between 1543 and 1549. The perils threatening the life of a Jewish court factor were vividly manifest in the fate of the Berlin mint master Lippold. After the sudden death of the elector, he was executed in 1573, charged with having allegedly poisoned his benefactor. Mordechai Meisel in Prague (1528–1601) fared better; he received a special writ of privileges granted in 1593 by Rudolf II in recognition of his services. Nonetheless, Meisel's entire assets were confiscated after his death; the justification given was that they belonged to his imperial lord, since Meisel had died childless.

Thus, the legal security of the Jews was dependent on the interests of the regents—and was to remain so for a long time to come. Jews were tol-

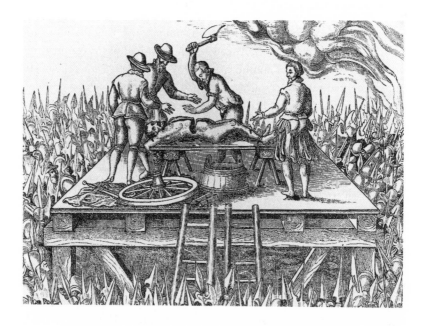

22　Torture of the mint master Lippold, January 23, 1573

erated as long as they "behaved properly," did not incur the wrath of the Christians, and were of material utility to their ruler. This did nothing to alter their social isolation. In the mind of the surrounding Christian society, the Jew had taken on the semblance of a despised and feared creature, only barely human. Many found the explanation to the riddle of their tenacious survival and steadfast refusal to be converted in the ancient legend of the Wandering Jew, for example, in the anonymous *Kurze Beschreibung und Erzählung von einem Juden namens Ahasver* (Short Description and Tale of a Jew Named Ahasver, 1602). Ahasver cannot die; as punishment for the crucifixion of the redeemer, he is condemned to wander eternally until Judgment Day, thus attesting everywhere to the truth of Christian tradition. "Now they no longer kill and torment us, they just expel us," said Maharal in a sermon in 1592, shortly after Emperor Rudolf had given him an audience.[32] These words of Maharal can be said to sum up the Jewish experience of the world at the end of the sixteenth century.

Yet a new age was dawning. Expulsions of Jews became more infrequent and isolated, the Church slowly lost its dominant position in matters affecting Jews, and a brighter future for the Jewish communities in Central Europe appeared to be at hand. In the East, as well, Polish Jewry took on new strength with its *Va'ad arba ha-aratsot* (Council of the Four Lands), its yeshivot, largely headed by members of immigrant families expelled from Germany, and a vigorously developing independent and distinctive corpus of custom. A new distinction began to be made at that time between the minhagim of "German" and "Polish" Jews.[33] In Germany itself, the venerable Jewry of Ashkenaz held fast to its ancient rites, usages, and traditions.

Part One
The Early Modern Period

1 | The Dawn of Early Modern Times

The late sixteenth century marked the onset of a new period in the Jews' settlement in towns and territories from which they had been expelled or where few Jews had lived before. The state as an absolutist polity became ever more dominant, and this had its effect on Jewish life in the new era. The seventeenth century was still young when the Jews, to their consternation, had to recognize that the modern state was no longer willing to leave the shaping of internal Jewish community life to their almost exclusive discretion. The strong position of the monarch and princes vis-à-vis the estates—already a key factor in political thinking in the late sixteenth century—would now free governance from the demands of the churches, the power of tradition, and the former authorities. Attempts were made to solve the problems of religious schism by transposing them to the plane of secular law. All this pointed the way to greater tolerance as well as to the rise of court Jews and the emergence of regional Jewish organizations (*Landjudenschaften*), corporate bodies recognized and supervised by the territorial prince. The basic contours of these two modern Jewish institutions were already visible in the sixteenth century.

The political and economic situation of the Jews now changed dramatically. One consequence of the Reformation was that it had forced the European states to be prepared to show greater tolerance toward adherents of other faiths. This toleration was embodied in the form of a religious peace buttressed by international guarantees in the Peace of

Westphalia (1648). Formally, tolerance was extended only to Christian minorities; in its broader effect, however, it was also of benefit to the Jews. There were increasing signs that Jews were being integrated to a certain extent into general life, a turn especially evident in the economic sphere. Two examples can serve to illustrate this. As early as 1598 it was noted that there were Jewish visitors attending the Leipzig Trade Fair, although they were subject to various discriminatory regulations. The charter of rights granted in 1611 by Emperor Matthias (1611–1619) to the Jews of Prague and all of Bohemia contains a first enumeration of the types of goods in which Jews were allowed to deal as peddlers. Up until that time the sole items they had been granted permission to sell, if at all, were goods held on pawn. In the area of culture as well, a more open attitude was now in evidence among the Jews—a new receptivity to the outside world uncharacteristic of medieval Ashkenazi Jewry, which had only begun to manifest itself in the sixteenth century.

Thus, at the turn of the century, the history of Jews in the Holy Roman Empire entered a new phase. All important new developments after the conclusion of the Thirty Years War (1648) had their beginnings long before its outbreak. This was in marked contrast to the situation of Eastern European Jewry. The middle of the seventeenth century for Jews there was a time of upheaval: many Jewish communities were destroyed in the pogroms of the Chmielnicki uprising (1648–1649), and the Swedish-Polish War (1654–1660) visited further sufferings on Jews in Poland. From this juncture on there is a parting of the historical ways: the Jews in the Old Reich experience a set of developments quite different in many respects from the history of Jewry in Eastern Europe, the Ottoman Empire, and the countries of the Mediterranean.

1. The Situation at the Beginning of the Seventeenth Century

As a result of the massive expulsions from virtually all urban centers during the fifteenth and sixteenth centuries, the majority of Jews resettled in numerous small localities; often there were only two or three Jewish families in a town or village. Many of the tiny principalities, those administered by imperial knights of the lower nobility and other petty absolutist polities, had granted them refuge for financial motives: the taxes levied on the Jews were a major source of revenue for these petty courts. As the sixteenth century came to a close, a new phase of Jewish migration in

Germany set in—this time not basically the product of expulsion and persecution, but motivated by the search for better living conditions.

The formation of a Jewish community in the Hofmark of Fürth exemplifies the way Jews were able to settle or resettle under certain favorable conditions in localities that had experienced a positive demographic and economic development. Both the margrave of Ansbach and the Bamberg archepiscopal see possessed sovereign rights there, and the nearby free imperial city of Nuremberg was also able to make its influence felt as a result of the land its citizens owned there. In 1528 the margrave initially granted permission to two Jews to take up residence in Fürth for a limited period of six years. The see followed suit in 1556 by admitting one more Jew. In 1573 it arranged for confirmation by imperial writ of its right to permit Jews to settle in Fürth. Vehement protest by the Nuremberg town council proved to no avail. By 1582 Fürth counted a population of two hundred Jews. The development of the Hofmark into a city was closely linked with this new Jewish presence in the town. In 1607 a Jewish cemetery was laid out, and the first synagogue was constructed in 1617.

Öttingen in the Ries and Glogau in Silesia were among the cities where sovereignty was shared by two authorities. There, too, conflicting official claims and interests had a favorable impact on the reconstruction of Jewish communities in these towns. The decision in 1602 by the count of Hanau to permit ten Jewish families to settle in his residential city was

23   Interior of the synagogue in Fürth (1705)

also characteristic of developments at the time: Jews were admitted simultaneously along with a small number of Calvinists in the hope that both groups would help promote commerce and manufacture in the city. However, the count initially tried to convert the Jews, obligating them to take part in a well-prepared religious disputation that took place under his direction. When his attempt at their conversion failed, he changed his tack and permitted the establishment of a Jews' Street with a synagogue. He also allowed the Jews to engage in commercial trade, imposing only minor restrictions. The count evidently expected to profit from such commerce because of the proximity of the Jewish trade center in Frankfurt am Main.

Characteristic for the new era was the permission granted Jews to settle in numerous localities in northern Germany, including towns where few Jews or none at all had lived in the medieval period. Thus, communities were reestablished in Hildesheim, Halberstadt, Minden, and Essen, and a number of new communities formed in Westphalia. During the course of the sixteenth century the territorial rulers in Hanover had repeatedly ordered the expulsion of the Jews there, but with little success, evidently because of the protection provided them by the city. After 1588, however, the situation was reversed: down to the nineteenth century Jews were permitted to reside in only one suburb, a township not under the sovereignty of the city of Hanover but subject directly to the duke. A set of different conditions was conducive to the beginning of Jewish settlement in Altona toward the end of the sixteenth century, a city where there had been no Jewish community in the medieval period. Altona was under the sovereignty of the King of Denmark, and it was he who opened the city's gates to the Jews. In 1641 King Christian IV issued a general charter of rights allowing the Jews to develop a regular communal life in the town.

Hamburg likewise had had no medieval Jewish community; here, too, Jewish settlement commenced toward the end of the sixteenth century, when a growing number of Marranos from Portugal obtained residence permits in the city by claiming to be Christians. Most were prosperous merchants with extensive business connections. Some also practiced artisan trades, particularly those, such as sugar extraction, involved in trade with Brazil. Consequently, the city had a compelling economic interest in their settlement. The "Portuguese" played a paramount role in the founding of the Hamburg Bank (1619), one of the first in Europe. The foreign commercial ties of the city expanded with each new wave of these immigrants. From 1601 Jews were also admitted in nearby Wandsbek, when it was realized how advantageous their presence was for the city of Hamburg. That same year the Marranos were permitted for a time to emigrate from Portugal and Spain, and their numbers in Hamburg rose. By 1646 there were an estimated one hundred "Portuguese" families there. Secretly, they set up three prayer rooms and established three separate communities, which united in 1652. The municipal senate had only permitted them to settle in return for a large fee; for a long period residence was conditional on their agreement to refrain from practicing their religion. However, under the pressure of economic interests, the senate later rescinded this restrictive condition.

The Hamburg burghers were far less willing than the senate to accept the presence of regular Jewish residents. One reason was that they feared competition; moreover, they were under the influence of the Lutheran clergy, whose militant intolerance toward other faiths also extended to Catholics and even Calvinists, an animus vented for many years in malevolent sermons from the pulpit. Though the senate retained the upper hand in a stubborn struggle with the citizenry, the Jews found themselves exposed to constant attacks by the burghers. For this reason a number of Portuguese families accepted a charter of rights offered in 1622 by the Danish king to settle in Glückstadt (Holstein). Nonetheless, the number of Jews in Hamburg soared, tripling from 1623 to 1663. The first Ashkenazi Jews now also came to live in Hamburg, though initially as "servants of the Portuguese nation." They relocated from Altona, fleeing from imperial, later from Swedish, troops, and they were repeatedly expelled. Not until the beginning of the eighteenth century were the "German" Jews treated as equals of the "Portuguese" in Hamburg.

A completely different set of conditions prevailed in Vienna, where a community, initially very small, though well-organized, was able to establish itself at the beginning of the seventeenth century. As the result of a Habsburg Jewry policy that oscillated between exploitation and expulsion, the number of Jewish families in Vienna in 1601 had plummeted to twelve. By 1614 their number had risen again to forty-four families. Most members were *Hofbefreite* (Jews protected by the court) or their employees and were permitted as such to develop their own community life and structures. They were active as wholesale merchants and court purveyors, enjoying an array of privileges that put them virtually on a par with the Christian nobility. Along with their entire retinue of servants, they were exempted from all taxes to the city and state. Though obliged to live in a ghetto, the *Judenstadt* (later the Leopoldstadt section of the city), separated from the city by a drawbridge, they had permission to buy and construct houses there and were under the sole jurisdiction of the chief marshal of the royal court. Since their economic activity was closely linked with state administration, they were granted freedom of movement in all towns where the emperor held court. Because of its wealth the small community was able, even then, to establish and maintain regular religious institutions. In many respects the Vienna community can be regarded as the prototype of a kehilla that developed from the nucleus of a wealthy family with close ties to the court of the ruler—a phenomenon that would soon become quite common throughout the empire.

At the end of the prologue it was pointed out that there were several large communities whose existence since the Middle Ages had not been interrupted by any longer-term expulsion and that had enjoyed continued growth. Prague was one such community: around 1600 it already had an estimated 6,000 Jews. Although a large fire completely destroyed all 318 houses of the ghetto in 1689, bringing much misfortune upon its residents, the Judenstadt was soon rebuilt. In 1702 there were 11,517 Jews again living in Prague, 28.9 percent of the total population. Throughout the entire early modern period the Prague ghetto was by far the largest Ashkenazi community and considered itself the capital of European Jewry.

By 1600 the Frankfurt ghetto had a population of some 2,200; since 1496 the number of houses in the Judengasse (Jews' Alley) had soared from 14 to 197. At the middle of the sixteenth century the Jewish community in Worms numbered 300; by 1610 it had more than doubled to 650. Both in Frankfurt and in Worms Jews made up 11 percent of the population. Despite this relatively strong concentration, also to be found in a number of other localities and regions, it should not be forgotten that the percentage of Jews was minuscule when compared with the total population of the empire, estimated in 1600 at between 18 and 20 million. In addition, the preponderant majority of Jews continued living in small to very small localities.

Although the only large-scale expulsion from an entire territory at the beginning of the seventeenth century was in Baden (1614), the Jews still lived in many places under a pall of constant insecurity and uncertainty. The sword of expulsion hung over their heads whenever privileges had to be renewed. In 1590 the duke of Brunswick-Wolfenbüttel ordered all Jews expelled from his lands, including those in Halberstadt. However, he was not rigorous in implementing this measure and, after repeated objections by the emperor, permitted them transit through his territories in 1594, later granting many the right to return. Even more characteristic for the new era was the expulsion of the Jews from Hildesheim in 1595. In response, the Jews took legal action, filing a complaint with the Imperial Supreme Court, which subsequently reversed the expulsion order (1601). In 1609 Jews were expelled from Hildesheim once again, because they had been blamed for bringing in the plague, but were soon allowed to resettle.

In southwestern Germany the threat of expulsion remained constant. In 1617 the Jewish community was expelled from Günzburg, a center for Jewry in this region. In the seventeenth century there were also entire states, such as Mecklenburg, in which Jews were denied the right of residence. In Lower Silesia the only town that allowed the Jews permanent residence was Glogau, and, in Upper Silesia, the town of Zülz. The Jews had been expelled in 1582 by an imperial edict from all other parts of Silesia. Then, during the Swedish-Polish War, large numbers of Polish Jews fled to Silesia, and in 1655, on the order of Emperor Ferdinand III, their settlement was "permitted in all localities of the Duchy of Silesia."[1]

Thus the situation of the Jews throughout the Old Reich was still far from uniform, and the Hebrew sources of the period often reflect a distinct sense of uncertainty about the future. One can gain some impression of what the right to residence in German cities meant for Jews then and later by considering their legal situation in a city like Worms, in many respects typical of the time. The Jews there were neither regarded as citizens nor so-called *Beisassen* (permanent residents, but with no civil rights). Rather, they were classified as *Hintersassen* (temporary residents) and later even as "serfs" of the city. Yet, however limited, their legal status had the advantage of its guarantee by the composite of three protective patrons: emperor, bishop, and city.

2. Events in Frankfurt am Main

For the Jews of Germany the seventeenth century began with an event that, suddenly and painfully, impressed upon their consciousness the fact that for them this was indeed the start of a new era. At the autumn trade fair in Frankfurt am Main in 1603, the lay leaders of a substantial number of communities from the south and west of the empire met to deliberate on certain deficiencies in the public life of the communities and decide how they could be remedied. Among the twenty-six participants who put their signature to the resolutions, seven or eight were rabbis, the remainder lay leaders. Autonomous Jewish jurisdiction was at the top of the list of the resolutions passed by the assembly. As on many similar occasions, Jews were urgently admonished not to bring their mutual disputes and quarrels before civil judges but rather, according to the precepts of religious law, to present them only to the rabbinical courts. Violators could expect severe warnings and harsh penalties. In order to enhance the effectiveness of the autonomous administration of justice, five rabbinical courts—in Frankfurt, Worms, Friedberg, Fulda, and Günzburg—were granted regional authority and the powers of appellate courts.

The assembly also decided to establish a fund for internal Jewish purposes, financed by a general tax: each Jew would pay one pfennig for every one hundred guldens of personal wealth. Individual assets were to be assessed by a committee of recognized reputable men, and the tax was to be remitted to specific offices located in the four above-mentioned communities (except Fulda), as well as in Mainz, Bingen, Hamm, Schnaittach, and Wallerstein (Ries). The assembly also reminded Jews it was prohibited to drink wine prepared by non-Jews or milk that had been produced under inadequate ritual supervision. It warned against frequenting taverns, renewed the prohibition on dealing in counterfeit or inferior coins or stolen goods, and ordered restrictions on expenditures for stylish apparel. Finally, the assembly issued a series of ordinances pertaining to the rabbinate: candidates for the rabbinate were only to be ordained by three competent rabbis; rabbinical supervision of ritual slaughter was to be made more strict; and the publication of new books was only permitted after approval by three rabbis. Rabbis were also prohibited from interfering in the affairs of other communities and rabbinical bans issued abroad were declared nonvalid. The assembly called on all rabbis in Germany to add their signature to the resolutions and to post them in all synagogues.

A Jewish informer—a butcher who had carried out nonkosher slaughter and had therefore been dismissed by the community—saw this as a welcome opportunity to take revenge. He managed to obtain a copy of the resolutions and then proceeded to denounce the signatories to the authorities, accusing them of plotting a highly treasonable conspiracy against the emperor and the empire. By means of artful intrigue, the informer succeeded in mobilizing the electors of Mainz and Cologne; they initiated proceedings against the Frankfurt community in the name of the emperor. Imperial commissioners then brought allegations against the

Jews at the city council, claiming that they intended to reduce the authority of the emperor and were thus guilty of conspiracy and lese majesty. The charges caused an enormous sensation. The protocols of the assembly and other documents of the community were confiscated. The indictment stresses that the convening of the "synod" in itself constituted a crime against the emperor, the empire, and the Church; the power of excommunication, the rabbinical criminal court, internal taxation, and the supposedly new ordinances on morality and religion were also criminal acts. These were all presumptions to authority that contradicted and were in conflict with the general pattern of the development of territorial states. Similar claims of authority had also characterized the expansion of regional rule in the sixteenth century.

In their defense statement the Jews affirmed their innocence and emphasized that, on the basis of longstanding experience, they could only assume that their assembly and resolutions would be favorably received by the emperor. And, in actual fact, such a meeting was nothing extraordinary. Due to the lack of a Jewish central authority in the empire, assemblies at which representatives of the communities discussed questions and problems of current interest and passed resolutions that were later published as *takanot* (ordinances) convened from time to time. Twenty-one years earlier, in 1582, an assembly had taken place where some of the resolutions adopted were quite similar. The representatives gathered together in Frankfurt truly had no reason to assume that the city magistrate and imperial court would have anything but understanding and sympathy for their enterprise. After all, the authorities in the past had generally regarded such "synods" with favor on account of their interest in effective Jewish self-administration in order to assure the smooth collection of taxes and levies. However, it emerged that there was a serious mistaken assumption here as far as the imperial government was concerned. Although the Frankfurt council eventually declared the resolutions harmless and unobjectionable, the main plaintiff, the elector-archbishop of Cologne, remained adamant. His aim was to extort as high an atonement fine as possible from the Jews, and he ultimately succeeded in his designs. After all, the resolutions, especially in the German translation available to the authorities, represented an ostensible challenge to the legal rights of the territorial princes, rulers, and authorities. The proceedings dragged on for many years, and the case was finally resolved in 1623: the community compensated the archbishop of Cologne for his "substantial expenses."

Even if this was certainly no "conspiracy," there are reasons to suppose that the initiators of the Frankfurt resolutions were well aware of the implications of their actions and the possible political provocation they entailed. This is reflected in their express declaration that there was no intention whatsoever to diminish the authority of the government and that supreme power over the Jews rested in its hands. In terms of their content, the resolutions differed little from the many takanot issued in earlier years. Josel of Rosheim and the assembly he convened had already struggled against many of the deficiencies and infractions that were the occasion for the Frankfurt resolutions. But the Frankfurt assembly obviously wished to achieve more than a mere improvement in the level of religious and moral life. It aspired to bring about a stricter internal management of community life, especially by regulation of the rabbinical court system and by a certain degree of organizational coordination of all Jews in Germany. It is out of the question that the participants were motivated by any political aims; nonetheless, it was not difficult to view the strengthening of rabbinical and community authority as a form of encroachment on the imperial sphere of power. The regional rabbinical courts that the assembly planned were all situated in free imperial cities or in territories immediately subservient to the empire—probably in order to avoid interfering in the authority of the territorial rulers. The territorial principle they embodied had, quite obviously, been influenced by developments in the empire. However, this orientation was precisely what had awakened suspicions among the highest imperial authorities.

The court proceedings by the state against the "conspiracy of the rabbis" brought an abrupt and sudden change in the political situation of the Jews as a religious-ethnic minority. After 1603 no further regional synod was convened, and in 1659 a final attempt to hold discussions in Hanau between rabbis from all over the empire proved a failure. A banding together of all Jews in the empire in the form of an association of individual members was contrary to the principle of the territorial state. As time went on the Jews in Germany saw themselves more and more as subjects of individual territories and not of the empire. Only in the imperial cities and in his hereditary lands did the emperor still have the prerogative of power over his Jewish subjects. The Jews realized now that the autonomy of community and religious life granted to them in the Middle Ages was no longer in harmony with the theory and practice of the territorial state. That state was prepared to permit a certain degree of tolerance toward Jews only if it appeared politically and economically expedient.

Viewed from this perspective, here was the beginning of a development that led directly to the Jewry policy of the Enlightenment and of liberalism. The events of 1603 thus appear to mark a turning point in the history of German Jewry.

The uproar over the "synod" heightened feelings of insecurity among the Jews. At the same time, the pressure of the imperial commission and the lack of imperial protection were an open invitation to the population to indulge in aggressive violence. That was not long in coming. As mentioned, the community representatives in Frankfurt felt there was need to take stringent measures to counter the trade in low-quality and counterfeit coins. Such coins were inundating the market, and the Jews were generally blamed for this, especially members of the Frankfurt and Worms communities. The resolutions passed by the Frankfurt assembly indicate that this allegation, which provoked popular anger, was in part justified. There were many cases at the time of Jews convicted for crimes involving coins. But the general mood of disgruntlement in the Frankfurt population had deeper reasons, which had little to do with the Jews. The free imperial city of Frankfurt was ruled by a patrician oligarchy that put the guilds at a serious disadvantage. Calls by the burghers for greater participation in the municipal government grew ever louder. Finally, the tension between the council and citizenry erupted in the form of demands against the Jews. In 1612 riots broke out both in Frankfurt and Worms.

Emperor Matthias's ascendancy to the throne and his coronation in Frankfurt in 1612 were the occasion sparking a political movement among the citizenry. When the council rejected the grievances, a citizens' committee was formed; it delivered its demands in a turbulent petition, took control of the city and appealed to the emperor. Complaints were voiced about patrician rule in the city. The citizenry demanded participation in municipal government, the reorganization of the tax system, the monitoring of municipal finances, and the creation of a standing citizens' committee. The movement was not just against the council, but was also directed against the Jewish community under the council's protective wing. The guilds in Frankfurt called for tighter restrictions on Jewish economic activity. Their spokesman was the pastry baker Vincent Fettmilch, a well-educated man who had nonetheless failed to secure employment with the city administration. Jews who ventured into the streets outside the limits of the Judengasse were often maltreated. The powerlessness of the councillors became evident in negotiations between the guilds, the council, and the imperial commissioners. Finally, the citizenry demanded

24 The Frankfurt Judengasse, section from the "Grand Bird's-Eye View"
by M. Merian the Elder (1628)

the expulsion of all Jews, except for the wealthiest families. In 1614 the
unrest erupted in an upheaval. Fettmilch assumed dictatorial powers in
the city and, after a courageous but unsuccessful stand by the Jewish residents, the Judengasse was plundered. The community sought refuge at
the Jewish cemetery, awaiting the worst. The insurgents forced some
1,380 persons to leave the city.

These events differed from medieval pogroms and expulsions in several respects. Not only were there hardly any Jewish dead or injured, and no Jew was compelled to accept baptism, but many of the persecuted Jews managed to find shelter in the homes of compassionate Christians in neighboring towns (including Offenbach, Hanau, Gelnhausen, and a number of localities in the Taunus) as well as in Frankfurt itself. Moreover, the fact that Emperor Matthias immediately intervened was indicative of the changed situation of the Jews. He placed Fettmilch under an imperial ban, and his authority, binding on the imperial free city, was sufficient to quash the rebellion. It collapsed, the former city council was reinstated, and Fettmilch and his coconspirators were later executed. The Jews returned to the city in a festive procession, accompanied by pipes and drums. The synagogue and many houses in the Judengasse were restored at municipal expense, and a large plaque was affixed above each of the three gates of the ghetto, displaying the imperial eagle and the inscription: "Under the Protection of the Roman Imperial Majesty and the Holy Empire." From this date on, the Frankfurt Jewish community held an annual commemoration of the deliverance with a local "Purim" celebration, preceded by a fast. Meanwhile, similar events had taken place in

25   The Fettmilch uprising of 1614

Worms. All the Jews were expelled from the city in 1615, their houses and synagogue looted and destroyed. Here the elector of the Palatinate intervened; the gang leaders were routed from the city, the Jews returned under a military escort, and the city was forced to pay them compensation.

Soon after the Jews returned to Frankfurt, the emperor issued a new *Judenstättigkeit*, as the legislation governing Jews was called in a number of towns. Thanks to this new decree, the Jewish community now had greater security than before. Henceforth the right of residence was unlimited—not restricted as before to a period of three years—and could be passed on to descendants. On the other hand, the Jewish population of Frankfurt was fixed at a maximum of five hundred households, only twelve marriages per year were permitted, and only six Jews from outside the city were annually allowed to take up permanent residence. In all other matters, including stiff ordinances designed to prevent closer social ties between Jews and Christians, the new legislation followed in the footsteps of the old. However, unlike previous *Stättigkeit* laws, it was not issued by the municipal council but decreed by the emperor himself, and only he could revoke it. In addition, the new law stipulated that all apprentices had to swear an oath they would not harass the Jews in any way. Both legally and politically, the outcome of the Fettmilch revolt underscored the fact that the worst pressures of the Jewish Middle Ages had come to an end.

3. The Jews in the Thirty Years War

The terrible suffering and devastation brought about by the Thirty Years War (1618–1648) in many areas of German-speaking Europe naturally wrought havoc in many Jewish communities as well. In 1621 the synagogue in Fürth was looted by soldiers, and the entire local community was destroyed in 1634. The homes of the Jews in Halberstadt were also plundered. The consequences of the war were particularly ruinous for the Jews in Bohemia and Moravia: numerous communities were completely devastated, and large numbers of Jewish refugees from villages and small towns in Bohemia and Austria sought refuge in Vienna and Prague. The Jews often suffered as much or more from the war's burdens than the Christian population. They were forced to quarter soldiers in their dwellings and frequently compelled to pay tribute far in excess of that demanded from their Christian neighbors. Nor were large communities, such as Frankfurt and Worms, spared the scourge of the epidemics that accompanied the fighting. There were even attempts to expel Jews from entire territories (such as Hesse-Darmstadt, 1628). Though the Frankfurt community provided assistance to refugees in transit, it was unable to absorb even a single uprooted family.

Nonetheless, the situation of the Jews in many localities remained more favorable than that of the general population. While the Christian population was decimated—in a number of regions drastically reduced by 60–70 percent—the Jewish population as a whole experienced only a minimal overall decline. The number of Jewish inhabitants in Frankfurt was 2,209 in 1624 and had dropped to 1,777 at the end of the war, a loss of about 20 percent. The Jews were not directly affected by the religious conflicts over which the war was fought, and their residential areas often suffered less than those of the Christian population—even though Jewish dwellings in a number of localities were deliberately plundered because they were believed to contain more valuable spoils. Many Jews were able to provide services useful for the conduct of the war in their capacity as middlemen, suppliers of goods, and credit agents; they soon became indispensable to both the Protestant and Catholic princes and military commanders. At the beginning of the war, with the empire in the throes of an acute crisis, the Jews constituted one of the few potentials the emperor was readily able to mobilize for his benefit.

From 1630 on, the Swedes in particular availed themselves of Jewish financial and commercial connections in the many German cities they occupied. As a consequence, Jewish involvement in economic and political life increased, but not before they had been forced to pay enormous war taxes levied on them by the occupying forces. Through their ramified network of far-reaching connections in Eastern Europe, Jewish entrepreneurs supplied entire armies with rations and fodder. Another major advantage for these Jewish contractors was the fact that so many Jews lived in villages and small towns and had for many years been engaged in trade between the countryside and the urban areas. They set up foundries and powder mills and supplied weapons, ammunition, horses, and clothing. For that reason the occupying troops, both Swedish and imperial, were often issued strict instructions to leave the houses of the Jews untouched. Thus, in 1636, Emperor Ferdinand II (1619–1637) ordered that Jews in Worms should not be harassed; they were not to be burdened by forced billeting of troops or compulsory loans. Not surprisingly, a Bohemian nobleman from the baronial family Lobkowitz attempted to salvage some of his valuables by hiding them in the Prague Jewish quarter.

The Jewish quarter in Prague was indeed a center of feverish business activity in the service of the emperor and his armies. When the imperial side was faced with a severe lack of funds at the outset of the war and feared serious defeat as a result, the Prague financier Jacob Bassevi (1570–1634), together with Prince Liechtenstein and General Wallenstein, leased the imperial silver mint. By a reduction in the silver content of its coinage, the emperor was able to raise immense sums for the conduct of the war. In the Battle of the White Mountain (1620), his army and that of the league emerged victorious over the Bohemians and recaptured the city of Prague. At the outbreak of the war a mob had stormed and pillaged the Prague Jewish quarter; now this was the only area of the city that, on specific orders from the emperor, was not plundered by his troops. After the emperor's entry into Prague, the Jews staged a festive procession in his honor, similar to that put on in Frankfurt after the quashing of the Fettmilch uprising. Henceforth, for more than one hundred years, the day imperial and league troops entered the city was celebrated as the "Prague Purim," with fasting and a subsequent festive meal. In recognition of his services, Bassevi himself was knighted by the emperor and given the title Ritter von Treuenberg. He was the first Jew in the Holy Roman Empire to be elevated to the hereditary nobility. Prince Liechtenstein, the imperial governor of Bohemia, allowed the Prague Jews to purchase a large number of empty Lutheran houses confiscated by the emperor. Since the citizenry and council of Prague had supported the revolt of the Bohemian estates, the expansion of the ghetto was carried out despite their vehement opposition. The Prague Jewish quarter now became a Judenstadt, a Jewish city. Emperor Ferdinand III (1637–1657) gave symbolic expression to the protected position of the Jews in Prague by permitting them to adopt, as a coat of arms, a Swedish helmet with a star of David, which was then affixed to all buildings of the Jewish community.

It is noteworthy that in the Thirty Years War the Jews—for the first time in their history—were often treated better than the rest of the population. That was certainly the distinct impression of a contemporary rabbi in Frankfurt am Main:

> We have seen with our own eyes and heard with our own ears that the living God dwells in our midst, ever standing by us in wondrous ways. . . . The soldiers, for years now on the march through the towns and villages, have often treated us more kindly than the non-Jews, so that Gentiles have sometimes brought their belongings to

Jews for safekeeping. Likewise, it was wondrously providential that the enemy troops failed in their designs to arrest Jews. And it proved an easy task to liberate those who had nonetheless been taken into custody, freeing them without a ransom or in return for only a small sum.[2]

The Thirty Years War was a time of rapid change for the Jews. Many new communities, urban and rural, were established specifically during this period; the number of members in some urban communities either grew or remained constant. In Vienna, as mentioned, a fully functioning community had formed, and, around 1618, its leadership board consisted of sixteen persons. It soon attracted outstanding scholars and developed into an intellectual center. Sometime between 1625 and 1627 the community appointed its first rabbi, the famous scholar Yomtov Lipmann Heller. The number of Jews in Vienna continued to climb throughout the war, and there were already more than two thousand Jews resident in the city by 1650.

Jews everywhere gained access to areas of the economy that had been previously closed to them. Thus, along with peddling, they were permitted in Frankfurt to engage in several branches of commercial trade even though they were not allowed to maintain shops or stands at the market and could only hawk their wares from door to door. Yet the war also had less favorable consequences for the Jewish population. The Jews suffered along with the Christians as a result of the general impoverishment of a large proportion of the rural population in the wake of the war. Jewish beggars and itinerants, not lacking even before it began, were a frequent sight during the war and increased immensely after its conclusion.

4. The Impact of 1648

In the history of European Jewry, 1648 was a year of tragic and dramatic events. While the belligerent parties were busy negotiating the Peace of Westphalia in Münster and Osnabrück, rebellious cossacks under Bogdan Chmielnicki swept down upon Jews in the Ukraine, at that time a part of the Polish state, perpetrating a horrible bloodbath and destroying hundreds of Jewish communities. The Jews in Eastern Europe also suffered badly during the Swedish-Polish War (1654–1660). Although there had been some earlier migration of Jews from east to west, a steady stream of refugees from Poland and Lithuania now poured toward the west and

south. In the sixteenth century the Jews in Poland had felt safer than their
coreligionists in Germany. Now that situation was reversed: they came
westward in torrents, seeking refuge in Germany, Austria, and Moravia.
The governments often disregarded existing laws, designating Jews who
lived on the Polish border and constituted a substantial majority of the
immigrants officially as "border Jews." Large groups of Jewish refugees
made their way to East Prussia and Silesia as well, and Polish Jews were
granted residence permits as "domestic servants" of local Jews in Breslau,
where they then became active as commercial agents for Jewish entrepreneurs abroad. In time they constructed five synagogues there. Refugees
fleeing from Poland were granted admission elsewhere as well, for example, in Hamburg, Dessau, and Fürth. The Jewish community in Moisling
near Lübeck, which played a dominant role in the Jewish population of the
East Holstein-Mecklenburg region into the nineteenth century, was
established by refugees who had fled from the cossacks. An entire yeshiva
with its director took flight from Cracow to Vienna.

Soon after the war's conclusion there were anti-Jewish reactions to this
inundation of immigrants. In 1650 the Moravian legislature passed a resolution that all Jews who had immigrated into Moravia after 1618 should
be deprived of their right of residence, since they had become "too numerous." With the departure of the foreign armies after the Peace of
Westphalia, various local authorities attempted once again to expel the
Jews. Their designs were successful in the free cities of Lübeck, Heilbronn,
Schweinfurt, Augsburg (though only partially there), and in a number of
cities in Upper Hesse (1662). Expulsion was the fate of the majority of
Ashkenazi Jews who had settled in Hamburg during the war. Nonetheless,
most rulers, including the great elector of Brandenburg, the elector of the
Palatinate, the duke of Hanover, the margrave of Ansbach, and others
refused to give in to the call of many urban citizens to expel the Jews.
Thus, Jews remained in Dessau, Halberstadt, Heidelberg, Herford, Cleves,
Landsberg, Minden, and innumerable villages. Elector Charles Louis of
the Palatinate (1632–1680) bestowed extensive rights and benefits on Jews
who were ready and able to lend a hand in the development of the city of
Mannheim. As a result, the Jewish population there tripled in a short span,
soaring from 125 households in 1698 to 380 in 1734.

The new political situation created by the Peace of Westphalia ultimately proved advantageous to the Jews. A large number of territorial
and urban regimes, each of which was able to pursue its own policies,
made Jews everywhere directly subordinate to local authorities. This

generally was a favorable development for the Jews as the era of absolutism came into full bloom. The old relationship of chamber serfdom to
the imperial sovereign was finally a thing of the past. The attempt by
Emperor Ferdinand II to reinstate the *güldener Opferpfennig* proved
abortive as early as 1635. Particularly now, after the conclusion of the
peace, the territorial sovereignty of the numerous princes and principalities, and their need for recognition, made it necessary to tap the economic potential of the Jews, which had so clearly proved its worth in the
recent war. There was now hardly a capital city, large or small, where at
least one Jewish family had not been permitted to settle. In the small
locality of Öttingen (Ries), the Jews on one side of the market square
were nicknamed the "Catholic Jews," those on the other side the
"Protestant Jews"—since one of the reigning dynasties of princes and
counts was Catholic, the other Protestant, and the boundary between
their two territories ran straight through the market square. Numerous
territorial changes now brought Jewish populations into territories that
had previously not tolerated Jewish inhabitants. Although this occasionally resulted in expulsions, it was also easier to draft laws on Jews
in such principalities, since there was no older Jewry legislation to be
taken into account.

The principle of tolerance and freedom of religion (notwithstanding
the official state religion) that had been laid down in the Peace of
Westphalia was valid for only the "three religions established in the
empire," namely Lutheranism, Calvinism, and Catholicism. It was not
applicable in the case of other Christian denominations and most certainly did not apply to the Jews. Yet the new religious peace had an impact
on attitudes toward the Jews, since the decision to separate politics from
religion was also advantageous for them. More and more Christians were
now traveling to Muslim countries, and the lands of other "infidels," and
demanded tolerance there. Consequently, it was impossible to deny tolerance to "unbelievers" in one's own country. Even before the religious
peace the authorities had grown accustomed to the fact that Jewish representatives now demonstrated a sensitivity for legal matters that had
already been given pointed expression by Josel of Rosheim. Most certainly the growing toleration of the Jews was influenced in part by
humane sentiments. Jews were now often invited on festive occasions to
participate in celebrations put on by the princes and cities. Nonetheless,
the actual intention was generally the age-old hope: the ultimate conversion of all Jews to Christianity.

In fact, even halfhearted toleration of the Jews aroused the opposition of the city populations and especially the guilds. Religious fervor and fear of economic competition both played a role here. In Halberstadt, during the Thirty Years War, the Swedish government had already defended the Jews against the allegations and violence of the guilds. After the city became part of Brandenburg, the new territorial ruler assumed this task of defense. The burghers of Vienna had greater success in their opposition to the Jews. Expulsions had already occurred on several earlier occasions there, and the Habsburg policy toward the Jews had long fluctuated between favoring the Jews and oppression. The merchants of Vienna, who in reality were only fearful of Jewish competition, were successful in their allegations that the Jews maintained treacherous links with the Jews of the Ottoman Empire. When he assumed the throne, Emperor Ferdinand III (1637–1657), bowing to pressure from the Vienna city council, initially refused to confirm the chartered privileges of the Jews. Yet, finally, he not only renewed their old rights, but expanded them—albeit in return for a substantial sum of money.

With the change of emperors in 1657, the city of Vienna launched renewed initiatives to expel its Jews. On the advice of his financial officials, Leopold I (1657–1705) at first—but not for long—resisted these pressures. Leopold's Spanish consort joined the Viennese merchants who

26   From a broadside on the expulsion of the Jews from Vienna 1670

were urgently petitioning for the expulsion of the Jews, blaming the presence of the Jews in the city for a miscarriage she had suffered. The expulsion order was sent to 1,346 persons of Vienna's Jewish community—as the Prussian envoy reported to the great elector in 1669—and they were compelled to emigrate in the summer of 1670. Most of them moved to Moravia, where many Viennese Jews had relatives. Others went to Bohemia and, via Moravia, to Hungary, particularly to the possessions of the tolerant Count Esterhazy in Burgenland, where the so-called seven communities soon began to flourish, with Eisenstadt as their center. Some families emigrated to Cracow, where many Viennese Jews had close trading ties with local Jews. Several large rural communities in southern Germany, such as Harburg (Ries), were founded by expellees from Vienna. Other communities, such as Fürth, absorbed a significant influx from Vienna. In 1683, for economic reasons, the emperor revoked the expulsion.

Thus, even in the early modern period, forced migration was the fate of the Jews in many German-speaking lands. The same year the Jews were compelled to leave Vienna they were also expelled from the Fulda rural districts. That was not the first time in this century: in 1641 they had suffered a similar expulsion. For other reasons, the Jews were forced to migrate from the large, ancient community in Worms: when Louis XIV invaded the Palatinate in 1689, the community was destroyed, along with the entire town. The Jews had tried in vain to curry the favor of the French with the payment of large sums. This later led to charges of treason leveled against them by members of the Worms town council. Not until 1699 did the Jews return to the city.

In Switzerland there had been no Jews since the end of the fifteenth century, after they had been banished from all cities there. During the seventeenth century they were permitted to settle in the canton of Aargau, but ultimately took up residence only in Lengnau and Endingen. For more than two hundred years these were the only localities in Switzerland where Jewish families were allowed to reside. The greater part of the Jews in these two communities stemmed from the Rhine region. The relative personal security and protection of property guaranteed to the Jews in Lengnau and Endingen are remarkable considering that Jews were strictly forbidden to live anywhere else in Switzerland. In 1689 they were accorded the special privilege of being allowed to lease a strip of land on an island in the Rhine for a cemetery. In use for many years, it became known as the *Judeninsel* (Jews' Island).

5. Admission of the Jews into Brandenburg-Prussia

Meanwhile, news of the expulsion of Jews from Vienna was received with special interest at the court of the great elector, Frederick William I of Brandenburg-Prussia (1640–1688) in Berlin. The Prussian monarch had spent his youth in Holland and absorbed the spirit of religious tolerance prevalent there. As a Calvinist, he was opposed to the orthodox Lutheranism many of his subjects espoused. For that reason he had few compunctions about pursuing a generous policy of immigration that ignored the wishes of the Lutheran church and promoting a realistic economic policy aimed at providing his economically backward country, thinly populated in the aftermath of the war, with new producers and consumers. Negotiations were held with representatives of the Viennese Jews. The result was that in May 1671 the great elector issued an edict permitting fifty Jewish families to settle in Berlin and several other cities in the Margravate Brandenburg, where their residence had formerly been prohibited. He had already granted Jews admission in East Prussia; in other territories acquired by the Peace of Westphalia—Cleves, Mark, Ravensberg, and the bishoprics of Minden and Halberstadt—small Jewish settlements already existed everywhere or were in the process of formation. Outstanding among these was the development of the Jewish community in Halberstadt. In the person of the great elector it had a constant protector who shielded the community against the hostility of the population and the municipal administration. The accommodating attitude of the monarch toward the Jews was based mainly on economic motives, yet religious factors also played a part. He hoped to be able to do missionary work among the Jews—an aim neither he nor his successors ever lost sight of. Thus, even here, the toleration accorded the Jews was only limited, conditional: the overriding consideration was economic utility, the ultimate goal their conversion to Christianity.

Initially, however, Frederick William insisted on a certain degree of tolerance toward the Jews, which repeatedly provoked the Lutheran population to protests and formal complaints. The edict of admission permitted the Jews to rent, purchase, or build apartments and houses; it granted them the right to unlimited trade and the display of their wares in open shops and at fairs. At first only wealthy merchants willing to invest their capital in their new homeland were accepted. They were given permission to settle for an initial period of twenty years; after its expiration, this dispensation had to be extended by new charters of rights and letters of protection. Since the 1671 edict did not allow for a synagogue, but permitted only religious services in private homes, the Jews had no right to appoint a rabbi. Nonetheless, the elector decreed in 1672 that the rabbi already recognized in the Neumark "should be the rabbi of all protected Jews throughout the entire Mark of Electoral Brandenburg."[3] In the city of Brandenburg the local populace was displeased about the new arrivals from Austria, and there was even physical violence. The elector reacted vigorously, taking the council to task and demanding that they protect the Jews. He chose to ignore petitions submitted against them.

The steadfast view of the great elector and his court that the economic activity of prosperous Jews was beneficial rather than harmful to the state was clearly at odds with the predominant opinion of all educated and experienced observers at the time. Some accused Jewish merchants of undermining regulated trade, undercutting prices, engaging in improper competition, and thinking only of their own profit rather than of what was advantageous for the state. Frederick William's tolerance went further than the Peace of Westphalia in respect both to Protestant communities and to Jews. However, a comparison with the Huguenots, a Calvinist minority that had also been allowed to settle in the kingdom, is instructive: it points up the fact that his government regarded the Jews, whom it had taken in so willingly, solely as agents of economic progress. In a 1685 Potsdam Edict Frederick William sanctioned the admission of Huguenots from France, Protestants who had been driven out of their homeland that same year, just as in 1688 he would also invite the hard-pressed Waldensians from Italy and Savoy. Almost twenty thousand Huguenots came to Brandenburg-Prussia. Both Jews and Huguenots were "imported surrogate citizens"[4] whose function consisted in eliminating the lack of manpower in the country, providing the state with additional tax revenues, setting up manufactories, and contributing to stimulation of trade and money transactions. Yet the two groups were treated quite differently both as persons and citizens. The Christian minority, on account of the desire to help fellow Christians, experienced no discrimination whatsoever, and was even granted a number of special privileges. By contrast, the Jewish immigrants were simply tolerated because of their usefulness—as was generally the case in the Old Reich.

2

The Court Jews

In political terms the absolutist state was bent on weakening the previous concentrations of power in public life, particularly the estates and the churches. An example reflective of the curbing of ecclesiastical power and the secularization of public life that was especially relevant for the Jews was the imperial edict on interest of 1695, which rescinded the prohibition on usury based on Christian principles and the associated threat of excommunication. As a result, moneylending became less and less a specifically "Jewish trade."

The economic system with which rulers tried to promote prosperity was mercantilism. Above all, mercantilism meant the accumulation of state revenues, population increase and, especially in Germany, fostering the immigration of foreigners whose activities bolstered the economy as a result of the new methods and skills they brought with them. The Jews could be utilized in an especially profitable way to realize these aims. The policies on Jewry pursued by absolutism were oriented to the principle of the need for an active balance of trade, and that to achieve that end, it was necessary to harness the economic and revenue-producing power of the Jews. State officials no longer hesitated to mobilize Jews for stimulating the economy and promoting the growth of the cities. Here and there, Jews were even permitted to purchase land, particularly those of Portuguese extraction.

1. Court Jews in the Economy and Politics

In the context of absolutism and its economic system, mercantilism, the court Jew (*Hofjude, Hoffaktor*) emerged as a totally new phenomenon in the history of Jews in the German-speaking countries in the seventeenth and eighteenth centuries. Jewish court agents and bankers had already existed in the Middle Ages, mainly in Spain, though also in Germany. In Saxony in the fourteenth and fifteenth centuries, for example, the margraves and later electors took Jews under their special protection into their service at the court. Jewish financiers attended to the business dealings of the bishops of Würzburg and functioned as bankers for the Cologne nobility. However, these were isolated phenomena, without importance for the fate of the Jewish communities and Jewry as a whole. This is also true in the case of the Jewish court agents who, from the middle of the sixteenth century, were active in Hesse-Kassel in financial and political matters but took no responsibility whatsoever for the collective obligations of the Jews. By contrast, what was characteristic of the court Jew, the focus of our interest here, was his close association with a community whose interests he championed. For that reason a Michel of Derenburg or the mint master Lippold, who are often mentioned as the first Brandenburg court factors, were not typical court Jews in the full sense suggested here. In their era, the middle and second half of the sixteenth century, there was no Jewish community in Berlin, and they left no mark on Jewish society. Mordechai Meisel and Jacob Bassevi were relatively more representative of the court Jew, since they were active within their respective communities in Prague and Vienna. Bassevi was officially appointed court Jew by Emperor Matthias in 1611 and was later confirmed in that post by Ferdinand II.

The need for court factors rose sharply in the Thirty Years War and its aftermath. The financial strength of the territories had been weakened by the devastations of the great war. Large banks and commercial enterprises such as that of the Welsers went bankrupt, the rich cities were impoverished, and the devaluation of coinage had ruined the credit system, bringing trade to a halt. On the other hand, the war required gigantic sums for the maintenance of the troops. Jews functioned as purveyors of supplies for entire armies. After the war's end most territorial rulers were plagued by a dire shortage of funds. The need for capital increased even more because the wasteful, lavish display characteristic of the absolutist princely courts demanded enormous expenditures. Huge amounts of money had to be raised for the construction of representative baroque palaces and dignified residences. The consequence of all these circumstances was the development of the court factor as a permanent servant of the ruler into an institution in all the larger and smaller territorial states. There was a natural and gradual process leading from Jewish provisioners for armies, without whom no war was waged in Germany in the seventeenth and eighteenth centuries, to the appearance of the court Jew. Hofjuden were soon much in evidence throughout the German-speaking countries and probably numbered in the thousands. Electoral Saxony provides an especially prominent example of this development at the time of its personal union with the Polish kingdom, when at least thirty-five Jewish families in Frankfurt were in the service of the court. A number of court factors were in the simultaneous service of several princes. Thus, the Frankfurt banker Moses Löb Isaac Kann was court factor in Mainz, Würzburg, Bamberg, and Vienna. There was also an entire series of dynasties of court Jews. Three generations of the Gomperz family served the prince-bishop of Münster, six served the Prussian rulers in an unbroken sequence; the dynasty of Behrend ministered to the elector of Hanover, while the Lehmann family served the Saxon court. For many years the names Oppenheimer and Wertheimer appear in the list of the court factors in Vienna.

The most outstanding and politically effective activity of the court Jews was doubtless the financing of the European wars in the age of absolutism, in particular the two large-scale military confrontations with France and the Ottoman Empire, from which the Habsburg rulers emerged victorious. The Viennese court Jew Samuel Oppenheimer (1630–1703) was the imperial army provisioner during the war in 1673–1679 against the hegemonic ambitions of Louis XIV in Europe. He had spent his youth in Heidelberg and was the first Jew to settle in Vienna after the 1670/71 expulsion. The imperial troops, which pushed back the Ottoman armies that had been on the advance since 1682 and thus eliminated the Turkish threat to Europe, were paid with enormous sums of money procured by Oppenheimer. He supplied the uniforms and rations, the horses, and their fodder, and even the rafts with which cannons, horses and soldiers were transported down the rivers. It was partly on his account that Vienna was saved during the siege of 1683, and he played a decisive role in the siege and capture of Buda[pest] in 1686 and Belgrade in 1688. When Louis XIV invaded the Palatinate in 1688, Oppenheimer

27   The court Jew Samuel Oppenheimer

took on the financing of a war on two fronts for a period of several years, able to place the potential of an extended network of Jewish financiers throughout Germany and the Netherlands at the emperor's disposal. Even the peace conferences, organized at huge expense, were financed by Oppenheimer: Karlowitz (1699) at the end of the Second Turkish War and Utrecht (1714) at the conclusion of the War of the Spanish Succession.

As purveyors to the courts, the court Jews procured every item deemed necessary, whether horses, cattle, jewelry, wines, or ermine. The construction of the spacious Karlskirche and the Schönbrunn Palace of the Habsburgs in Vienna was financed with Jewish credit. Immense amounts of capital had to be raised for rulers who desired to become king or wished

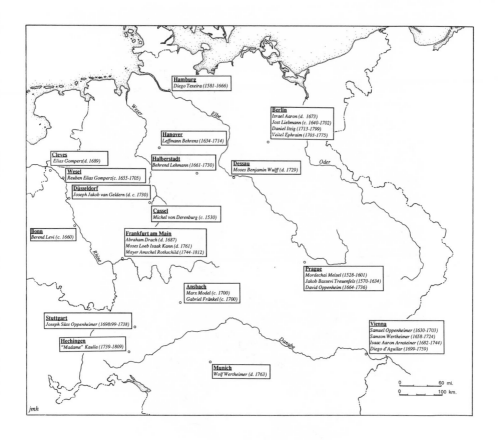

MAP 3   Significant Court Jews in German Lands

to achieve some other higher status associated with greater power. Elector
August II (the Strong, 1670–1733) of Saxony promoted his election to the
Polish throne in 1694 by the payment of millions of thalers to the Polish
nobility—funds that his court factor Behrend Lehmann (Issachar
Bermann Segal, 1661–1730) had to procure. Lehmann achieved the highest standing among northern German court financiers, engaging simultaneously in a wide array of varied activities as a court banker, court jewel-
ler, army provisioner, and political agent—a diversity unique among
court factors in Germany. Without his help and that of other court Jews,
August would not have become king of Poland. Shortly before, Leffmann
Behrens (1643–1714), the court Jew of Duke Ernst August of Hanover,
had procured the rank of electoral prince (1692) for the duke in return for
an extraordinarily large payment to the imperial treasury (estimated at

1.1 million thalers). In 1701 Behrens was similarly involved in helping to obtain the Prussian crown for Frederick I.

Court Jews were drawn into diplomacy and gained international importance, not just through the procurement of higher offices for their sovereigns but above all via transactions with subsidies. Subsidies were monies extracted by many German rulers from foreign states through treaties of alliance, especially with France, England, and Holland, in payment for troops placed at their disposal for military purposes. Court Jews were generally active as middlemen in these transactions and often garnered large fortunes as a result. To mention but one example: the entire array of financial dealings of the private treasury of the Duke of Hanover was in the hands of Jewish financiers, headed by Leffmann Behrens. It was this treasury through which nearly two million thalers flowed, a sum paid by the French crown to the duke as subsidies in its war against Holland (1672–1678).

Court Jews were also active in other areas of the economy. Some established manufactories, that is, early industrial enterprises, at a time when such ventures were still considered very bold and Christian merchants were little inclined to undertake such risks. However, this was always done with the support of the authorities. Hofjuden leased state monopolies, such as lotteries, salt, tobacco, and the mint (a topic treated in greater detail below). In a number of manufacturing branches, such as silk and lace manufacture, they initially enjoyed a monopoly. The Behrens firm in Hanover ran a large cloth manufactory and a tobacco factory. However, the main commercial activity of the court Jews was and remained the trade in diamonds and precious metals. In various ways, then, the Jews did a great deal to stimulate trade and commerce in the German-speaking countries.

But what was it that made the Jews, in particular, likely candidates for employment as court factors? The decisive element was that they were dependent, for better or worse, on the grace, if not the mood, of the ruler. Thus, a sovereign could put pressure on his court factor without having to fear that the latter had any dangerous lust for power, or that, for whatever reason, he might seek to establish contact with the estates or other interest groups. Moreover, the court Jew had to take on all tasks demanded of him, if he did not wish to risk his position, fortune, security—indeed, jeopardize his very life. Thus, far more than Christian financiers, his services were utilized to implement a cheapening of coinage (reduction in silver content), a system of financial procurement that filled the coffers of the ruler at the expense of the population. Such practices were bound to provoke the ire and hatred of the impoverishing population against the *Münzjude,* the Jewish minter.

Coinage inflation was of central importance for the fiscal monetary policy of all absolutist states, especially as a device for financing wars. Coins were taken out of circulation, melted down, reminted with a lower silver content and returned once more to circulation. Thus, inferior coins had been inundating Central Europe since the early seventeenth century, and especially since the start of the Thirty Years War. The Jews were the principal instruments of these dealings, such as the so-called *Kipper und Wipper* devaluations of 1619–1621, in which Portuguese Jews in Hamburg played a role as minting entrepreneurs. As experts in trade with precious metals, Jews were the main suppliers of silver to the German mints throughout the entire seventeenth and eighteenth centuries. When they bought up full-value silver coins returning inferior equivalents, the consequence was devaluation of the currency and staggering inflation. The Münzjuden acted everywhere as the agents of the ruler, following his precise orders and, if these were given in writing, destroying the instructions after concluding the manipulation. It was not as if the princes were unable to resist the tempting offers of the minting entrepreneur—rather, they exploited the Jewish court factors for this despised but very lucrative business. The right to mint coins was a prerogative of the territorial prince by which he was able to procure funds, and whereas the Christian entrepreneur could warily decline, the Jew simply had no choice.

Thus it is evident why the rulers preferred—and often were compelled—to entrust these dealings and other business to court Jews rather than to Christian merchants and guilds. The latter were neither in a position nor prepared to do what the court Jew, under compulsion, was ready and able to provide the court. In the frequent instances where absolutist courts attempted to replace Jewish factors by Christians, the latter were often unreliable and unknowledgeable. The court Jew was peerless when it came to reliability, because he could not afford to disappoint the expectations of his sovereign. He was also more adaptable than his Christian competitors, since he was far less obliged to follow the traditions and norms of conduct of business that were considered binding in Christian society. He was thus in a far better position to assist the sovereign in the economic and structural reorganization of the state. Another salient element was his readiness to assume risks, unparalleled in commercial circles of the day—though, of course, it also eventuated in numerous bankruptcies. Provision of coinage was one of the most fluctuation-prone and dangerous undertakings, although also among the most lucrative.

On occasion, high-ranking princes in financial straits turned directly to Jewish creditors. For example, Emperor Leopold I found himself in this predicament after his requests for loans had been arrogantly and disdainfully rejected by the Austrian aristocracy. It was far easier for the emperor to deal with the Jews: after all, they were totally subject to his power and dependent on his mercy. For that reason they were also cheaper and more unassuming than their competitors. Bereft of civil rights and belonging to an oppressed minority, they often had to content themselves with promises, protection, and special privileges—in the fond hope that somehow they might turn these into cash. Yet thanks to their far-reaching network of connections, they frequently had more capital at their disposal than did their competitors, enjoyed better credit possibilities, and could afford to wait, putting up with longer repayment terms. Mindful of the general disadvantage Jews suffered under, court Jews sometimes also deliberately underbid their better-off competition in order to wedge their way into a particular branch of business. Similarly, and to a greater extent, court Jews made use of a ramified system of bribery in order to win over court officials, all the way up to the top echelon of ministers. At the time in Europe this system was the general norm; in many territories bribes contributed regularly to the income of officials.

What has been said so far certainly does not exhaust all the reasons underlying the special suitability of the Jews for the function of court factor. Above all, consideration should also be given to the extensive network of family and personal ties that enabled them to arrange credits and procure materials quickly and to make use of agents, middlemen, and traveling merchants dispersed across the length and breadth of entire countries. Most of the families of court Jews married among themselves. Thus, for example, the imperial chief court factor Samson Wertheimer (1658–1724), the successor to Samuel Oppenheimer, was his nephew. Leffmann Behrens's mother was the aunt of the Berlin court Jew Jost Liebmann. One son of Leffmann Behrens married the daughter of Samson Wertheimer, while another married a daughter of Elijah Gomperz, army provisioner of the great elector. Leffmann's daughter married David Oppenheim (Worms 1664–Prague 1736), the chief rabbi of Nikolsburg and later of Prague. His grandson was wed to a daughter of Behrend Lehmann.

The families of court Jews were evidently interlinked by a carefully thought out and well-planned marriage policy. In any event, it can be demonstrated that virtually all of the many hundreds of court Jews were related by marriage. This was a fact of considerable advantage for their financial, diplomatic, and dynastic services, because they utilized their sons and relatives as agents and heads of commercial enterprises. In addition, this arrangement provided them with some guarantee that delicate matters the sovereign wished to keep secret, such as coinage dealings, could be treated with proper discretion. Three of the most powerful families of court Jews were jointly involved in the acquisition of the Polish crown for the Saxon elector and the royal crown for the Brandenburg-Prussian elector.

Another factor was the mobility of the Jews. Not every small locality could boast a Christian wholesale merchant, but it was possible for court Jews to send a representative to the tiniest residential town, who then often became independent and, with time, started up his own business. The fragmentation of Germany into numerous small states was a blessing for the Jews in this respect too, as was their dispersion across Europe. In Hamburg and Amsterdam their wealthy Portuguese coreligionists also contributed to concentrating New World trade in jewels and precious metals in Jewish firms as a result of the uninterrupted business connections they maintained with the Iberian peninsula and the Spanish territories across the Atlantic. In this way they made it significantly easier for the court Jews to supply their rulers.

Among the Sephardim there were only a handful of court Jews in the strict sense. It may be that their Iberian pride kept them from assuming the subservient position of a court Jew, or that, as cosmopolitans accustomed to life in urban centers, they found it difficult to adjust to the small residential towns in the various principalities. The outstanding exception of a court Jew from a Portuguese Marrano family was Diego d'Aguilar (1699 Portugal–1759 London), who reorganized the state tobacco monopoly in Vienna in the period 1723–1739 and granted the imperial court large loans. As a rule, the Sephardi envoys differed from the typical Ashkenazi court Jews by their greater involvement in political activity rather than economic dealings. Among the Sephardi Jews in Hamburg there was a Portuguese and a Spanish representative. The latter, Jacob Rosales, mediated between the imperial and Swedish parties at the peace negotiations in Münster and Osnabrück. Diego Texeira, an outstanding member of the Portuguese community, became envoy of the abdicated queen Christiana of Sweden in 1654.

The ability of court Jews to establish and maintain connections domestically and abroad was typically manifest in the transfer of subsidies. The Hanover-French subsidy deals linked agents and bankers in Hanover, Hamburg, and Paris. Leffmann Behrens had agents working for him on a regular basis in Amsterdam, Brussels, Bückeburg, Celle, Düsseldorf, Frankfurt am Main, Goslar, Hamburg, Hildesheim, Cologne, London, Lüneburg, Münster, Vienna, and Wetzlar. These agents, in turn, employed subagents, who accepted orders for them in many small localities to procure items for the regents, their courts and armies. For their coin dealings the entrepreneurs had at their disposal a veritable army of Jewish peddlers, out collecting broken and old silver, as well as coins no longer in circulation. Via the large number of contacts and agents, court Jews obtained information rapidly from all quarters, data whose value for them and their ruler was inestimable. The unparalleled success of Samuel Oppenheimer as purveyor for the Austrian armies was made possible only by the creation of a huge network of agents for whom he acquired privileges, safe conduct, passes, contracts, and special benefits as well as the prerogative to live in places where a Jew had never before been granted right of residence.

In order to provide all these services, and especially to acquire freedom of movement and unlimited economic activity, the more important court Jews had to be freed in part from the restrictions that separated Jews from the burghers. Thus they were generally exempted from the body tax (*Leibzoll*) and other special levies on Jews. As a rule, they were also excused from having to pay protection fees. At the trade fairs many of them enjoyed equal rights with the Christian merchants. A number were allowed to carry weapons and live outside the ghetto, if one existed. In addition, the court Jews possessed certain special prerogatives distinguishing them from ordinary citizens, such as the right empirewide to claim the special protection of the authorities. Their most important privilege was direct access to the prince. They were subject to the direct jurisdiction of the *Hofgericht*, the royal court of law.

To a substantial degree the institution of court Jewry was based on the personal ties of the court factor to the ruler. At times the sovereign assumed the attitude of a patron toward his court Jew and the latter's family. Thus, in 1740, the prince of Sachsen-Anhalt placed a room and the garden of his Dessau palace at the disposal of his two Jewish court factors for the wedding of their children, and he and other members of the royal family showered the nuptial couple with sumptuous gifts. When a court factor of the great elector, Elijah Gomperz, celebrated the wedding of his son in his own palace in Cleves and the young prince of Brandenburg-

Prussia (the later King Frederick I) happened to be in the city, Prince Frederick and the governor, Prince Moritz von Nassau, let it be known they wished to attend the wedding. And so they did. "For a hundred years no Jew had had such high honor."[1]

The position of the Jewish Hoffaktor at the princely court was ambiguous. On the one hand, the court factors acquired respect, rank, and titles, such as court and chamber agent, chief factor, and chief war factor. Behrend Lehmann, whom August the Strong had appointed Polish envoy in Lower Saxony, advanced for a time to the post of lord of the Castle of Seeburg in the county of Mansfeld, where, as a large estate owner, he was master over thirteen villages. And Samson Wertheimer, the imperial chief court factor in Vienna, dubbed the *Judenkaiser*, was assured upon appointment of unconditional exemption from all taxes and levies and granted unimpeded freedom of movement and residence throughout the empire. On the other hand, however, the court Jew did not act as a free agent but as a servant to his sovereign. He generally received only a modest salary, even though he could amass a large income from other sources. Despite all his special benefits, he was always perceived to be a Jew and treated accordingly. In official documents, correspondence, and bills Leffmann Behrens was generally referred to simply as "the Jew."

Finally, the court Jew, though indispensable to his prince, had neither equal rights with Christian burghers nor was he socially acceptable. Thus, on occasion, the court Jew even had to serve court society as an "object of amusement." In Warsaw August the Strong indulged in the "joke" of forcibly cutting off the beard of his court Jew Behrend Lehmann by his own hand—even though Lehmann had promised him five thousand thalers if the monarch allowed him to cut off his beard himself (a beard was obligatory for Jewish males). And King Frederick William I beat his court Jew after he dared to appear in the blue coat of a Prussian grenadier. To be sure, such scenes were reported to have occurred occasionally with Christian officials as well.

The total dependence of the court Jew on his ruler and his officials finds pointed expression in a letter written by Ruben Elias Gomperz of Cleves to his agent in Berlin: "I'd risk my lifeblood for His Majesty my King and my dearest [code name for a Prussian official] as well, because I can see they are sincere, united with me in heart and soul. If, God forbid, that was not so, dear brother, I would have to run away from here, and go begging with my wife and children, God forbid."[2]

Gomperz was well aware just how vital for him his personal connections with the sovereign were and how closely bound up his own fate was with that of his ruler. Any change of rulership could endanger his position. Consequently, he also tried to maintain good relations with the heir to the throne. In addition, he often secured several different residence permits for himself, which could prove quite handy in an emergency. Wealthy as the court factors were, they constantly had to provide loans, cash advances, and presents. They knew that they or their heirs could be forcibly deprived of their assets—because they were often made the scapegoat for policies they had only implemented but not initiated themselves.

The court factors also knew they were a thorn in the flesh of the people, because of their great wealth and the outward splendor in which they lived, and an easy target for the arrows of their enemies. The tragic fate suffered by Lippold and the expropriation of the possessions of Mordechai Meisel were already mentioned. Bassevi was arrested in 1631 after the death of his patron, Prince Liechtenstein, and his entire fortune was confiscated. General Wallenstein arranged for his release, but when Bassevi died shortly after Wallenstein's murder, all his special privileges were declared not transferable to his survivors. The powerful Viennese chief court factor Samuel Oppenheimer suffered a similar fate, though on a much greater scale. When he died the imperial treasury owed him more than five million guldens, but the state canceled this debt and imposed compulsory bankruptcy on the house of Oppenheimer. Even earlier, Oppenheimer had been forced to forfeit a portion of his outstanding debts when he was arrested on the basis of a trumped-up charge. Shortly before his death, the mob, due to some trifling offense, was permitted to loot his house in Vienna.

The most tragic and therefore best-known case was the trial and execution of his relative Joseph ("Jud") Süss Oppenheimer (1698/99–1738), the court factor of Duke Charles Alexander of Württemberg. By a combination of shrewdness, ambition, and unscrupulousness, Süss had succeeded early on in rising to the post of secret adviser to the duke in financial matters and affairs of state. This alone would have sufficed to alienate the highest officials and turn the representatives of the estates into his sworn enemies. But the situation was compounded by another factor: he approved and was an ardent supporter of the duke's self-aggrandizing policies. Moreover, Süss led a life of extravagance and profligacy. In practice, he had ceased living in accordance with Jewish tradition and was a decided outsider in Jewish society. In his position of trust with the duke, he overstepped the customary bounds of a position as court factor. His

ambition knew no limits. Süss became the chief adviser on economic policy to the duke of Württemberg, introduced reforms in administration
and finances, in particular the separation of state and court finances, a
reduction in the salaries of officials, improvement of the mint, exploitation of natural resources, monopolies on salt, wine, and tobacco. All these
were heavy blows to established interests. Moreover, the duke had added
to his own unpopularity by converting to Catholicism and his efforts to
bolster the Catholic Church in a Protestant territory.

Upon Charles Alexander's sudden death in 1737, Jud Süss was arrested
that very night. He was subsequently tried on charges of obtaining office
by devious means, lese majesty, high treason, draining the country dry,
and other crimes. Yet the decisive factor in his conviction was the fact that
he was a Jew, and he was exposed as such to his enemies' lust for revenge.
In contrast with others who had been implicated in the duke's policies but
were protected by family ties or other significant links to the leading
strata of Württemberg society, Jud Süss was an ideal candidate to be the
sole scapegoat. He was executed as a Jew, and as a Jew his body was then

28   Public execution of Jud Süss Oppenheimer in Stuttgart, 1737:
Jud Süss in an exalted position (*upper left*); Jud Süss on the day of
his execution (*upper right*)

put on public display. Accordingly, his coreligionists regarded him as a martyr. Moreover, in his prison cell a repentant Joseph Süss Oppenheimer had returned to the Jewish tradition and had refused baptism as a condition for his release. An appeal was sent out to the Jewish communities to light a candle in his memory for the period of an entire year.

Jud Süss differed from most court Jews, who generally adhered quite strictly to Jewish tradition, in his secular lifestyle. That deviation from traditional paths was reflected in the preserved inventory of his library: for the most part it contained legal works and fiction, along with language textbooks and reference works, but had virtually no Jewish literature. Yet, beyond this, there is another reason why he cannot be viewed as the "prototype of the court Jew": in contrast with all other prominent Hofjuden, Süss was totally absorbed in court life and had no interest in Jewish concerns. To be sure, other court Jews also pursued policies aimed principally at promoting their own economic advantage and showed little consideration for the interests of others, except in the royal court. But their activity was indirectly of benefit to the Jewish people, because the welfare of the community was inextricably bound up with their own. The fact that, on the other hand, they tried to elude shared financial responsibilities did not cause them any greater pangs of conscience than, for example, the tendency of well-to-do citizens to shift the main burden of taxes to the shoulders of those less fortunate.

2. Court Jews and the Jewish Community

A significant number of court Jews began their official public career when they were appointed by the sovereign as the responsible leader of all Jews in the territory. Thus, in 1651, the bishop of Münster named a wealthy Jew as *Befehlshaber und Vorgänger* (commander and chief) of all Jews in the Münsterland district in Westphalia. He had to make sure the annual protection tax was collected; in addition, he was responsible for resolving disputes among his fellow Jews as first juridical instance and had to propose a rabbi for this purpose. In a quite similar manner, a year earlier, the great elector had appointed his veteran agent Berend Levi as "commander and chief" over the Jews in the Brandenburg lands west of the Elbe. Later this office was assumed in the duchy of Cleves by the community leader Gumpert Salomon, and after him always by a member of the Gomperz (Gumperts) family. The most important task of such territorial lay leaders was to collect the special levy on Jews. This

function was so closely bound up at times with the finances of the court
Jew that he was permitted to obtain what the sovereign owed him by collecting the taxes on Jews.

If taxation had been the sole or most important internal Jewish activity for the typical court Jew, his position in the community would have
been little more than that of a feared tax collector or, at best, a respected
notable. But the court Jew's function and status went far beyond this. Not
every court Jew was as wealthy and endowed with such an expansive
sense of public spirit as Behrend Lehmann in Halberstadt, yet he set an
example for many others. Lehmann embodied the ideal of the court Jew
who, while attracted to court life and the baroque lifestyle, basically
remained faithful to Jewish tradition. He combined charity toward his fellow Jews with a public-spirited concern for the non-Jewish population of
his town. For example, Behrend Lehmann imported marble pillars for the
Holy Ark of the synagogue in Halberstadt; after extensive fires had devastated large sections of the town, he contributed generously to support
the reconstruction of the homes of the poorer residents. Like other court
Jews, he sought in the honors bestowed on him in the Jewish world a sub-
stitute for the distinctions and rituals of court life that were denied to him
as a Jew.

The typical court Jew was a benefactor and advocate of his community, championing its interests. Court Jews often took Jews without a residential permit into their homes as servants, shielded them from depor-
tation, and thus assured them a basis for existence. They established
charitable institutions and foundations, some of which continued to
function down into the twentieth century. On countless occasions, and
often successfully, court Jews endeavored to thwart a planned expulsion,
liberate prisoners, prevent violence, and block the dissemination of anti-
Jewish publications. In short, wherever distress and danger threatened
the Jews, the Hofjude came to their aid. Behrend Lehmann was able to
obtain special conditions for the protection of Jews in Halberstadt from
Frederick I and Frederick William I of Prussia. As envoy of the king of
Poland, he also took steps to ensure the welfare of the community in
Lissa. Court factors from Poland who managed the estates of magnates
negotiated with him and other court Jews in Germany on mutual inter-
ests. Samuel Oppenheimer's agents traveled through Hungary, Slovakia,
and the Balkan countries to ransom poor Jews taken prisoner in the
Turkish wars. When court Jews were given respectful mention in the
Hebrew literature of the day, as a rule it was with the title *shtadlan*

(intercessor), that is, an advocate who championed Jewish interests with the authorities, like Josel of Rosheim.

Quite a few communities, including Magdeburg, Königsberg, and Breslau, had originally come into being through a special circumstance: a court Jew who moved to a residential town where no other Jews were allowed to live would hire a large number of Jewish servants and workers for his house and staff. Gradually, these persons became independent, and the core of a small community crystallized. The remarkable growth of the Halberstadt community around the turn of the seventeenth century was the merit of the agent (*Resident*) Behrend Lehmann; throughout his entire life Halberstadt remained the hub of his economic enterprises. Although Jews were not tolerated in Saxony, many foreign *Messjuden*, that is, visitors to the trade fair, in service to the Saxon elector, settled there with special royal permission and acted as a magnet, attracting other Jews to take up residence. The Jewish community in Vienna owes its resettlement and rapid growth after the expulsion of 1670 to the court Jews Samuel Oppenheimer and Samson Wertheimer.

However, the bonds of solidarity of the typical court Jews with their community did not prevent friction and conflict with community lay leaders. The source of such discord generally lay in certain autocratic proclivities among the court Jews. They viewed themselves as an aristocracy, and were generally regarded and treated as such in the community. The numerous benefits and prerogatives by which they distinguished themselves from other Jews were a major cause of disagreements among themselves and with the communities. The court factors were not under the jurisdiction of the rabbinical judiciary; like the officials at the royal court, they were subject only to the Hofgericht of the sovereign. Thus, to a certain degree, they stood apart from Jewish law, beyond its sphere of authority.

Just as the court Jews identified their own welfare with that of Jewry as a whole, they also combined what was useful for their people with what was advantageous for their own families. In other words, they were constantly concerned with ensuring that their influence and position benefited their own family members, in the same manner that was amply manifest at the royal court. Their own selfish inclination to nepotism was not the only factor that played a role here. Another crucial consideration was that the public good (naturally, as they interpreted it), and the discretion imperative to much of their ramified activity, would be best safeguarded if close relatives occupied important positions in the communities. We thus have a long list of leading kehilla officers who were closely related to court Jews and who, in the majority of cases, probably owed their appointment to the influence of family members.

Several examples can serve to illustrate this nexus. The Berlin court Jew Jost Liebmann and his energetic wife and successor Esther succeeded in arranging for Jost's brother to become provincial chief rabbi of the Neumark. Later they also arranged this for the latter's son, who was also Esther's son-in-law from a first marriage. Her son Abraham was appointed rabbi of Halberstadt and several towns in the surrounding area. Baruch Gomperz, the son of the Cleves court Jew Ruben Elias Gomperz, became the first territorial rabbi of Silesia and was also a minting entrepreneur on the side. The father-in-law of the Mecklenburg court Jew Ruben Michael Hinrichsen, who possibly stemmed from a Portuguese family, became the chief rabbi of Mecklenburg-Schwerin. Rabbi Moses Kann, the long-time chief and provincial rabbi of Hesse-Darmstadt, was a son of the Hesse-Darmstadt court factor Löb Kann-Bing in Frankfurt am Main. These few examples culled from a multitude of similar cases point up the close interconnection between typical court Jews and internal Jewish community affairs. Intermarriage between wealthy entrepreneurial families and the class of the learned was a longstanding and widespread practice in Jewish society, as was the participation by scholars in the business dealings of prosperous merchants.

The communities did not always keep their silence regarding the autocratic and nepotistic tendencies among the court Jews, some of whom functioned as head parnasim in communities or Landjudenschaften, governing in the style of true despots. The Halberstadt community made protestations to the king in Berlin against the appointment of Abraham Liebmann as municipal and district rabbi. His special privilege as the sole judge in cases involving money and debts also provoked ill will in the city council and among the members of the Jewish community board. The Jews in Paderborn and Cleves were adamantly opposed to Berend Levi, who had been forced upon them. They rejected him, contending that he was not "tractable and modest, as befits a community leader, but rather tyrannical and irascible."[3] They argued that he was not a shtadlan for the Jews but functioned on behalf of the elector—in order to generate funds for him. Feuding was also frequent among the various dynastic families of court Jews: for years relations between the Gomperz, Behrens, and Lehmann families were marked by tensions, though this did not prevent them from intermarrying.

Following the principle of noblesse oblige and in recognition of the central importance accorded study and scholarship in Judaism, many court Jews were able to achieve remarkable benefits for Jewish culture and intellectual life in their communities and states. Here too they emulated the practices of the royal courts. It was an old custom among Sephardi Jews for wealthy heads of family to set apart study rooms in their own homes, or in buildings specially erected for the purpose, and to defray the costs of their maintenance. This practice now spread among Jews in German-speaking Europe in a similar socioeconomic situation. In this way the affluent Jews strengthened their relation with the class of scholars, and the regular daily study of these scholars became an act of piety that redounded to the religious merit of the patron.

One of the earliest so-called *Klausen* (houses of study) was founded in 1689 by the court Jew Joseph Elias Gomperz in Cleves. At the same time Leffmann Behrens (popularly known as Lippmann Cohen) established a bet hamidrash (house of study), to which he invited Talmud scholars, in his own home. He also financed the publication of new books in the field of Talmudic research. Behrens built a synagogue for the Hanover community, as did Jost Liebmann in Berlin, who himself was a "fairly knowledgeable student of Torah."[4] A number of court Jews stemmed from families of scholars or were, like Liebmann, well-versed in Torah studies. Samson Wertheimer had studied at the yeshiva in Frankfurt am Main and was a Talmud scholar. A preserved volume of his notes on sermons attests to his remarkable learning. The Hungarian Jews appointed him their chief rabbi, and many large communities bestowed the honorary title of *chief rabbi* on Wertheimer, an appellation with which the emperor also distinguished him in his hereditary lands.

In 1703, in Halberstadt, Behrend Lehmann built a Klaus for three scholars to serve as a study house and residential quarters, along with a library and synagogue. He justified his request for a building permit by stating that the German Jews should no longer be compelled to send their children to Talmud schools in Metz, Prague, and Poland. How energetic and decisive he was in his concern for the function of this institution is reflected in a Hebrew letter he wrote to the Halberstadt community from Minsk when the community was trying to turn the Klaus into a children's school: "The Klaus, which I built for the scholarly study of the Torah, with permission of the elector and your consent, was specifically meant for this purpose [i.e., for adult study], and I spent large sums on its construction."[5] He also writes that he paid a third of the entire tax revenue of the community, although he was resident there only on occasion. At the same time he issued a threat: if his wishes were not respected, he would settle elsewhere, since he could live anywhere he desired, and in the future would only pay four thalers annually to the community. Lehmann's charities also extended to the publication of numerous rabbinic works. In 1696 he had the Talmud reprinted in Frankfurt an der Oder at his expense, as is duly acknowledged on the title page; he then distributed the bulk of the edition cost-free to numerous communities and yeshivot. All the commendations that the rabbis from Nikolsburg, Posen, Frankfurt am Main, and Amsterdam prefaced to the Lehmann edition of the Talmud speak of him with great praise. The study houses and presses of the court Jews attracted scholars from Poland to Germany, where they made a major contribution to lifting the cultural level of the Jews and deepening their knowledge of Judaism.

3. The Historical Significance of the Court Jews

What was the importance of the court Jews for Jewish and for European history? What impact did they have on the later development of Jewish life in the German-speaking countries? Court Jews, like all Jewish "advocates" before them, struggled to ameliorate the difficult conditions under which the Jews lived even as they also tried to further their own personal self-interest, both economically and socially. But the time was not yet ripe for Jewish emancipation. The court Jews were themselves neither "emancipated" nor "liberated." Precisely the fact that, despite all their external success, they had no rights as burghers is ample indication of just how far the absolutist state was still removed from realizing the idea of Jewish emancipation. Likewise, the court Jews were not "assimilated," unless by assimilation one means essentially economic integration, for the economic activity of the court Jews was now no longer isolated from the general economy, as it had been in the medieval period. It was a part of the commerce, finance, and administration of the states in which they dwelt. When the emperor confiscated Samuel Oppenheimer's estate in 1702, the move came as a severe blow for numerous Christian banking houses that had worked together with Oppenheimer. Since the court Jews maintained constant close contacts with non-Jewish society, both economically and personally, it is possible to contend that their way of life prepared the path for the transition of Jews from the isolation of the ghetto into European society.

However, if Jewish assimilation means intellectual and cultural accommodation to Christian society coupled with a simultaneous abandonment
of identification with the Jewish world and its values, then Jud Süss, to be
sure, was already on that path. Yet the typical court Jew was certainly not
assimilated in this sense. If Behrend Lehmann signed his name in German
script and Leffmann Behrens spoke flawless standard German, these were
instrumental achievements, necessary for dealing with the authorities. In
the wealthy class of the urban Jews such accomplishments were no longer
a rarity. It was also more and more common for pious court Jews to have
their portrait painted by a professional artist. As long as court Jews were
active as "advocates" for the interests of the Jewish community, refused
to engage in any business for their sovereigns on the Sabbath, and as long
as the library of a Viennese court Jew contained only rabbinic and other
traditional Jewish literature, while not boasting a single volume in a language other than Hebrew and Yiddish—no one could contend that they
were endeavoring to assimilate.

Yet in the age of Enlightenment this picture gradually changed. The
close ties to tradition that had characterized the typical court Jew began to
loosen in later generations. Samuel Oppenheimer still wore a beard, but
his son Emmanuel was clean-shaven. As time passed traditional forms of
living disappeared and conversions to Christianity became common
among the descendants of the leading and well-known families of court
Jews. Thus, by the end of the eighteenth century, the entire family of the
prominent Berlin Münzjude Daniel Itzig was baptized. Nonetheless, conversions to Christianity became frequent in families of court Jews only
after the middle of the eighteenth century, when they were generally no
longer uncommon in Jewish circles that had been influenced by the
Enlightenment.

The importance of court Jewry for general political and economic history has also been overestimated. Court Jews did not have a major part in
the colonial expansion of the European peoples or the development of the
capitalist economic order. No large-scale enterprises were financed by
Jews, and none can be compared with the Fuggers or Welsers. Their activity was almost exclusively restricted to the requirements of the royal
court, the military, and the need for luxury items of a small upper class. A
comparison between Jewish court factors in Germany and in Poland dis-
credits the thesis that Hofjuden were the principal figures behind the genesis and growth of the mercantilist-absolutist economic system. In truth,
they adapted everywhere to the system that was already in existence and

required their services. In Poland they served the existing feudal system; in Germany they helped create and maintain a new system but cannot be regarded as its initiators.

Nonetheless, the court Jews had a decisive role in the financing, and thus the development and expansion, of the modern state. They were the "agents of absolutism," and as such became one of the foci in the power struggle between the sovereign and the estates. They made a key contribution to the development of Austria as a great power; they also had a significant part in the rise of Prussia—because the machinery of the Prussian state, far more highly developed than that of the Habsburgs, also found it necessary to make use of the services of Jewish firms and entrepreneurs. Bavaria was the sole state that, for a long time, had no desire to engage Jewish army purveyors. They did not become a regular fixture there until the beginning of the eighteenth century; even then, no more than 20 percent of total credit, at the most, was obtained from Jewish lenders. In the second half of the eighteenth century the Kaulla family then played a significant role in the economic and financial policy of various German states.

In internal Jewish affairs the numerous communities, synagogues, study houses, printing presses, and charitable institutions in particular established by the court Jews were of lasting value. Despite occasional tensions, the court Jews earned the recognition and gratitude of their Jewish contemporaries. Yet contemporary Jews also criticized various aspects of their way of life that seemed worthy of reproach. The most vehement and fearless critic among the rabbis of his time, Jacob Emden of Altona (1697–1776), depicted the profligate life of a court Jew, holding it up as a negative example:

> That man resembled those wealthy at the time in a certain state, who set up a house of study in their home and house scholars there. These scholars are to pursue their studies assiduously so as to expiate all the wrongdoing of the rich. They apparently believe that God can be bribed, so that the scales can be balanced and one act compensated by the other. Others engage a scholar who gives instruction at appointed times, so that, like a scapegoat, he can take all their transgressions upon himself, a ransom for their souls. They eat, drink, and make merry day in, day out, satisfying their cravings and pursuing their passions. Yet they say to themselves: our soul is saved; after all, we have a scapegoat who expiates our sins. And what

does God do? He sends them dishonest persons, worse and more sinful than they, people who pretend to be pious and holy—and yet commit the most grievous crimes, themselves sinning while leading others astray. They even unmask themselves in public, as in a case thirty years ago in a well-known house of study.[6]

As always, Emden was ruthless in his criticism, generalizing from what was an individual instance. But already, during the Thirty Years War, Joseph Juspa Hahn (c. 1570–1637), a member of the Frankfurt rabbinical court, felt it necessary to set down rules of behavior for the Jewish merchant in his book of morals. These included the following: one should avoid dealing with goods that might entail too great a risk and try not to disgrace the Jewish name; unfair competition is absolutely forbidden; employees should be paid promptly, their wages should not be withheld; the rich should not flaunt their wealth, but should be content with little.[7]

These admonitions, especially the last, attest to the fact that certain tendencies had already surfaced at an early juncture among the wealthy, later to erupt in full bloom in the grandiose life led by many court Jews. They seemed to be governed by an insatiable desire for material success and social advancement, obsessed with the notion they had to vie as Jews with the ostentatious lifestyle of the great and wealthy families in the state. They built palatial residences for themselves, appointing their interiors with elegant furniture and silver dishes. Along with resplendent urban mansions, some court Jews even acquired country estates. Behrend Lehmann rode in a coach drawn by six horses, attended by four liveried servants. In this respect, the court Jews were clearly the forerunners of later German Jewry. There, too, a similar phenomenon was often in evidence: wealthy Jews, freed from the yoke of discriminatory pressure, appeared to be making up with a vengeance for what they had been so long denied in the ghetto.

The success of the court Jews exacted its due. Their exorbitant profits were gained by high risks whose dangers they ultimately were unable to escape. These Jewish parvenus were not only subject to the normal run of business hazards that Christian wholesalers and financiers often took upon themselves but also exposed themselves to perils that endangered them alone, simply because they were Jews. Their vulnerable position left them a preferred target for the aggressions vented by the Christian population. Ultimately, the largest firms established by the court Jews collapsed. Some of their number, such as Jost Liebmann's widow Esther and the grandsons of Leffmann Behrens, were charged with crimes and arrested. In the history of Central Europe, the court Jews were an integral part of a new economic and political system. In the annals of their own people, they marked the advent of a new era—and the continuity of an ancient fate.

3

The Jews in the Age of Mercantilism and Early Absolutism

In the aftermath of the Thirty Years War economic policy in the German territories was reorganized and geared to centralization even more strongly than in the countries of Western Europe. In the area of trade that often entailed eliminating guild restrictions on production and the promotion of manufacturing. This particular type of mercantilism, closely associated with the concept of cameralism (from "cameral" government, i.e., government by a cabinet of ministers), was most pronounced in Brandenburg-Prussia. Government policy there aimed at strengthening the state by vigorous stimulation of its economy. In the main, this was facilitated by a process in which the government gradually (though often reluctantly) recognized the relative autonomy of economic life and sanctioned legal norms and agreements with increasing reliability. In the realm of public finances the state was now also prepared to enter into arrangements with private economic interests that were clearly capitalist. It was a development that offered the Jews new vistas for economic activity.

1. Branches and Centers of Jewish Trade

Jews were still denied entry to the branches of trade dominated by the guilds. As neither Christians nor burghers, Jews were unacceptable to the guilds. Still, in the eighteenth century, this prohibition on admission of Jews as members, implicit in the guild charters and regulations, was expressly confirmed. The constant complaints by the guilds and professional organizations against the Jews reflect more than competitive envy: they indicate a profound sense of discontent regarding the emergence of new economic patterns that diverged from the established bourgeois, guild-based system of trade. The Jews were excluded de facto from crafts by the Jewry codes, even in villages where crafts were not organized on a guild basis. Yet now it was often easier to circumvent trade prohibitions, given the increasing political, social, and economic decline of the guilds. New branches of trade and manufactories were introduced and promoted by the territorial rulers, effectively bypassing the guilds. Despite the still massive restrictions, the Jews were now able to strike out in new directions. Their wish to cast aside moneylending, an activity imposed on them for centuries, was the prerequisite for expanded occupational mobility. In turn, such enhanced mobility enabled them to take an especially active role in modern trade and commerce. These changes contributed to an expansion of options, opening up doors previously shut to Jewish economic activity. In our discussion of the court Jews, we have seen how the absolutist state was able to harness the economic potential of a small elite. Let us now examine the effect of that same policy in relation to Jewry as a whole.

Times had changed: the Jews in German lands no longer earned their livelihood almost exclusively by lending money. In smaller towns and the countryside they were still channeled into the role of moneylenders, and in the larger cities a sizable number of pawnbrokers continued to ply their customary trade, while also dealing in commodities. However, more and more Christian merchants now sought to enter the money market. At the same time, from about the beginning of the seventeenth century, there was a trend among Jews—still excluded from artisan crafts—to enter commercial trade. Yet they had to choose carefully, engaging only in those trades where one might expect to encounter minimal obstacles and reap relatively large gains. One early such example was the purchase of booty from soldiers who had served in the Thirty Years War. The silk trade was an example of a different sort. In Halberstadt this sphere was for many years exclusively in Jewish hands; silk merchants there obtained the precious cloth from the numerous Jewish silk manufacturers in Amsterdam and, later, Berlin.

The great elector had been instrumental in initiating Jewish trade, since he understood the potential inherent in it for stimulating the economy. However, he was also capable of dealing with the Jews in an extremely harsh and heavy-handed manner, using force if he felt the situation warranted it. Trade in silver was especially well developed among the Jews in Halberstadt and the Harz Mountains. In 1665 the elector informed the Halberstadt administration that the mint in Berlin required a quantity of silver and that, in his view, the Jews in his lands were the most suitable agents for procuring this metal. The Jews in Halberstadt declared their readiness, yet maintained they could not deliver the silver at the elector's stated price. The result was that the monarch thereupon banned the Jews from all free trade in precious metals under penalty of loss of their entire assets. Yet, that same year, he granted special protective rights in Halberstadt to a small number of Jewish traders in fine jewels. Trade in nonprecious metals was another of the leading enterprises among Jews in Halberstadt. Throughout the seventeenth and eighteenth centuries, its Jewish community was the largest in the entire kingdom of Prussia. Since the not-too-distant major commercial centers of Leipzig and Magdeburg did not allow Jews to reside there, important Jewish entrepreneurs who might otherwise have moved to these cities also chose to live in Halberstadt. In various localities the newly developing trade in tobacco was left to Jewish enterprise, and on occasion Jews also leased the salt monopoly.

Jewish merchants frequently did not restrict themselves to a fixed set of commodities but traded in any products they could obtain. This is also reflected in an often quoted observation by Glückel of Hameln: her father traded "in jewelry and, like a Jew, in anything else which could be profitable."[1] What that might mean in concrete terms is reflected in the response by a Jew in Dringenberg (near Paderborn) to the question of how he made a living, replying that he had no less than the following items in stock: grain, textiles, leather, tar, fish oil, food oil, cheese, herring, butter, linseed, steel, silk, and buttons.

The Jews introduced the practice of door-to-door peddling in the countryside—making a virtue of necessity, since it was generally forbidden for them to operate retail stores. Thus Jews turned themselves into "mobile shops"; instead of providing customers with a desired item from a store shelf, they sought them out at home—no matter whether the potential client needed the merchandise at the moment or not. In this way they provided an important service to the villagers they visited when "on the road." At a time when demand in the villages was also on the rise, and the closest shops could only be reached by embarking on a difficult and expensive journey, inhabitants in many areas of the coun-

tryside were dependent on the Jewish peddlers. The Jews provided a significant service to the rural community—not only as vendors but also as
buyers of agricultural products the farmers had for sale. They put up the
money or purchased the grain in the field before harvest and then traded
in this produce. Jews were particularly involved in the horse and cattle
trade—an area that was not controlled by an urban guild and thus stood
open to Jewish businessmen. Dealing in these animals was generally
connected with the sale of their meat—initially for reasons that were
purely religious. Trading in the ritually forbidden hindquarters of
kosher slaughtered animals was expressly permitted to the Jews in
Prussia by a decree of the elector. However, the guilds often complained
bitterly about such meat, which was less expensive for the consumer
than what they offered.

One can see here how competitive envy on the part of guilds was at
odds with the interest of the broader population in obtaining cheaper
products. For example, the Halberstadt administration noted in its report
to the elector in 1671 that there had been a decline in the price of meat in
various localities as a result of marketing practices by Jewish traders.
Although there was usually no competition with Christian merchants
and artisans in the villages, tradesmen at first voiced vehement opposition
to peddling, especially in Hesse, where Jewish trade in livestock had
increased enormously. At the beginning of the eighteenth century the
guilds in Giessen complained that the Jews were dealing in goods they
had obtained from rich Jews in Frankfurt am Main and that money was
thus flowing out of the state, passing across the border of Hesse to a free
city. Nonetheless, Jewish door-to-door peddling established itself, over the
course of time, in many German states and principalities as well as in
Bohemia and Moravia. The vocation was handed down from father to son,
and each "village traveling salesman" (*Dorfgeher*) usually traded on his
own "territory" (*medine*, Yidd. "state" or "country"), that is, the sales
area he had inherited from his father and grandfather.

The numerous decrees enacted by local governments pertaining to
Jewish commercial activity reveal contradictory tendencies. Thus, for
example, in Brandenburg-Prussia extensive restrictions and strict control
were imposed on the one hand, while permission to settle, protection,
concessions, and various rights were willingly granted on the other. In
contrast with the great elector, his successor King Frederick I (1688–1713)
was less open to the idea of promoting commerce; he believed artisan
crafts and manufacturing were the basis for the prosperity of the state.

For that reason he continued to insist that there be restrictions on Jewish open retail shops and free trade by Jews in Berlin and several provinces. However, in other provinces of his kingdom, especially East Prussia, he encouraged Jews in the interest of increasing settlement and stimulating the economy. It was now forbidden for Jews to buy stolen goods; unlike in the medieval period, they were not protected by any right of receivership. Jewish trade in money was still lucrative, yet one always had to be mindful of the associated risks and heavy losses that had bankrupted many a moneylender, despite his substantial assets—bankruptcies in which lenders not only lost their fortune but also were imprisoned. Often, however, the Jewish moneylender was not the actual owner of the capital he lent; his funds were borrowed from other Jews as well as from Christian merchants.

A large commercial center came into being in the Frankfurt Judengasse. The Jews there had established a network of agents and intermediaries among their rural coreligionists, and these ramified ties enabled them to engage in all sorts of extensive business dealings. Though the majority remained secondhand dealers, some advanced to become bankers, agents, dealers in agricultural products, clothing, shoes, and furniture, or the owners of hosiery factories and other manufactories. Many Frankfurt Jews kept vaulted storerooms outside the ghetto where they stored and even sold their wares. Thus, the competition between Jewish and Christian merchants in selling goods steadily intensified during the second half of the seventeenth century, and the burghers demanded that the town council protect them by imposing rigorous controls on Jewish residence. Indignant over the passivity of the town council, they appealed to the imperial court, and the Jewish question thus became the point of departure for a prolonged constitutional dispute that raged on for many years. Similar to demands a century earlier, the burghers called for an active role in municipal administration, the remedying of various grievances—and, as before, the elimination, or at least restriction, of Jewish competition in economic life. The Jews, for their part, petitioned the imperial council in Vienna for assistance. For a long time no decision was reached, probably because the imperial court did not wish to undermine the financial power of the Frankfurt Jews, who cooperated closely with the imperial court Jews. And so the situation remained little changed—despite constant protests from the citizenry.

In Prague there were a large number of Jewish craftsmen, in part catering to the love of luxury among wealthy Jews and Christians in the city.

At the secondhand market (*Tandelmarkt*) Jews were the only dealers. It was situated outside but not far from the ghetto, and from time immemorial Jews had been permitted to trade there—they owned all the stands and vaults. The important commercial function fulfilled by the Jews of Prague is reflected in the petitions for their return submitted on the occasion of their expulsion in 1745. The nobility complained that there were no buyers for the products of their estates, and even the guilds of tailors, shoemakers, and furriers, for whom the Jews were no competition, "fervently wished . . . to have the Jews back in Prague again,"[2] probably for similar economic reasons. The Jews in Moravia expanded the old Jewish trade in clothing, a specialty that had evolved from pawnbroking, and had received a powerful new impetus by the provisioning of the armies. Jews there gradually developed this branch into massive home production, and finally into a large-scale Moravian textile industry.

There were two innovations in the field of Jewish mercantile law and its practical application that facilitated transactions in goods and money among Jewish merchants in the domestic market and abroad. Both

29 Jewish tailor and Jewish butcher in Prague with guild emblems (1741)

reforms had originated in Poland and then spread to Germany. Documents similar to bills of exchange were issued among Jewish businessmen in Poland, their purpose to provide simple instruments, in the form of debentures, for noncash transactions. On these so-called *memranen* (from Heb. *hamir,* "exchange") the debtor wrote his name in the center of a piece of parchment, recording the sum owed and date for payment on the back. The fact that Prussian professors of law in the eighteenth century felt obliged to provide information on this practice proves that these debt vouchers, which circulated from hand to hand, were also accepted and honored by Jewish dealers in Germany.

Another innovation that went much further was the so-called *heter iska* (Hebr. and Aram. "transaction permit"); it too first arose in Poland and then spread rapidly throughout the Jewish world of trade. This regulation provided Jews with a device to circumvent the biblical prohibition on interest. Without some means to bypass that injunction, internal Jewish trade in money and goods would have been unable to develop. On the basis of this expedient, creditor and debtor signed a document with a set text, formally transforming the debt relation into a kind of partnership. The lender became a fictive partner of the borrower, thus making it possible to view the payment of interest as the return of a portion of business income. The basis of this technical fiction in banking went back to Talmudic sources, but its simplification as a generally valid norm—although it provoked vehement disputes among scholars—ushered in a new era in the history of Jewish trade in money and goods, dispelling religious misgivings about new forms of internal Jewish economic activity.

The participation of Jews in fairs in German towns reflects their increased role as tradesmen, the new dynamism of Jewish economic activity, and the important part played by the Jews in the general development of mercantilism. Glückel of Hameln remarks that her husband regularly visited the trade fairs held in Leipzig, Frankfurt am Main, Frankfurt an der Oder, Naumburg, and Brunswick. She herself continued these journeys after his death: "I afflicted myself: in the heat of summer and in the snow of winter I went to fairs and stood there in my shop all day."[3]

The trade fairs were so central to Jewish economic activity that the provincial rabbi in Deutz, Joseph Juspa Kossmann (d. 1758), wrote in his compendium of Jewish customs that visiting the fairs was of such importance as to be permitted even on the intermediate days of the feasts of Passover and Tabernacles.[4] The principal fair was in Leipzig, held twice a year. The first mention of Jews as guests there was in 1598. Between 1675 and 1764 a recorded total of 81,937 Jews visited the Leipzig Fair. The number of German communities represented among the trade fair visitors rose from 12 in 1673 to a peak of 103 in 1763. The second largest number of Jews came from Bohemia, Moravia, Austrian Silesia, and Hungary. Prague regularly accounted for the largest contingent of Jewish visitors to the fair. Jewish fair guests from abroad came, in particular, from Zhitomir, Constantinople, Rotterdam, Amsterdam, Copenhagen, Venice, and Belgrade.

The Jews made a notable contribution to the development of Leipzig into a commercial center, especially as an international hub for the fur trade. In the period 1675–1764 the city of Leipzig and the government of the elector of Saxony took in a total of 719,661 thalers in revenues from the body tax levied on the Jewish visitors to the fair, supplemented by the far higher amounts collected in duties on goods. The elector and the Leipzig city council welcomed Jewish participation in the fairs. Yet local merchants felt threatened; fearing the competition of the Jews, they struggled by all available means against Jews participating in the fair and did not shrink from even resorting on occasion to violence. Yet the elector and the council were resolute and did not give in to merchants' demands, although they did subject Jews attending the fair to strict surveillance. They were only allowed to travel to Leipzig on certain roads; everywhere, they were required to pay tolls and transit fees. Every *Messjude* always had to wear the yellow Jewish ring on his person and show it to all council personnel or municipal police officers on demand. Upon entering the Leipzig city gates, Jews had to pay the body tax, and it was forbidden for them to stay in Leipzig except during the period of the fair. In addition, Jewish merchants were obliged to pay much higher duties for the goods they brought to the fair than did their Christian counterparts. Finally, a careful register was kept of all Jewish visitors. In contrast with Leipzig, the fairs in Frankfurt am Main and Frankfurt an der Oder treated the Jews as complete equals and did not even levy a body tax.

2. The Regulation of Jewish Existence

Although the absolutist-mercantilist state in Germany, especially Brandenburg-Prussia, regarded Jewish settlement and economic activity as a necessity, it was unable to cast off deeply ingrained ideological reservations. State policies were marked by contradictory tendencies: on the one hand, the Jews were offered an incentive for trading in the country. On the other, the authorities yielded to popular pressure, fueled by competitive envy and religious hatred, enacting a multitude of anti-Jewish laws and ordinances. Since the Jews often felt constrained to overstep the legal restrictions imposed on them, they left themselves vulnerable. They were entwined in a vicious circle deriving from a stereotypical image rooted in traditional religious prejudices. The severity of Jewry legislation forced them to circumvent and violate those laws (indeed, as will be seen, it often pushed them beyond the law, toward a life of crime). That, in turn, reinforced negative public opinion, leading to further restrictions and difficulties. One example that illustrates this nexus between public opinion and concrete anti-Jewish measures is the advice given by the landgrave George II of Hesse-Darmstadt (1605–1661) to his successor in his last will and testament:

> In order to plant honest religious faith in the country, our son . . . should be wary of the Jews. For they are an idle and useless people. They do not live by the labor of their hands in accordance with the divine design but rather lie about in indolence, greedy for gain, waiting in the lurch to seize what they may. In the most reprehensible manner . . . they suck the Christians dry, blaspheme, desecrate, and vilify the Son of God and dishonor God with their daily superstitious prayers. And whoever, for the sake of mere pernicious pleasure . . . protects the Jews, prefers a sackful of Jewish money to the honor of God. . . . If one allows the Jews to implant themselves too firmly in a country, it will later prove difficult to get rid of them.[5]

After this preamble, and in keeping with what the cities had demanded, the landgrave recommended to his successor that the Jews be expelled from Upper Hesse. As mentioned above, that expulsion was carried out in 1662.

The Renaissance had not ushered in any radical change in the sociopolitical position of the Jews. The weakening of the papacy and the strengthening of the hand of the territorial rulers vis-à-vis the emperor left the Jews at the mercy of the caprice and respective needs of the local rulers. Nowhere were they full citizens of the city in which they resided. Although Jews had to bear the burden of all duties required of citizens, except for the quartering of soldiers, they were excluded from townsmen's trades and denied the right to hold public office. By grievous humiliations, Christian society repeatedly reminded the Jews that they were outsiders. At best, they were *Schutzjuden*, i.e., Jews tolerated only on the basis of a protective relation provided by a patron.

The details of such "protection" had been set down in general *Judenordnungen* and, in part, in special "letters of protection" (*Schutzbriefe, Geleite*). By dint of these, Jews were entitled to settle and to engage in commerce. In the age of absolutism a change was introduced in the granting of protection: instead of the previous individual or special letters, collective general letters of protection were now usually issued. That is to say, the sovereign granted a large number of persons the privilege of protection in a *Generalgeleit*, after checking on each individual included in the letter. The period of protection, formerly limited to just a few years, was gradually expanded until it finally was granted as a rule for the entire lifetime of the protected individual. One important feature of these letters of protection was the specification of a precise territorial area in which they were valid. The patron could cancel the privilege at any time, and there was generally a fixed number of authorized protected Jews.

Not every Jew shared the relatively favorable lot of the Schutzjude. It became more and more common to require proof of assets as a condition for the granting of protection. In the old communities of Bohemia the right of Jews to engage in commerce was contingent on the full or partial ownership of a house. Whoever was not a homeowner was usually denied the right to trade, did not pay a share of the collectively remitted protective fee, and was assigned no "family status" allowing marriage, when this institution was introduced in 1726. As a rule, all kehilla employees came under the umbrella of protection. The upshot was that all sorts of fictive officials were appointed, such as a second or even third cantor. Coverage by the protective privilege was also extended to everyone belonging to the household of a protected Jew, especially family members and servants.

Jews who were not "protected" were considered to be *unvergleitet*, that is, without formal protection. They had no right of residence and were generally able to eke out only a meager existence by manual labor. Despite strict measures by state and provincial governments prohibiting Jewish beggars from taking up residence, Jews from the countryside and abroad slipped illegally into cities everywhere without any official protection. The number of Jews in this category was often substantial. Around 1700 there were 117 Jewish families living in Berlin; 70 were protected, 47 unprotected, the latter category also including several officials of the community. In addition, the files mention some 1,000 Jews termed vagrants or beggar Jews (*Betteljuden*). From time to time expulsion decrees were issued against the latter, but these had no lasting effect.

In order to acquire the status of a protected Jew, one first had to deposit the "admission fee," usually a quite substantial sum. Then a carefully calculated protection fee, levied annually, had to be paid for obtaining the right of residence and a permit for business, including the right to engage in pawnbroking. The admission edict for Jews in Brandenburg-Prussia set down an annual protection fee of eight Reichsthaler. Because of his thriving business, one Jew who wished to relocate from Goslar to Halberstadt in 1664 was granted protection on the condition that he pay a double fee. Later on the protection fee was graduated in accordance with the individual's total assets. In many urban communities a collective fee was fixed— for example, 1,000 ducats in Berlin in 1700—and was then apportioned by the community lay leaders among individual members. In Mainz the protection fee was a standard 24 guldens for every individual, supplemented by a number of other fees. Emigration out of a sovereign territory was often even more costly than settling there. According to the Judenordnung of 1679 in Hesse-Kassel, no wealthy Jew was allowed to emigrate until he had obtained a formal exit permit, the charge for which was a third of his assets. Further determinations of the legal situation of protected Jews appeared in the form of Jewry regulations and police ordinances.

It is difficult to summarize the multitude of prohibitions protected Jews had to accept on the basis of conditions for admission and the various Judenordnungen. Basically, everything that was not expressly permitted was forbidden. Several examples can serve to illustrate the myriad ways in which the Jews' lives were hemmed in. In localities where they had no right of residence, they were allowed to engage in trade only if accompanied by a military escort; the soldiers were supposed to prevent their staying in town overnight. Jews were not permitted to keep Christian domestic servants, and only a "Sabbath woman" was allowed to perform certain services on the Sabbath forbidden to Jews by religious law. Except for their seat in the synagogue, their own house was the only real estate allowed to the Jews, and even that not as a general rule. The Frankfurt town council maintained its claim to supreme right of ownership over all Jewish houses in the ghetto. Excluded from every trade considered "honorable" at the time, only rarely were Jews permitted to deal in new goods, as opposed to secondhand items, though the extent of such trade increased with time. Often the only avenues that remained open to them were credit transactions, pawnbroking, dealing in secondhand goods, and changing money—all sources of income in public disrepute. Yet even dealing in money was restricted, as many letters of protection stipulated the highest permissible interest that could be charged for loans. Often it was forbidden for Jewish physicians to treat Christian patients. In a typical case, a Jewish doctor was first prohibited from practicing his profession; then he was forbidden to engage in commerce; finally, he was forced to request permission from the sovereign to earn his living by moneylending. Only very gradually was permission given for the construction of new synagogues; down to the beginning of the eighteenth century it was usually forbidden. Where no synagogues existed, worship was conducted in prayer rooms. The latter were permitted only in private homes—even then, often on the condition that the meeting room should not be visible from the street. The foundation stone for a community synagogue in Berlin was not laid until 1712.

These prohibitions were compounded by a slew of diverse levies, taxes, and duties imposed on the Jews, which were, after all, one of the main underlying motives for their toleration. A distinction should be made between regular taxes and occasional special levies, though it is difficult to say which constituted a greater burden. Protection fee (*Schutzgeld*), poll tax (*Geleit*), residence (*Stättigkeit*), and Jews' tribute (*Judenzins*) are various designations for more or less the same regular annual payments that every protected Jew had to remit. Many special imposts were levied on the

30 Synagogue, Heidereuther Gasse, Berlin, built 1712–1714

community, though these differed from locality to locality. In a listing of the thirty-four different levies and taxes the Jews of Frankfurt am Main were obligated to pay, two taxes are noteworthy: the crown tax (paid to the court of the Roman emperor or king, when he was in Frankfurt, particularly on the occasion of his coronation) and the so-called Jews' tickets (a fee for permission to leave the ghetto on Sundays and holidays). Common custom required that at specified times the communities present costly gifts to every higher municipal official. Governments also tried repeatedly, and sometimes successfully, to impose special-purpose levies on the Jews, particularly for financing military ventures.

In addition to such special imposts, far higher general taxes and duties were collected from Jews than Christians. To mention but a few examples: in Prussia Jews had to pay twice as much excise tax as the Christian merchants; the property tax enacted by the Bohemian parliament in 1636 was almost ten times higher for Jewish houses than Christian dwellings. In the bishopric of Paderborn Jews were obligated in 1704 to bear an equal share of the local tax burden together with the Christian inhabitants, on top of numerous special taxes and levies. However, all trade restrictions on them were simultaneously abolished.

The most humiliating burden placed on the Jews was clearly the body tax (*Leibzoll*). No Jew, except for those few who enjoyed special privileges, was allowed to pass through any city gate or across the border of one of the many territories without paying a toll for his person as he did for the load of goods he was transporting or an animal he was taking to the weekly market or the slaughterhouse. The body tax made traveling almost anywhere more difficult, and even the Jews who went to the Leipzig Fair and enjoyed many special benefits were not exempted from it. Virtually no Jew was spared the demeaning situations that were a regular daily occurrence when the body tax was paid. Even in the age of Enlightenment it was abolished in only a handful of German states; not until the end of the eighteenth century was it finally eliminated. Originally, the great elector had exempted the Jews he invited from Vienna to settle in his lands from the body tax, but that dispensation did not last long. The Leibzoll was reintroduced in 1700 by his successor Frederick I, though only for a short period. After that it was abolished for Prussian Jews traveling inside Prussia, but remained in force for Jews, throughout the entire eighteenth century, on journeys to and from other German territories. Only in a few cases was the Leibzoll eliminated in a specific sovereign territory after payment of a cancellation fee, such as in

Cleves. After the count of Hanau permitted a number of Jews to settle in his residential city, they were exempted from the body tax when they journeyed to Frankfurt am Main.

Anti-Jewish prejudice was even more conspicuous in the justice system than in the institution of the body tax. Sentences handed down against Jewish defendants generally appear to have been more severe than in the case of Christians convicted of the same offense. The execution of Jews was sometimes carried out in an especially degrading form on the gallows: the condemned prisoner was strung up by his legs, head down, between two live dogs, and left to dangle until he died, a slow death which often took several days. With Christian offenders, as well, the severity of punishment was graduated in accordance with social status, especially when it came to the use of torture, which remained in force in several German territories down to the beginning of the nineteenth century. Consistently, however, the treatment of Jews was more merciless than that meted out to other prisoners. When rabbis were allowed to give comfort to their brethren sentenced to death on the way to the gallows, voices were raised in complaint about this "annoying innovation in the empire."[6] It is thus no surprise that many decades were to pass before the medieval Jewry Oath, one of the worst and most debasing harassments that had been devised against the Jews, was completely abolished. As late as 1787 the emperor felt it necessary to admonish his subjects to adhere to the regulations of the Imperial Supreme Court regarding it: "In future, the Jewry Oath is to be administered in the same manner and with the same formulas as were customary in the past."[7] Special oaths for Jews in Germany did not finally disappear until the era of emancipation in the nineteenth century.

A further serious affront to the Jewish minority, singling them out and discriminating against them in contrast with all other groups in the population, was the collective responsibility imposed on every Jew, the Jewish community as a whole, and particularly the community's lay leaders for the obligations and transgressions of each individual member. If a Jew did not discharge his financial obligations to the state, the Jewish community was held responsible. There were also localities where Jewish heads of households were obliged in certain cases, under threat of penalty, to carry out police surveillance of their fellow Jews. Certain Judenordnungen imposed the duty on every Jew and Jewish community to hand over offenders to the authorities. As will be seen below, this burden of collective responsibility was made even more onerous during the course of the eighteenth century.

Their social and legal inequality notwithstanding, the absolutist state expected the Jews to demonstrate their loyalty to their sovereign and participate in patriotic celebrations and holidays. Long before the beginning of emancipation, Jews endeavored to live up to the expectations of the state. When one reads how the new Roman emperor King Joseph II received a deputation from the Frankfurt Jews on the occasion of his coronation in Frankfurt am Main in 1764, accepted their expensive gifts, and spoke with them "as one converses with a friend,"[8] it is easy to forget just how difficult it had been for those very same Jews to obtain cancellation of a regulation specifically prohibiting residents from leaving the ghetto on the day of the coronation.

Under absolutism, however, the protected Jew enjoyed certain legal privileges. By virtue of his letter of protection, for example, he had full and unlimited access to the legal process. An official statement from 1712 points this up: based on experience, Jews were "sufficiently assured . . . that legal assistance has never been denied them, but rather that they, like their Christian neighbors, have received impartial justice."[9] As long as the protected Jew adhered to the rules of the letter of protection, his patron promised him protection in and out of court, as was guaranteed to other subjects and burghers. Glückel of Hameln corroborates this in her account of the murder of two Jews in Hamburg in 1687 and the manner in which the murderer was apprehended, brought to justice, and executed—thanks to the persistence of a Jewish woman and the probity of the authorities in Hamburg and Altona. The Hamburg senate was steadfast and refused to be put off by the "commotion" this incident provoked in Christian circles. Rather, it sternly admonished the population "not to molest the Jews on the streets and in their homes." In another case, the Hamburg council announced that the Jews promised a reward of one hundred ducats for anyone who could furnish information about the murder of a Jew.[10] In the principalities Jews everywhere incorporated prayers for the sovereign and his family into their public worship as well as sermons on the occasion of public commemoration days or victories. This was not only due to a sense of obedience as loyal subjects and a desire to follow the words of the ancient prophet (Jeremiah 29:7). By means of such prayers and sermons Jews also acknowledged and expressed their gratitude that the sovereign protected them against the burghers, clerics, and other elements in the population that were hostile to them.

Remarkably, unlike other communities in the empire, it was not the custom in the Frankfurt community to say a prayer every Sabbath for the city magistrates, even though that omission was taken very much amiss. Perhaps this was some sort of protest by the Frankfurt Jews against the way the city was squeezing them into an ever more cramped living area, to a degree more insufferable than elsewhere in Germany. Another possible factor was that the ghetto in Frankfurt am Main, as mentioned earlier, was "imperial" and that, by leaving out the prayer, the Jews avoided the dilemma of having to decide to whom they were actually obliged to pay homage—to the free city or directly to the emperor. In any event, they were not afraid to take an open stand against evident neglect and abuse. After being forced to wait longer than Christian merchants at the town post office, they demanded and achieved the establishment of a post office of their own in the ghetto. In Fürth the powerful and wealthy community forced the municipality, against the wishes of a hostile mayor, to invite their representatives to participate in the meetings of the municipal council. Respected Jewish merchants were already addressed as "Herr" by the authorities, no matter how indignant many theologians and burghers were about this demonstration of respect. The tone of their petitions and religious defense changed, becoming more confident, self-assured, and spontaneous.

In examining the attitude of the Jews to the absolutist state, it should not be forgotten that the Judenordnungen, with their regimentation and discriminatory regulations, were certainly not the same everywhere. Even the conditions of protection for Jews in one and the same locality or territory could differ, depending on the specific sovereign to whom they were subject. Thus the conditions of the "knightly" Jews in Bamberg were more favorable than those of the "episcopal" Jews, subordinate to the bishop. Sometimes the sovereign granted the Jews rights that were bound to appear extremely generous judged by the standards of the period. For example, in 1691 the elector Frederick III of Brandenburg introduced new regulations pertaining to the legal, economic, and religious situation of the Jews in the principality of Halberstadt. Inter alia, these regulations stated:

> 1. The Jews are free to practice their commercial trade buying and selling in the city and the entire principality of Halberstadt, freely, securely, and unimpeded, to travel from one locality to another and transport their goods. . . . 4. Jews are permitted to slaughter for home consumption. They may sell to non-Jews the animal parts they are forbidden to eat by religious precept. . . . 7. Public religious

worship is permitted. 8. Jews from outside the principality are given special permission to travel and stay in Halberstadt.[11]

On various occasions this same elector turned to other princes in order to assist his protected Jews in collecting their outstanding debts. In 1690, in the duchy of Cleves, he approved an extremely favorable charter of rights for the Jews. Despite objections from the estates, there was a resolution appended to the charter at the request of the Jews: among other things, it promised them once more "swift and impartial justice in all their legal disputes." The charter also contained permission, not granted in earlier letters of protection, for the unhindered observance of their "ceremonies and festivities."[12]

In conclusion, it is appropriate to ask: how did the legal situation of the Jews compare with that of other groups in the population? In several provinces in the eastern parts of the empire, there was a rural peasantry compelled to live in total dependence on the landowners—in practical terms, largely in a form of serfdom. "Feudal services and dues restricted the freedom of movement [of the serfs] as much as the prohibition to pursue a trade, along with the dependence on the knight's consent when wishing to marry, and on his disciplinary and patrimonial powers." Similar conditions prevailed in other provinces as well. Thus, a widely traveled enlightener remarked in the 1780s: "In most of Germany's provinces the peasant lives under a kind of oppression and slavery—one that is truly often more harsh than serfdom in other lands."[13] Most Jews were spared the extreme material and legal hardships endured by the peasants and serfs. However, although they were generally better off, in two respects their status was less tolerable than that of any other group in the population. First, only the Jews lived under constant fear that they might be expelled from one year to the next simply because their "protection" was not renewed. Second, in the eighteenth century conditions for residence worsened only in the case of the Jews—a topic that will be examined in the following chapter. In sum, lawmakers everywhere in the Old Reich until the era of emancipation proceeded on the assumption that the Jews formed "an alien nation within the state, hostile to the Christians."[14] Life under these circumstances represented a unique fate shared by no other group in the population.

4

The Jewish Minority in the Enlightened Absolutist State

1. Jewry Policy in the Eighteenth Century

The enlightened ruler governed according to principles of reason and fairness as "first servant of the state" (Frederick II) to promote the general welfare and advancement of all his subjects. One might therefore expect that the Jewish minority, which had been forced into the role of pariah, was able to note a steady improvement in its situation in the age of enlightened absolutism. In reality, however, that was not the case: the Jews continued to be viewed as a separate special group, a "Jewish nation," despised as a collective, although some hoped to gain economic advantage from individual Jews. This was primarily due to the reluctance of most Enlightenment thinkers to revise and abandon their old prejudices against the Jews. Down to the end of the eighteenth century their attitudes were still far from genuine tolerance. The continuous growth in the Jewish population, the influx of Jews into the cities and urban economic life on the one hand, and the counterpressure of the rising Christian middle class on the other, prompted the lawmakers to repeated attempts aimed at restricting the size of the Jewish population and circumscribing its position.

Already in the final years of reign of the great elector there was a perceptible change in Jewry policy. Although the government was open to negotiation, taxation was made more ruthless. Fiscal considerations in state administration loomed ever more important, overshadowing the interest in stimulating the economy, a factor that determined the direction initially taken by the great elector's policies regarding the Jews. This was intensified under his successor, Frederick William I. The general living conditions of the Jews deteriorated. In the course of the eighteenth century the range of occupational options open to the Jews was further curtailed and new restrictions were even imposed in many localities on door-to-door peddling. On the one hand, Jews found it more and more difficult to practice a profession; on the other, they were constrained to bear ever heavier financial burdens. Thus, in 1768, the entire Prussian Jewish community was required to pay the sum of twenty-five thousand thalers in protection fees. In addition, there were diverse new levies devised by inventive officials. For example, the Halberstadt Jews had the following annual obligations: a tax for military service, levied because the Jews were not considered fit for the military and earmarked to help finance the pay of the special bodyguard of Frederick William I; a calendar tax (obligatory subscription for printed Christian calendars); a levy for the municipal lending house (*Mons pietatis*); a jewelry tax (on trade in luxury items); finally, a shop fee (for a permit to operate one's own store). There were additional levies on a large number of special occasions, including marriages and divorces. Such regulations were also valid in other parts of the territory. Increased difficulties were likewise encountered in connection with the granting of protection. In many places there was a rigorous expulsion of poor, "unprotected" Jews; the children of protected Jews were not accepted for permanent residence unless the parents were wealthy or had proven their worth by the establishment of manufactories.

In numerous German territories the government bureaucracy began to treat and administer all matters pertaining to Jews in special departments, often called Jewry commissions (*Judenkommissionen*). The Prussian bureaucracy in particular was constantly occupied with Jewry legislation. Complaints lodged by the Berlin guilds against the Jews were a major contributing factor. Such complaints reflected not only competitive envy; far more, they attested to the profound dissatisfaction among guild members with new economic forms that differed significantly from the guild-oriented trade of the townspeople. Four times over the course of half a century, the government issued a new Jewry law, generally under the official name of *Judenreglement*. Individual ordinances were also enacted from time to time. In 1700 King Frederick I confirmed the previous restrictions on trade and, in addition, prohibited Jews from home ownership. In the *Reglement* of 1714 King Frederick William I revoked many earlier restrictions, permitted Jews once again to open retail shops, and allowed their admission to several artisan crafts; he also granted them permission to purchase houses. However, these mitigating measures, for which the king made the Jews pay him the sum of eight thousand thalers, did not remain in effect for long. Vehement protest from the Christian merchants continued unabated, especially because of the fact that the number of Jews, particularly in Berlin, was constantly on the rise—this despite the strict conditions for taking up residence laid down in the laws of protection. Fictitious servants and community officials settled in the community, Jews from outside and Jewish beggars slipped into the kingdom unnoticed. Sometimes officials interfered, as in Czernikau (West Prussia), where twelve "privileged" (*ordentliche Schutzjuden*) and twenty-four "unprivileged" protected Jews (*ausserordentliche Schutzjuden*) lived, but fifty persons were listed as community employees. (After a careful examination the Prussian officials declared that fifteen employees were enough.)

In 1720 the king set up a Jewry commission once again, following another such body already established in 1708. The job of the commission was to keep a reliable check on the number of Jewish inhabitants throughout the land and the taxes they paid. The result was the General Jewry Regulation of 1730, whereby stringent regulations once again restricted trade by Jews; artisan crafts were closed to them, except for a small number that were not part of the guild system, and peddling was also prohibited in the cities. They were not allowed to purchase houses, inclusion of children in the letter of protection was made more difficult, and the number of Jewish families in Berlin was officially limited to one hundred. Jewry commissions were also set up in other German territories at the time, such as the Judenschaftliche Kommission in Hesse-Kassel, made up of councillors of the royal treasury and formed at the beginning of the eighteenth century. These commissions also drafted legislation that generally made the situation for Jews more onerous, though there were exceptions. In Fürth, for example, the dean of the cathedral issued a Jewry regulation that was basically a compendium of old charters and ordinances, containing little that was new. In any event, the dominant trend in legislation on Jews in the first half of the eighteenth century is unmistakable: laws became more severe and rigid, and all prospects for an improvement in the situation of the Jews evaporated—a hope that had still existed at the end of the previous century.

In an important sense the Prussian *Generalprivilegium* of 1730 governing all Jews in the monarchy represented the final break with the

Middle Ages, marking the victory of the centralized absolutist polity over the corporative state. From that juncture on, the Jews no longer lived by royal decree but by state law, and the protective relationship based on revocable privileges had thus been eliminated. Nonetheless, the regime of the enlightened sovereign Frederick II (1740–1786) continued the inhumane policies toward Jews of his predecessors. Notwithstanding the tensions in his youth between himself and his father Frederick William I, he adopted his father's aversion to the Jews. He did not believe that in their mass they possessed those virtues requisite for integration into civic society. With his sometime friend Voltaire, Frederick II shared a profound intolerance for the Christian church and for Judaism, the matrix from which it had sprung. He was also intolerant of those who adhered to religious orthodoxy of any type. In Frederick's eyes, Jews were not human beings but members of a tribe—unable to grasp the achievements of the new enlightened age and unworthy of their benefit. In his "Political Testament" (1752), Frederick the Great berated the Jews as the most dangerous of all sects: he alleged they were harmful to Christian trade, arguing that the state should make no use of their services. His "Testament" of 1768 reiterated the same ideas. In the rationalist political philosophy upon which the reformist absolutism of his state was founded, the welfare of all its subjects—the "greatest happiness of the greatest number," as it was later formulated—was regarded as the most important internal function of the state. Though the Jews too were subjects of the state—if only tolerated ones—the state was not interested in their welfare. Rather, they remained nothing but an instrument for furthering the welfare of the state and its development into a great European power.

Thus Frederick II promoted and favored the thin stratum of affluent Jewish entrepreneurs, granting individual Jews various privileges and special rights. In his eyes, they were untypical of the Jews as a whole. The general charter of rights for the Jews in Breslau (1744)—who were, for the most part, either court factors or enjoyed expanded protective privileges—had already pursued a similar tack: the only Jews granted special rights were those who had demonstrated their utility in trade with Polish Jewry.

Frederick II increasingly restricted the extent of the economic activity of the "common" Jews, while raising their taxes and levies. Certain branches of trade, such as wool and woolen products, were now closed to them. There was mounting pressure on wealthy Jews not to squander their time with petty commerce and to embark upon more useful enterprises, such as the establishment of manufactories and factories. Frederick II also obligated all Jews to supply silver to the mint, and in the course of his long wars he engaged more *Münzjuden* and war suppliers than all his predecessors. In the Seven Years War (1756–1763) Prussian mint entrepreneurs earned 29 million thalers for the king by manipulation of coinage. The most prominent Jewish coin entrepreneuers in Berlin were Veitel Heine Ephraim (1703–1755) and Daniel Itzig (1723–1799). The often questionable coins whose supply Ephraim organized were commonly called "Ephraimites"— though not to his greater fame or glory. Itzig was appointed by the king to the post of chief lay leader (*Obervorsteher*) of the Prussian Jews. He finally became the first Prussian Jew to receive a patent of naturalization for himself and his family. While a small group of privileged Jews grew rich in the wars by leasing the mint and supplying war provisions, the great mass of poor Jews bore a heavier tax burden than the Christian population as a result of special war levies. Dragging on the heel of the many other taxes and payments, these extra levies proved most oppressive.

For the age of Enlightenment the measures instituted by Frederick II in the course of tightening the policy of collective Jewish responsibility were especially retrogressive. A collective obligation for the payment of protection fees binding on all Jews had been introduced as early as 1674. It led to extremely stringent and disastrous mutual policing within the communities. In a cabinet order issued in 1747, Frederick II proclaimed that the elders, or the communities they represented, bore collective responsibility in the case of robberies where a member of the community was involved. This collective responsibility also extended, inter alia, to damage incurred as a result of bankruptcies, the buying of stolen property, or the acceptance of stolen goods as pawned security. A year later a new ordinance was announced prohibiting Jews from shaving their beards—to make sure they would be readily recognizable. (Frederick's intention was to make it easier for the authorities to apprehend Jewish thieves.)

The crowning achievement of the Prussian bureaucracy in the field of Jewish legislation during the reign of Frederick II was the lengthy Revised General Code (*Revidiertes Generalprivilegium und Reglement*) of 1750. Rigorously classifying the Jews into groups of the privileged and less privileged, it differentiated among six classes. The first, smallest, and wealthiest class was that of the *Generalprivilegierte* or the "generally privileged." These persons were permitted to settle in the area set aside for Jews without a special permit and could purchase houses and land. As merchants they enjoyed the same rights as Christians and, in exceptional cases, they were allowed to acquire citizenship and were able to pass these rights on to their children. The second class consisted of *Ordentliche Schutzjuden* or "privileged protected Jews." They did not have the right of free choice of residence and their status could only be passed on to one of their children. *Ausserordentliche Schutzjuden* or "unprivileged protected Jews" made up the third class. They were permitted to take up residence only by virtue of the useful professions they practiced as physicians, opticians, painters, engravers, and the like. A father from this class could "place" one of his children—that is, include the child in his right of residence—but only if the child had assets of at least one thousand thalers. The fourth class consisted of community employees, including the rabbis. Class five was made up of the "tolerated," that is, "unprotected" Jews, who required the patronage of a "protected Jew" in order to stay in Berlin. They were only permitted to marry if their intended spouse was from the two highest classes. This fifth class also contained the children of those "privileged protected Jews" who could not inherit their father's status, along with the children of the "unprivileged protected Jews" and the employees of the community. The servants and domestics employed in the homes and commercial enterprises of the Generalpriviligierte comprised the sixth class. Their stay in Berlin was dependent on the duration of their employment. Aside from further strict restrictions and prohibitions aimed at preventing the Jewish population from multiplying, other noteworthy paragraphs of the code specified that the total protection fee fell due at the end of every quarter and the entire Jewish community of each province was responsible for its payment. Further, Jews entering the city of Berlin were only allowed to use two gates in order to ensure proper surveillance.

There can be no doubt about the lawmaker's intention: the introduction to the legislation underlines the need to curb the growth of the legitimate resident Jewish population and to put a halt to the illegal influx of unprotected Jews. Nonetheless, a contrary aim is also evident—economic exploitation. That this was indeed the monarch's intent is confirmed by a later series of supplementary laws, especially that of 1769, which obligated the Jews on certain specific occasions to purchase a large amount of inferior porcelain from the Berlin manufactory and to market it abroad. Several generations later one could still "admire" remnants of this *Juden-Porzellan* in Jewish homes, since it was not always possible to sell all the porcelain in foreign markets. The law also dissolved the Jewry Commission, a measure contemplated even earlier, and assigned all "Jewish matters" to the General Directorate or the departments of military matters and state-owned estates (*Kriegs- und Domänenkammern*).

Inclusion of Jewish affairs within the general government bureaucracy brought the Jews one step closer to liberation from their pariah status but did not offer the greater majority any alleviation of their situation. Still, the support of Jewish entrepreneuers and factory owners, to whom the state in effect granted civic rights, can be regarded as a harbinger of an as yet distant emancipation—although this certainly had not been Frederick II's intention. Instead of the court factors his predecessors employed, who were active on a large scale in advancing the economic and personal interests of the sovereigns, he now entrusted his economic enterprises to a considerable number of Jewish agents. They assumed specific, well-defined tasks, becoming in reality an integral part of the machinery of his government administration. Looking back upon Frederick II's Jewry policy, it remains doubtful whether the enormous bureaucratic apparatus, without which it could not have been implemented, was justified by the revenues brought in by the Jews. The protection fees raised during his reign amounted to less than 1 percent of total state income.

Despite the fact that the legislation concerning Jews constituted an enormous economic burden for those affected, and the broad mass of Jews continued to pursue petty trade, peddling, and dealing in secondhand goods as their main livelihood, individual businessmen did succeed in amassing capital and expanding their commercial activity. The descendants of these Jews were able to play a greater role as entrepreneuers in the economic life of the city and often the state as well. Thus the rise of the Jewish middle class, which owed its beginnings in large part to court Jewry, progressed substantially under Frederick II. One consequence of the ordinances with which he restricted Jewish economic activity was that activity was intensified in the few branches of trade still open to the Jews, where they gained a certain edge over their Christian competitors. Like the court Jews, the Jewish merchants were constrained to be bolder and more ready to take risks, since they had had to accustom themselves to higher levels of insecurity. They gravitated to niches of commerce that were not yet "occupied" or discovered fresh avenues of enterprise. Jews were able to import new types of commodities, such as chocolate and coffee, for which they enjoyed a monopoly. In foreign trade they also benefited from the wide network of connections they maintained with Jews all over Europe. In the 1770s the palette of economic activity of a sizable segment of Berlin's Jews was already quite diverse. A list of industrial firms in Jewish ownership mentions manufactories for a broad array of goods: silk, wool, thread, liquor, leather, linen, gold, and silver.

In general, despite the worsening of their legal position over the course of the eighteenth century, it appears that overall pressure on the Jews diminished. Application of the laws was not always, nor everywhere, strict and unrelenting. The fact that officials now took an active interest in Jewish affairs proved an added strain on the Jewish population, since there was a steady stream of new levies and taxes. Yet such bureaucratic activity was ultimately beneficial, because it often led to a modicum of concern for their welfare. In particular, senior officials, who had developed a more liberal, freer conception of the state and human society, occasionally lent a sympathetic ear to Jewish requests that their burdens be eased. Thus the obligation to display the Jewish badge was gradually either abrogated or made less strict in most localities. In Frankfurt am Main, for example, the Jewish badge was abolished by the Imperial Court Council in 1728.

Despite the yoke of repressive legislation, the number of Jews in the lands of the Old Reich mounted steadily throughout the eighteenth century, keeping pace with the growth in the general population. By 1700 their numbers in the German territories had risen to approximately 25,000; around the middle of the eighteenth century this figure had reached an estimated 60,000 to 70,000. In large measure, that growth was the result of Jewish immigration from Poland. In 1709 a total of 3,024 Jews were tallied in Frankfurt am Main, nearly 10 percent of the entire population. Despite the prohibition in force on the settlement of unprotected Jews, the Jewish population in Prussia increased substantially. Instead of the officially allowed limit of 120 families in Berlin, there were actually 333 around 1743, and the total number of Jewish residents was 1,945. In 1784 there were 3,670 Jews living in Berlin, out of a total population of 145,000 (8.1 percent). In Halberstadt there were 192 Jewish families in 1728, with another 120 families in the town's environs. In Cleves and Mark, as well, the recorded Jewish population that year was relatively large: 175 families. The number of Jews in Worms was approximately 500 in 1744, about 15 percent of the total population. In Prague, the largest Ashkenazi community in Europe, there were an estimated 11,000 Jews in 1700, one quarter of the city's inhabitants. The main community in Moravia, Nikolsburg (Mikulev), rose from 146 families in 1657 to more than double that figure by 1690, and reached 620 families by 1724. In the electorate of Bavaria, where the ordinances of 1553 and 1616 had prohibited Jews from taking up residence, there were individual cases of Jews who had nonetheless settled in the state. According to the police regulations, a total of 1,750 Jews with passes or permits from the sovereign were tolerated and granted entry as court factors or their protected relatives. Around the middle of the eighteenth century special Jewry criminal law was abolished there.

In Bohemia and Moravia the economic and political situation of the Jews differed from that in the other territories within the Old Reich. During the Thirty Years War, which had begun with a revolt by burghers and noblemen against Catholic Habsburg rule in Bohemia, many estates owned by the insurgents had been confiscated after the victory of the Catholic armies and incorporated into estates belonging to magnates loyal to the emperor. Since difficulties arose connected with the sale of products from these expanded estates, the magnates (who controlled their territories like independent princes) settled Jews on their lands, obligating them to purchase the surplus from the estates. In the agreements with the newly admitted Jews, the obligatory purchase of various products, especially wool, leather, and cheese, was specified under "duties of the Jews," with notation of the maximum prices and dates for payment. While some Jews purchased and sold products put on the market by serfs, others leased manorial trade houses and factories where, among other things, brandy and leather were produced. There were also several Jewish customs collectors. Thus the Jews fulfilled vital economic functions in Bohemia. They were also permitted to earn their living as craftsmen and worked even for non-Jewish customers in the villages, where the guilds did not wield as much power. The distribution among occupational branches was far more "normal" in Bohemia (outside of Prague) than in Germany: in 1724 15 percent of the Jews were moneylenders, 20 percent craftsmen, and 13 percent leased factories. In 1724 Jews in Bohemia were distributed over 169 cities and 672 villages and were thus unusually decentralized. In Moravia, by contrast, there were no Jews in the villages before 1848, aside from leaseholders of manorial trade houses. Moravian Jews were concentrated in 52 communities, while in Bohemia there were some 200 outside of Prague.

In the wake of their liberation of Bohemia and Moravia from Protestant rule, the Habsburg authorities tightened their policies toward non-Catholics. Thus, in the 1720s, they established ghettos in many places in order to displace Jews from the center of a locality to its periphery, a move the traders and craftsmen also welcomed. In 1727, at the insistence of the Church (though not always with general approval), population transfers aimed at separating Jews and Christians were carried out in numerous Bohemian and Moravian provincial cities. Freedom of movement was largely prohibited. One year earlier Emperor Charles VI (1685–1740) had decided to restrict the number of Jews in Bohemia, Moravia, and Silesia. Although Charles was one of the most anti-Jewish monarchs of the Habsburg dynasty, that did not prevent him from granting favors to his court Jews, from whom he anticipated financial advantages. It was he who issued the notorious *Familiantengesetz* (Familiants Law), which Jews termed a calamity (*gezerah*). To begin with, the law established a fixed and constant number of Jewish families: 8,541 in Bohemia, 5,106 in Moravia, and 119 in Silesia. Then it stipulated that, in any family, only the eldest son was allowed to marry—though not until after the death of his father and once he had reached the age of twenty-four. Only the wealthy were able to arrange for a special dispensation for marriage by payment of a large sum. In 1738 Charles VI expelled the Jews from Silesia. That same year he also intended to expel all poor Jews from Bohemia, including many immigrants from Poland, but this plan was not implemented: for economic reasons the estates in Bohemia opposed any effort to reduce the number of Jews.

This brings us to the expulsion of the Jews from Prague in 1745. Empress Maria Theresa (1717–1780), who was under the powerful influence of the Church, had adopted the anti-Jewish animus and aims of her father Charles VI. In addition, she initiated a systematic internal policy to make her vast empire uniform in religion as well. Earlier, Catholic Cologne (which tolerated no Jews) banished the Protestants in 1714, and in 1731–1732 in Austria, under the pretext that their community leaders were rebels, the fanatic archbishop of Salzburg had brutally driven out nearly twenty thousand Protestants from his lands. An occasion for the expulsion of the Prague Jews presented itself when, during the War of the Austrian Succession (the second Silesian War), Prague was conquered in the late summer of 1744 by the Prussian army. Without any foundation, the Jews were accused of providing assistance to the enemy and committing treason against Austria. Thereupon Maria Theresa signed a decree of banishment against the Jews of Prague in December 1744, extended a bit later to all Jews in Bohemia and Moravia.

Jews from Prague and Vienna were quick to react: they immediately dispatched letters to the larger Jewish communities in England, Italy, Denmark and elsewhere in Europe, and also in the Ottoman Empire. The court Jews throughout the Habsburg Empire and the large communities in Frankfurt am Main and Hamburg launched a feverish campaign aimed at preventing the expulsion. At the center of their efforts in Vienna were Diego d'Aguilar, a court Jew from a Portuguese Marrano family mentioned earlier, who in 1742 had already performed yeoman service in helping to prevent a banishment of Jews from Moravia, and Wolf Wertheimer (the son of Samson). In Frankfurt am Main Moses Kann-Bing petitioned the archbishop of Mainz, with whom he was on close terms, and succeeded in convincing him to send a personal letter to Maria Theresa. Just two weeks after promulgation of the decree various royal courts in Europe had already begun to intercede at the Habsburg court in Vienna on behalf of the Prague Jews. The Italian communities were even able to persuade the pope himself to intervene; the Ottoman sultan dispatched a special courier bearing a personal letter.

In the meantime, negotiations to end the war were successfully concluded at the beginning of May 1745. Three days after conclusion of the Peace of Dresden, the empress signed a decree postponing the expulsion of the Jews of Bohemia and Moravia indefinitely. The pressure of the diplomatic protests, the peace negotiations, and the expostulations of government officials all had their impact on the empress. However, the decision came too late for the Prague Jews, who had already been forced to leave the city with their elderly, sick, women, and children at the end of March 1745. The wealthy moved to various communities in the empire, Holland, and Italy; the poor migrated through Saxony to Prussia, and most from there went on to Poland, while a smaller proportion managed to reach Holland. The departure of the Jews from Prague plunged all of Bohemia into a temporary economic crisis, especially because many producers required the services of the Jews as middlemen and salesmen. Even guilds, which had earlier issued urgent calls for the expulsion, now had second thoughts and wanted the Jews back. In the summer of 1748 the Jews were finally permitted to return to their homes in Prague.

This was to be the last expulsion of Jews in the Old Reich, even if Maria Theresa remained hostile to them. (Legend has it that many years later, upon giving a private audience to a wealthy Jew, she chose to sit behind a curtain as if by doing so she intended to avoid the danger of infection.) Her major reforms, especially the transformation of the Austrian-Bohemian half of the empire into a modern, unified bureaucratic state, proved advantageous for the Jews, however unintended that benefit may have been. The representatives of the central government in the various provinces became accessible to the Jews and often protected them from encroachments by local officials.

For the Jews of Europe what had transpired in Prague proved a new type of experience and a trial. This was the second time that the solidarity of leading Jewish communities and personalities had been put to the test. A century earlier, after the pogroms of 1648/49 in Poland, they had not been found wanting and had provided the necessary mutual aid. The main challenge then had been the ransoming of the large numbers of Polish Jews taken prisoner by the cossacks and offered for sale into slavery. Faced with the expulsion from Prague, the communities now passed a new test of solidarity by utilizing diplomatic channels and making their political influence felt.

2. Relations Between Jews and Christians

Public opinion regarding the Jews was still dominated by the familiar prejudices and traditional stereotypes. Once again, a comparison with the Huguenots is instructive. Whereas these foreigners were treated as a highly privileged and unstigmatized group, Jews were stereotyped, even by otherwise enlightened people, as necessarily godless, dishonorable, filthy, and uncultured. It was a notion deeply etched into the consciousness of the Christian population. Even the enlightened encyclopedias, in their numerous articles dealing with the Jews, retained an attitude of intolerance. The religious peace between Christian denominations only "rubbed off" a bit on relations toward the Jews, but no more than that. Whenever there was talk of tolerance in Germany, what was generally meant was still exclusively the various churches; the synagogue remained apart.

Old prejudices took on new accents. Although the rationalist thinkers of the eighteenth century shook the traditional religious world view to its foundations, they usually remained hostile to a Judaism whose outlook and precepts were, in their view, not worthy of a life guided by reason. Moreover, a critique of Christianity was simultaneously a critique of Judaism as well, since Christianity did not deny its Jewish roots. The Deists of that period, who rejected divine revelation, likewise wrote disparagingly about the Jews, who still clung to their ancestral Sinaitic faith. Even those few who were favorably disposed toward Jews as individuals were unable to shake off a certain ambivalence toward Judaism as a religion.

At times Christians accused Jews of ruthlessness and a lack of business ethics, maligning them as merchants motivated by pure and unadulterated selfishness who violated their own precepts of Jewish morality. In arriving at this judgment critics generally overlooked civic disabilities as a factor explaining that their practice of an ethics valid within their own group did not extend beyond it. As a rule, the rabbis preached against dishonesty in dealings with Christians, even though they recognized that their listeners had sometimes been constrained to employ means they would certainly have avoided were their situation more favorable. An important legal opinion in this connection was authored by Yair Ḥayim Bacharach (1638–1702), who served as a rabbi in Koblenz and Worms. It includes these words:

> The exceedingly wise elector Charles Louis, of blessed memory, would often converse with my brother-in-law Isaac, who served as rabbi of Mannheim and the Palatinate. On one such occasion the elector complained to him about [his Jewish] coreligionists . . . "Not only do they themselves transgress against the laws, but they corrupt the . . . judges by bribes." . . . My brother-in-law replied that by no means did he wish to excuse . . . this lawlessness. He expounded at length on the gravity of their sins, from a Jewish as well as a general moral . . . viewpoint. But he urged that the following point be taken into consideration: "It is well known that religious hatred exceeds all other types, and . . . members of one and the same religion are good friends. . . . When a Christian and a Jew appear before a court, the heart of the judge is undoubtedly inclined toward the Christian, and he suspects the Jew of falsehood and treachery. . . . For that reason, by bribing the judge, the Jew is only attempting to neutralize his prejudice." This is, of course, no justification, but the moral judgment on bribery thus appears in a different light.[1]

The legend of the Wandering Jew, who was suddenly sighted in streets and lanes all over Germany, was especially widespread and provided new fuel for the longstanding traditional fear of the Jews. Like the witches in the sixteenth and seventeenth centuries, the Jews were a marginal group, excluded from society—a minority that served as the target for projected fears and hatreds. This probably also helps to explain why, in the extensive contemporaneous literature on the Jud Süss affair, there was not a single German or foreign author who chose to distance himself from the distorted image of the court Jew.

Traditional hostility toward Jews was provided with a pseudoscientific foundation in a book published in 1700 by Johann Andreas Eisenmenger entitled *Entdecktes Judenthum, oder gründlicher und wahrhafter Bericht, welchergestalt die verstockte Juden die Hochheilige Drey-Einigkeit . . . erschrecklicher Weise lästern und verunehren* (Judaism Unmasked, or a Thorough and True Account of How the Unrepenting Jews Horribly Blaspheme and Dishonor the Holy Trinity). Despite its decidedly medieval theological approach and style, it became a perennial source book for various forms of modern antisemitism. Eisenmenger (1654–1704) was professor of Oriental languages in Heidelberg, and had acquired his considerable knowledge of Talmud from Jews in Frankfurt am Main and Amsterdam. In his treatise he gathered together all rabbinic statements that were apt to make the teachings of Judaism appear despicable—especially those that supposedly vilify Christianity and the non-Jews. Although he does not falsify his rabbinic sources, and his translations are exact, Eisenmenger's description of Jewish beliefs and views differs substantially from what the Jews themselves have actually derived from those same sources. Printed in 1700, the book consisted of two thick volumes and ran to more than two thousand pages. The Frankfurt community, which had already in 1595 successfully petitioned the emperor to halt the distribution of a new edition of Luther's *Von den Juden und iren Lügen* (Of the Jews and Their Falsehoods), attempted, through the agency of Samson Wertheimer and Samuel Oppenheimer in Vienna, to achieve an imperial ban on the distribution of this book. Once again, the community was successful, but Eisenmenger appealed against the imperial injunction, and the court case dragged on for many years. Ultimately, it was reprinted and published in 1711 with the permission of the Prussian king Frederick I. Although Eisenmenger's book was banned in some localities, such as Bamberg and Mainz, because of its provocative content, it found its way into many proper and upstanding middle-class homes. We know, for example, that the library of Goethe's father in Frankfurt am Main contained a copy.

Frederick I also interfered in the internal affairs of the synagogue by reviving an ancient measure that had, up until then, been resorted to only in the early Byzantine empire and in a few isolated instances during the Middle Ages in Europe. In response to a denunciation from a baptized Jew, the king issued an order in 1703 that Jewish worship should be carefully monitored so that in the prayer *alenu leshabe'ah*, the Jews did not mock the Christians and their messiah in word and gesture. Since about 1400 the ancient accusation that the Jews blasphemed Christianity in the synagogue—part of the standing repertoire of Christian polemics—had made special reference to this prayer and to the passage: "They [the non-Jews] fall prostrate before empty vanities and pray to a God who can offer no salvation." Although most Jewish commentators interpret this sentence as a reference to heathen idolatry, Ashkenazi Jews, in a form of self-censorship, had long since deleted it from their prayer books. Yet since many continued to recite it from memory, Frederick I issued a strict ordinance stipulating that this sentence not be uttered. In some cities monitors were actually stationed in the synagogue to make sure the passage was omitted from worship. Until 1788 in the Königsberg synagogue there was an inspector's chair set up for this purpose, occupied by one of the theology professors who was paid a special fee for his services.

Under the influence of Lutheranism, the right to public worship in religions other than Protestantism was still highly controversial and hotly disputed. Down to about the middle of the eighteenth century, in Prussia, even private Catholic worship was only permitted in the case of diplomats, soldiers, and skilled workers. Even where Jewish settlement was tolerated the authorities were reluctant for many years to grant permission to build a synagogue. Thus, in many localities, "off-the-street synagogues" were set up in private houses, not visible from the thoroughfare. Even where private prayer rooms were officially tolerated, the number of worshippers was restricted, and they were only permitted to enter and leave the building in small groups. In Halberstadt even an existing synagogue could be torn down in 1669 by order of the provincial estates. Individual customs and usages of the Jews, which were part of their religious practices, were also perceived as irritants. The sale to Christian butchers of ritually prohibited parts of the animal was an old bone of contention; the Shabbos goy—a non-Jew who performed certain services for Jews on the Sabbath—was an object for regulation by state ordinances throughout the seventeenth century in Upper Hesse. The "Sabbath cord" (eruv), a ritual arrangement to delimit an area within which it was then permissible to carry objects out into the street on the Sabbath (otherwise forbidden by Sabbath law), in various localities provoked prohibitions and formal proceedings. Christian ministers sometimes complained to the government about the disturbances to public peace and quiet caused by Jewish religious services, such as the blowing of the ram's horn (shofar) on the Jewish New Year, especially if a Jewish holiday happened to fall on a Sunday.

If a Jewish scholar had a penchant for mysticism and this became known, he might become embroiled in embarrassing and unpleasant investigations. The suspicion against purported Jewish magic and occult arts led on occasion to merciless persecutions. The chief rabbi Tsevi Hirsch Fränkel, who had served in Ansbach since 1709, was sentenced to life imprisonment after an "obscene and superstitious book" containing instructions for exorcising spirits and other charms had been found in his possession. In the course of the investigation, Jewish holy books in synagogues and private homes were confiscated throughout the entire margravate. The Frankfurt rabbi Naphtali Cohen (Katz) was accused of having started the great fire in the Frankfurt ghetto (1711) by his experiments with "practical Kabbala." It had broken out in his house and destroyed virtually the entire Judengasse and the synagogues. Although released after his arrest, he felt compelled to leave the city.

In all regulations pertaining to Jews in the early modern period, especially in territories with a strong Lutheran element in the population, the governments believed it was necessary to work toward a strict segregation of Jews from Christians and to prevent the latter from developing a sense of respect and appreciation for Jewish customs and traditions. To achieve this end, lawmakers, in the first place, sought to thwart any attempt by Jews to deprecate Christian belief and give the Christians cause for irritation. Hence the prohibition against Jews leaving the ghetto on Sundays and Christian holidays and the numerous ordinances devised to make it more difficult for Jews to practice their religion in a manner that might attract attention.

Yet the authorities went further, seeking to bring about the Jews' speedy conversion. Ecclesiastical means of compulsion were mobilized in a bid to bring Jews closer to Christianity. The practice introduced by the Roman Catholic Church in the Middle Ages to force Jews to listen to missionary sermons was now often declared to be among the legal obligations incumbent on Jews, under threat of penalty—especially in Protestant territories but also for a time in Catholic Vienna. Thus Duke George William of Brunswick-Lüneburg ordered in 1689 that all protected Jews had to attend Christian worship once a year, where the fundamental principles of Christianity would be expounded to them. In Hesse-Darmstadt some of the early Jewish provincial assemblies (*Judenlandtage*, see chapter 6) in the 1640s and 1650s were not convened for fiscal purposes but for Jewish edification: the Jews were gathered together and forced to listen to the sermons of missionaries in addition to the reading aloud of the *Judenordnung*.

That same code of regulations forbade Jews to own books against the Christian religion, a transgression that was to be uncovered by "assiduous inquisition." Now and then Hebrew books supposedly containing such objectionable passages were confiscated, as occurred in Fürth in 1702. In this instance, as in similar cases, the investigation was the product of denunciations by baptized Jews, though sometimes such inquiries were also provoked by rivalry between competing publishers. In 1714 the Hebrew books of the Jews in Halle were first confiscated and then returned; in Vienna copies of the Talmud were taken away in 1722. Censorship of Hebrew books in Prague was so strict that Rabbi David Oppenheim, who was a renowned bibliophile and owned the most valuable private Hebrew library ever assembled (in 1715 it consisted of seven thousand printed volumes and one thousand manuscripts), feared that some of his precious books and manuscripts could be confiscated or damaged. He therefore transferred his library from Prague to the house of his father-in-law Leffmann Behrens in Hanover (1702), where he believed it would be safe (later, in 1825, the Oppenheim collection was purchased by the Bodleian Library in Oxford). Jewish books were actually burned in 1744 in Prague.

If the aim of all these measures of coercion was to bring about a movement toward baptism among the Jews, then they proved a failure. The compulsory sermons were generally discontinued after a few years. Although cases of conversion were on the increase from the beginning of the eighteenth century, the underlying reason was not legal constraints but material distress—or indeed the allurement of possible integration into Christian society. There is no doubt that the preponderant majority of such converts came from the ranks of the Jewish beggars in German lands and abroad. Driven by the hopelessness and desperation of their lives, they sought and found material sustenance and security in the bosom of the Church. Conversely, the prosperity and numerous Christian contacts of the families of court Jews promoted the opportunity (and readiness) to assimilate, a process that, as we have noted, often led in their grandchildren's generation to the baptismal font.

The determination of the Jews to remain Jews seldom yielded to duress. Yet it did succumb to kindness and accommodation, which was the favored tactic of the Pietists, adherents of a current within Protestantism centered on the heightening of piety in practical life and the fostering of brotherly love. Philip Jacob Spener (1635–1705), the leader of the Pietist movement, who served many years as a minister in Frankfurt am Main and had frequent contact with Jews there, had attempted to attract Jews to Christianity without coercion through love of humanity, sermonizing, and conversation. He never spoke of the "obstinate," but always of the "poor" Jews. He declared that they had not forfeited their "merit" and nobility. Spener therefore demanded respect for the Jews and freedom of conscience, even if he had initially been in favor of obligatory sermons. In fact, virtually all leading representatives of early Pietism were intensively concerned with the question of the conversion of Jews. Under their influence, homes for proselytes and other institutions for the care and welfare of baptized Jews were established. With the support of the king, Johann Heinrich Callenberg (1694–1760), professor in Halle, the principal bastion of Pietism, founded an Institutum Judaicum for the training of missionaries. He also established a press for publications in Western Yiddish, including a dictionary and translations of several books of the Bible.

The Pietist movement and the occasional friendly contact between Jewish and Christian scholars did not fail to have an impact on the relation of Jews to contemporary Christianity. The distinction between polytheism and Christian belief, already made at times by rabbis in the medieval period, gained broader acceptance. Jewish authors now regularly prefaced their works with the comment that wherever non-Jewish peoples were termed idolaters, the reference was to the peoples of classical antiquity and not the European peoples of the present age. That was not only a stratagem to preempt interference by state and Church censors but was often the result of honest conviction. Thus, for example, Rabbi Yair Ḥayim Bacharach indignantly denounced the "false piety" of those who refused to pronounce certain Christian proper names and even the names of certain coins, out of a timid apprehension about possible polytheism. He noted that such persons only served to increase Jew-hatred among the nations.[2]

Rabbi Jacob Emden (1697–1776) of Altona wrote about Christianity in a spirit of tolerance unparalleled in rabbinic literature. Not only were the Christians not polytheistic, he contended, but Christianity was much closer to Judaism than had been commonly assumed. For that reason a Jew was obliged to approach an honest Christian with respect, tolerance, and a generous sympathetic attitude. In commenting on the question of the extent to which Jews were obligated by religious law to convert those of other faiths, Emden emphasized that it was a duty to dissuade potential proselytes, even from the start. He also commented on the relative tolerance of the authorities of the day: "[The sovereigns] of the peoples who rose up as successors [to the peoples that have disappeared from history's stage] and have seized hold of power are 'merciful kings.' We live in their shadow among the nations. Through God's great mercy, he has permitted us to find favor and compassion in the eyes of the nations' kings."[3]

The disputation between an apostate and the chief rabbi of Schaumburg-Lippe, Joseph Samson of Stadthagen (d. 1715), ordered in 1704 by the elector George Louis of Hanover to be held in his palace in the presence of the royal court, attests to the new attitude. Jewish-Christian disputations were still quite frequent in the seventeenth century, as Joseph Juspa Hahn noted when he gave his readers instructions on how best to refute the arguments of Christian disputants. However, the disputation in Hanover, about which a detailed report has been preserved in Hebrew,[4] was the only public event of its kind in the later period. Although the rabbi may have embellished his report, suggesting, for example, that he emerged victorious from the encounter, there can be no doubt that during this disputation the royal family in Hanover revealed a remarkably tolerant attitude toward Judaism and the Jews.

Christian Hebraists now demonstrated a new open-mindedness toward Judaism. The aims they pursued in their Hebrew research were, at least in part, thoroughly scientific, even if usually linked with a covert hope for Jewish conversion. They recognized that Judaism, like Rome and ancient Greece, was an integral part of Western tradition. Europe's scholars had felt indebted to that tradition in their struggle, buttressed by a growing scientific and historical understanding, to reshape their worldview, even in the age of the most bitter religious wars. At the same time, they wished to use their studies to bolster the Christian understanding of the Bible and religious tradition through research in Hebrew sources. A further and very powerful motive was their desire for as accurate a picture of the Jews and Judaism as possible—an interest one might today term anthropological. Thus numerous illustrations increasingly appear in books on Jewish customs. The four-volume work *Jüdische Merckwürdigkeiten* (Jewish Curiosities, 1714–1718) by Johann Jacob Schudt (1664–1722), Orientalist and principal of the classical secondary school in Frankfurt am Main, described the customs of the Jews, especially in Frankfurt. It remains still today an important source for the history and life of the Jews in Germany.

The biographies of several outstanding Christian Hebraists attest to their close personal ties with Jews. The legal expert and Orientalist Johann Christoph Wagenseil (1633–1705) frequented the ghetto in Vienna as a young man and had acquired his knowledge of Judaism there. He defended the Jews against blood libel and popular animosity due to usury, for which he alleged the Christians themselves were to blame, and expressed his frank admiration for the Jews' way of life and fidelity to their faith. Yet Wagenseil also published works intended to expose Jewish vilification of Christianity, especially a collection of Jewish polemical writings against Christianity, brought out under the title *Tela ignea Satanae* (The Flaming Arrows of Satan) in Altdorf in 1681. Like his colleagues, he was especially interested in the Jews' conversion. The two Swiss scholars, Johannes Buxtorf the Elder (d. 1629) and his son Johannes Buxtorf the Younger (d. 1664), were similarly ambivalent about the object of their study. Buxtorf the Elder published a manual on Hebrew letter writing in 1610, but also authored the book *Synagoga Judaica* in 1603, a compendium of numerous old and familiar attacks against Jews and Judaism, which went through several printings. Johann Christian Wolff (1683–1789), by contrast, was recalled most favorably by Rabbi Moses Hagiz, who spent several years in Altona. Hagiz noted that he came to the house of the "great, wonderful, and eminent scholar," the famous preacher in the grand and celebrated city of Hamburg, Professor Jochanan Christoph Wolff. The latter invited him into his enormous library and discussed scholarly questions with him there.[5] Aided by David Oppenheim's aforementioned library, Wolff would compile his monumental four-volume bibliography *Bibliotheca Hebraea* (Hamburg, 1715–1733).

In statements made by high-ranking officials in scholarly circles, one could sometimes hear and read that the Jews too, like the Christians, were human beings. It became possible for large Jewish communities such as those in Frankfurt am Main, Hamburg, Halberstadt, and Fürth, by virtue of their numerical, economic, and even intellectual strength, to assume a confident and assertive stance toward the authorities. Nonetheless, public opinion, even in educated circles, was still little inclined toward a just and fair assessment of the Jews, and they were forced to endure countless humiliations. The presence of opposition to the first halting attempts to include the Jews in the early modern process of creating a bourgeois (*bürgerlich*) society were clearly apparent, for example, among the vilifiers of Jud Süss.

In many localities, well down into the eighteenth century, any Christian could demand three dice of a Jew he encountered outside the ghetto. This old custom, originally bound up with the body tax, may have been seen as appropriate punishment for an ancient transgression: the casting of lots for the clothing of the crucified Jesus. If the Jews so challenged were not carrying dice, they either had to buy their release with money or were made the victim of all sorts of harassment. A similar irritant was the Jewish obligation in some places since the Middle Ages to present the pastor of the local church with an annual gift of two silver spoons. In university towns Jews often suffered from the vulgarities and badgering of the students. Glückel of Hameln wrote: If a university is there, it is a "bad place" for Jews.[6]

Jews also remained the repeated target of violent excesses, especially when they were blamed for economic distress. In 1699 in the diocese of Bamberg a food shortage developed after the prince-bishop sold the grain from his estates to Dutch Jews. Riots directed against the Jews ensued. The bishop who, already in 1666, had forbidden the harassment of Jews on the street, punished the rioters with a heavy fine. In the seventeenth and eighteenth centuries social tensions and economic problems in Altona erupted into anti-Jewish violence on four separate occasions. An economic crisis in Hamburg in 1730 likewise triggered an anti-Jewish disturbance.

Compared with their responses in the Middle Ages, the Jewish reactions to such lawlessness were now far more forceful. The position and activity of the court Jews probably contributed to this posture, as did the pride of the Portuguese Jews, who, rather than endure insufferable taxes and humiliating ordinances, migrated in large numbers from Hamburg to the more tolerant city of Amsterdam. The intense campaign against the publication of Eisenmenger's *Entdecktes Judenthum* was an example of a more vigorous political defense of their interests. Glückel of Hameln repeatedly wrote of the need for "revenge" when Jews were murdered, that is, to pursue, apprehend, and punish the culprits. A prominent Moravian chief rabbi noted in one of his responsa that the leaders of the community had ordered the relatives of a murdered Jew to pursue the murderer and hand him over to the authorities, even if that should involve a major expenditure of funds.[7] Such actions—and, in particular, the public manner in which they were conducted—attest to the genesis of a greater confidence and self-assurance.

5

Community, Society, and Domestic Life

1. Community Administration and the Rabbinate

After having examined the external conditions of Jewish existence, let us turn our attention to community life. It was marked by the presence of two salient parallels between the administration of a Jewish community and a municipality. Burghers and community members respectively were under a regimen of strict supervision, enforced by a multitude of officials, dignitaries, and employees, controlled by the town council, the community lay leaders, or elders. Since the Middle Ages the community had experienced a process of structural change: in the tug-of-war between the key figures the decisive locus of power had shifted from the circle of scholars to the wealthy laymen. Both in the Jewish community and in the city the propertied class was now the dominant stratum. The public functioning of all branches of community life was regulated by precise statutes and regulations.

The earliest completely preserved community statutes date from Cracow (ostensibly 1595), but there were the beginnings of a community constitution in Frankfurt am Main as early as the middle of the sixteenth century and in Prague before 1600. As a rule, each kehilla was a compulsory association to which all Jews who lived in the locality belonged. After 1648 numerous community officials came from Poland, especially rabbis, cantors, ritual slaughterers, and synagogue caretakers. In several large communities additional officials were employed. Thus there is mention of

Jewish night watchmen in Frankfurt am Main and a Jewish police unit in Hamburg. The most important institutions of the community were the synagogue, the community hall (often housed in the rooms of the synagogue building), the study room (likewise frequently a part of the house of prayer), the school for poor and orphaned children, the ritual bath (mikveh), the community oven (where Sabbath foods were kept warm), the cemetery, the poor house and hospital (*hekdesh*), and a number of religious-cultural and charitable organizations.

Both in the city council and the communities the oligarchy was based on wealth and public standing. Thus, for example, individuals in Fürth with assets of less than six hundred guldens were excluded de facto from the leadership of the community. Moreover, only those who had belonged to the community for at least twelve years were eligible for office. These conditions were eased for learned men who had been given the honorary title of *ḥaver* (scholar). The members of the community board (in Frankfurt am Main and Friedberg the communal leaders originally responsible for construction work in the ghetto were termed *Baumeister*, "master builders") were closely related to one another. Acceptance of an honorary office in management of the community was often regarded by the government as a duty that could not be declined. In Berlin it was only possible to be released from the obligation of having to assume the office of chief elder against the payment of one hundred Reichsthaler. The main employees of the community were the rabbi, the community scribe, and the community beadle (Hebr. *shammash*, Yidd. *shammes*). An honorary position associated with very special functions was that of shtadlan, the representative of the community to the outside world.

The procedure for selecting lay leaders was in keeping with contemporary conceptions and the oligarchical character of community leadership. The class-based election system that had been introduced in most communities mirrored, as it had in the cities, the socioeconomic situation, which was anchored in the communal constitution. This was a system that assured the well-to-do a predominant position. In many communities the elections were indirect: the main lay leaders were chosen by from three to seven electors; the rule provided that they could not be related to each other (and were thus called *kesherim*, from *kasher*, "suitable, without blemish"; in some places they were also termed *borerim*, i.e., "electors"). The others were chosen by the community leadership or the electors in cooperation with the elders. In separate divisions the first, second, and third electors were selected, with members of the higher tax groups possessing greater influence. In Berlin, where the elders were initially not elected but rather appointed by the authorities, the electors were determined by drawing lots, selecting three from among the most wealthy, two from the middle economic range, and one from the poorer Jews.

The election of community functionaries was rarely for life. Nonetheless, the dominant tendency had been to retain the previous incumbent in office wherever possible. The state authorities also felt that a certain continuity was appropriate. In Frankfurt am Main, by contrast, lay board members were originally elected for life, and supplementary members were co-opted by the board itself. In Prague community board members were not chosen for life; likewise, there was no co-optation by the board. In 1617 a conflict in Frankfurt over this question was brought before the rabbis of Fulda, Hildesheim, and Metz for adjudication. The city council was also drawn into the matter and passed ordinances from time to time. Finally, agreement was reached on an electoral system that paved the way for new members to be admitted while also taking into account the merit of the older leaders who had been active for many years on behalf of the community. However, in numerous other communities it remained the rule that the body of all Jews was organized like a guild whose board generally added to its number by co-optation. In Frankfurt am Main the electors were required to swear an oath in the synagogue before the open Holy Ark that they would only elect worthy men to the board and only those who were "impartial," that is, not closely related to each other.[1] The elections were subject to confirmation by the authorities. In Berlin the government issued the following regulation in 1722–1723 for the constitution of the board: it should consist of two chief elders appointed for life, one of whom, in addition to a salary from the royal treasury, was given an annual supplementary honorarium of three hundred thalers by the community; furthermore, there should be five elders, four treasurers, four wardens for the poor, and additional members of the board. Every three years the board was to be elected anew. Several of the earlier members were always to retain their office.

Even if it appears that the electoral regulations were gradually altered yielding to pressure from the majority of the community, the rule of the board over the community remained untouched. With few exceptions, the government recognized the decision of the board members on the admission or expulsion of a Jew wishing to settle in the locality. If a Jew dared to settle in the town against the will of the board but with the permission of the authorities, he was regarded as a *Beisitzer*, that is, an inhabitant without right to residence, and was excluded from the economic, religious, and social life of the community. The cancellation of the right of residence of a community member was the most effective instrument available to the local leadership to maintain order and discipline. The Frankfurt community had the right to annul the *Stättigkeit* (right of residence) of any member, usually as a form of punishment. Naturally, they were also permitted to expel Jews who had settled in the town without formal Stättigkeit. This total power invested in the local leaders derived from medieval legal usage (*herem ha-yishuv*) and was probably also approved by rabbinic scholars. Nonetheless, it appears to have owed its effectiveness, at least in part, to the external paradigm of the guild masters, which also had, like the municipal administration, a shaping influence on community governance.

The board members exercised their control with the complete approval—indeed the active support—of the authorities. In Berlin the authorities constantly expanded the disciplinary powers of the community board members; in so doing they underscored their insistence that the Jews must acknowledge collective responsibility for one another. Among others, these powers included a say in questions regarding a person's right to settle, written references in connection with the issuance of letters of protection, surveillance of aliens, prevention of unauthorized infiltration, and tax assessment. No house could be sold without the approval of the board members. They enjoyed the special protection of the state, which in the Prussian *Reglement* of 1700 expressly specified that, along with the regulation of internal Jewish affairs, it was the main task of the elders to tend to state interests as they concerned the Jews. The chief elders in Berlin, who received an annual payment of one hundred Reichsthaler, were responsible to the government for everything that occurred in the Jewish community. Whenever a case necessitated it, they had to inform the Jewry Commission.

Under these circumstances it was only natural that the rabbi was, as a community official, subordinate to the lay board members. This was manifest, for example, in the fact that rabbis were as a rule appointed for a period of only three years, after which it was up to the community, generally under the rather autocratic direction of the lay leadership, to either reappoint or replace him. Appointment of a rabbi for life tenure, as in the case of Rabbi David Oppenheim in Prague, was a rare exception. According to a regulation introduced in many communities, only a rabbi from outside the community could be employed; he was to be unrelated to local residents and without any appreciable following in the local community. This was to prevent the formation of factions among the members, lessen the danger of a struggle for the office, and preserve the independence of the rabbi from family and other special interests. That, for example, was one of the reasons underlying the opposition of the Prague community to the appointment of a son of the "Great Rabbi Löw" (Maharal) as rabbi. Indeed, Maharal himself had not been appointed to the rabbinate until quite late in his life. Only when matters of religious law were involved were the board members and the entire community subject to the leadership and decisions of the rabbi, in his capacity as teacher of religious law and head of the rabbinical court. Even then the initiative seldom lay in the hands of the rabbi. As a rule, he expressed his opinion in response to a query or in the course of a discussion. Nonetheless, he could take the initiative and comment from the synagogue pulpit on events and developments in the community. Despite his dependence on the lay leaders, a strong and forceful personality might influence the community, even in a direction not agreeable to the board. This became a source for communal conflicts, which will be dealt with below.

The board members and the entire community generally gave the rabbi the honor and respect due him. To the outside world he was not only a religious official in the narrow sense but, together with the lay leaders, represented the community. He also had a certain right to participation in administrative acts in which a particular state interest was involved. Thus, time and again, especially in smaller communities, he also fulfilled a decisive function in the allocation of taxes. Rabbis and local officials performed their duties with great seriousness and solemnity. Scrupulous attention was given to titles and honors. Thus, for example, the prerogative of the rabbi to be publicly honored by being "called up" to the reading of the Torah on certain Sabbath days and festivals was precisely set down. In many communities, no scholar, no matter how eminent, could be called to the reading by the honorific title *morenu* (our teacher) if he was not an officiating rabbi.

Yet even in the bestowal of honorary titles the powers of the rabbi were limited, and the board members made sure that no one in the community advanced socially without their approval. Accordingly, the rabbi was contractually obligated (in his *Rabbonusbrief* or letter of appointment) at the time of his employment not to bestow any honorary titles—such as *morenu* (or, in many localities, even the less prestigious title *ḥaver*)—without the approval of the lay leaders. This regulation was applied even in the case of rabbis of international renown. On the other hand, the board members were restrained from allowing an outside scholar to deliver a public lecture without the express consent of the rabbi. The rabbi was permitted to charge a fee for the bestowing of titles, the issuance of *hekhsherim* (ritual permits confirming that a particular food is kosher) for wine, meat, and cheese from outside the community, the testing of ritual slaughterers, the issuing of a marriage license, interrogating witnesses and pronouncing court decisions, issuing various types of documents, and many other sundry rabbinical services. These fees made up a large part of the rabbi's income—often the bulk—though it should be noted that in many writs of appointment the community agreed to provide suitable lodgings for the rabbi and his family at its expense.

The proper domain of the rabbi was naturally the Jewish court. As a rule, it had autonomous power to adjudicate in all civil cases between Jews, as well as in marriage disputes, the appointment of guardians, the preparation of wills, and, of course, in all proceedings against individuals who had broken religious law. Scholars in the community who belonged to the ranks of the *bene yeshiva*—that is, older community members who in their youth had attended a yeshiva and, due to their knowledge of the law and to their piety, were counted among the prominent intellectuals in the community—functioned as adjunct members of the rabbinical court. In Prague the chief rabbi had five "senior jurists" (*Oberjuristen*) as associates, and, in order not to bother them with minor cases, a small-claims court was set up, headed by six "junior judges." In special cases the members of rabbinical courts in larger communities were invited by other communities to judge a case.

In carrying out a verdict, especially if it involved a punitive sentence, the rabbi was dependent on the cooperation of local board members. In many communities the lay leader in office for the month (*parnas ha-ḥodesh*), in Prague termed *Monatshalter* (officer of the month), was invested with all disciplinary powers within the confines of the community. He convened the meetings of the board, which he chaired, and exercised a number of important powers and responsibilities in connection with the current affairs of the community. According to the Mainz *Judenordnung* of 1741, it was incumbent upon him to sit in on the court of the rabbi together with the officer of the previous month, authorize the verdict by his signature, and see that it was carried out. The rabbi was not empowered to impose fines, even for religious transgressions, such as irregular attendance at public prayer, without the consent of two members of the lay board. Likewise, the religiously grave *herem*, which in effect excommunicated the banished individual temporarily, was only valid if confirmed by two board members. The procedure of ban was used both as a punishment and a means of compulsion.

There were also other means of punishment and disciplinary measures available to the Jewish courts, and these could likewise be included as part of the pronouncement of the ban: physical punishment, abrogation of resident rights, forfeiture of religious functions and honors, loss of the capacity to testify in court or to swear an oath, loss of eligibility to be appointed to community offices, and a prohibition on eating outside the home. By means of the "little ban" (*hakhrazah*, "proclamation"), a convicted offender was publicly called upon to atone for or redress his transgression. Whoever remained in hakhrazah seven days without doing what had been demanded of him was placed under a full herem. In minor matters the board member in office for the month could reach a decision on his own and even had a limited ban at his disposal. Thus, to a certain extent, board members and rabbis found themselves mutually dependent on each other.

The basis of internal community finances was formed by the mitzvot and by the direct and indirect internal taxes. The category of mitzvot comprised the numerous ritual acts and honorary offices in the synagogue for which the members applied, often paying substantial amounts for the privilege. Among the internal taxes was that on meat, usually charged when kosher meat was purchased. These payments were in addition to the broad range of protection fees, levies and duties, regular or one-time, that Jews were obliged to render to the state. The annual protection monies and special taxes were paid to the state and city by the community, and the burden was distributed among the members according to their assessed wealth. The respective wealth of each taxpayer was estimated by tax assessors (*ma'arikhim, shama'im*). These assessors swore an oath not to estimate taxes too high, because of animosity, or too low, because of affection or consanguinity. Taxes were remitted only in the case of the needy or for the rabbi and certain community employees. In the eighteenth century the Berlin community made a special exception for Moses Mendelssohn, freeing him from tax obligations in acknowledgment of his meritorious deeds on behalf of Jewry and scholarship.

A Friedberg statute of 1633 indicates the pressure the community exerted on its members to persuade them to make truthful statements in estimating their assets as required for the apportioning of the tax burden and to pay their taxes promptly. It stipulates that when a member objects to the assessment made, the tax assessors bring him before the open Holy Ark, where he must make his statement under oath. If a member is tardy in payment of taxes, he cannot wed in the community. If he has the ceremony performed elsewhere, he is not permitted to stay overnight in Friedberg, and whoever puts him up will be placed under the ban.[2]

2. Institutions and Associations

The central institution of the community was, of course, the synagogue, and, where one did not yet exist, the prayer room set up in a private home. The high socioreligious value attached to public prayer was underscored by the custom that men and women always wore a special cloak when coming to the synagogue. Over and beyond its religious functions, the

31   Blessing of the new moon. From Paul Christian Kirchner,
Jüdisches Ceremoniel (Nuremberg, 1724)

synagogue generally served as a meeting room and study house, sometimes also as a courtroom. The synagogue courtyard was the scene for various religious ceremonies, especially weddings, as well as the burning of leavened bread on the eve of the Passover festival, occasional funeral speeches, and the prayer for the new moon (*kidush levanah*). The synagogue formed the social focus for the Jewish community, as a sociopolitical and not only religious body. When one reads that the many money dealers in Hamburg, who were busy running to and fro the entire day seeking their livelihood, headed for the synagogue as evening approached, it is important to note that this daily convergence on the synagogue was not just due to religious habit but also reflected a need for ongoing social contact. In numerous communities the lay leaders issued synagogue codes that regulated everything in the synagogue, down to the minutest detail, under threat of penalty for infractions. Where there was a synagogue private communal worship was generally forbidden. Nonetheless, in Berlin around 1774 there were no less than 22 private prayer rooms for a Jewish population numbering 2,200.

At the very heart of the community's social life stood charitable activity. Indeed, it is possible to say that the combination of sociability and charity gave the kehilla its special stamp as a community. Charity also imbued sociability with a religious dimension. The most important charitable activity in the community occurred in the framework of voluntary associations, the foremost of which was the "sacred fraternity" (*hevrah kadisha*). In the narrower sense this was a burial society, yet it fulfilled a number of other religious, social, and even financial functions. The fraternal society accompanied and took care of each family of a seriously ill community member from the onset of disease to the setting of the gravestone in the case of death. If the family involved was in financial distress, the hevrah granted it material assistance. It also aided poorer members of the community, provided for the dowry of brides, wine for circumcision ceremonies, and street illumination in the ghetto. For that reason the society was also dubbed *kippe* (from Hebr.-Yidd. *kupah*, "cashbox"), since it was frequently the communal institution best situated financially. Admission into the hevrah was an honor. There was a membership fee, and some statutes indicate that membership in the hevrah, which was costly, was also a kind of insurance, by which members were entitled to preferential treatment for their daughters and relatives in the distribution of funds for bridal dowries.

As far as can be determined from the historical sources, this society did not exist in German lands until the sixteenth century, yet it had already appeared in Spain in the medieval period. This Sephardi influence in Germany, demonstrable in certain other spheres as well, may be due to Portuguese Jews who came and settled there or the mediation of Ashkenazi communities from northern Italy. Another possibility is that social and demographic change in the Ashkenazi communities created analogous situations to those that had existed in Spain, making the formation of such fraternal societies necessary. Important among such prerequisite factors was the relatively large growth of the Jewish population in many towns and the crystallization of socioeconomic differences to a degree previously unknown. A number of burial societies in the countryside were formed by cooperation among individuals from various localities in the area, since, by themselves, the small communities were unable to maintain burial functions.

In addition to these internal factors, there was the organizational and social paradigm provided by the Christian guilds. As in the guilds, the members of the burial fraternities were graded in a hierarchy of leaders, "seniors," special functionaries, and ordinary members. They were all subject to strict rules of discipline. Here, too, the influence of the guilds is unmistakable: the fact that Jews were denied entry to all guilds may have strengthened their desire to create a kind of "guild" of their own, even if its actual function was totally different. Like a regular guild, the ḥevrah gathered at specified times for prayer and study. Its members enjoyed certain special rights and privileges in the community, and once a year they met for an exclusive festive banquet. In many respects, they formed the elite of the community. Carefully framed statutes assured that only the best—in both religious and material respects—were accepted into the society as members. They had social obligations among themselves and were expected to lead an especially strict religious and moral life. Only the leaders (gabai'im) of the fraternity had the right to recommend candidates for membership or election to office. At the end of the seventeenth century, in Fürth, a fraternity of circumcisers was also organized. It introduced protective measures for the safety of the infants and passed regulations aimed at excluding unqualified candidates for the office of circumciser.

With the upsurge in the kabbalistic current, which will be discussed below, that influence was also felt in the voluntary associations of the community and in domestic religious customs. In accordance with the example of the pious societies in Safed, the center of the new kabbalistic school inspired by Rabbi Isaac Luria, associations were founded whose members vowed to lead an especially pious life in which penance and supplication for redemption played a central role. Among other things, they pledged to make a general, mutual confession on specific days of the month. Each member was also obliged to reprimand his fellow immediately if it became known that he had committed some moral infraction or ritual transgression. Each evening all persons who might have offended an individual member during the day by word or deed were to be expressly granted forgiveness. Before sleep many regularly said the confession of sins prescribed for the seriously ill on their deathbed. Special procedures of atonement were recommended to association members, especially fasting, the most common instrument of pietistic devotion. There were those who fasted a full forty days before Yom Kippur, the Day of Atonement, interrupting the fast only at night.

Over the course of the eighteenth century the importance of the fraternal societies waned. They were no longer able to be as generous with their funds as before. Moreover, other associations that fulfilled some of the same tasks previously within the competence of the burial societies had arisen. Thus, with ongoing modernization, the function of bridal insurance was sometimes removed from the responsibilities of the ḥevrah kadisha—for example, in Berlin, where Moses Mendelssohn took part in setting up a marriage association whose members could assure the bridal dowry of their daughters by making regular contributions.

Beyond the circle of influence of the fraternity, and sometimes parallel to it, the community took pains to ensure that a hostel and infirmary were available for travelers or the indigent sick and that a physician, a pharmacist, and diverse medical institutions were on hand for the community members. It also assumed a certain supervisory function over the circumcisers, midwives, and wet nurses, and undertook rigorous measures if the community was threatened by pestilence or epidemics. Medical care for community members was often of far better quality than that available to the Christian population. Large communities employed a community physician, though for this they needed the formal permission of the municipality and, at times, even of the sovereign. Permission was not always granted, and, when it was, often with certain restrictive conditions attached. When the Frankfurt community wished to appoint the famous doctor and scientist Joseph Solomon Delmedigo (1591–1655), the Christian physicians expressed adamant opposition, but in 1631 the city finally gave its permission. In 1645 Delmedigo moved to Prague, where the community had worked out a set of special guidelines for physicians (*hanhagat ha-rofe'im*).

An important honorary office in the community was that of the supervisor of charity (*gabai tsedakah*), to whom a number of officials were subordinate. Their job was to provide for the poor, the sick, mothers in childbed, the homeless, as well as impoverished brides. The expenses for charity were largely covered by the donations everyone customarily pledged upon receiving the honor of being "called up" for the reading of the Torah. A collection box for the support of the poor and sick was also passed around at every public and private festivity in the community. Regular collections were conducted on behalf of the Jewish communities in the Holy Land and, from time to time, for ransoming Jews who had been taken into captivity or for alleviating hardship in communities ravaged by fire, epidemic, or other calamities.

3. Community and Family Life

The significant demographic upsurge in the Jewish population in Central Europe during the early modern period mentioned earlier should be viewed in connection with both the charitable activity of the Jewish communities and certain developments in Jewish private and family life. Despite the often catastrophic living conditions in the ghettos, conditions of health among Jews were not worse than in the general population, nor was there higher mortality. It is likely this was largely due to the strong bonds of solidarity linking all members of the community and providing them with access to welfare institutions. Additional factors favoring a rapid growth in population were early marriage, relatively low infant mortality, and the emphasis on personal hygiene (as contrasted with the often appalling sanitary conditions outside the home). In comparison with the general population, it may be observed that Jews in this period had a better diet and suffered from less drunkenness and violence.

On the whole, the urban community over this entire period presented a picture of prosperity, despite the heavy burden of taxes and levies. The growth in trade with goods, money changing, and coinage transactions, in part through the ramified network of the court factors, led to a rise in the standard of living of a majority of the urban Jewish population. The memoirs of Glückel of Hameln not only describe the life of an important stratum of affluent Jewish families in northern Germany but also mirror a socioeconomic situation in which wealth and prosperity figure as central themes. As in other periods and locales of Jewish history, here, too, economic advancement led to a pronounced urge to adapt to the surrounding milieu and a growing hunger for general education, quite apart from the aura and allure of the lifestyle of court Jewry.

This phenomenon was most conspicuous in clothing. One glance at the numerous contemporaneous illustrations depicting Jews suffices to convey the extent to which they were endeavoring to embellish their traditional dress with a modern and stylish flair, with no lack of extravagance and splendor. The moral sermons of the rabbis are an eloquent testimony to the trend. They speak of women's clothing that must not be decorated with gold and silver and should not be made of velvet, damask, or satin; on weekdays no silk should be worn either. In general, apparel should display neither beauty nor wealth. Bright colors were not permissible, and only a single ruff was allowed. Shoes could be only of simple leather; hats could not be too fancy. Men were not to wear blond wigs, nor gold or silver buttons. Neither men nor women were allowed to don jewelry that was overly expensive and ostentatious.

In the large communities the lay leaders, in cooperation with the rabbis, issued dress codes identical in numerous details with similar regulations introduced by the Christian authorities. In their responsa, as well, the rabbis commented on the new fashions if they appeared to them to clash with religious law. Rabbi Jacob Emden in Altona dealt with the question whether it was permissible for married women to cover their hair with a wig instead of the previously customary bonnet and arrived at a negative ruling.[3]

32 Jewish traditional dress in Fürth (1706)

The dress codes pursued three aims: in the realm of religion they were to remind Jews of the duty of chastity and modesty as well as the maintenance of external features distinguishing them from non-Jews; "politically," any unnecessary provocation of non-Jews should be avoided; the social motive was a condemnation of the craze for stylish fashion as a temptation to splurge on clothing, incurring expenses for which one had no funds. Hirsh Koydanover, born in Vilna, the son of a Frankfurt rabbi (d. 1712), expressed his indignation over the new fashions in his ethical work, *Kav ha-yashar*:

> Women have to be more reserved than men. They should not dress according to whim and go attired in the manner of non-Jewish women, as I observed only recently. [First,] these Jewish women cannot be readily distinguished from Christian women. The consequence is that men commit a sin when they look at them. Second, they provoke feelings of enmity among the non-Jews, when they see that Jews are dressed more elegantly than the princes. Third, they cause their husbands serious difficulties by forcing them to purchase clothes that are beyond their means. Among men, as well, the craze for fashion leads to terrible consequences: they shave off their beards, and none can see that they are Jews.[4]

In Metz, at the beginning of the eighteenth century, Jewish men began to wear wigs in accordance with the latest fashion. At that same time the author of a religious vademecum for everyday life noted that many men had replaced their full beard by a far smaller one.[5] The similarity between the repeatedly articulated prohibitions and warnings proves what little effect they had and just how great was the power of fashion they were attempting to combat.

Conspicuous consumption was also evident in social life. There were repeated ordinances issued against putting on wasteful banquets. These rules limited the number as well as the sumptuousness of the feasts but permitted the wealthy, in contrast with the poor, to serve more lavishly. Limits were also placed on the number of musicians and minstrels, and the regulations inform us that at banquets held on weekdays in wealthy families, especially wedding dinners, there were also music and performances by jesters. A responsum written toward the end of the seventeenth century notes that there were numerous occasions when a family sat down with guests for a festive meal that did not take place on a Sabbath or holiday. Since, according to Talmudic regulations, pious schol-

ars are not allowed to take part in any festive meal that is not an obligatory religious meal (se'udat mitsvah), religious songs were sung at the
table, and a guest knowledgeable in the Torah was probably asked to say
a few edifying words, in this manner fulfilling the precept.[6]

Making loud noise in the synagogue, such as on Simḥat Torah (Rejoicing
in the Law), was also the object of regulations. In Frankfurt am Main a play
printed for the Purim festival in 1708 was confiscated and burned by the lay
leaders because it was "very silly and lacking in taste . . . to say nothing of
the godlessness with which they present the pious Mordechai as a nasty,
obscene, vulgar old man."[7] Many regulations dealt with card playing,
which was apparently so widespread that it could not be totally proscribed;
on days when no prayer of supplication (taḥanun) was said (i.e., days of
happy remembrance or the intermediate days of a feast), it was expressly
permitted. Dice games, however, were completely prohibited, and ordinances were issued against gambling, under penalty of a ban. The only
game the rabbinate did not object to at all was chess. The casual frequenting of taverns and coffeehouses was reprimanded, and already in 1687 the
statutes of the triple community of Altona-Hamburg-Wandsbek forbade
going to a bowling alley, a comedy, or a fencing school on the Sabbath or a
holiday. The background to all these phenomena was a strongly pronounced craving for a life of luxury and wealth. An examination of the
numerous ethical books, in part still only available in manuscript form, suggests that this topic preoccupied the religious leaders and social critics of the
time far more than in previous eras.

Even more than domestic and private life, public worship in the synagogue reflected the joy in worldly pleasures of the urban community and
a new sense of religious aesthetics that differed markedly from naive
medieval piety. The traditional, learned, and pious figure of the precentor
no longer satisfied the community. It wanted musical edification, stimulation, and a vocally pleasant performance, one that gave beloved traditional tunes their due while simultaneously offering the ear something
new. Thus the prayer leader became a cantor, able not just to intone the
old tunes but also to incorporate contemporary popular melodies, occasionally even operatic arias, into his repertory. In this way Ashkenazi synagogue music took on an increasingly Baroque stamp. Attempts were
even made, within the framework of what was permitted by religious law,
to introduce instrumental music into the synagogue. Thus musicians in
the Meisel Synagogue in Prague played "a beautiful song before the
entrance of the Sabbath" on an organ and stringed instruments. There are

similar reports from other communities.[8] In Frankfurt am Main Jewish instrumentalists were brought in from nearby Offenbach for the close of Simḥat Torah.

Jewish professional musicians and instrumentalists have been documented since the sixteenth century and throughout the entire early modern period, especially in Bohemia, but also in Germany. During the seventeenth century Prague and Bohemia had their own social class of Jewish musicians. As early as 1580 a Jewish band played at the wedding of a Bohemian nobleman, and in 1641 the Prague archbishop bestowed (or reconfirmed) the right of Jews to play at Christian baptisms and weddings. Despite objections by Christian musicians to the Jewish competition, the privilege was later renewed. Paul Christian Kirchner's *Jüdisches Ceremoniell* (Jewish Ceremonies), published in 1734 in Nuremberg, contains an illustration of a wedding procession led by a cellist and two fid-

33   Jewish wedding procession. From Paul Christian Kirchner,
Jüdisches Ceremoniel (Nuremberg, 1724)

dlers. The Jewish minstrel was an indispensable member of Jewish society in the eighteenth century, popular not just among Jews but among Christians as well.

In many communities living conditions were in stark contradiction to the desire for luxuriousness, splendor, and an outwardly contemporary way of life. The fact that Jews lived in special sections of the town was not necessarily in itself a symptom of official discrimination. In Bamberg in 1687 the community unsuccessfully requested that the prince-bishop provide them with a remote place where they might erect their houses so as to be protected from the animosity of the population. A similar petition is documented for Vienna at the time of Emperor Ferdinand II. Yet in many ghettos and Judengassen (Jews' Alleys), for example, in Frankfurt am Main and Worms, Jews were literally crammed into a crowded space, and hygienic and sanitary conditions were in a permanently sorry state. For that reason even the front yard of the synagogue could, at times, hardly be used for religious purposes. In Frankfurt vernacular the Judengasse was known as "New Egypt," and the young Goethe wrote about the "extremely unpleasant impression" he had, while casting only a fleeting glance inside as he passed by the gate, of the crampedness, filth, and throngs inside.[9] Although he also turned up his nose at the "accent of an unpleasant speech" he heard spoken there, there is nothing spiteful in his remarks on the Jews and their street. At the end of the eighteenth century Bettina von Arnim could still write about the "purgatory of the Judengasse" in Frankfurt, where neither air nor light could penetrate. Since the city did not permit any expansion of the quarter, the Jews were compelled to build storey upon storey, so that the roofs of opposite houses almost touched. At the end of the seventeenth century 3,000 persons lived here in 200 dwellings, and on average there was only one room to a family. A similar situation existed in Hotzenplotz (Moravia), where 596 Jews lived in 39 houses, sixteen or more to a house. By contrast, the occupancy ratio in the Christian population there, numbering 1,977 persons, was six to a house. Yet, despite such crowding, paintings and sculptures sometimes embellished the interiors of the dwellings of wealthy Jews.

A look at Jewish family life shows that the purity of morals in Jewish families was generally maintained, even when the conditions of protection for Jews, and the *Familianten* laws in particular, made it exceptionally difficult to marry off the children. Yet there was no lack of complaints about lax sexual morals, and rabbinical responsa often mention that the bride and bridegroom nowadays openly embrace and kiss in the presence of others before the wedding. The fact that the birth of an illegitimate child was not too rare an event is attested by a record of the circumcision custom in the Fürth community, according to which illegitimate children were not circumcised in the synagogue, as was traditional usage.[10] The general practice of early marriage, especially in wealthy families, served to prevent violations of sexual morality to only a limited extent. When many children died in the Prague community in 1611, the rabbi, Solomon Ephraim Lunschitz, issued a number of ethical rules, principally pertaining to chastity and abstinence, in order to avert any further calamity. Among other things, he ruled that an unaccompanied woman was not allowed to enter the house of a non-Jew for the purpose of trade. Girls were not permitted to go out walking alone or in pairs either during the day or at night. Jewish prostitutes were no longer tolerated in the city and were required to leave. At the end of the seventeenth century the Hamburg board members issued a regulation that a woman was not allowed to go to the opera unless accompanied by her husband. In the middle of the eighteenth century the rabbis and lay leaders of a *Landjudenschaft* felt it necessary to prohibit men and women from dancing with one another at weddings and youths and girls from sleeping the night in a common room.

Family life revolved to a large degree around marrying off the children. Limitations on young couples starting a family, imposed by the rigorous paragraphs of laws and letters of protection, were only a part of the obstacles, although the most decisive, blocking the path to marriage. Particularly for economic reasons, the Jewish community itself also reserved the right to limit the annual number of marriages and thus curb the growth of the Jewish population. In Altona, for example, there was a regulation that no Altona Jew could marry without the approval of the chief rabbi and the community lay leaders. If a Jew from Altona secretly married a woman from outside the town—an act by which she acquired the right to residence in Altona without a formal decision by the lay board—he was severely punished. As a rule, parents claimed the right to determine the choice of a spouse for their children. Increasingly, in rich families, wealth was preferred over scholarship, a development bemoaned by the rabbis. Many also avoided marrying their children to immigrants from Poland. Money outweighed distinguished lineage (*yiḥus*)—an attitude quite divergent from the traditional view. The size of the dowry was crucial. In wealthy families it was the custom of the young couple to board with the parents of the bride for a period of two years (*auf Kost*) after the wedding.

Degrees of piety differed. The family of Glückel of Hameln, for example, was exceptionally devout. The entire family would fast the day before Rosh Hashanah (New Year), an ascetic practice called the "fast of the righteous" in halachic sources. Her husband, who was constantly on business trips, did not leave the city during the entire year of mourning following the death of his father so as not to miss even one *kaddish* (prayer for mourners) in the synagogue. Yet, even in less learned families with no penchant for asceticism, the lifestyle was marked by a piety that manifested itself in all phases and situations of life. This is attested by a multitude of prayer books and other publications for religious use.

The special character of domestic religious life in the Jewish communities in German-speaking Europe was distinctively reflected in a popular pious genre: the small devotional books containing prayers, blessings, and other extracts from the siddur (prayer book) for daily use. These little books could be found everywhere in great quantities and in various editions, and some contained Western Yiddish translations of the Hebrew texts. They also included a large number of religious table songs (zemirot). The religious table song was an especially popular custom in these circles, probably connected with the fact that for the greater part of the year, in many small communities, there could be no common public prayer because there were not enough men for a quorum (minyan, ten adult males at least thirteen years old). The chanting of the table songs, a tradition often cultivated with deep emotion, compensated the family, as it were, for the lack of communal synagogal worship.

Such popular piety was quite compatible with a certain laxity in the observance of the religious law. In 1771 the rabbis and board members in Mainz issued a regulation stipulating that girls were forbidden, under penalty of a fine, to comb their hair on the Sabbath and holidays. Another Sabbath prohibition that often was not taken very seriously was the law against carrying on the street where there was no "Sabbath wire" (eruv, surrounding a given settled district and symbolically "mixing" private and public domains in order that an individual might carry from one to the other or within the latter). Some circumvented the regulation to drink milk only if milked from a cow under Jewish supervision. There were more and more instances of Jews filing cases against one another in secular courts instead of the rabbinical court in the community. In Frankfurt am Main dissatisfaction was expressed that Jews were turning to the municipal council with complaints against fellow Jews for any and every trifle and even calling the police to the house of Jewish neighbors. This

went so far that at times there was a special prayer (*mi-sheberakh*) recited
in the synagogue against slanderers. There was a frequent tendency to
take traditional laws and customs lightly, a development that became ever
more pronounced in the course of the eighteenth century. It is thus
understandable that the Mainz Judenordnung of 1741 mentions a supervisor who, as a kind of police officer watching over public morals, had to
see to law and order and make sure religious duties were fulfilled.

4. Education

The education of the children, training them in religious tradition and
grooming them to start households of their own, was among the most
important concerns of the community and the family. In accordance with
the well-known passage in the *Sayings of the Fathers* (*Avot* 1:2) about
the three pillars on which the world rests, many community regulations
began with the first pillar, Torah, that is, education and instruction.
However, the community itself only took care of the education of the
impoverished and orphaned in schools for children between the ages of
six and thirteen. The community's view was that children's education was
primarily a parental concern and duty. Accordingly, instruction for children from somewhat better-off families often began from their fourth
year, in small private schools, run by the teachers at the parents' expense.
Families that could afford it took in private tutors who generally also lived
in with the family.

Most of the school teachers and private tutors stemmed from Poland,
Lithuania, or Bohemia; as a rule, they came for just a short period and
soon returned to their homeland. Usually they taught eight to ten hours
a day, generally in the same room they lived in. For that reason, their
instruction was called *ḥeder* (Hebr. "room"). Considerable criticism was
voiced of their training and teaching methods. Yet this criticism of the
teachers, whose quality varied enormously from place to place and school
to school, should not obscure the fact that there were also many well-
functioning schools with excellent and extremely dedicated teachers. In
the second half of the eighteenth century Prague had more than sixty-
three schoolmasters, two of them women. In Hamburg in 1764 there were
twenty-eight Jewish school teachers and eleven school employees. In rare
and isolated cases Jewish pupils also attended Christian schools.

Instruction of Jewish children revolved almost exclusively around the
sacred books: the prayer book and the Bible for the younger pupils,

Mishnah and Talmud for the older ones. The only nonreligious subject generally taught was basic arithmetic. The wealthy families had their children instructed in foreign languages, with the aim of acquiring at least a reading knowledge; already at the end of the seventeenth century rabbis were lamenting the "new fashion" of teaching children French even before they were able to pray. This trend involved Jewish families not only in Alsace and Lorraine, but in Hamburg, Frankfurt am Main, and even small provincial towns. Yet, on the whole, the educational system in the communities, faithful to the norms and principles on which it was based, succeeded in raising a young generation that remained attached to Judaism, its laws and philosophy, despite the changes in living conditions they experienced.

Boys, who finished elementary instruction at the age of thirteen, then usually entered the business of their father or of their future father-in-law. However, especially in the countryside, parents often sent their children off to work at a more tender age, since they could not manage without their extra earnings, however meager. In wealthy families, and when a pupil showed special aptitude, parents generally wished for their sons to attend a yeshiva until marriage. In such cases the son was frequently sent off to "learn" in Poland, Bohemia, or Moravia. Marriage often simultaneously marked the beginning of occupational life, except when a rich father-in-law enabled the young married man to continue his study of Torah for several more years.

Almost everywhere there was a society for adult education, the so-called *shas hevrah* or *shas kippe* (Hebr. *shas*, acronym for *shishah sedarim*, the six orders of the Mishnah and Talmud), and other societies for the less learned. Where they existed, the *Klausen* maintained an active program of instruction for community members along with the regular classes for their scholars and advanced students. A rabbi commented, "When I was a rabbi and head of a yeshiva in Frankfurt, many [groups and classes] used to gather there every day at noon in order to learn, each headed by someone well versed in the Torah. He would teach them, each [group] according to their [level of knowledge]."[11] Nonetheless, the knowledge of Jewish literature was not very well developed among the majority of the Jews in Germany. Many of those ignorant of Torah believed they were not obliged to learn if they contributed to the maintenance of a Klaus or enabled students or scholars to study in some other way.

If instruction for boys was often deficient, the girls were in a far worse situation. The contemporary sources do mention that girls also learned

French and were often given piano lessons, because it was a part of middle-class education. However, a ḥeder for girls of the type in Hamburg where Glückel of Hameln received Jewish elementary instruction was a rarity. In his critical book on ethics, the learned merchant Isaac Wetzlar (first half of the eighteenth century) lamented this deficiency:

> How can one justify the fact that our young daughters do not receive any instruction in the Bible, a subject through which they would at least learn to understand the holy language that is called our mother tongue by the other nations? Then they would not find it difficult to comprehend the meaning of the words in which they pray to God. . . . Yet no one protests that they study foreign languages, French and Italian—and even do so with non-Jewish teachers. . . . Many pious women weep bitter tears over the fact that they stand in the synagogue and pray, yet do not know what they are praying. They hear the reading from the Torah and do not understand what is being read. . . . Among other peoples the women know the Bible better than do our own.[12]

Glückel of Hameln is tangible proof that there were also women who were the equal of many men in Jewish and general education. She was well versed in the Bible and exceptionally widely read in the Western Yiddish literature of her time; as a result, she was also familiar with the Hebrew sources. Glückel began recording her memoirs in 1690 at the age of forty-four after the death of her husband. She did not write to instruct others, but "to soothe her spirit and shorten her sleepless hours at night." Glückel was a wealthy merchant's wife and continued on with her husband's business as a widow. He had been one of the four Hamburg members of the Ashkenazi community of Altona who bore the heaviest tax burden. Glückel's name appears in the 1690s in the lists of the Jewish guests attending the Leipzig trade fair. Socially, she belonged to the circles of the court Jews, was a sister-in-law of Leffmann Behrens and was also related by marriage to Elias Gomperz. Piety and a sense for business are the two central themes running through her book. News reports about special events in the community alternate with accounts about births and marriages in the family (the latter always replete with an exact indication of the size of the dowry). The many quotations from pious books in her memoirs are not mere embellishment but intended to give all life situations a religious meaning.

The widows of many court factors took over their tasks when they died. Thus, after Elias Gomperz died in 1689, his general charter was renewed for his widow; when the Mainz court factor Issachar Homburg died in 1759, his wife Blümle, who had considerable standing at the court, was allowed to continue his job of supplying the army. The crown princess of Saxony had her own female court Jews. "Madame Kaulla" (1739–1809), the matriarch of the influential Kaulla family in southern Germany, particularly active in Württemberg, was Germany's most important female court factor in the second half of the eighteenth and the beginning of the nineteenth century. She also exercised a beneficial influence on Jewish society. The increasing activity of women in the communities is reflected in the fact that women's charitable organizations were formed in the course of the eighteenth century and worked together with the men's fraternities.

5. Tensions and Conflicts

Social tensions arose in a number of communities, occasionally generating crises and conflicts. The wealthiest were assured power by means of the class-based electoral system, especially when it came to the key issue (and for the poorer members the most critical one): the assessment of taxes. Many quarrels in the community were related to the apportionment of the tax burden. The oligarchy in community administration, firmly established since the sixteenth century and seemingly unalterable, time and again provoked the majority. Especially in Prague and Frankfurt am Main, there was constant strife and turmoil.

In Prague, after the decision in 1577 that community officials should be reelected on an annual basis, the same individuals nonetheless remained in office for many years, and fierce feuding ensued between the factions of the ghetto. In 1645 a new electoral system was introduced, with secret balloting and compulsory voting, under penalty of the ban. One year later the poor were also granted the franchise but had to pay a monthly fee for this privilege. The Prague chief rabbinate suffered in particular as a result of these tensions and wrangling over voting rights and remained unoccupied for a long period after 1679. One faction even managed to obtain an ordinance from the Bohemian Chamber that prohibited the community board from bestowing the office of chief rabbi on anyone. The belligerent parties constantly appealed to the government, in this way reinforcing the claim of the state that it had a right to confirm the elections to the rabbinate.

In Frankfurt am Main the Fettmilch uprising, which had developed out of a social movement calling for more democracy in the representation of the townspeople in the municipal council, made a powerful impression on the Jewish population. Thus the demand was raised to expand the board so that all circles within the community would be represented. Thereupon a new system was instituted, on the basis of which every person who had assets of three thousand guldens (later reduced to one thousand) and had been married for at least five years was eligible for office. At the same time, the number of members of the board was increased from ten to seventeen. Despite these moves, oligarchy remained firmly entrenched: in the eighteenth century the same families (often even the same men) still retained the highest offices. In the last third of the seventeenth century there was a first successful attempt to break the power of the heads of the Kann family, yet after the turn of the century they regained their former dominance. This bid was evidently influenced at the same time by mounting tensions among the Frankfurt citizenry, increasingly discharged in the form of protests against the autocracy of the councillors. But the prosperity of the Frankfurt community suffered badly as a result of two large conflagrations that gutted the ghetto in 1711 and 1721, and concerns for everyday survival displaced the discord and contention of community politics. The board member Isaac Kann and his supporters were left a free autocratic hand to do as they pleased, at times flouting the statutes.

Around the middle of the eighteenth century the struggle against the dominant regime erupted anew; this time the members of another wealthy family, the Kulps, played a leading role. The community split first into two, later into four factions. The struggle raged on for twenty years, prompted intervention by the city council and even by the emperor in Vienna, and shook the community to its foundations. Yet, although the city once even found it necessary to deploy soldiers in the ghetto to preserve law and order, there was no violence. The struggle was waged using all means of power and pressure available to the faction leaders. The heads of the two warring families had connections to the highest echelons: Judah Kulp was imperial court factor and Isaac Kann was factor to the court in electoral Mainz. Moreover, Kann's elder brother Moses was a distinguished scholar, a Klaus rabbi in Frankfurt, chief rabbi of the landgraviate Hesse and son-in-law of the great Viennese court Jew Samson Wertheimer. The strife ended with an imperial decree and an internal code of regulations for the community, a document of many sections that had been finally agreed upon. The absence of the chief rabbi, Jacob Joshua Falk, and the simultaneous embroilment of the Frankfurt community in the Hamburg amulet controversy contributed significantly to the dispute's vehemence and protracted length. Both topics will be dealt with below.

Competition among the merchants, most of whom traded in the same lines of goods, was the source of numerous tensions and conflicts in the communities. In the countryside squabbles often erupted when a "village traveling salesman" (*Dorfgänger*) going across country encroached on the "sales area" (*medine*) of someone else. Many regulations in the ordinances of the Landjudenschaften attest to that. The communities were also torn by tensions over the question of additional Jews moving in—a result of fears about possible competition. In general, the lay leaders were prepared to take stringent measures in order to prevent competition from nonprotected Jewish peddlers and were vigorously supported in this by the authorities. Naturally, that often sparked serious internal conflicts; so did the collective responsibility placed on the entire community, and particularly the local board, which forced them to take action against individuals for the sake of protecting the community as a whole. In such cases the traditional mutual solidarity among Jews, rooted in religious precept, found itself facing a difficult dilemma.

A similar situation emerged in many localities because of the influx of Jewish refugees from Poland beginning in 1648. As already pointed out, the drives to collect funds to assist the victims of the pogroms reflected the presence of a strong sense of Jewish solidarity. But the homeless were not always accepted with open arms by the communities; at times they were made to feel that, although they were Jews, they were outsiders: not "Ashkenazis" but "Polacks." Thus the Berlin community requested the government in 1714 not to issue letters of protection to new arrivals and threatened illegal settlers with banishment. In Hanover the local community board did not permit Polish Jews to take up residence. This attitude was evidently accommodated to official policy there, which, since the ascendancy of Frederick William I to the throne, had been actively working against the settlement of Polish Jews.

However, there were also amicably arranged agreements between estranged neighboring communities and factions within these communities. One example is the resolution of the tensions in Hamburg and Altona. In Hamburg the three original Portuguese communities differed in their socioreligious conditions and outlook. Harmony among the Portuguese was disturbed for a long period because of wrangling over inheritance, disputes about religious views, and the machinations of informers and renegades. This was compounded by the antagonism between Sephardim and Ashkenazim; communal friction was rife, even if not readily evident to outside observers because of the many features they shared in common. At the beginning of the eighteenth century some Hamburg Ashkenazim had succeeded in partially adapting to the better-placed Portuguese, narrowing the gap economically and in social terms. However, a total convergence was not yet possible; in certain spheres, marriage in particular, the Portuguese did not wish to surrender their exclusivity. In 1670 a formal agreement was concluded between Ashkenazim and Sephardim in Hamburg, followed in 1710 by official recognition of the "German" community and its legal parity with its Portuguese counterpart. Yet there were also internal tensions within Ashkenazi society in Hamburg and Altona, mainly over the question of the ownership and use of the Ashkenazi cemetery. Another source of friction was the fact that Altona Jews had the right to enter Hamburg and hawk their wares from house to house. To compound matters, Jews also came from other areas, attempting to "slip in" and settle in the town. Toward the end of the seventeenth century an amicable solution was arrived at—indeed, a formal unification. An association of communities was set up between Hamburg and Altona, which the community in Wandsbek also joined, creating the aforementioned "triple community" (Dreigemeinde) Altona-Hamburg-Wandsbek. Above all, it consisted of a single rabbinate located in Altona, the seat of the chief rabbi and of the Jewish court.

Joint committees of the triple community worked out statutes that differed from those of other large communities mainly in that the permissible number of "protected" Jewish families was not limited in the three communities—not even in Hamburg, despite its generally restrictive policy on Jews. However, the admission to community membership was contingent on the approval of the lay boards. The candidate's reputation was examined, and he had to furnish proof of a minimum amount of assets. As in the Portuguese community, the decision on admission or rejection of an applicant was made primarily based on the desire that the number of the poor and needy should be kept to a minimum. The character of the leadership was just as oligarchical as in other communities. But, in contrast to Frankfurt am Main and Berlin, at least the wealthy all enjoyed parity in that there were no class differences among them (except in the composition of the admissions committee), nor was any preference given to certain families. The election of the chief rabbi was by a joint committee of the three communities, in which Altona always retained an absolute majority.

6. The Jews in the Countryside

Since the expulsions of the Jews from the cities at the end of the Middle Ages, the preponderant majority lived in small towns and villages. In the seventeenth and eighteenth century the proportion of rural Jewry within the total Jewish population in German lands was far in excess of 90 percent, and at the beginning of the nineteenth century 80 percent of German Jews still lived in the countryside. In the southwest of the empire there were a large number of localities with a sizable percentage of Jewish inhabitants. Here and there they even formed a majority, as in Gailingen and Randegg in the Lake Constance region, localities that were commonly known as "Jews' villages" (*Judendörfer*). Such small village communities were not kehillot in the urban sense: that is, with religious and social institutions and facilities, an administration, and a rabbinate. Only a portion of the larger rural communities had an appointed rabbi. Most banded together in the Landjudenschaften, through which they could obtain the most necessary communal functions even without possessing a communal organization of their own.

The Jews in rural areas often lived under less oppressive conditions than urban Jewry and thus frequently developed a feeling of belonging. Yet, analogous to the situation among many Christian village inhabitants, this sense of identity among rural Jews was not oriented to the empire, that is, *reichsdeutsch*, but was provincial, indeed even local in its attachment. Jewish-Christian relations in the countryside were often closer and more amicable than in the cities, and there were numerous reports of close social ties between Jews and Christians. Rabbis complained that in small villages Jews spent the Sabbath with non-Jews and frequented non-Jewish taverns, a practice they decried as detrimental to the character of the Jewish day of rest.

The rural Jews differed from their Christian neighbors not only in their ethnic and religious affiliation but in their economic activities as well. Rural Jewry was not a Jewish peasantry; the typical rural Jew was dependent on peddling for a livelihood. He also fulfilled an important function in the network supplying the court factors. In 1669 Samuel Oppenheimer was able to rely on a "hinterland" in Lower Austria where

34 Decorated wooden synagogue in Bechhofen (Franconia)

477 Jewish families lived scattered over some 70 localities. Likewise, the rich Jewish merchants in Berlin would have achieved nothing without the raw materials they were supplied by the country Jews in the eastern Prussian provinces. For the Jewish peddlers, traveling from locality to locality earning a livelihood was extremely toilsome and strenuous. On the road the entire week, they lived on cold food, enjoying a warm meal at home only on the Sabbath.

The religion of rural Jews had stood the test of many trials and temptations, but it was not learned. Although the typical rural Jew rooted his behavior in practical religious law and custom, his knowledge of Judaism was otherwise often meager, his ability to study the religious sources yet more limited. Still, even among uneducated rural Jewry there was great respect for education, and even the tiniest village communities generally employed a teacher. Moreover, the relative lack of learning among most males in the village communities narrowed the religious-cultural gap between men and women in comparison with the urban communities. This may have been one of the underlying reasons why rural Jewish women often had a more respected and independent position in the family and community than their counterparts in the towns. In the countryside, more than in the city, it was specifically the Jewish woman who was the guardian of tradition.

In the period under scrutiny life in the communities, both urban and rural, was grounded in the teachings of the written and oral Torah. It was not just external constraint that held the Jews together in their communities—more important as a cohesive bond was the determination to give expression to the relevance and binding force of Jewish law and custom. The authority and power to implement decisions wielded by the rabbis and community boards were anchored in this desire. Their activity and resolutions had to be in full harmony with Jewish laws and traditions and the values cherished by the community.

6

The *Landjudenschaften*

For the great majority of Jews in Germany from the sixteenth century down to emancipation the *Landjudenschaften* were the standard form of organization. These were corporate self-governing bodies set up to administer Jewish affairs autonomously. In a certain sense they represented a continuation of the occasional assemblies convened by the rabbis and community representatives in the Middle Ages. Yet they were based on needs and perceptions that derived from the situation of Jews in the German lands in the early modern period. One of the most conspicuous factors operative here was the extensive dispersion of the Jewish communities in the wake of the numerous mass expulsions. As a result a sizable proportion of the Jewish population was living in very small towns and villages. Many small Jewish settlements found they were unable to develop any viable fabric of community life and maintain communal institutions. Yet, given the unrelenting external pressures, an organized banding together of all Jews, some of whom lived extremely isolated and far apart, was an existential necessity for preserving their Jewish identity. On the other hand, the smaller communities were now more stable, which made solid organizational structures both possible and meaningful. Another factor was the progressive territorial fragmentation of the German lands and the claims to sovereignty of every small potentate, which also stimulated interest in the formation of a Landjudenschaft. Thus an official territorial Jewish organization was now a necessity, since in deliberations and decisions on central Jewish concerns—such as apportionment of taxes and the steps that had to be taken with the authorities to secure Jewish existence and ease its burdens—the dynastic and legal situation in each principality had to be taken into careful account.

1. The Organization of the Landjudenschaften

The degree to which the organization of the Landjudenschaften was determined by the prevailing territorial realities is illustrated by the example of the electorate and bishopric of Mainz, which was divided into an upper and lower archdiocese. Analogous to this structure, there were two Landjudenschaften, and only the chief rabbi was officially responsible for both. This expressed a longstanding predilection in Ashkenazi communities to remain as independent as possible from external Jewish bodies and authorities, which they did not trust to take local traditions and conditions into proper account. Another element was the traditional dependence of Jews living dispersed in smaller localities on a nearby larger organized community. This was expressed in practical terms in two ways: by subordination to the larger community's local legal jurisdiction and the obligation to contribute to the taxes and other levies imposed by it. The Jews dependent on using community institutions located else-

35   Seal of the Bamberg Landjudenschaft

where preferred the organization of a Landjudenschaft, in which they enjoyed parity with many others, to dependence on a single larger community in which they would have no influence whatsoever. The Landjudenschaft was thus a comprehensive association encompassing all Jews in a sovereign territory who possessed the right of residence, that is, of all "protected Jews." They belonged to the association as individuals directly, not via a local community. Only those Jews who were under the protection of noble lords of the manor were exempted from membership in the Landjudenschaft.

Thus the Landjudenschaft represented an attempt, by and large successful, to realize the abiding aspiration among Jews for banding together communally in a form adapted to the conditions of the early modern period. This process was promoted by the fact that the state had a parallel interest in an organization of this type. With its well-developed structures the Landjudenschaft provided the territorial sovereign with an excellent means for watching over the Jews and exploiting them for the good of the principality, with no extra incurred expenses. From the unified and self-contained community—whose genesis had been in part voluntary, in part created by ordinances of the sovereign—a compulsory association evolved, one to which every Jew resident within the territorial borders was required to belong.

Already in the fifteenth century there had been corporate bodies of Jews in the Rhineland and Franconia, loosely structured organizations whose principal purpose was defense or rescue operations. Landjudenschaften in the full sense of the term, that is, associations marked by a new, previously nonexistent level of structural unity and continuity, could be found in virtually all the territories of the empire from the beginning of the seventeenth century, the period of transition in German Jewry from the Middle Ages to the early modern age. It was probably no coincidence that roughly simultaneous with this development innovations also appeared in Jewish communal organization outside Germany. In Poland the Council of the Four Lands (Va'ad arba ha-aratsot; the often encountered translation of "synod" for the Hebrew term va'ad is misleading) was already in full bloom in the first half of the seventeenth century, as was the formal organization established by the Moravian Jews. It is quite possible that the banding together of Jewish settlements in the German territories was influenced in part by the example of communal organizations in Poland and Moravia. However, the two organizational forms differed in several important points, an aspect that should be stressed if we wish to grasp the special character of the Landjudenschaften in Germany.

The Landjudenschaften were not associations of communities, as in Poland, Lithuania, Bohemia, and Moravia, or later on in Burgenland—countries with a high Jewish population density—but rather were organizations made up of individual members. All heads of families were obliged to personally attend the gatherings of the Landjudenschaften, while in the community associations only the local board members were expected to do so. In contrast with the situation in the countries of Eastern Europe, where distances were great and community structures diverse, within the generally small territories of the empire there could be a much closer and more cohesive form of cooperation among members in the Landjudenschaften. On the other hand, it never proved possible to form an umbrella organization of all Landjudenschaften, recognized throughout the empire, as in Poland and Moravia. The internal makeup of the Landjudenschaften also differed from the organizational structures in the East. Far more than in Eastern Europe, the management and administration of the rural corporative bodies lay in the hands of the local lay leaders, among whom the court Jews were a predominant force.

Fundamental for the genesis of the Landjudenschaften was the ancient desire for autonomy—both vis-à-vis the state and the communities and associations outside of one's own territory. The aspiration for independence and resistance to outside interference were powerful motives for joining together, especially in an era when territorial sovereignty was on the rapid ascent. Initially, the German territorial estates (*Landstände*) may also have exercised a certain influence as a corporative model. Thus larger and more wealthy communities generally remained outside the contiguous Landjudenschaft or gradually developed a special niche within it, as in Mannheim and Fürth. Another important motive was the necessity to raise funds to cover the costs for communal offices and functions, such as the salary of a rabbi or the purchase and upkeep of a cemetery. All the families dispersed throughout a small principality formed a single "territorial community" (*Landgemeinde*, Hebr. *kehal medinah, bene medinah*), with the entire array of institutions otherwise characteristic of the local community. The Landjudenschaften assumed many of the functions, duties, and powers of a local gemeinde that were not bound to a locality—as was, for example, the operation of a synagogue. In particular, like every other Jewish community, they were autonomous in legal matters and administration. However, over the course of time, especially in the eighteenth century, this autonomy was curtailed by the state and then eliminated entirely when Jews were granted civil equality.

How can we account for the fact that the Landjudenschaften, with their tight corporate organization based on the principle of compulsory association, were able to function as an institution for nearly two hundred years? This was due in large measure to the continuing interest and strict supervision of the authorities. On the one hand, the strengthening of the centralist tendencies of the territorial states no longer permitted Jews to maintain their own community system, independent of the state. On the other hand, the states sought to make use of the Jewish organization for their own purposes. Initially, rulers regarded the Landjudenschaft basically as an effective and convenient instrument for Jewry taxation, an expedient tool and little more. Down to the end of the seventeenth century they had little interest in the details and internal functions of the Jewish organizations insofar as their own fiscal interests were not involved. Later on officials increasingly interfered in the life of the individual and society. The ordinances of the Landjudenschaften had to be approved by the authorities.

There were Landjudenschaften in almost all the territories of the Holy Roman Empire, especially in ecclesiastical states. In structure and administration they patterned themselves on the respective corporative forms of the Christian environment. The earliest known example of a Landjudenschaft is documented in Alsace. Josel of Rosheim notes in his memoirs and elsewhere that in 1510 he was elected "leader and head" (*Vorgänger*) of the "*gemeiner judischheit*," that is, the corporate Jewish body of Lower Alsace, "to watch carefully over the community and administer its affairs."[1] Until its stepwise annexation by France, Alsace belonged to the empire and had a dense Jewish population, with two separate Jewish territorial corporate organizations, highly developed at an early point, in Upper and Lower Alsace. In German-speaking Lorraine, as well, there was a Landjudenschaft, subordinated to the French king after annexation.

The relatively high proportion of Jews in the Hessian territories also led there to the genesis of corporative associations at an early juncture. Already in 1569 the Jews in Upper Hesse had a board composed of three lay members. In 1650 there is official mention of a "Jewry of the [Hessian] landgraviate" and a provincial assembly of the Landjudenschaft, assessment of wealth, and an election of board members, "all as before."[2] The rural Jewish communities in Hesse-Kassel and in the territories of electoral Cologne were formed at the end of the sixteenth century.

When the number of rural Jews in Bohemia rose sharply in the second
half of the seventeenth century and they were assessed by the Prague lay
board to pay more than a third of the total sum of taxes, they felt they had
a justified grievance and took action. In 1659 they formed an independent
autonomous body: the Bohemian Landjudenschaft, with its own tax
administration and deputies.[3] Until the end of the Thirty Years War the
board of the Prague Jewish community was the only representative body
of the entire Jewish population of Bohemia recognized by the state
authorities. After that the institution of the deputies and adjuncts of the
Bohemian Landjudenschaft came into being. That same year (1659) it
drew up a "police code," which stipulated the number and powers of the
deputies, the system of election and taxation, and other matters. The first
deputy of the Landjudenschaft was the so-called *Primator*. Independently
of Prague, the Moravian Jews had already formed a "legislative corporate
body" in the sixteenth century, attested to by 311 ordinances codified in
1650, most of which are older.

For the period from 1616 to 1821 Landjudenschaften have been documented in a total of thirty larger territories within the borders of the Old
Reich (excluding Bohemia and Moravia). This figure should be supplemented by an even larger number of Landjudenschaften in the smaller
territories, though these are difficult to distinguish from the local community organizations.[4]

The lay leaders of the Landjudenschaft had virtually unlimited power
over Jewish society. They regulated religious, social, and economic life and
issued ordinances that had to be approved by the government, a procedure
that generally was a mere formality. They conducted all negotiations with
the authorities and submitted petitions, as a rule drawn up by non-Jewish
lawyers. Since the board members often managed affairs as they thought
best, they sometimes faced opposition within the communities, even if
they were seldom guilty of a genuine abuse of their powers and position,
judged by the ethical standards of the day. Their handling of finances was
often subjected to severe criticism, especially by poorer members of the
Landjudenschaft, who attempted—though usually with little success—to
alter the tax assessment to their benefit and to the disadvantage of the
rich. Any obstreperous opposition was soon silenced—by fines, dispossession of rights, and imposition of the ban, with the support of the rabbinate and the authorities.

Of most far-reaching consequence was the extensive prerogative of the
board members to decide on permission for a Jew from outside to settle in

the territory—or even on the right of a son to succeed to the place of his father. The sovereign, who was the sole holder of the *Judengeleit*, that is, the right to admit or expel Jews, had transferred its implementation in individual cases to the Landjudenschaft. After the set number of "protected" Jews had been decided upon, along with the number of indigent Jews beyond this figure that were allowed to stay, the board members had a free hand in the granting, withdrawal, or denial of the right to residence. Usually, protection could only be obtained through their mediation with the authorities. In practice, the board members of the Landjudenschaft held the lease on the Judengeleit, and this was the basis of their power.

The lay leaders and other officials were elected by the general assembly of the Landjudenschaft. This assembly was called the "Jewish provincial assembly" (*Judenlandtag* or *Juden-Convent*, Hebr. *yom ha-va'ad*), and, in principle, was convened every three years. That was linked with the standard three-year cycle of the elections for officials, whose origins lay in the distant medieval period. Nonetheless, board members sometimes did not call an assembly for many years, supposedly "in order to economize on expenses and effort for the entire community," until the government intervened. The Judenlandtag, which lasted three to four days, met only with the permission of the authorities, who made participation obligatory for all heads of families liable for taxes, including widows. They had to appear at the assembly in order to be assessed for taxes, which, officially, was the sole purpose of such plenary meetings.

In accordance with the regular agenda of the assembly, discussion was held and decisions made on all matters affecting Jewish communal life, foremostly on taxes and other sundry community levies. They were apportioned among all those liable to pay taxes, based on the estimate of the assets of every head of household. Along with the tax burden, the method of payment was also determined for the period up until the next assembly. At the same time, new elections were held for all board members and officials, including the rabbi—all for a three-year tenure. In addition, the assemblies audited Landjudenschaft finances and issued ordinances dealing with religious, social, and economic matters. Such ordinances (*takanot*) were often subsequently published. The rabbis also took advantage of the assembly to carry out the annual examination of the ritual slaughterers and "meat inspectors."

The "small council" (*va'ad katan*) convened at shorter intervals. It consisted of the territorial rabbi, the chief board member, the parnasim, the elders and adjuncts—some twenty to thirty members in all. This body was the decision-making organ of the Landjudenschaft between assemblies. The chief board member (*Obervorsteher, Obervorgänger,* or *Oberparnas*) was the chief official of the Landjudenschaft; his associates were the elders and adjuncts (*tove medinah, ikore medinah*), assisted by the assessors (*shama'im*), led by the chief assessor, the tax collectors, auditors, scribe (*sofer medinah*), and messenger (*shamash medinah,* Judeo-German: *kahals meshores*). In addition, electors and administrators of charitable funds were also appointed—and, from case to case, persons to draw up statutes. The territorial rabbi, scribe, and messenger were salaried officials; all others served in an honorary capacity. In the main, the functions and titles of the honorary officials and dignitaries were identical with the corresponding functions in the communities mentioned earlier. The extremely important office of advocate to the government (shtadlan, syndic) was generally held by the chief board member, who usually was identical with the local court Jew. Members of the same family often retained this office within the family dynasty for generations; indeed, the honorary posts were frequently in the hands of certain families on a continuous basis.

There were thus clear parallels between the development of court Jewry and the Landjudenschaft. Both institutions had external functions, serving the state, and internal functions for the Jewish inhabitants. Often enough, the formation of a Landjudenschaft followed from the strong position of a court Jew. Just as the court Jews stood in the service of the absolutist prince, the Landjudenschaften were dependent on the respective sovereign. No resolution, election, or appointment by the plenary assembly and the small council was valid without governmental approval. In the eighteenth century the states intensified their supervision of the Landjudenschaften and dispatched commissioners who took part in the assemblies, sometimes even chairing the proceedings, in return for a high fee. With slight differences, the organization and officials outlined here were common to all Landjudenschaften.

The elections at the assembly closely resembled the community elections described in the previous chapter. Here too, with time, the system of the three-class election was introduced in Prussia and elsewhere by government order. Only those who had lived in the country for a long period and had attained a specified minimal age were eligible as candidates for the office of board member. As everywhere under absolutism, the entire system had a highly patriarchical character. As a rule, the chair at the assembly was held by the community rabbi or the chief board member;

with the backing and protection of the authorities, he managed the proceedings with a strong hand and little concern for democratic principles. Nonetheless, it did occur that a Landjudenschaft, after a protracted struggle, was successful in having a chief board member who had embezzled funds dismissed by the authorities. Around the middle of the eighteenth century cases multiplied in which Landjudenschaften succeeded in their attempt to curb the powers of the chief parnas—a development clearly influenced by Enlightenment conceptions.

Quite naturally, the principal topic of negotiations and deliberations at the assemblies—taxation—was the subject that provoked the fiercest disputes. Before the formation of the Landjudenschaften, the "protection fees" (*Schutzgelder*) had to be paid by every Jew, on the basis of individual letters of protection, directly to the royal treasury. Now they were collected communally and transferred in a lump sum. Every head of family newly admitted as a resident in some locality in the territory had to pay the Landjudenschaft a one-time fee for new members (*me'ot hakdamah*). The assets (*erekh*) of each taxpayer were determined at the assembly by Jewish assessors selected specifically for this office, and the procedure often led to heated dispute. Many of the less well-off were incensed that they were at all obligated to take part in the assembly, because the rich paid nowhere near their proper share when taxes were divided up, and tried wherever possible to shift the tax burdens to the others. There was an upper limit for the amount of declared wealth, and this alone was a clear instance of preferential treatment for the wealthiest heads of families. If someone believed he had been overtaxed, he could lodge a complaint with the government official and seek his decision.

However, it should be borne in mind that the lay leaders, most of whom were among the wealthiest members, guaranteed the tax obligations of the community by means of their assets. Moreover, the unjust distribution of the taxes between rich and poor, and the undemocratic election system, were quite in keeping with concepts of public law at the time. The board members were strict in gathering in taxes. If internal means of pressure in the case of individuals and the threat of exclusion from all affairs of the Landjudenschaft against entire rural communities proved to no avail, the lay leaders had no choice but to request official intervention by the government against dilatory taxpayers. At times the government responded to repeated requests by the board members by calling in the military.

Yet the central role of taxation on the agenda of the Landjudenschaften should not obscure the fact that there were other discussions and decisions on a variety of matters that reflected concern for Jewish values. Thus the taxpayers of the Landjudenschaft Hesse-Kassel agreed at the end of the seventeenth century to establish and maintain a provincial yeshiva, since the numerous small rural communities were unable to support a yeshiva of their own. This yeshiva existed for many years in Witzenhausen.[5]

2. The Territorial Rabbinates

As religious head of the community and its judge in all internal Jewish quarrels and complaints, the chief rabbi (*abad,* abbr. of *av bet din,* "head of the court") enjoyed particular respect; as a rule, his authority went unchallenged and was absolute, both externally and within the community. Since the second half of the fourteenth century, princes had claimed the right to appoint—or at least to confirm—the rabbis in their territories. After the expulsions of the fifteenth century there was a sharp decline in the number of rabbinical courts; at the beginning of the seventeenth century no more than ten were still in existence. These courts, which could be found in free imperial cities, ecclesiastical territories, and in the Habsburg possessions, now took on a supraregional importance, extending far beyond the respective territorial borders. Increasingly, the rulers in the sovereign, absolutist-centralist states insisted on the independence of "their Jews" from rabbinical courts outside their territory. For example, the community in Mainz remained without an official rabbi from its reestablishment in the late sixteenth century down to 1630; as a result Jews in Mainz turned to rabbis in Frankfurt, Worms, and other localities. This situation led in 1602 to an ordinance issued by the elector stipulating that the Jews of Mainz and the entire archdiocese should only consult the rabbi of Bingen, located inside the territory. Gradually, some twenty territorial rabbinates were formed, along with a number of provincial rabbis of a lower grade (*dayane medinah*). Thus the rabbinical courts of the free cities forfeited much of their previous influence.

The ability of a rabbi to act unencumbered by rabbinates outside of the territory was so important to the sovereigns and the Jews of their territory that in several states the territorial rabbinate actually predated the establishment of the Landjudenschaft. Thus, already around the year 1525 in Günzburg Rabbi Jonah Weil served as Swabian chief rabbi. In 1618/1619 in the territory of the prince-bishop of Bamberg, for the first time, all the protected Jews of the territory sent a petition to the government asking for permission to choose a chief rabbi. Their request was granted though not implemented until 1658. The territorial rabbinate in the county of Lippe came about in a similar manner. In 1684 the representatives of the Jews asked the count for permission to maintain a rabbi of their own, and the sovereign consented. Although the Jewish community as such had presented the petition here, there was as yet no separate organization with lay leaders, deputies, and a treasury.

In many cases the first territorial rabbis were appointed by the sovereign himself. The initiative to appoint the first territorial rabbi in Hanover (1687) was launched by the court Jew Leffmann Behrens, but the rabbi was installed in office by the duke. The later territorial rabbis were chosen by the community of the residential city where they had their official residence. A similar method was used in other territories as well, such as in electoral Mainz. Although the Mainz rabbi automatically became territorial rabbi, and all Jews of the territory contributed to his salary, he was always chosen by the Mainz community alone. On the occasion of the appointment of a territorial rabbi in Hesse (1655), the landgrave emphasized that this was being done for the benefit of his own financial interests. One advantage of having one's "own" rabbi was that the Jews of his territory did not need to travel to Fulda or Friedberg to consult a rabbinical court. But the chief consideration here was fiscal: to make sure that fines did not flow across the border into state treasuries outside the territory. The sovereign also had an interest in confirming and controlling the area of activity and powers of the rabbi. When the Jews in Hesse-Darmstadt engaged a rabbi on their own initiative in 1729, an investigation was ordered. Many sovereigns insisted on swearing in the territorial rabbi. For example, the Fürth rabbi Baruch Rapoport was simultaneously to be entrusted with the rabbinate in Schnaittach, but only on the condition that he be officially sworn in. He steadfastly refused this offer for many years, agreeing only to a "handshake" ceremony, which was finally granted him. Thus the rabbis became Jewish officials authorized by a territorial sovereign and enjoying the trust of the government.

The chief rabbi exercised considerable authority. He had the right of approval over all resolutions of the individual community and those passed in the Landjudenschaft. He and the provincial rabbis made halachic decisions and were consulted on all matters pertaining more generally to Jewish communal affairs. They were responsible for the exact observance of ritual and religious law in the communities. For example, they were entrusted with the duty of making sure, under threat of penalty, that daily public prayers, requiring a quorum of at least ten males aged thirteen or older, were regularly held. Although, in many instances, rabbinical disciplinary powers were restricted by the community administration, if the chief rabbi also fulfilled the function of a shtadlan, his authority was virtually unlimited. When he traveled through the principality, an obligation in some territories, he was often received like a visiting prince.

Yet, despite his reputation and authority, the rabbi was subordinate in certain respects to the lay boards. The chosen rabbi received a formal writ of appointment from the board members, the already mentioned *Rabbonusbrief*. If he refused the appointment, the second candidate on the selection list was chosen. Usually his appointment was limited to three years, and it was up to the board members whether he was reappointed after expiration of his term. But there are also documented instances where the contract of the territorial rabbi did not contain a clause specifying a limit to his tenure, a procedure that became the general rule from about the beginning of the eighteenth century. His salary was modest, and his income consisted, as in the case of the community rabbis, more of earnings from fines and fees for official services than from a fixed salary. He had to report the fines he imposed to the treasury and pay a portion of this as due to the state. If he needed financial assistance, such as for his daughter's dowry or in the case of illness, he was dependent on the beneficence and goodwill of the lay leaders. In exercising his religious office, he usually enjoyed a free hand.

Salaried rabbis were not permitted to engage in business dealings, and this was often expressly forbidden by a clause in their writ of appointment. However, in itself it was not perceived as detrimental at the time if the rabbi was also a businessman—as long as the duties of his office were an honorary function and he was not a paid employee of the community. The first territorial rabbi of Hanover, a relative of Leffmann Behrens, was a very wealthy money dealer who took no salary for his services. That was also the case with Samson Wertheimer, who was simultaneously chief court factor, rabbi in Vienna, and chief rabbi in Hungary, and with his son-in-law Bär Eskeles, a banker, who was also the chief rabbi of Nikolsburg and the territorial rabbi of Moravia. It was no rarity for the same man, at one and the same time, to be a court Jew, chief board member, and territorial rabbi; in many other instances territorial rabbis were related to board members and families of court Jews. Certain rabbinates remained for generations in the hands of one and the same family dynasty, usually the wealthiest in the land. Although an attempt was made to exclude by law any kinship between the territorial rabbi and the parnasim (in electoral Hesse the territorial rabbi was not allowed to be related either to a board member or to two very wealthy protected Jews), there were often complaints about his dependence on the latter.

The territorial rabbis did not always live on a constant basis in the main community of their district. Frequently, they even resided in an extraterritorial community with which they had ties. For a time the territorial rabbi in Trier lived in Metz, where he was the head of a respected yeshiva. After his appointment, the Moravian chief rabbi Eskeles retained his residence in Vienna. The first chief rabbi of Hesse-Darmstadt mentioned in official documents, Samuel Schotten, was head of the Frankfurt *Klaus,* and for thirty-four years (1685–1719) administered his office in Darmstadt from Frankfurt. Given the lack of competent rabbis, it was sometimes unavoidable that great rabbinical personalities were brought in from the outside to arbitrate in difficult cases. Thus a dispute in the Jewish community in Hesse-Darmstadt was resolved by a judgment of the chief rabbi of Worms, Samson Bacharach. At times a territorial rabbi was also responsible for areas that lay outside his district. Thus the Jews of the archbishopric of Cologne had a rabbi who was resident in Deutz or Bonn and was also responsible for Jülich-Berg. The chief or territorial rabbi of Friedberg also serviced the principality of Hesse and a number of smaller territories that were unable to maintain a rabbi of their own. A number of village communities that had the means engaged a religious teacher (*moreh hora'ah* or *moreh tsedek*) whose qualifications were not the equal of the territorial rabbi but sufficed for the daily religious needs of the small community.

3. Later Developments

Even if neighboring Landjudenschaften provided each other occasional mutual assistance and cooperated to a certain degree, there was a stubborn resistance against expanding the territorial corporate body into an organization encompassing all the Jews of a large state. That became evident at an early juncture, for example, in Brandenburg-Prussia.

In 1650 in an attempt to place all the Jewries in the territories of Brandenburg-Prussia under a central direction for fiscal reasons, the great elector appointed Berend Levi from Bonn as "commander and leader" of the

Jews in all districts of Brandenburg west of the Elbe. The plan failed, however, due to the combined opposition of the Jews, the cities, and the estates, none of whom were eager to let their rights be curtailed. The first steps in the direction of cooperation among all the Jews in the various Prussian provinces were taken in 1713, when the elders and local lay leaders of all Jewries requested the king to reduce the sum of 20,000 thalers demanded of them for confirmation of their privileges. It appears that these corporate Jewish bodies succeeded in agreeing on a formula for distribution of the levy without the intervention of the authorities. Nonetheless, such common actions did not lead to a permanent central institution.

Only after a common chest for the tax revenues from all Jews in Prussia was created by royal resolution did the representatives of the various provinces begin to meet, once every five years, starting in 1728, in order to set the proportion of taxes due from each Landjudenschaft. These "general assemblies" (*Generalversammlungen, Generaljudentage*) were held alternately in Berlin, Brandenburg, and Spandau until the era of emancipation. In 1775, at the suggestion of the Berlin community, the king appointed a "senior state elder of all Jewries" whose activity was to encompass all communities and Landjudenschaften in the entire monarchy.[6] This development marked some progress, principally under the pressure of centralist government measures, in coordinating the various Jewish corporate bodies with their partially contrary interests.

In other states, such as Hesse-Darmstadt and electoral Mainz, the only Jews attending Jewish territorial assemblies toward the end of the eighteenth century were the deputies. Although the Judenlandtag is still repeatedly called a gathering of all Jews, it appears to have changed more and more into an assembly made up of community board members, community representatives and delegates. On the one hand, this may have been due to the steadily increasing size of the Jewish population, which made it technically difficult to organize a general assembly of all taxpaying heads of households. On the other hand, it reflected a development characterized by the growing bureaucratization of procedures under the petty princes in matters pertaining to Jewish life and a tendency toward less democracy within the leadership of the Landjudenschaften. The authorities were increasingly inclined to create commissioners and agencies designed to make Jewish affairs more amenable to control. The dominance of the Jewish leadership stratum and the antagonistic interests of the upper, middle, and lower classes rendered it virtually impossible to develop a form of democratic self-governance.

There was a similar pattern in the territorial rabbinates in Bohemia and Moravia. In Bohemia the territorial rabbinate had already come to an end in the first half of the eighteenth century when the chief rabbi David Oppenheim set up twelve district rabbinates. Although he hoped in this way to serve the advancement of traditional religion, by the end of the eighteenth century the spirit of the Josephinian Enlightenment had penetrated the Bohemian district rabbinates, spreading from there to the rural Jews of Bohemia. By contrast, in Moravia, where the territorial rabbinate was far older than that in Bohemia, no district rabbinates were formed and, under an ongoing conservative territorial rabbinate, the Enlightenment could make headway there more slowly.

In several German territories, such as Upper Hesse, territorial Jewish assemblies still continued to be held into the first quarter of the nineteenth century. In Hesse-Darmstadt the organizational framework of the Landjudenschaft and territorial rabbinate remained in existence into the twentieth century.

Despite the unpleasant concomitants, the creation and maintenance of the Landjudenschaften was a remarkable achievement, the product of a lively and dynamic Jewish public spiritedness, receptive to external stimuli. In the main, the self-governance granted to the Jews by the state undoubtedly served as an instrument of regimentation and discipline. Yet, at the same time, it was also a form of self-determination, and was perceived by Jews as a token of respect for their distinctive character and the means that rendered Jewish existence possible. In the decline of the Landjudenschaften in the age of Enlightenment, one can discern early signs of the dissolution of Jewish communality.

7 | Intellectual and Religious Life

1. The Traditional Jewish Centers of Learning

At the beginning of the seventeenth century the study of the Torah in Germany was still generally at a low level. The extreme degree of dispersion of the Jewish population over a huge number of small localities initially hampered any significant improvement in the intellectual sphere. In many localities there were none who could boast of a solid grounding in Jewish knowledge. One consequence of this was that poor, nonlearned Jews occasionally moved to regions where they were unknown, passed themselves off as scholars, and did serious harm. In Poland storekeepers who had a certain background in Talmud could devote themselves to traditional learning while their wives attended to customers. In Germany it was forbidden almost everywhere for Jews to operate open retail shops. Outside the cities Jews earned their living by peddling, an occupation that precluded the possibility of spending several hours in regular daily study. In the cities, as well, work was so strenuous that little time remained for study. In addition, there was a tendency in Germany toward a kind of "division of labor" between those who studied and those who worked: several scholars who dedicated themselves totally to learning in a *Klaus* fulfilled the duty of constant study of the Torah "by proxy" for the entire community. Conscientious community members usually contented themselves with one hour of study a day.

From the middle of the seventeenth to the mid-eighteenth century

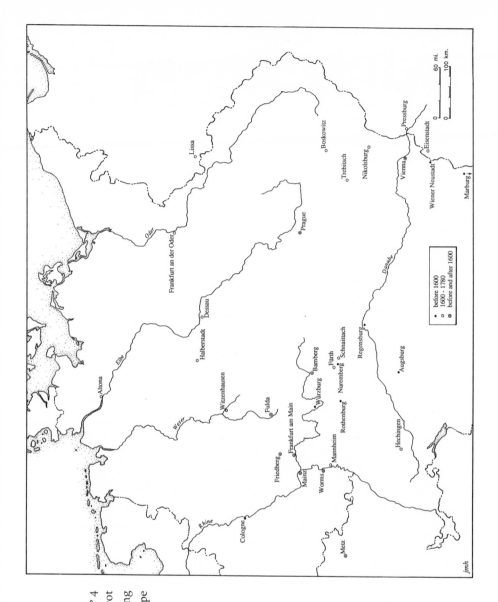

MAP 4

Significant Yeshivot
in German-Speaking
Central Europe

Legend:
- before 1600
- 1600 - 1780
- before and after 1600

Places labeled on map: Altona, Lissa, Frankfurt an der Oder, Dessau, Halberstadt, Witzenhausen, Fulda, Friedberg, Frankfurt am Main, Mainz, Worms, Cologne, Metz, Mannheim, Rothenburg, Würzburg, Bamberg, Fürth, Nuremberg, Schnaittach, Regensburg, Augsburg, Hechingen, Prague, Boskowitz, Trebitsch, Nikolsburg, Vienna, Pressburg, Eisenstadt, Wiener Neustadt, Marburg

Rivers: Oder, Elbe, Weser, Rhine, Danube

Scale: 60 mi. / 100 km.

imh

there was a major change. It began with the migration of Jews fleeing from Poland and Lithuania, whose ranks included numerous scholars. Sometimes together with their pupils, these learned Jews were accepted by communities in Germany, and in some cases appointed community or Klaus rabbi. The "Polish spirit," later so sharply criticized by Jewish enlighteners and historians as supposedly ushering in "a new Middle Ages for European Jewry," actually sparked certain positive changes.[1] Despite its weaknesses, examined below, it led to a reinvigoration of intellectual life and scholarly activity—not only in the field of Talmud study but in other Jewish disciplines as well.

Most of the urban communities that developed in the seventeenth century into large kehillot (at least as measured by the criteria of the time) followed the old German-Ashkenazi traditions and maintained a yeshiva. The most respected such academies in Germany were located in Frankfurt am Main, Worms, Altona, and Fürth. Yet the chief city in the empire when it came to Talmud studies was undoubtedly Prague, a community headed by scholars who had been the disciples of Maharal. Solomon Ephraim Lunschitz (1550–1619) was a famous preacher and the head of the rabbinical court; Yomtov Lipmann Heller (1579–1654) was an eminent expert on Halacha, whose commentary on the Mishnah was soon regarded as one of the main works of rabbinic literature. Since many Prague scholars directed a yeshiva, there were a number of them in the city. The communal bodies maintained strict supervision over the students who flocked there. At the beginning of the eighteenth century the rabbis David Oppenheim (a nephew of the court Jew Samuel Oppenheimer in Vienna) and Abraham Broda headed two large yeshivot that served several hundred students. The last Talmud scholar of world renown in Prague, Ezekiel Landau (1713–1793), was also the last head of its largest yeshiva, which he directed from 1754.

If Prague was the hub for Talmud study in the east of the empire, Frankfurt am Main and Metz were the two most important study centers in the west. The directors of the yeshivot there came mainly from Poland and Lithuania, at a time when the Eastern European yeshivot were in decline. No other institution of its kind in Europe could compete with the intellectual level and achievements of the Frankfurt yeshiva. The Metz community, with its celebrated yeshiva, belonged to the German-speaking Jewish culture area until the French Revolution, and, as late as 1789–1790, there was still a newspaper published there in Western Yiddish, although longtime residents in Metz were also fluent in French. The region extending from Metz in the west to Prague in the east formed a single unit as far as Ashkenazi tradition, Torah study, and communal institutions were concerned.

An important yeshiva developed in Fürth from the nucleus of the local Klaus that had been established by the wealthy rabbi Bermann Fränkel (d. 1708), who also served in Schnaittach and Schwabach. This yeshiva too flourished under the direction of scholars from the East. In Halberstadt, as well, the activity and donations of the court Jew Behrend Lehmann led to the creation of a center of Talmudic learning. Eminent scholars were active in Vienna on the eve of and during the Thirty Years War and attracted pupils who were given lodging, board, and instruction in the Klaus that had been set up there. Outstanding scholars came with the wave of thousands of refugees from Poland seeking refuge in Moravia around the middle of the century and led to a blossoming of Talmud studies there. The Nikolsburg yeshiva was among the most important in Europe. One major reason why traditional intellectual life in Moravia was at such a high level was because of a special ordinance there that made it binding on every community with at least thirty heads of household to maintain a yeshiva, no matter how small.

In the larger communities the yeshiva was the focal point around which the circle of *lomdim*, scholars resident in the locality, crystallized. They were supported financially by the community and individual donors, as were the *bene yeshiva*—scholars who, on the basis of community laws, had certain duties and rights alongside the rabbi in the framework of communal ordinances. As earlier, in the ordinances of the Polish, Lithuanian, and Moravian communities, the concern for the continued existence of the Talmud academies and the progress of the young scholars was often expressed in the statutes of the communities and *Landjudenschaften*. The number of students whose support was undertaken by the community was often agreed upon as part of the contract with the rabbi when he was appointed. Generally, the aim was a compromise between the demands of the rabbi and the usually more reserved position of the community board. Thus, Rabbi Joseph Teomim of Lemberg (c. 1727–1792), who was appointed in 1781 by the community in Frankfurt an der Oder, requested he be given ten to twelve pupils (*baḥurim*) for Talmud study; however, the community did not wish to commit itself to a fixed number and only made general promises.[2]

The community and rabbi also reached an understanding regarding the rights and duties of the baḥurim and the conduct expected of them.

Thus, in 1766, when Rabbi Aryeh Leib Gunzberg from Lithuania (1695–1785), author of the widely esteemed Talmudic work *Sha'agat aryeh* (The Lion's Roar), was appointed in Metz, the community inserted a number of rules of conduct for his baḥurim in his contract, including a prohibition on their accepting a teaching post in the community. No reason is given for this regulation, but it is likely that the community wanted to prevent students from settling in the town by such an arrangement.

In Berlin, where there had been a regular house of study (bet hamidrash) since 1743, the fixed number of Talmud students was not supposed to exceed forty. If there were more than forty baḥurim in the town, community officials were obliged to make a selection from among them of the forty they felt were especially worthy candidates for support. The others were forced to leave the city so that they would not become a burden to the community. Special boards were responsible for the administration of the house of study and also the educational institution set up in 1774 according to the will left by Veitel Heine Ephraim and operated as a yeshiva down to the middle of the nineteenth century.

The fact that despite the many educational institutions in Germany gifted and wealthy pupils still went off to Poland and Bohemia to study at yeshivot there probably had more to do with the wanderlust of the students than their academic ambitions. In the eighteenth century the conditions for an intensive and very advanced study of the Talmud were more favorable in the lands of the Old Reich than in Poland and Lithuania, where constant war and economic adversities had led to the closing of many houses of study. At that time there were probably more students from the East attending the yeshivot in the west than vice versa. Although there were still some eminent scholars in Poland with whom students could pursue their studies on a private basis, baḥurim from Germany did not have to travel to Poland to study with fine Polish scholars, since there was now no lack of them in the German communities.

There were now quite a few outstanding scholars born in the empire as well. Only a few typical representatives can be mentioned here. Yehudah Mehler, born in Bingen in 1660 and one of the most important rabbis in Germany in the seventeenth and eighteenth centuries, served until his death in 1751 as rabbi of the archbishopric of Cologne, the archbishopric of Münster, and the duchy of Cleves. He was resident alternately in Deutz and Bonn, where he maintained a renowned yeshiva. Rabbi Nathaniel Weil (1687–1769) taught in Prague and was an exception among yeshiva principals, since he studied all six orders of the Mishnah with his students—even those sections missing in the Babylonian Talmud and thus usually not taught in the Talmud academies. He later became rabbi in Karlsruhe, but was not allowed to open a yeshiva there. Rabbi Yair Ḥayim Bacharach (1638–1702), an outstanding Talmud scholar who also possessed considerable general knowledge, was the most typical exponent of the new intellectual orientation that began to take hold among scholars in Germany. He was a direct descendant of Maharal and served as a rabbi in Koblenz and Worms. Bacharach emphatically cautioned against the abstruse and misleading, overly analytic methods of pilpul, recommended curricular reform, and insisted that the most important aim of study was its practical application in life. With that orientation, he trod in the footsteps of Maharal, who had been publicly scathing in his criticism of traditional instruction and customary teaching methods. Maharal's critique of education was continued by his disciples and by Isaiah Horowitz, and never ceased to be voiced in later generations.

However, even in Germany, some were loathe to give up the highly casuistic forms of Talmud exegesis that were common currency in Polish yeshivot. Pilpul was a method of dialectical analysis of a Talmudic text through which the justification or the verbal formulation of a statement was questioned, especially by posing a presumed contradiction, and was then resolved with just as hypothetical and generally far-fetched an argument. The formal logic and inventiveness of the pupil, as well as the educational aim of sharpening his intellect, were more important here than the search for truth. Though overstating the case, a visitor to Frankfurt am Main in the 1730s reported that hundreds of students of Talmud "wasted their time with hairsplitting."[4] In 1714 a Christian Hebraist in Germany even published a methodological introduction to pilpulistic exegesis of the Talmud as practiced in many Polish and German yeshivot.[5]

However, the greatest scholars, Bacharach in particular, publicly distanced themselves from these teaching methods, and when confronting textual or logical difficulties, tended more toward text emendation than overly subtle mental acrobatics.[6] By contrast, Tsevi Hirsch, the head of the yeshiva in Halberstadt who hailed from Poland, used to say in commenting on text emendation that it was "easy to just erase something" that did not seem to fit.[7] The conflict between these methods and views pointed up the existing rift between the scholar typical of German Jewry and his typical Polish colleague. This was probably in part what Rabbi Jacob Emden was alluding to when he complained that most posts for rabbis in Germany were occupied by scholars from Poland and Polish elementary teachers had taken over most of the jobs as teachers. At the same time, he may have been expressing his annoyance that he had been passed over for the post of Hamburg chief rabbi—and that a Polish scholar had been selected instead.[8] Although the "Polish spirit" was heavily represented in Germany by rabbis and teachers, the western Ashkenazi tradition held its ground with remarkable tenacity. Neither the western Ashkenazi pragmatic teaching methods nor the typical western Ashkenazi religious outlook, more open to the needs and demands of workaday life than the eastern perspective, could be displaced. In the first half of the eighteenth century a scholar who served in Germany and Moravia wrote, "The Jews in Germany stick to the advice of Rabbi Yishmael (who in the Talmud [Tractate *Berakhot* 35b], recommended that the study of Torah should be brought into accord with one's occupation) and at that they have succeeded."[9]

2. Rabbinic Writings

Literary activity in the field of traditional Jewish scholarship was intensive and diverse. Several outstanding examples must suffice here. Especially characteristic of Jewish scholarship in Germany as a genre were books on customs (minhagim) in the communities. The most important work in this area was *Josef omets* (1723) by Joseph Juspa Hahn (Nördlingen) (1570–1637), who served as a judge on the rabbinical court in his native city of Frankfurt am Main and was head of the yeshiva there. In his book he presented a precise description of the customs of the Frankfurt community but went far beyond this framework, sketching the portrait of a vibrant community animated by a lively intellectual spirit and internal intellectual tensions. In its religious tendency the book bears affinities to the tradition of the medieval Jewish mystics, the Ḥaside Ashkenaz: for example, in its recommendation that in observing the commandments one should strive to make their fulfillment even more stringent, or in the way it reproduces, with naive faith, the contents of the *Sefer ḥasidim*. Its popular homiletics, interspersed with many tales and parables, is likewise reminiscent of the *Sefer ḥasidim*, as is its repeated demand for total honesty and uprightness in daily dealings with one's fellows, especially when financial affairs are involved. The parts of the book that treat details of everyday life bespeak a certain sense of comfortable domesticity. Hahn is proud of Ashkenazi tradition and unwavering in his insistence on observing Ashkenazi customs, even when they are obviously mistaken. He has enormous respect for Eastern European scholars but does not hesitate to debate with them on halachic questions. In particular, he rejects the pilpul-based method of study dominant in the east, preferring the practically oriented approach prevalent in Germany. The author notes repeatedly that he does not engage in kabbalistic studies but has some knowledge of the literature from the circle around the kabbalist Isaac Luria and occasionally recommends kabbalistic customs. Typically, his rejection of unscientific hairsplitting is in keeping with a remarkable interest in Hebrew language and grammar, a distinct predilection for textual criticism, and his extensive knowledge of literature. Hahn is thus an Ashkenazi scholar astride two eras, with one foot still in the Middle Ages, the other already firmly planted in the modern period.

Rabbi Joseph (Juspa) Schammes (1604–1678) wrote an extensive work on the religious life and customs of the Worms community, which he served for many years as beadle (shammash).[10] He appreciated the pomp and circumstance with which the Jews of Worms celebrated their domestic and public festivities, describing them down to the smallest detail. In the many sections devoted to synagogue rites and customs he follows the organization of the minhagim collections of the fifteenth century, taking Maharil as a model, especially in regard to the central importance he ascribes to the cantor and the traditional liturgical melodies. Reflective of their strong organizational development since the end of the Middle Ages, the community and its institutions are far more prominent in Schammes than in the works of Maharil. The book presents the various phases in the life of a Jew from the cradle to the grave and provides profound insight into contemporary Jewish history. Schammes likewise busied himself collecting the old Jewish legends in Worms, stemming largely from the time of the *Haside Ashkenaz*, and editing their publication under the title *Ma'ase nisim* (Miraculous Deeds). Less ambitious, but far more suitable for daily use in the synagogue and at home was the collection of customs and traditions of the Fürth community, published there in 1767. It is noteworthy that in the sphere of ritual and synagogue tradition as well, western Ashkenazi usage was able to hold its own, maintaining itself despite the powerful influx of Eastern European elements.

The responsa literature, so richly represented in Germany and Austria in the fifteenth century, did not blossom again in significant quantity until the eighteenth. Nonetheless, two large works of responsa appeared in the seventeenth century that exerted a strong influence on the practical application of Halacha in the modern period and provide invaluable historical source material. In *Havat Yair* (1699) Rabbi Yair Hayim

Bacharach produced a work repeatedly cited by modern halachic research, a veritable treasure trove of sources and an important documentary for the outstanding, in many respects pathbreaking personality of its author. The second work of note is the responsa collection by the Moravian chief rabbi Menaḥem Mendel Krochmal, *Tsemaḥ tsedek* (1675). His legal decisions gained considerable influence in the rabbinical world, especially regarding the question of remarriage by women whose husbands had disappeared in the Thirty Years War (Hebr. *agunot*) and in matters of community organization, in which he often decided in favor of those economically less fortunate.

Rabbi David Oppenheim, the court factor who occupied the Moravian chief rabbinate at the end of the seventeenth century, left numerous legal opinions; like most of his many manuscripts, these were left unpublished.[11] His addressees were scattered across the entire Ashkenazi Diaspora, from Brest-Litovsk to Rotterdam, and his responsa even reached as far as Jerusalem. Among the topics his legal decisions deal with, questions about agunot and problems pertaining to the validity and application of community ordinances are especially noteworthy. His brother-in-law, Rabbi Jacob Reischer, born and educated in Prague, was gradually recognized by rabbis of his time as the preeminent halachic authority. His legal opinions address questions sent to him not only from throughout Germany but a number of other countries as well, including the Holy Land. They attest to his sovereign knowledge of the entire rabbinic literature, especially in the field of jurisprudence, and his penchant for lightening the stringency of the law if entire communities, rather than individuals, were involved. He often tried to justify the old local customs of German communities, even if they were difficult to harmonize with the halachic norm. Reischer sanctioned the reading of news on the Sabbath in time of war, which some considered a violation of the Sabbath law, arguing that after learning the news it might be necessary to take immediate action. In terms of content and style his responsa reflect a Jewish life largely guided by the still unquestioned authority of religious law and its interpreters.

However, all these writings must stand in the shadow of two works that rank among the classics of responsa literature of all time. Rabbi Jacob Emden's *She'ilat Yavets* (1739–1759) is an important document of the time that, quite apart from the depth and keenness of its halachic argumentation, illuminates contemporary problems, especially where tradition clashes with the views and demands of the modern era. Rabbi Ezekiel Landau's monumental *Noda bi-hudah* (1776–1811) contains 860 responsa, some of which caused a sensation in the rabbinical world because of their tendency to accommodate to the aspirations and necessities of the modern age. To mention just one example: though he harbored certain reservations, Landau was the first rabbi to permit autopsies on the basis of religious law. His many legal opinions were authoritative for all Ashkenazi communities.

There were also a number of new publications in the field of jurisprudence, generally in the form of commentaries and supercommentaries on Joseph Caro's classic, the *Shulḥan Arukh*. Among the multitude of new interpretations (*ḥidushim*, "novellae") on Talmudic literature, only those key authors will be mentioned here whose writings are printed in modern editions of the Talmud or are used as special printed texts in Talmud academies. The commentaries of Rabbi Meir Schiff (Maharam, 1605–1641), who was born in Frankfurt and served as rabbi in Fulda, exemplify the German teaching method, which took pains to avoid the exaggerated pilpul. The four parts of the novellae by Rabbi Jacob Joshua Falk (1680–1756), *Pene Yehoshua* (The Countenance of Joshua, 1739–1780), appeared after he had relocated to Germany and were reprinted in numerous editions. In contrast with the authors of previous centuries, Falk was able to explain various Talmudic passages in a fresh and original way, even though his conception generally followed that of the medieval authors. He possessed the energy and boldness to explicate the Talmud with the eyes of a scholar from about the thirteenth or fourteenth century, one who knew nothing of the later excesses of pilpul. In so doing, Falk paved the way for a renewal and rejuvenation of Torah study on the basis of reason and incisive logic.

Publications in the field of ethics generally took the form of a commentary on Talmudic or later rabbinic texts. This is also true in homiletic literature. Rabbi Jacob Emden's three-part commentary on the prayer book (1745–1748) was widely read. In addition to explanations on the texts of prayers and a compilation of the regulations and customs on weekdays, the Sabbath, and holidays, it also contained ethical and theological treatises. In the realm of Jewish philosophy in the Old Reich, after Maharal of Prague, no important Jewish thinkers appeared until Mendelssohn. Likewise in biblical exegesis, long closely linked with philosophy, no work of major importance was produced. Scholarship was exclusively concerned with the oral law of the Mishnah, the Talmud, and other areas of rabbinic literature; scholars who pondered God, the world, and man tended to venture into the field of mysticism.

3. Literature in Western Yiddish

The rise of a Jewish middle class in the cities and the extent to which Jews were dispersed over innumerable small and even smaller localities made written correspondence in the Western Yiddish colloquial language a vital necessity. This, in turn, led to an enormous growth in Western Yiddish literature, whose beginnings date back to far before the seventeenth century. One factor influencing the expansion of this literature was that women were becoming increasingly important as consumers of culture.

Knowledge of Hebrew was in general decline, and few were still familiar with its literary treasures. Already, in 1688, the lay leaders of one Landjudenschaft complained about the leaders of another because the latter had written a Hebrew letter they were unable to understand. Records of Landjudenschaften, originally kept in Hebrew, shifted in many cases to Yiddish around the middle of the eighteenth century. Even as the medium of prayer, Hebrew increasingly became a foreign language, in some Jewish circles only partially understood. For that reason, for example, a prayer book published in Prague in 1718 contained the literal translation in Yiddish above each line in Hebrew, and apparently many families sang some of the beloved Sabbath zemirot in their Yiddish version. Given this situation, a rabbi suggested that persons who understood no Hebrew, especially women, should pray in "German"; another intended to write a compendium of the Sabbath laws accompanied by a "German" translation because so many contemporaries, as a result of ignorance, were violating important religious precepts.[12]

That Western Yiddish literature was mainly meant for a female readership is reflected in the fact that its language was generally called *Weiber-Teitsch* (lit. "women's German"). The characters used in Yiddish books had developed from the so-called Rashi script and were known as "women's script." In addition, the female reading public had an evident influence on the style and themes of this literature. Moses Altschul, who lived in the sixteenth century, wrote in the introduction to his *Brantspiegel* that it was meant for female readers—and for men similar to women with regard to the low level of their education.

Published in Basel in 1602, the *Brantspiegel* was the first book on ethics written in Yiddish and was widely read in Germany. Its seventy-three chapters contained popular philosophical sermons mixed with tales from the Talmud and Midrash. The author expatiated on wise men and fools, on good and evil women, on trust in God, modesty, charity, and chasteness; he also included lengthy commentary on religious laws for women, especially regarding married life and the kitchen, and underscored women's duties in child rearing and attendance at the synagogue.

Western Yiddish literature provided Jewish women with basic Jewish knowledge and a certain general education, enabling them to make up for their lack of formal schooling. The authors repeatedly stressed that by making use of the "German" language they were answering a crying need.

Naturally, the most important popular publications were the Bible translations. A Yiddish version of the Pentateuch had been completed in Cremona in 1540 and was reprinted in 1544 in Augsburg. The first independent translation of the entire Bible, by Yekutiel Blitz, was published in 1678 in Amsterdam, as was a similar translation by Joseph Witzenhausen, finished in 1687. Paraphrasings and rhymed renderings also appeared, and a popular *Teutsch-Humesch* (The Pentateuch in Judeo-German, c. 1590) was widely read.

By far the most popular of the Yiddish Bible versions for generations was *Tsenno-renno* (the name is a corrupted form of the first two Hebrew words of Song of Songs 3:11). The work is a paraphrase of the weekly sections of the Pentateuch and the corresponding sections from the Prophets (haftarot) and the scrolls (megillot) read on particular holidays, accompanied by illuminating extracts from rabbinic historical and agadic (legendary) literature. First published in Lublin and Cracow at the beginning of the seventeenth century by Jacob ben Isaac Ashkenazi of Janov, it was later brought out in Basel in 1622 and went through forty-three printings by the end of the eighteenth century. *Tsenno-renno* was charged with emotionality, greatly loved by women, and could be found in virtually every Jewish home.

Books on moral instruction began to appear in greater numbers from the start of the eighteenth century, possibly under the influence of the pietistic movement in Germany. Yehiel Michal Epstein, rabbi in a number of different communities in Germany, published the Yiddish book *Derekh ha-yashar la-olam ha-ba* (The Straight Path to the World to Come) in Frankfurt am Main in 1703. The book was meant for "ordinary people, women, and girls" and contains a compendium of religious laws in the manner and spirit of Rabbi Isaiah Horowitz's *Shene luhot ha-berit* (The Two Tablets of the Covenant), a work much venerated in scholarly circles (see below). *Simhat ha-nefesh* (Joy of the Soul), by Elhanan Henle Kirchhan of Frankfurt, appeared in 1707 and, in but a few years, went through six printings; it stresses the joys of a moral life and contains poems and songs (with musical notes) for domestic celebrations.

One such book with a special character was the *Liebes-Brief* (Love Letter) by Isaac Wetzlar from Celle, written in 1749, of which several manuscripts existed, though it never appeared in printed form. The author, a respected and prosperous merchant, had acquired a vast Jewish knowledge in his youth. The work has a pronounced penchant for social criticism and is thus a rich source for information about the contemporary situation in the communities. Wetzlar is extremely critical of the community leaders, the parnasim and rabbis, contending that the latter neglected their duties as pastors, educators, and judges and were more interested in their income than the welfare of the community. Like other authors, Wetzlar holds up the Sephardi communities as a model for emulation, especially in regard to synagogue discipline and education. He reserves special criticism for scholars who pore over the Talmud day and night but whose studies have no connection with their practical life and the life of the community. In many passages Wetzlar's sensitivity for the views of Christian society is evident; he apparently had close contact with non-Jews. This may also account for the similarities between certain tendencies in his book and aspects of contemporary Pietism.

Another book with ideas and sentiment kindred in some ways to pietistic views is the devotional volume *Liebliche Tefiloh* (Delightful Prayer) by Aharon b. Samuel. The work, published in Fürth in 1709, had an unusual fate. The author lived in a small town (Hergershausen) and described himself as a "simple person, not learned." He stressed the religious importance of devotion, especially private devotion, and accordingly authored a large number of prayers in Yiddish for various life situations. He evidently did not have a very high opinion of a solid grounding in Talmudic learning, and this reinforces the assumption that he was religiously a nonconformist. It is thus not surprising that all the copies of his book that could be found were confiscated by the Jewish authorities. They were later uncovered in 1830, stored in the attic of the house of study in Hergershausen.

The renowned and much cited work of memoirs by Glückel of Hameln belongs in some respects to the genre of morality literature because the book is replete with edifying reflections and moralizing commentary. The deeply religious consciousness of the author, in which it is difficult to separate her faith in God from superstition and her trust in God from fatalism, did not perceive any disharmony between the worldly wealth of a person and his nullity in the eyes of God. Glückel's book articulates her times and a certain modernity of mind, reflected in her keen interest in life and aptitude for vivid description. As autobiography, her book belongs to a rich genre of narrative literature in Yiddish that was quite multiform in her era.

The classic *Ma'ase-Buch* (Book of Deeds), the first and most important collection of prose tales from Jewish sources in Yiddish, was first published in Basel in 1602; it contains 257 tales, drawn mainly from the Talmud and Midrash. This book and books like it were meant to displace the profane popular literature, rich in non-Jewish motifs, that had already made its appearance in the sixteenth century, but they did not succeed in that aim. A multitude of new publications also appeared in the field of secular narrative literature. There were also highly popular epic poems from German literature in Yiddish translation, such as *Kaiser Oktavian, Die schöne Magelone, Eulenspiegel, Schildbürger,* and many others. Events of topical interest among German Jewry and in the empire were celebrated in songs and ballads, such as the Frankfurt "Vinzlied" (Song of Vincent), which dealt with the return of the Jews and the downfall of their enemy Vincent Fettmilch, or the song commemorating the election and coronation of Leopold I in 1658, "Ein schön Lied, wie es zugegangen ist in Frankfurt mit der Wahl und Krönung Leopold."

Western Yiddish literature made a singular contribution to enhancing the level of Jewish and general education among Jews in the Old Reich. It was the instrument that helped enrich the intellectual life of many Jews who no longer had a solid grounding in Hebrew but whose knowledge of standard German was still deficient.

4. Hebrew Printing

All these cultural achievements could only be realized on the basis of a ramified network of Hebrew presses whose relatively rapid development in many German cities has rightfully been termed nothing short of "phenomenal." In the sixteenth century Hebrew book publishing in the lands of the empire was established on a continuous basis only in Prague and, later, in Frankfurt am Main. However, the Jews of Frankfurt, until emancipation, were never allowed to set up their own press, so that all Hebrew prints there were produced in Christian printing houses, although Jews were also employed as printers. Hebrew publishing elsewhere, as in Augsburg, Freiburg, Heidelberg, Isny, Konstanz, and Thiengen, was on a temporary basis, usually at the initiative of itinerant Jewish publishers, often supported by Christian Hebraists. In Hanau, for example, there was a Hebrew printing press in existence from 1610 to 1630. Jewish publishing and printing presses did not begin to thrive until after the Thirty Years War, when such presses advanced to the forefront of Hebrew book production in Europe at that time, both qualitatively and in terms of volume. The court Jews had a significant role in this development. The Hebrew printing houses in the empire now supplied the large Jewish book market in Eastern Europe, where Hebrew book publishing had been virtually shut down after the pogroms of 1648/49 and did not recover until the eighteenth century.

Significantly, the first large-scale publishing enterprises arose at the instigation of the territorial rulers, who had a variety of motives for promoting Jewish printing. The count of Hohenlohe gave a Jewish master printer permission to open a press in Wilhermsdorf since he needed a potential buyer for the output of the paper mills in the territory. This permit led to the establishment of a press that, starting in 1670, went on to publish many beautifully produced Hebrew books. The duke of Sulzbach, who promoted the founding of a large press in his city, had interests of a different kind. With a strong penchant for mystical-theosophical studies, he brought the Christian theologian and poet Knorr von Rosenroth to his court and asked him to publish his *Kabbala Denudata*, a book on the basic principles of the Kabbala as elaborated in the *Zohar*, the classic work of Jewish mysticism. At the same time, a large-format deluxe edition of the *Zohar* in Hebrew was published in Sulzbach. This was the beginning of a long tradition of Hebrew book production in Sulzbach, which from 1684 to 1851 was a major center of Jewish book production worldwide, publishing some seven hundred Hebrew and Yiddish works during this period. In fact, in respect to the number of books produced for specifically religious purposes, Sulzbach ranked as the world leader. Another important printing house owed its foundation in 1694 to the Dessau court Jew Moses Benjamin Wulff. It was initially set up in Dessau and was later active in the nearby towns of Halle, Jessnitz, and Köthen. In Halle a large edition of the *Shulḥan Arukh* was brought out, financed by the wealthy court factor Assur Marx. The press in Jessnitz was distinguished by its special interest in scholarly works on non-Talmudic subjects, a topic that will be treated below.

The important press in Dyhernfurth in Lower Silesia was established by the magnate of the town, who granted the learned bibliographer

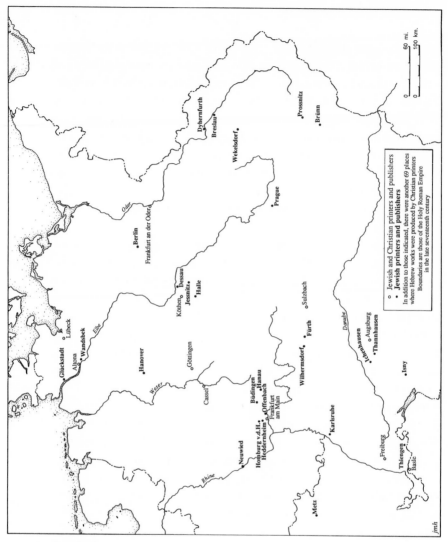

MAP 5
Sites of Major
Hebrew Printers and
Publishing Houses

○ Jewish and Christian printers and publishers
● **Jewish printers and publishers**
In addition to those indicated, there were another 69 places where Hebrew works were produced by Christian printers Boundaries are those of the Holy Roman Empire in the late seventeenth century

60 mi.
100 km.

Lübeck
Glückstadt
Altona
Wandsbek
Berlin
Frankfurt an der Oder
Dyhernfurth
Breslau
Wekelsdorf
Prossnitz
Brünn
Köthen
Dessau
Jessnitz
Halle
Prague
Hanover
Göttingen
Cassel
Büdingen
Hamau
Hedernheim
Offenbach
Frankfurt am Main
Homburg v.d.H.
Neuwied
Karlsruhe
Wilhermsdorf
Sulzbach
Fürth
Ichenhausen
Augsburg
Thannhausen
Isny
Freiburg
Thiengen
Basle
Metz

Oder
Elbe
Weser
Rhine
Danube

jmh

Shabbetai Bass (1641–1718) from Prague a permit to publish books in the hope that the opening of a Hebrew printing house would be beneficial for the development of this recently founded town. At the same time, he gave permission for Jews to settle there in connection with the press. With the exception of Glogau and Zülz, this was the first time in one hundred years that Jews had been able to live in Silesia. Bass laid the foundation stone for a new community consisting of his own family and those of the Jewish journeyman printers and apprentices he had brought along from Prague and Cracow. Immigrants from Poland made a substantial contribution to the development of Hebrew printing in Germany and not only in Dyhernfurth. In the Dessau presses, as well, there were compositors and proofreaders from Poland, while most journeyman printers in Sulzbach hailed from small localities in Bavaria. The Dyhernfurth press published hundreds of Hebrew and Yiddish works of all kinds over the many years of its existence. Another printing house worthy of mention was the one set up in Fürth in 1691 by the court Jew Mordechai Model from Ansbach. It concentrated on rabbinic works of various kinds. In the eighteenth century a number of other printing houses were set up in the town so that Fürth also grew into a center of Hebrew publishing in the Old Reich.

Hebrew publishing in Germany made a notable contribution to raising the level of Jewish intellectual life in the lands of the empire and Eastern Europe, especially by repeatedly reprinting the Babylonian Talmud with its dozens of tractates and a series of commentaries and glosses. Since the Amsterdam edition of 1644–1648 a half century had passed without the publication of a complete edition of the Talmud. Persecutions and wars had destroyed many volumes, and there was a universal shortage of copies. For that reason Behrend Lehmann arranged for publication of the abovementioned Talmud edition in Frankfurt an der Oder. This was the first complete edition of the Talmud published in Germany, and it was followed by two further editions brought out later in the same locality. The Talmud was also reprinted in 1721/1722 in Frankfurt am Main (and, in part, in Amsterdam), financed by the Viennese court Jew Samson Wertheimer, in cooperation with his son-in-law Moses Kann in Frankfurt. This edition became the basis for almost all later reprints of the Talmud. Yet after being confiscated by the censors, it remained under lock and key for over thirty years, until the influence of Rabbi Moses Kann brought about its release in 1753. Other complete editions of the Talmud were published in Prague, Berlin, Sulzbach, Vienna, and Dyhernfurth; a few tractates also appeared in Fürth. Distribution of books within the empire and to the east and west principally made use of the fairs in Leipzig and elsewhere. From a religious perspective Hebrew publishing was a meritorious enterprise and, simultaneously, a lucrative business in which large sums of capital could be invested.

Some idea of the importance of this network of book production and distribution for intellectual life can be gained by considering that the first edition of the Talmud in Frankfurt an der Oder—some five thousand copies—was soon sold out and that the Talmud was reprinted ten times during the eighteenth century, each printing numbering several thousand copies. Experts estimate that about a third of all Hebrew books published down to the end of the eighteenth century were produced by presses in Germany, prayer books of all types making up at least half. As already indicated in the case of the Frankfurt edition of the Talmud, the authorities and their investigative commissions kept an eagle eye on Jewish book production. For example, they demanded that all Talmud editions be reprints of the Basel edition of 1571–1581, from which all "offensive" passages had been expurgated. On the other hand, the communities insisted that no book should be published without the approval (*haskamah*) of famous rabbis. This prevented the printing of works with an obviously heretical content but did not hinder the publication of a spate of books of inferior quality. Despite the traditional character of the works produced, there can be no doubt that Hebrew printing provided a powerful stimulus for the movements paving the way for the Jewish Enlightenment of the eighteenth century and its break with the past.

5. The Mystical Current

Educated circles in the seventeenth century were in a state of intellectual and religious ferment. Humanism and the Reformation of the previous century had weakened or eliminated powerful conventions from the medieval past, although these had not yet been supplanted by a new culture. It is true that the intellectual situation within Jewry had not experienced a similar upheaval, yet here too there were numerous signs pointing to incipient ferment.

From time immemorial mysticism in Judaism as elsewhere had been an element that bore within itself a dynamic force: the power to shatter, shake up, and shape anew. In the sixteenth century, in Germany and other centers of Jewish settlement, a process was set into motion in whose course the Kabbala, until then treated as a body of esoteric teachings, increasingly began to emerge into the Jewish public sphere. More and more *ba'ale shem* (Hebr., masters of the Name) appeared on the scene, miracle workers to whom troubled and afflicted Jews flocked hoping to make use of their purported magical powers to ease their distress. Some eminent scholars also achieved renown as kabbalists and performers of miraculous deeds. Outstanding among these was Rabbi Elijah Loanz (1564–1636), a grandson of Josel of Rosheim and at various times a rabbi in Fulda, Hanau, Friedberg, and Worms. Among other works, he authored kabbalistic commentaries on the Song of Songs and Ecclesiastes. In his *Shene luḥot ha-berit* Rabbi Isaiah Horowitz (ca. 1565–1630) meshed the written and oral Torah with the teachings of the Kabbala. His personality and intellectual outlook had a lasting impact on the communities in Frankfurt am Main and Prague, where he was active as a rabbi. Horowitz spent his final years in the kabbalistic center of Safed in the Holy Land. Rabbi Naphtali Bacharach, born in Frankfurt am Main, published his magnum opus *Emek ha-melekh* (Valley of the King) in Amsterdam in 1648, a work that presented a detailed account of the kabbalistic teachings of Rabbi Isaac Luria (1534–1572), who originated from an Ashkenazi family, lived in Egypt and died in Safed, making them accessible to a broader public. The book was generally recognized as the authoritative source for knowledge on Lurianic Kabbala, which also enjoyed particular popularity at that time in Germany. Along with the influx of emigrants from Poland into Germany from the middle of the seventeenth century on, came many itinerant preachers who spread kabbalistic ideas. Before the expulsion of 1670 the Vienna ghetto was a hub of kabbalistic learning. Yet it should be noted that veneration for Lurianic Kabbala and an active interest in its teachings was by no means in contradiction with an emphatically rationalistic tendency, as manifest especially in the thinking of Rabbi Yair Ḥayim Bacharach, mentioned earlier. Just as in the European academic world of the seventeenth century, so too among the Jews, mysticism and science lived in harmony with one another.

Many of the customs influenced by Lurianic Kabbala were magicoreligious practices intended to accelerate the coming of a redeemed world and the advent of the *olam ha-tikun*, the universe of true order. This type of piety contained a strong messianic component. Since all human action was understood to have an effect on hastening or impeding future redemption, each and every custom, even the most insignificant, became an object of religious fervor. In Germany this spiritual movement led to an even more painstaking observance of the most minor religious customs. Later on, in Eastern Europe, its impact was felt in the ecstatic religiosity of Hasidism, which was necessarily somewhat lax in its attention to individual rites, though not in the observance of directly given ritual commandments.

The powerful influence of Lurianic Kabbala continued on well into the eighteenth century. It manifested itself in the synagogue liturgy, especially in a new arrangement of prayers expanded by psalms and songs on the eve of the Sabbath, as well as in an exuberant Sabbath celebration in the home, with spirited singing of table songs written specifically for the purpose and with the kabbalistic custom of speaking only Hebrew on that day. Mystical and pietistic customs grew widely popular. Respected rabbis lived an ascetic life marked by much fasting and frequent ritual immersions. Especially noteworthy among them was the Frankfurt rabbi Naphtali Cohen (in office from 1704 to 1711), a mystic who also engaged in the practical Kabbala using incantations, amulets, and magical healing methods. The internal life of the communities, it was apparent, had become permeated by kabbalistic ideas.

8 Toward a New Era

1. The Sabbatian Movement

The strong messianic element in Lurianic Kabbala has given rise to the proposition that it was the decisive motive force underlying the messianic movement that swept through the entire Jewish world in 1665/1666, engulfing all of Jewry in the feverish expectation of imminent redemption. The appearance of the supposed Messiah Shabbetai Tsevi (1626–1676) in the Orient in 1665 unleashed a blaze of excitement and enthusiasm whose intensity and diffusion in 1666 wherever Jews lived was unparalleled in the long history of Jewish messianism. Undoubtedly, the epochal historical events in Jewish history in the preceding decades also contributed their share to this wave of excitation. Both the catastrophe that befell Polish Jewry and the readmission of Jews to England in 1656, which was viewed as almost a miracle, were interpreted at the time as portentous steps on the path to final deliverance. The unanimity in messianic expectation in all Jewish communities in Europe, Asia, and North Africa was of enormous importance in itself for bolstering the belief of the Jewish masses in the Messiah and the imminent fulfillment of his religious-national mission.

The written messages sent by the "prophet" of the Messiah, Nathan of Gaza and the reports of his first appearance and early success in Gaza and Smyrna triggered a swell of enthusiasm everywhere. Many followed the call to repentance with fervor: they prayed, fasted, flagellated themselves, undertook ritual purifications and mortifications of the flesh, sold their possessions, and prepared for departure for the Holy Land. They even followed the call of the Messiah to change the days of mourning into festivals of rejoicing. This time, they believed, it was finally, finally true; and it was up to them whether redemption would become reality.

The communities in the empire, as in other lands, were swept up by the general frenzy. A flood of writings inundated the communities, especially in the south. However, the messianic fervor displaced the halachic tradition less in Germany than elsewhere, and fasting on days of mourning was still observed. We have a report on the events in Hamburg from the pen of a reliable eyewitness, Glückel of Hameln: "The joy when letters arrived [with news of Shabbetai Tsevi] is not to be described. Most of the letters were received by the Portuguese. They took them to the synagogue and read them aloud there. . . . Some people sold home, hearth and everything they possessed, awaiting redemption."[1]

Indeed, the sense of joyous expectation in the Hamburg Portuguese community was especially great. With the arrival of "good news" about Shabbetai Tsevi, festive services were held in the synagogue, including prayers normally recited only on holidays. The leaders of the communities met and decided to send representatives to Constantinople "in order to pay the homage due to our King Shabbetai Tsevi, the Anointed One of the God of Jacob (may His reign unfold and His name be made eternal)." This plan was not carried out, yet it was decided "to offer the houses of the community for sale by putting up notices . . . in order to gradually eliminate the burdens and debts of the community and prepare ourselves for the path which, with divine assistance, we soon hope to travel."[2] The "believers," that is, those who were convinced that Shabbetai Tsevi was indeed the true Messiah—in Hamburg they made up the overwhelming majority—founded a new yeshiva in which ecstatic sermons were preached about the Messiah and the imminent deliverance of Israel.

Along with Hamburg, Vienna, Prague, and Frankfurt am Main were important centers of the messianic movement. Christian observers recounted that in Frankfurt four hundred heads of household were preparing for the trip to the Holy Land and that indeed many of them had already departed. In Mainz a study circle met daily with Rabbi Yair Hayim Bacharach from Worms "on account of the glad tidings." The rabbi was following the events with keen interest. There was a large messianic movement among Jews in Franconia as well, especially in the Nuremberg area. The margrave of Ansbach prohibited the Jews from sending their property outside the country and emigrating without a permit. Many Christians refused to pay installments on debts owed to Jewish creditors, since they would, after all, soon be leaving; for their part, the Jews wished to collect on their outstanding debts as quickly as possible. This gave rise to tensions, sparking excesses and violence.

Elsewhere, too, Christians reacted in a similar way to the messianic movement among the Jews. In Hamburg the Portuguese community, whose preponderant majority had been seized by messianic fervor, petitioned the senate because the non-Jewish mobs had disturbed the peace. The community also asked the senate to ban the public distribution of pamphlets on the messianic expectation. Because the community feared mob violence, they enjoined their members from speaking with Gentiles about the messianic movement. It was reported from Frankfurt that the Christians were annoyed with the Jews, who had claimed self-importantly that new times were in the offing and that their sufferings would soon be at an end.

So powerful was the general expectation and enthusiasm that even the many rabbis who were not among the "believers" capitulated in the face of the crowd's exuberance. In Germany only a single rabbi spoke out publicly and unhesitatingly against the Messiah: Jacob Sasportas (ca. 1610–1698), from Oran in North Africa, an eminent Talmudic scholar. He had wandered for years around Europe, never staying longer than a few years in any one place, and had just arrived in Hamburg in November 1665, a few weeks before the first reports about Shabbetai Tsevi. Sasportas stayed on in Hamburg with his family and was supported by the community as a private scholar. In contrast with the communal rabbi, who placed himself at the head of the "believers," Sasportas spoke and wrote in protest against the messianic "swindle." He gave an urgent warning about the bitter disappointment that was bound to follow upon the heels of the frenzied enthusiasm of the moment. In part probably also moved by personal motives (Sasportas was embittered that no important community had wished to engage him as their rabbi), he had, with great foresight, exposed the prophecies and commandments of the purported Messiah to be nothing but trickery and sham.

Shabbetai Tsevi's arrest by the sultan (February 1666) and his captivity in Gallipoli under very favorable conditions served many "believers" as persuasive proof of his messianic mission. But his forced conversion to Islam (September 1666) put an abrupt end to the mass movement. Disillusionment in the communities was universal, profound, and bitter;

they had hoped and prayed in vain and fasted for nothing. The rabbis and community leaders immediately began removing all traces of the Sabbatian madness from the liturgy and communal records. It was to disappear like a bad dream.

Neither the initial success of Shabbetai Tsevi nor the catastrophic conclusion to this episode led to a deep rupture with tradition, for messianic expectations in Jewish tradition had long been marked by contradictions. Thus, after the supposed Messiah had converted to Islam, it was possible to return to traditional normalcy. Yet, clandestinely, underground in Jewish society, a hard core of "believers" remained. They divined a deeper significance precisely in the apostasy of the Messiah and for generations remained loyal to the Sabbatian spirit of the partial or total abrogation of the Law. They formed an explosive oppositional group capable of shattering the framework of the community, anchored by the rabbinate in the moorings of religious law. For many decades after the death of Shabbetai Tsevi these Sabbatians clung to their convictions. Their influence was felt especially in literary spheres but had a social impact as well.

Under the leadership of the Sabbatian Judah the Pious (d. 1700) from Lithuania, a "sacred brotherhood" (havurah kedoshah) was formed. After many wanderings in Europe that took the brotherhood through Germany and Austria, it journeyed on pilgrimage to Jerusalem in 1700 but collapsed soon after the sudden death of Judah the Pious. Part of this group returned to Germany and remained for years in Mannheim, finding refuge in a newly established Klaus. In this way a secretly active branch of the Sabbatian sect arose in the city, and its influence also extended to the community in Frankfurt am Main. In more than one case the rabbis and community leaders felt it necessary to pronounce a ban on Sabbatians who confessed their heresy.

A whole series of publications with Sabbatian tendencies (not always readily recognized) appeared in Germany, such as some of the writings by the Sabbatian Nehemiah Hayon (ca. 1655–ca. 1730) published in Berlin. Communities from far and wide banded together in the struggle against the sect, and in 1725 each of the three large communities in Amsterdam, Hamburg, and Frankfurt am Main published a special proclamation, partly in Hebrew, partly in Yiddish, in which they pronounced the ban on the sect. The movement was particularly deeply rooted and widespread in Bohemia and Moravia, where some of the most influential Jews became its secret adherents. One of the centers of the pseudomessianic movement of Jacob Frank (1726–1791) was also located there. Frank, a sectarian and adventurer from Poland, had proclaimed himself a reincarnation of Shabbetai Tsevi; in 1759 he converted to Roman Catholicism, along with many of his followers, after having first embraced Islam. The emergence of these "believing" Frankists was the last phase of the Sabbatian movement. From 1773 to 1786 Frank lived in Brünn and then moved with eight hundred devotees, some of whom were still attached to Judaism, to Offenbach, where he held court until his death.

Although one should not overestimate the numerical importance and influence of the Sabbatians and Frankists within Jewry in the German-speaking lands in the eighteenth century, it is evident that they contributed to the wave of radical change that seized hold of Jewish society. In several cases it is even possible to establish that certain leading Frankists in Prague, for example, were identical with the spokesmen of the movement for a Jewish Enlightenment (maskilim). But that is not the crux of the matter. The decisive point is that these movements contributed to shaking the foundations of Jewish tradition by their ideologically motivated rebellion against the domination of the existing rabbinate and its orthodoxy. The fiasco of the messianic mass movement, which had received the blessing of many rabbis, dealt a heavy blow to their standing and image. Virtually all had fallen victim to the messianic delusion and its allure and had failed to see through its deceptive character. They had also failed in their role as the appointed teachers and mentors of the communities. As a result, some rabbis and scholars rationalized the downfall of the Messiah by retroactively endowing his appearance with a mystical theological dimension, thereby achieving their own rehabilitation as well.

With the collapse of the Sabbatian movement Lurianic Kabbala—indeed, even the Kabbala as a whole—was widely discredited. After all, it was Lurianic Kabbala that had intensified the longing for messianic deliverance to fever pitch, largely making the Sabbatian wave possible. Thus one can note in subsequent generations of Jews in Germany a kind of traumatic anxiety about a possible repetition of the case of Shabbetai Tsevi and of the dreams of premature salvation it engendered. That which Gershom Scholem termed "fear of the Kabbala" (*Kabbalaangst*) was also in part a consequence of the Sabbatian movement and its aftermath.

A Jewish merchant who had studied many years in the yeshivot of Prague and Frankfurt am Main, and had a profound respect for the "sacredness" of the Kabbala, spoke out against the "new fashion" among students of the Talmud to delve into kabbalistic literature on their own, since they could easily become ensnared in the Sabbatian net.[3] A certain dejectedness seized hold of many, and some felt a sense of discontent with existing religious and intellectual life. The internal struggle with the Sabbatian "heresy" clearly altered the shape of traditional society. Up until that point it had been rent by disputes and internal tensions, but for centuries there had been no sects and splinter factions that did not apostatize.

One can certainly view the remnants of the Sabbatian movement in the eighteenth century as a serious challenge to the principles of traditional rabbinism and to the community leadership in the lands of the Old Reich. As such, it was indeed a forerunner of the Haskalah and the later movement for religious reform—though only in its negation and certainly not in the positive development of its mysticism. Although Jewish Enlightenment was vigorously opposed to the mysticism of the Sabbatians, Sabbatianism, in its revolt against the existing rabbinical order, had been its pioneer.

2. Scientific Attitudes Among the Rabbis

In other respects, as well, traditional society was no longer quite the same. Since the onset of the early modern period the image of the rabbi and scholar had changed, a process that probably began in the circle around Maharal in Prague. One of the changes was that instead of the common sophistic, hairsplitting exegesis of rabbinical sources, there was now a concerted effort, using rigorous hermeneutic rules, to examine these materials in order to derive their meaning. Along with mastery of rabbinic scholarship in the narrower sense, the tendency now arose in the eighteenth century to deal with "metahalachic" and general scientific disciplines. This overcoming of the earlier distance from science and philosophy, an aspect of Ashkenazi culture that had long differentiated it from the Sephardi world of learning, is probably also bound up with the circumstance that, with the rise of humanism, the sciences had emancipated themselves from Christian theology.

One of the first rabbis in whose approach one can discern this shift was the already mentioned Yomtov Lipmann Heller. He not only wrote a monumental commentary on the entire Mishnah but also dealt intensively with philosophical and intellectual works by Spanish-Jewish authors. Rabbi Yair Hayim Bacharach left an extensive list of his own writings, most of which have been lost. The areas of knowledge this catalog includes reflect a remarkable universality: homiletics, philosophy,

Kabbala, contemporary history, local history, chronology, genealogy, liturgy, religious poetry, questions of natural science, customs and usage, Hebrew linguistics and grammar, Talmudic lexicography and methodology. The Frankfurt Klaus rabbi Samuel Schotten knew Latin and had a significant knowledge of astronomy, which he imparted to his pupils. He also initiated them into Hebrew grammar and mathematics. The Prague rabbinical adjunct Jonah Landsofer (1678–1712) printed excerpts from Euclid's geometry at the end of his work of responsa, with illustrations, because of its "enormous utility for our teachings."[4]

It was also significant that men who were not particularly distinguished as Talmud scholars authored works that broke new ground in Jewish scholarship. Especially important among these was Shabbetai (Meschorer) Bass, mentioned above. Born in Poland, he fled to Prague in 1655, where he worked as a cantorial assistant. There he studied the general sciences as well as Latin. Among the many books he published, the work *Sifte yeshenim* (The Lips of the Sleeping, 1680) was a pioneering enterprise. It was the first Hebrew bibliography to follow a lucid scheme of classification based on scientific criteria.

During the first half of the eighteenth century a number of works were published that pointed to a new interest in humanistic disciplines: Hebrew dictionaries, writings on Hebrew linguistics and grammar, popular-scientific treatises in Hebrew, exegetical works marked by an appreciative approach to the natural sciences and mathematics as indispensable tools for a proper understanding of the Bible and Talmud, systematic guides to Talmud study and a better understanding of medieval philosophy, introductions to arithmetic and algebra. These writings came out of the same printing houses that also published rabbinic works, and many had certificates of approval from renowned rabbis and the heads of rabbinical courts.

With the tacit consent of the Dessau chief rabbi David Fränkel (1707–1762), and even perhaps under his direct influence, the Hebrew press in Jessnitz, not far from Dessau, brought out a series of works whose first publication or reprinting pointed to this significant intellectual change. It is especially apparent in the first publication after two hundred years of *Moreh nevukhim* (*Guide of the Perplexed*) by Maimonides, which appeared there in 1742 with the implicit approval of Rabbi David Fränkel, though without his specific approbation. The very fact that the press in Jessnitz was allowed to reprint this work, which rabbis in Ashkenaz had never been particularly fond of, attests to a certain shift in the intellectual stance of the rabbinate in Germany. The publication of a manuscript 130 years old by David Gans (see the prologue) on astronomical and cosmological topics, *Neḥmad ve-na'im* (Nice and Pleasant, 1742) points in the same direction. In the realm of traditional studies Fränkel arranged for a magnificent new edition of Maimonides' codex *Mishneh Torah* (Repetition of the Law), which had not been reprinted in full since the Amsterdam edition of 1702. However, Fränkel's greatest literary achievement was his own major work, *Korban ha-edah* (Sacrifice of the Community, 1743–1760), a commentary on large parts of the Palestinian Talmud, which until then had never been interpreted systematically and in terms of textual criticism, since, for most questions of Jewish law, the Babylonian Talmud was accorded greater importance and authority. Fränkel's commentary broke fresh ground for Talmud studies, opening up a new scientific dimension. It is thus not surprising that this rabbi was the teacher and mentor of Moses Mendelssohn.

The Breslau businessman Rabbi Isaiah Berlin (1725–1799), renowned for his Talmudic learning, likewise combined rabbinic scholarship with source-critical methods in his research on the Talmud. The Berlin chief rabbi Hirschel Lewin (1721–1800) was head of a thriving yeshiva and well-read in secular literature as well. He admired Moses Mendelssohn and published an approbation, with detailed arguments, on *Alim li-terufah* (Leaves of Healing), the prospectus in which Mendelssohn announced his work on the Bible. Even Rabbi Jonathan Eybeschütz (1690–1764), who rejected the rationalistic tendency of the time, and whose own works, especially his famous commentaries on sections of the *Shulḥan Arukh* dealing with penal and ritual law, are still completely in the old traditional rabbinic style, respected Mendelssohn. In one of his homiletic treatises he noted emphatically, and with long-winded justification, that all sciences— mechanics, optics, astronomy, medicine, botany, chemistry, painting, logic, music, and law—are important for Torah study.[5] His exposition is vividly reminiscent of certain remarks by Italian rabbis, such as Judah Moscato, in the sixteenth century.

Rabbi Jacob Emden (1697–1776), one of the towering authorities of the eighteenth century, embodied an approach marked both by greater open-mindedness and a view still oriented to the clearly delineated limits of scientific pursuits. He was the son of Rabbi Tsevi Ashkenazi, author of the famous collection of responsa *Ḥakham Tsevi*, and had traveled far and wide with his father across Europe, from Hamburg-Altona to Amsterdam and Lemberg. In Saloniki and Belgrade Ashkenazi had become familiar with and developed enormous admiration for Sephardi culture; his interests broadened to languages, natural science, and philosophy. In his autobiography, in itself a rarity in the rabbinic world, Emden writes of himself that he was fluent not only in German, but in Dutch as well, and also had a passable knowledge of Latin. His hunger for learning was omnivorous: he had great interest in an array of subjects, including astronomy, physics, botany, medicine, the art of politics, and history. However, his support for scientific study had its limits. In one of his responsa he answers in the affirmative a medical student who had inquired as to whether his studies were permissible in the light of Halacha.[6] He made a strict distinction between areas of knowledge that

36   Jacob Emden, *Sefer ḥinukh* (1758–1762).
Representation of the three monotheistic faiths

were permissible in terms of Halacha, and that he himself was interested in, and philosophy, which he vehemently rejected on Jewish religious grounds. Consequently, he also spoke out denouncing the reprinting of Maimonides' works in Jessnitz, which he believed posed a threat to the purity of the religious faith of his contemporaries. This dividing line between the natural sciences and philosophy was already to be found in the Middle Ages among certain Jewish scholars who had a favorable attitude toward general education.

The motive Emden mentioned that lay behind his zeal for secular studies was the duty of every Jewish scholar to strive to be the equal of Christian scholars in general education. As generous as he was regarding the acquisition of general knowledge, and despite his tolerant view of Christianity, Emden was rigorous in his opposition to anything in Judaism that smacked to him of heresy, and he pursued every suspicion in his writings with an extreme single-mindedness. Yet he was certainly not overly strict in the observance of religious duties and protested against the "added stringencies being invented every day."[7] He was even critical of the classical work of the Kabbala, the *Zohar*, being the first rabbinic scholar to examine it from a text-critical perspective and coming to the conclusion that the ancient sacred text contained sections that had been interpolated centuries later.

Jacob Emden was also scathing in his criticism of the social contacts between Jews and Christians that were becoming more intensive at the time: "[Our Jewish contemporaries] are no longer mindful of the fact that they are in *galut* [exile]; they mingle with non-Jews, adopting their customs, and are a great disgrace. The holy seed mixes with the peoples of the earth."[8] In making this remark, Emden was probably thinking primarily of the limited circle of the court Jews. However, he himself shared some of the responsibility for this development. As a result of his uncommonly tolerant treatment of Christianity, mentioned earlier, he promoted an attitude toward non-Jews that was less encumbered by Jewish theological reservations than in the past.

Despite his recognition as a learned scholar, Emden's desire to have a formal appointment as rabbi met with only modest results. Although he was named communal rabbi in Emden in 1729, he remained in the post only four years and then lived as a private scholar in Altona. Emden was independently minded, a lone spirit who heedlessly expressed his clear-cut opinion at every opportunity, and thus had little prospect of emerging victorious in any contest where a rabbi was to be selected. It is apparent from his autobiography that, more than in the case of many other prominent contemporaries, the motives informing his thought and action were an amalgam of the objective and the personal. He was a Janus-faced figure: deeply bound to tradition, yet surprisingly flexible and progressive— very much a product of the new era.

In sum, Jews in the German-speaking lands were no longer inclined to isolate themselves in matters of culture to the same degree as they had in the early modern period. Since the influence of Lurianic Kabbala was certainly not conducive to an involvement with the general sciences, the varied and diverse phenomena included here under the concept of "scientific attitudes among the rabbis" are all the more remarkable. This scientific stance was still untouched by modern, historical-critical methods of research; nonetheless, it was marked by distinct traces of the impact of the spirit of the times. Undoubtedly, one contributing factor was the fact that Jewish and Christian scholars knew one another and had contacts of which only a small portion are documented. Although it would be mistaken to regard this new ideal of education among the rabbinical scholars as a rupture with traditional Jewish scholarship, nonetheless, especially with the turn away from Kabbala, one could see within it the seeds of the later "scientific study of Judaism," *Wissenschaft des Judentums.*

3. Venturing Into the Outside World

Just as the rabbis became more receptive to outside influences, so one can also discern a certain receptivity in broad circles of the Jewish communities to the non-Jewish culture of their environment. And, yet, this new open-mindedness did not lead to a break with the traditional lifestyle or to a distinct change in the conception of self.

Long after the middle of the eighteenth century all Jews still spoke the Western Yiddish dialect, a language very difficult for non-Jews to understand. For pupils in the Talmud schools the reading of German books as entertainment was forbidden, and it was also frowned upon in many strictly religious homes. Nonetheless, German newspapers (*Gazetten*) were widely read, and even Rabbi Jacob Emden permitted the reading of such papers, save for the business section, on the Sabbath.[9] Although most scholars, rabbis, and older persons still wore clothing in the traditional Jewish style, and Jews were often readily identifiable by their beards, head coverings, and the like, most urban Jews now dressed in the manner customary in the towns. Many Jewish men still used their own first name in combination with that of their father, yet by this time quite a few old established families had adopted a family name. In the seventeenth century a number of Jews had already been able to read and write letters in the German language—court Jews and others who had frequent dealings with non-Jewish society. In the eighteenth century, simply for reasons of business and legal necessity, every better-off merchant could read German and also knew a bit of Latin. In some circles of the rising Jewish middle class the knowledge of French was valued. When, in 1711, Jews were forced to seek temporary lodgings with Christians (this too a new development) after the great conflagration in the Frankfurt ghetto, they surprised many of their hosts by their level of general culture.

Gradually, German universities began to admit Jews to attendance at lectures and later on to the examinations as well—though only at Protestant universities. In Catholic territories, almost throughout the entire eighteenth century, Jews were excluded from university education, in accord with what the Basel Council had stipulated back in 1434. The small university in Frankfurt an der Oder was the first where Jews matriculated and were permitted to take degrees, including many Jewish students from Poland. The Prussian University of Halle, founded in 1694, was one of most heavily attended universities in German lands in the eighteenth century, and the number of Jewish students there was relatively large. Halle was a major center of tolerant Pietism, and since the university also had a strong pietistic tendency, it was favorably disposed toward the presence of Jewish students. Moreover, since its medical faculty was internationally renowned, medical students, which made up the preponderant majority of Jewish students, preferred Halle over other universities. Between 1724 and 1800 an estimated 150–180 Jews studied there; of these 59 were able to complete their studies with a doctorate in medicine. After Halle the second largest group of Jewish students was at the Berlin College of Medicine. Ever since its founding in 1737, the Hanoverian university in Göttingen—which rose to become the leading German university from the middle of the eighteenth century on—had accepted Jewish students without any restriction, virtually all of whom chose to study medicine.

There was considerable freedom of research and teaching, as well as religious tolerance, at the universities of Halle and Göttingen. This served to make it easier for Jewish students to study there, even though the missionary intention in admitting them was often patent. Another factor was the pietistic inclination toward the Old Testament and the Hebrew language, which is why Jewish scholars (some of them baptized Sabbatians) were engaged as teachers. They gave private lessons in Hebrew and Semitic languages to professors and students of theology and Semitic philology. However, this did nothing to alter the pronounced Christian character of the universities. For example, Jewish students were required to swear a Christian oath upon receiving their doctoral degree. They were also often forced to pay higher fees than others and to put up with harassment, abuse, and religious provocations. Jews who taught Hebrew at the university were expected to behave in a subservient manner toward every student; in terms of their status and remuneration they were on the bottom rung of employees. On the other hand, the Jewish communities in the university towns often provided for the needs of the university students, in a manner analogous to the traditional assistance granted to Talmud students. They also offered students the opportunity to further their Jewish knowledge concomitant with study of secular disciplines at the university.

There were excellent reasons why so many Jewish students in the pre-emancipatory period chose to study medicine. There had been Jewish physicians in Germany throughout the Middle Ages, even at the princely courts. Jews had always pursued the profession of medicine, since, in religious law, a high value was placed on caring for the sick and their healing. Consequently, it was easier for traditional Jewish society to accept medical study than any other profane disciplines. Yet external factors also favored the choice of medicine. In many localities it was no longer permitted to practice as a physician without the required academic training and degree. In addition, all the other courses of study led to professions that were closed to Jews. Medicine was different—even if leading thinkers, such as the founder of Pietism, Philip Jacob Spener, still felt that Christians should not seek out the services of Jewish doctors and midwives. Although in the sixteenth and seventeenth centuries Jewish students from Germany still found it necessary to go to Italy and Holland to study, medical faculties by the eighteenth century were increasingly open to Jewish applicants. However, since other faculties were initially closed, even young Jews who preferred to study philosophy, mathematics, and natural sciences had to register as students of medicine. This probably accounts for the fact that many of the first Jewish scholars to devote themselves to other secular disciplines possessed a university degree in medicine.

According to his own report, Tobias Cohn Harofe ("the Doctor,"

1652–1729) from Metz was one of the first two Jewish students to attend a German university, namely, in Frankfurt an der Oder. In 1678, when he had sent a written request to the great elector for admission, the latter not only approved the request but even granted him an annual stipend. Cohn later wrote an encyclopedia of medicine and the natural sciences in Hebrew, *Ma'ase Tovyah* (The Work of Tobias, 1707), reprinted in Jessnitz in 1742. He was principally active as a court physician in Turkey. Asher (Anselm) Worms (1695–1759), who was a doctor in Frankfurt am Main, had a broad general knowledge and was well-versed in Jewish literature. He was the author of a tripartite work on the tradition of the biblical text (Masora), entitled *Seyag la-Torah* (Fence Around the Torah, 1766), but was not regarded as a rabbinic scholar in the traditional sense. In his youth he published a mathematics textbook in Hebrew, *Mafte'aḥ ha-algebrah ha-ḥadashah* (Key to Modern Algebra, 1721), referring to himself there as "candidate for the rabbinate, for medicine and philosophy, and student in the Frankfurt Klaus."[10] Despite his secular education, Jonas Jeitteles (1735–1806), the Prague physician and scholar, did not disdain tradition, so that Rabbi Ezekiel Landau, the chief rabbi of Prague, had no reservations about striking up a close friendship with him. Yet Jewish physicians were foci of profane learning within the communities, and circles of those hungry for knowledge often formed around them. Thus a strictly conservative community such as Fürth was understandably cautious: on one occasion it employed a community doctor only on condition that he maintain a traditionally Jewish external appearance—that is, grow a beard and set aside his wig and sword.

The aspirations among the Jewish intelligentsia for knowledge beyond the perimeter of Jewish religion, especially when it came to learning German, were often preceded by external pressure and material necessity. The *Judenordnung* of George II of Hesse-Darmstadt (1629) had already stipulated that promissory notes over twenty guldens had to be written in German. During the seventeenth century regulations of this kind appeared in many localities. In 1728 and 1737 the granting of letters of protection in Hesse-Darmstadt was not only made conditional on the proof of minimal assets of six hundred guldens but also on language skills, that is, the ability to read and write proper German—and not Yiddish, which was considered disreputable as an inferior jargon and thieves' argot. Court Jews, whose relatives and servants were in daily business contact with Christians, as well as the many Jewish peddlers in the countryside, were all constrained for practical reasons to learn

German. The Jewish entrepreneurs and manufactory owners had to conform to the values of the state and bourgeois society and to acquire the requisite knowledge for business in their field.

How the needs of occupational life impelled Jewish merchants to become informed on mundane topics that were indispensable for the practice of their profession is illustrated by the almanacs (*luḥot*) that began to appear regularly from the middle of the eighteenth century. These almanacs contained lists of the fairs and markets with their exact dates in the Christian calendar, the birthdays of the sovereigns (extremely important dates for the many court factors), meteorological and astrological forecasts, medical advice, and much more. All this was in addition to the basic function of the calendar to provide exact information on the religious-ritual cycle of the Jewish year, such as the dates of the new moon, festivals and fast days, precise times for the beginning and end of the Sabbath, etc. The basic tone and tenor of the almanacs was pious, with no trace of an enlightened spirit. They were a faithful reflection of the intellectual and social situation of a Jewish society that, though still totally contained within the framework of Jewish tradition, was now increasingly exposed to non-Jewish cultural and social influences.

Change originated, to a significant degree, with the Portuguese communities, especially in Hamburg and Amsterdam, the latter a community often visited by merchants from Germany. A Sephardi community had also been established in Vienna after the Peace of Passarowitz (1718) between Austria and the Ottoman Empire, which granted all Ottoman subjects, regardless of religion, freedom of movement in Austria and the right to engage in trade there. As a consequence, Ottoman Jews—in contrast with those Ashkenazi Jews who did not belong to the circle of the court Jews—were free to settle in Vienna and engage in commerce and trade. Private prayer rooms were soon established there, forming the nucleus of a Sephardi religious association (1736) that continued in existence down into the twentieth century.

Thus Ashkenazi Jews had ample opportunity to observe a Jewish tradition that, unlike their own, had never excluded science, philosophy, and even art. Although the Hamburg Portuguese community was not the equal of its illustrious counterpart in Amsterdam, it too could boast physicians, scholars, linguists, poets, and philosophers; in Hamburg, as well, the Sephardi Jews developed a vibrant and intense intellectual life. The Christian faith of many educated Portuguese, adopted under duress, had shaken their religious foundations to the core and made room for a measure of secularization that led in the seventeenth century to serious internal and external conflicts. Thus, for example, in 1627 the Amsterdam Jew Uriel Acosta (1585–1640), who was opposed to all religious authority, was placed under the ban in Hamburg, where he had lived for a time, and became the focus of continuing discord.

Proud of their tradition and way of life, the Sephardim regarded themselves as the social and cultural equals of the Christian world around them. Ashkenazi Jews who came in contact with their Sephardi brethren often admired their community and felt the urge to criticize their own. The aesthetics and good manners that prevailed in the Portuguese synagogue, their urbane sophistication and penchant for philosophy, were highly seductive for many Ashkenazi Jews. In particular, they were intrigued by the well-organized school system of the Sephardim, which took the demands of professional life into consideration and avoided teaching methods that were not conducive to learning the skills useful for practical life. Yet self-criticism in the Ashkenazi community was often also a consequence of growing contacts with the non-Jewish culture and their tendency toward a more positive evaluation of the Gentiles. "What will the goyim [non-Jews] say?" was the question many an Ashkenazi Jew asked himself in view of the uncouth behavior, noisy commotion, and lack of formal structure that had established themselves in numerous synagogues. A short path led from that point to the insight that the synagogue was in need of renewal.

4. Social Problems Within and at the Periphery of the Communities

In the course of the eighteenth century Jewish commerce gradually lost its earlier importance for German economic life. State policy, especially in Prussia, favored local manufactories and restricted foreign trade by means of export prohibitions and high tariffs. This deprived a significant segment of the rising Jewish entrepreneurial class of its former economic basis. A social stratification evolved and a widening gap between the poor and the wealthy. An ever larger proportion of German Jewry sank to the level of paupers. Despite the absence of extensive occupational differences, the rise of a numerically still small Jewish upper middle class contrasted with the growth of a Jewish underclass. In many towns the Jewish merchant class, already economically independent, increasingly adopted bourgeois features. Yet the typical image in the eyes of the Christian bourgeoisie—a perception that would become highly significant for the later course of emancipation—was that of the "beggar Jew," the *Betteljude*.

The overwhelming majority of Jews belonged to the poorer economic classes; the living conditions of roughly 25 percent of the Jews resembled those of the German lower middle class. At most, some 20 percent were well-to-do; at the extremes, economic misery stood counterposed to considerable affluence. Conspicuous wealth was in evidence, particularly among the court Jews, who together with their retinue made up at most only 2 to 3 percent of Jews in the German lands. However, decisive social differences were often based more on legal status than material possessions. For example, there were four "classes" (*Stände*) of Jews in Bohemia, whose rank ordering was linked to rights connected to the ownership of real estate: 1. home owners with an unlimited right to trade, 2. leaseholders with limited trading rights, 3. tenants without trading rights, and 4. servants without any legal rights whatsoever. Fundamental to the internal social stratification was a bifurcation into two groupings. On the one hand, there were dealers in goods and money granted special privileges by the authorities (and from whose ranks the intellectual leadership was recruited). On the other, there were those dependent for their livelihood and residence permit on the former: private tutors, male and female servants, and community employees. This class division was often very sharp and sanctioned in community regulations. Thus, for example, the wealthy in Frankfurt were permitted a larger number of festive meals at a wedding than were the "middle" classes.

Since indigent Jews, as a rule, were not accepted into the communities as members with full rights, the figure for the average income of members was rather high. However, it is difficult to construct an accurate statistical picture since the comparative numerical relation between rich and poor Jews fluctuated from year to year. In general, there was a demonstrable process of progressive impoverishment. Thus, for example, in Halberstadt, where most of the 117 Jewish families owned their own homes in 1699, the number of Jews in need of support increased from year to year, especially on account of the influx of poor Jews from outside the city. The result was that in 1740 one-quarter of the Jews in Halberstadt were unable to pay their levies. The migration of penurious Jews into the communities continued, despite many drastic ordinances issued by the authorities to stem the flow. Poor Jews were also not always welcomed with open arms by the Jewish residents. The communities were always prepared to help out temporarily, but they were less inclined to offer permanent residence and opportunities for employment. People feared competition as well as opposition from the Christian population. In addition, entire communities now had to bear collective responsibility in all cases of bankruptcy and business failure. As a result, they were left with little choice but to prevent the influx of Jews with no visible means of support and to banish destitute Jews from the town.

Social distress was relieved in part by private initiative and in part by the community administration. The orphans' home in Fürth, donated in 1763 by a private businessman, was the first of its kind in Germany. Jews in transit and the poor who lived in a given town were usually housed by the community in a poorhouse. At the community office they could also obtain so-called vouchers (*Pletten*, from *Billetten*, tickets), that is, a written order for accommodation, entitling them to lodging and board at the home of a member of the community. Members were obliged to take their turn in housing the needy for a short period and providing meals for students if there was a local yeshiva. In many communities, both large and small, this system of Pletten was a well-organized and effective welfare institution. For example, the responsible Jewish community official (the *Plettengabbe* or "voucher manager") of the community in Gochsheim near Karlsruhe, which consisted of only 26 families, distributed 1,650 vouchers in a single year, while the larger community in Schnaittach passed out nearly 10,000. Although only those beggars and needy who had an honest reputation were allowed to partake of the benefits of this institution, their numbers were always large. They would equip themselves with letters of recommendation from the rabbi or lay leader of their permanent place of residence and then make the rounds of the communities in order to feed their families or accumulate a dowry for their daughters.

The Jewish poorhouses, at times praised by sympathetic Christian observers as especially progressive institutions, provided care mainly for the local elderly, sick, women, and children. Poor Jews from outside the community were questioned after arrival about their assets and, in the case of a negative decision by community officials, were forced to move on. Those who were permitted to stay enjoyed the community's hospitality but continued to be treated as outsiders. In Hamburg, for example, all aliens—the indigent and transient, servants and foreign teachers—were buried in a special cemetery. Nor were they allowed to marry within the communities. Moreover, according to a Hamburg community statute of 1726, it was prohibited to collect funds publicly from community members to assist local or nonlocal poor, although the injunction proved difficult to implement in practice. A broad stratum of Jews with few or no means, including a large number of private tutors, female domestics in every family, and community employees, often eked out their livelihood in extreme misery.

Some 10 percent of the total Jewish population in Germany in the eighteenth century was made up of vagrants and itinerants with no fixed residence; in Franconia and Swabia they probably even accounted for more than a quarter of the total. This development had been abetted in particular by the oppressive Jewry policy with its diverse restrictions on Jewish settlement, mounting taxes, and rules excluding Jews from commerce and artisan crafts. It was compounded after the pogroms of 1648 by the immigration of an entire class of homeless and impoverished Jews from Poland, estimated at between ten and fifteen thousand persons. Given such conditions, it is not surprising that the Betteljude became a frequent phenomenon and one that took on ever more ugly forms. Thus, simultaneous with the rise of court Jewry, a large segment of German Jews at the opposite end of the social scale declined into "Jewish beggary." Faced with the staggering social problem presented by mendicancy, a rabbi in the eighteenth century wrote, "There are countless poor; hundreds, thousands of them are hanging about everywhere."[11]

Betteljuden, an official term at the time, were described as "vagabonding casual workers without a letter of protection, surrounded by suspicion and subjected to regimentation from all sides."[12] From the beginning of the eighteenth century we hear of edicts against "vagabond beggar Jews." In many principalities they were not permitted entry, and they were driven from Prussia in 1750. Many such Jews were tramps who had no other occupation—they had, so to speak, inherited their way of life. Since they were not accepted into the communities, they had no chance of improving their economic situation. The community regulations stipulated that they be compelled to move on as soon as possible so that they would not become a long-term burden on the hospitality of community members. To assure this, a Jewish guard was posted at city gates. A further decline was unavoidable: from mendicancy down into the depths of acute social distress where prostitution and illegitimate children became common phenomena. And, from there, in turn, it was but a short step into the underworld of criminal activity.

Poverty and a lack of legal status were not the only causes that could result in a life of crime—even the widespread occupation of peddling was

a possible avenue to criminal activity. Although peddlers had a fixed residence, they were constantly traveling through the countryside. Barely
scraping together enough to support their families, they often spent the
night in out-of-the-way lodgings and easily became involved with dubi-
ous company. This phenomenon intensified during the eighteenth century, but its roots extend back to the period of the great persecutions of
the mid-fourteenth century. Already from that era there is documentation of itinerant Jewish beggars, tramps, and impoverished Jewish
vagrants who joined bands of thieves and robbers. A picture of this development can be gained in particular from linguistic research on German
"thieves' cant" (*Rotwelsch*), a secret argot with a number of very clear
Jewish lexical traces. The first published dictionary of this jargon, the
Liber Vagatorum (1510), already contains a small vocabulary derived
from Hebrew and Yiddish. A list of expressions used by a Christian gang
and recorded by the police in 1687 provides a lexicon some 20 percent of
which could only have originated from Jewish vernacular speech, even
though few Jews (or even none) belonged to this specific gang. Despite
such usage, only a Jew who himself was (or had been) a member of such
a gang could understand the Jewish jargon of thieves.

Initially, Jewish criminals were only found in Christian gangs of
thieves, but in the eighteenth century a growing number of independent
Jewish robber bands appeared, which, in turn, occasionally also had
Christian members. The participation of Jews in German gangs proved a
source of surprise for Christian society, since this clashed with the passive
endurance of suffering otherwise ubiquitously associated with Jews and
their traditional image. The technical accomplishment and mastery
demonstrated by Jewish thieves in burglaries of well-protected houses
and factories caused considerable amazement, the more so since Jews were
still excluded from all artisan crafts. The police were even more impressed
by how difficult it was to penetrate the Jewish gangs, by their circumspect
planning, and by the disciplined execution of their projects. Their proven
powers of physical resistance under torture were likewise formidable. The
general opinion was that Jewish criminals were more dangerous than others, because they were more crafty and devious. They were bound
together by closer ties and, because they were more mobile than the
Christian outlaws, they could elude justice more easily. The territorial
fragmentation of Germany obstructed the effective pursuit of the gangs,
which were always able to escape over some border. Northern and western Germany were the principal terrain in which Jewish gang activity was

concentrated; Hamburg and Altona were among the main bases. The fact that there were fewer Jewish gangs operating in southern Germany was probably due to the relative economic backwardness of the region and to the lack of large cities. The wealthy bourgeoisie and the growing industrial base in the north and west offered greater enticement.

What were the relations between these Jewish gangs and respectable Jewish society? In the first place, it should be noted that, despite all their depravity, members of the Jewish robber bands lived as Jews and generally adhered to traditional Jewish lifestyles and customs. As a rule, they did not undertake any expeditions on the Sabbath and kept the dietary laws. For the most part, the Jewish robbers were married, had children, and, if they had the right of residence, returned from their raids to their families, as others might come back home from a business trip. Their family life did not differ substantially from that of their respectable fellow Jews and was in distinct contrast with the practice of concubinage customary among most Christian outlaws. Jewish criminals clung to their faith even at the gallows, although they might at least have mitigated their fate by baptism. Their steadfastness was acknowledged even by settled, law-abiding Jews. Still, they were largely isolated from the community, and, already in 1675, a regulation of the community in Frankfurt am Main notes that "the rabbis of Germany have banished and excommunicated the itinerant thieves and excluded them from all that is sacred and holy in Israel."[13] Although it was strictly prohibited to engage in commerce with such persons or to offer them lodgings for the night, it is reported that they often visited the synagogue. They intermarried almost exclusively among themselves, so that an expert could write in the nineteenth century: "I believe I can prove by means of a genealogical table that at least several hundred of the most notorious Jewish bandits now alive form one single family."[14]

Jewish thieves stole not only from Christians; in fact, Jews were the preferred victims of some individual bandits. For that reason Jews resident in localities near the scene of a crime sometimes turned willing informants. On the other hand, there were Jewish fences for stolen goods and landlords who, because they were ready to arrange a hiding place for their larcenous coreligionists, facilitated the remarkable mobility. There is also evidence attesting to the cooperation of Jewish gangs with settled agents (wire pullers, called *Baldober*, from Hebr. *ba'al ha-davar*, lit. "master of the affair"). In one instance, even a court factor, Mendel Garbe in Meiningen, was arrested and subsequently executed for his indirect role in the robbery of a gold and silver factory by a Jewish gang. Some Jewish thieves underwent baptism, though not many. One did it so as not to be deported from Berlin, but continued to live secretly as a Jew and attend the synagogue.

Strange as it may sound, precisely in this milieu of robber gangs a form of cooperation evolved between Christians and Jews that was based on complete equality. Beyond this, the Jewish gang members, for all of their lawlessness and depravity, presented the image of a new type of Jew, one who was—paradoxically—self-emancipated. Court Jews and Jewish bandits indeed had this in common, that each in their own way attempted to overcome the pariah status of the Jew, offering defiance to a society that rejected them. The police officials often noted that a Jewish thief spoke "pure" German (probably meaning the local dialect) or standard German with only a slight Jewish accent. But for the Jews in Germany, their brethren who had strayed into a life of crime were both a terrible reality and an abiding burden. They also helped shape the distorted image of the Jew as unworthy of calling Germany his home.

Another marginal group consisted of those Jews who decided to convert. It would be an exaggeration to speak of a large movement toward baptism before the end of the eighteenth century. In fact, Christian contemporaries were sometimes astonished at the small number of conversions to Christianity despite the oppressive situation most Jews found themselves in—a plight from which they could rapidly have escaped via baptism. Nonetheless, the number of conversions increased toward the end of the seventeenth century, and in the following century it mounted into the hundreds. Only a small segment of these converts came from the ranks of the wealthy and learned; most were beggars or robbers condemned to death who could save their lives by conversion. In Bohemia and Moravia the familiants legislation, aimed at limiting the growth of the Jewish population, played an important part in the movement for baptism among the lower Jewish social strata.

Toward the end of the eighteenth century the picture changed: while, in the past, Jews who went the route of baptism came mainly from a lower social and cultural milieu, those interested in changing their faith now came increasingly from prosperous and educated circles, especially the families of court Jews. There were almost no candidates for conversion from the socially more insulated middle class. One convert said that in his case it was the "constant contact with Christians" that had induced him to be baptized.[15] Yet even converted Jews were viewed with suspicion by

Christian society. Characteristic of the reserved attitude toward them is a 1769 letter by the Prussian king in which he remarks that "only rarely among the Jews is the change of religion sincere and undertaken for honest reasons."[16]

5. The Gradual Decline in Jewish Communal Autonomy

The struggle for the autonomy of the Jewish community in Germany was originally an internal Jewish dispute involving an attempt to prevent interference by external Jewish authorities in the powers of the local community and its rabbinate. After the establishment of the Council of the Four Lands in Poland in the sixteenth century, the struggle was often waged against this body, which regarded itself as the supreme Ashkenazi authority. On various occasions, rabbis and communities in Germany had protested against meddling by the council in their local affairs. In some circles, however, the *Va'ad arba ha-aratsot* was regarded as a court of appeal, and generally it intervened only if German communities called upon it to do so. Such was the case, for example, when the Hamburg Ashkenazi community became embroiled in a suit in 1660 with the community in Altona about the right to own its own cemetery.

Increasingly, however, the communities saw themselves under threat from a much more powerful party—the state. Analogous to its policy vis-à-vis other corporate bodies, such as the guilds and estates, the absolutist state attempted to dissolve Jewish self-governance. The notions of raison d'état and the sovereignty of the ruler displaced all previous political theories and religious ideologies. Religion was transformed from a guiding principle into a welcome instrument of domination. Consequently, in the age of Enlightenment the interference of the state in the autonomy of the community became regular policy. It was based on the theory of natural law, which postulated the direct relation between the state and the individual subject as a fundamental principle. However, the attitude of the absolutist prince toward Jewish autonomy was complex, shaped by a variety of conflicting interests. On the one hand, such autonomy contradicted the conception of the centralist state and its opposition to corporate bodies of any kind. On the other hand, the ruler did not wish to abandon this tried and tested machinery of taxation, which relieved him of the necessity to collect the taxes of each protected Jew individually. For that reason the princes did nothing to destroy the organizational frame of community administration, while systematically curtailing all the internal functions of autonomy that were unrelated to taxation.

In a highly effective manner the policies of the absolutist state accelerated the decline of the Jewish communal corporate body as an independent administrative authority. Many governments, in particular that in Brandenburg-Prussia, created a special supervisory organ (the *Judenkommissionen* already mentioned) to watch over community governance. They also sent trusted agents to attend all Jewish court proceedings and meetings and report to the government on everything transacted there. Many functions of the territorial rabbinate were gradually transferred to the central state administration. Although the government recognized the community administration as a Jewish authority, it was now seen principally as a conduit in the communication and channeling of its orders to the community members. The government did not countenance independent action by the community leadership, not even when matters were involved where the government was in total agreement with their content. After the Frankfurt community passed a dress code in 1715 in order to curb extravagant expenditures on clothes (municipal ordinances of a similar nature had been issued for the Christian burghers as well), the city intervened and imposed a fine on the board—since it had been so presumptuous as to preempt legislative authority.

37 Johann Jakob Schudt, *Neue Franckfurter Jüdische Kleider-Ordnung*
(New Frankfurt Jewish Dress Code, 1716)

Governments even intervened in purely religious matters, especially when differences arose within a community—such as who should blow the shofar in the synagogue on the New Year or whether the rabbi was allowed to introduce a small change in religious services. Such interference was more common in the larger states in northern and eastern Germany; in the ecclesiastical territories in the southwest, and especially in tiny principalities and areas administered by imperial knights of the lower nobility, the Jewish communities and *Landjudenschaften* retained a greater degree of self-government and autonomy.

With the onset of the early modern period instances of state interference in the appointment of local rabbis multiplied everywhere, while the size of individual rabbinate districts was increasingly reduced. The authorities also meddled in the elections for community board members. During a fierce dispute that rocked the Frankfurt community in the period from 1615 to 1628 regarding the composition of the lay board, the magistrate, on its own initiative, constituted the board anew, even appointing some of its members. After one of the parties to the altercation appealed to the Council of the Four Lands, it issued a strongly worded protest stating that such interference in the right of self-determination for Jews was unprecedented. In 1722 in Königsberg King Frederick William I directly appointed the rabbi and the four parnasim. In 1729, when a vacancy arose in the Berlin rabbinate, the elders received a royal directive, unexpectedly and without evident reason, to elect a young man from Leipnik as community rabbi. Protest by the elders proved of no avail.

Only on rare occasions in the Middle Ages had there been interference with the autonomy of the rabbinical court. In the early modern period the power of the judiciary had been preserved for the simple reason that the state authorities did not wish to be bothered by the internal squabbles of the Jews. Despite this, litigation by Jews against one another before secular courts became ever more common, even in questions of religious law and custom. That factor contributed to the weakening of rabbinical authority within the communities. But the decisive element in hastening the decline of rabbinical jurisdiction, and thus the power of the rabbis, was the restriction of the competency and effective domain of the Jewish judiciary imposed by the absolutist state. Even if relevant legislation in the numerous German territories was anything but uniform, the tendency to curtail the powers of the Jewish courts was common to all, aside from a few exceptions, such as Fürth.

The new Jewry regulation in Hamburg in 1710 made Jewish divorce dependent on a decision in the Christian courts; it prescribed Christian guardians for Jewish orphans along with the Jewish guardians appointed by the rabbis, and restricted Jewish jurisdiction in cases involving marriage and inheritance. The authority of the rabbinical court, previously binding on all community members, was increasingly reduced to that of a court of arbitration whose authority rested upon the assent of both parties. The privileges and ordinances issued by the Prussian crown in these matters were, for a time, neither consistent nor uniform. When Rabbi David Fränkel was appointed to the rabbinate of Berlin in 1743, he received express confirmation of his rabbinical jurisdiction and as chief rabbi of the Kurmark Landjudenschaft he was granted the right in 1751 to punish recalcitrants. The Breslau chief territorial rabbi Jonas Joseph Fränkel, whom the king had granted a general charter with rights equivalent to those of Christian merchants because of his extensive trade connections abroad, was given jurisdiction in connection with small cases. However, the Prussian General Jewry Code of 1730 in most instances permitted the rabbi to engage in only the amicable arbitration of disputes. Finally, the General Code of 1750 eliminated the jurisdiction of rabbis "in civil cases . . . since the rabbi and elders are not entitled to any genuine jurisdiction" and accorded their judgments merely the character of legal opinions.[17]

Already at the beginning of the eighteenth century the experienced and worldly wise chief rabbi of Schaumburg-Lippe was well aware of the decline of the Jewish court: "It is widely known that we dwell in the midst of the nations and are not authorized to pass judgment in accordance with the laws of our religion. This is especially true in the small towns and villages, where our brethren are scattered."[18]

Even where the jurisdictional powers of rabbinical courts had been retained, the parties to the action could appeal against their verdicts to the general secular courts. Often, Jewish courts lacked the power to carry out their judgments, even where rabbinical administration of justice had continued in force. In order to enable Christian judges to adjudicate in cases between Jews in accordance with Jewish law, the Prussian government in 1778 ordered the chief rabbi Hirschel Lewin to prepare a German compendium of Jewish laws pertaining to inheritance, wills, guardianship, and marriage insofar as they concerned rights of ownership. The book, written with the assistance of Moses Mendelssohn, bore the misleading title *Die Ritualgesetze der Juden* (Jewish Ritual Laws).

There is no doubt that this development was directed against the rabbis and had indeed already been discernible in the early history of court Jewry. To a certain extent, the court Jew (often also himself serving as rabbi) replaced the imperial or territorial rabbi in the eyes of the sovereign. The fact that the monarch gave preference to the court Jew for the position of chief rabbi or head parnas was undoubtedly due to the special position he enjoyed as the most prominent Jewish personality but was in all likelihood equally influenced by the general secularization of state governance and efforts to negate and eliminate the purported "domination by the rabbis." In Christian eyes the rabbis epitomized much that was despicable about the Jews. This was probably one of the reasons why, according to a Prussian law of 1712, Jews with the title of rabbi were prohibited from entering the state along with beggar Jews and schoolmasters. The attitude is further illustrated by the fact that rabbis were not excused from the ancient and humiliating practice of the Jewry Oath, which was exacted, for example, from the Berlin chief rabbi Hirschel Lewin when he assumed office in 1773.

The rabbis' prerogative to impose a ban with the approval of the community board had been the quintessence of their power since time immemorial. It was thus to be expected that the absolutist state would endeavor to bring about its elimination. Rabbis now retained the right to issue a *herem* solely in connection with disputes in the synagogue, and, even then, they could only exercise it together with the elders, contingent on permission from the authorities. The Prussian Jewry Code of 1730 still contains the regulation that a Jew, with the knowledge of the authorities, could be excommunicated without any restriction. However, the Code of 1750 prohibits even the so-called secret ban against Jews whose behavior is "not in keeping with the views and wishes" of the rabbi and the elders—that is, punishment for religious transgressions.

6. Internal Weakening of Rabbinical and Community Authority

The restriction and ultimate elimination of rabbinical supervision over the community and of rabbinical legal jurisdiction was a postulate of the modern state. It far preceded the modern currents within Judaism that swept away the traditional community power structure. However, it is evident that even the internal standing of the community leadership was already in question here and there in the seventeenth and eighteenth century and had begun to totter. The oligarchical composition of the community boards and their autocratic regimes provoked repeated opposition and unrest among community members. The struggles over elections to the lay board led in some cases to virtual anarchy. With the ever heavier burden of taxes, squabbles erupted between individuals and the community or Landjudenschaft. The slandering and persecution of the Prague rabbi, Yomtov Lipmann Heller, was initiated by community members who felt their interests had been damaged by his allocation of taxes. The preference of many sovereigns to entrust the leadership of the communities to their court Jews, who then often acted high-handedly on their own, marked a further weakening of community self-determination and the authority of elected community organs. One consequence was that community members now pursued their religious, social, and intellectual needs in semiprivate associations.

The dependence of the rabbis on the community board played into the hands of the antirabbinical tendency among the authorities. Even in the exercise of their religious office rabbis were not independent, and their rights of jurisdiction were also challenged by elements in the Jewish community. It occurred, for example, that a rabbi announced in the synagogue the threat of a possible penalty if certain religious rules were not observed. The board thereupon pointed out to him that he had no right to issue any instructions without its consent, and took the occasion to further inform him that he was not entitled on his own to appoint a scribe for ritual purposes or to extend the contract with the ritual slaughterer. If influential factions or persons in the community so desired, rabbis were harassed and removed from office. To be sure, some rabbis enjoyed exceptional status—those who were great scholars and widely admired personalities—but even they were not safe from provocations. At times tensions arose surrounding the rabbi if he had come from Poland and was unfamiliar with local custom or had scant regard for established minhagim. An even more critical attitude prevailed in some partially acculturated circles toward the many *heder* teachers who had come from Poland. Not only was their Eastern Yiddish dialect difficult for the children to understand, but they were not always greatly pious or learned.

The zeitgeist, decisively stamped by mercantilist and physiocratic ideas, viewed churchmen and the clergy as politically and economically useless figures. That anticlerical spirit also penetrated into Jewish circles and contributed to diminishing the standing of the rabbinate as an insti-

תואר פני הרב המאור הגדול ה"ה מו"ה יהונתן אייבעשיץ זצ"ל
רב דק"ק אלטנא מקדם בפראג.

JONATHAN EYBSCHÜZER

Ober-Rabbiner zu Altona

Verlag u. Eigenthum v. Wolf Pascheles Prag.

38 Jonathan Eybeschütz (Eybschüzer),
rabbi of Altona-Hamburg-Wandsbek

tution and of the individual rabbis. Another compounding factor was that rabbis, even the most respected, had faults that would come to light and evoke disapprobation among community members. Thus people spoke disparagingly about the nepotism and venality that had become common practice in the filling of vacant rabbinical posts. They talked for hours, and not very respectfully, about the latest reports from the scene of bitter controversies that raged between and about various rabbis.

Among these controversies the so-called amulet dispute between Jacob Emden and Jonathan Eybeschütz that erupted around the middle of the eighteenth century took on a special importance. Far more than in the case of earlier disputes, it was waged with the active participation of the entire rabbinate in Europe and thus provoked an unprecedented impassioned echo in the communities. When Eybeschütz became chief rabbi of the triple community Altona-Hamburg-Wandsbek in 1750, both he and Jacob Emden, who lived in Altona, had eminent reputations in the Jewish world. Soon after Eybeschütz took up his new post, Emden accused him of Sabbatian leanings. The evidence consisted of amulets that had been written by Eybeschütz. Many rabbis gave women amulets upon request to protect them against childbed fever—a common malady to which many mothers still succumbed at that time. There was thus nothing suspicious in preparing such amulets. But the accusation against Eybeschütz was that his amulets contained hidden allusions to Shabbetai Tsevi and his alleged magical healing power. Emden's father, Tsevi Ashkenazi (Ḥakham Tsevi), had been a staunch opponent of Sabbatianism and its adherents, and his son continued the struggle. His press printed no less than twenty-four polemical tracts against Eybeschütz and the Sabbatian heresy.

Both the community leaders and the Hamburg senate disapproved of Emden's high-handed actions against the chief rabbi, regarding them as interference in their area of competence. The King of Denmark, under whose protection Jewish jurisdiction was exercised and to whom Eybeschütz appealed for help, also offered him his support. Emden was, as a result, forced to leave Altona for a time. Rabbis of large communities abroad, including Lublin and Nikolsburg, placed a ḥerem on opponents of Eybeschütz. The Council of the Four Lands in Poland dealt with the case and, in the autumn of 1753, after some initial hesitation, acquitted Eybeschütz of all charges by a majority decision and ordered all polemical pamphlets published against him to be burned. In Frankfurt am Main the dispute poured oil on the flames of the partisan struggle, discussed earlier, that had split the community into two hostile camps. The chief rabbi there, Jacob Joshua Falk, was one of the leading personalities convinced of Eybeschütz's guilt and called on him to repent. This call, which was made public without Falk's knowledge, antagonized the many supporters of Eybeschütz in the community and Falk had to leave the city. The controversy about whether or not Eybeschütz was a Sabbatian reflected the deep dismay engendered by the suspicion that a universally respected rabbi, despite his attachment to the Torah, should nonetheless have allowed himself to be led astray into such heretical beliefs.

Although there are few contemporary sources documenting the amulet dispute's major role in weakening rabbinical authority, there can be no doubt that the splits it engendered within community boards and in the rabbinate caused lasting damage to these institutions. A major factor was the unprecedented manner in which Emden had personally insulted the Hamburg chief rabbi, attempting to vilify Eybeschütz and degrade him in the eyes of his many admirers and readers of his works. The frequent use of the rabbinical power of the ban against men who were suspected of sympathizing with Sabbatianism—not just in the amulet controversy but in a host of other cases as well—diminished the effect of this means for preserving rabbinical authority. A rabbinate divided against itself and rent by internal quarrels and hostilities was hardly in a position to forcefully confront the challenges of Enlightenment.

In the controversy surrounding the "Cleves *get*" in 1766–1767, rabbis and rabbinical courts from various communities likewise fought against each other with fierce antagonism. The matter in dispute was the validity of a divorce letter (*get*) from the hand of a man who had not been of sound mind at the time of the divorce. The rabbi in Cleves maintained that the divorce was valid—contrary to the opinion expressed by others, especially the rabbis in Frankfurt, who were absolutely convinced that their position was the correct one. In addition, the Frankfurt rabbis insisted they had the sole judicial competence to deal with the matter. Both affairs, the Hamburg amulet controversy and the Cleves divorce, undoubtedly had a detrimental effect on the standing of the rabbinate. Moreover, the amulet controversy strengthened the already mentioned tendency of German Jews to turn away from mysticism and heightened their readiness to participate in the Enlightenment.

In conclusion, it should be emphasized that the Jews, a number of whom had attained high levels of culture and education during the period treated here, were still remote from the Haskalah (the Jewish Enlightenment) understood as a historical concept. The Haskalah signified more than an open-minded cultural attitude and growing social contact with Christian circles. Above all, it marked a change in self-understanding regarding the primacy of Jewish tradition, which had previously been unquestioned. In the period before Mendelssohn, that shift had not yet occurred. To be sure, there were already certain tendencies toward convergence with Christian society and assimilation on two social planes: within the high-placed circles of the court Jews and, far below, in the shady demimonde of Jewish beggars and bandits. Biting critique of various phenomena in Jewish society had appeared, seeming to herald the transition to a new era. Yet most Jewish scholars, as well as the vast majority of community members outside learned circles, did not deviate from traditional Jewish norms and ideals. Their self-conception continued to be that of a group religiously and nationally set apart, whose allegiance was to the observance of religious law.

Part Two
The Jewish Enlightenment

9 | Beginnings of the Haskalah

1. The Setting

Not until the second half of the eighteenth century, when Europe and Germany already stood under the full impact of the late Enlightenment, did a nucleus of adherents of *Aufklärung,* known as maskilim, emerge within Jewish society. Inspired by the European Enlightenment, they initiated a parallel Jewish movement, the Haskalah (from Hebr. *le-haskil,* "enlighten, clarify with the aid of the intellect"), a term that illuminates the common ground shared by both currents. Berlin was its point of origin. It was there that the leading figure of the Jewish Enlightenment, the philosopher Moses Mendelssohn (1729–1786), lived and worked from 1743 until his death. His creativity and activity stand at the very heart of this intellectual movement.

As described at the end of part 1, the seeds of enlightenment were already discernible before Mendelssohn, but they did not fuse into a sociocultural movement powerful enough to effect a major shift in consciousness until the middle of the eighteenth century. Prerequisite was the creation of a social domain where, beyond the pale of the coercive power of normative Judaism, Jews could meet on a secular plane to engage in critical thought and work. The result proved to be more than a fleeting flare-up of ideas supported by a few isolated individuals. The coming together of Jewish intellectuals not identical with the rabbinical elite, men who scrutinized the Jewish religion, its laws and way of life, on the basis of Enlightenment ideas, catalyzed a necessary process of ferment. The stage was set for a confrontation between innovators and their opponents, and forces were set free that pushed unceasingly in the direction of a restructuring of Jewish society.

The initiators of this turn were children of the old Jewish community; without exception, they had all had a highly traditional education. Mendelssohn, born in Dessau, capital of the tiny principality of Anhalt and home to only a few dozen Jewish families around 1729, was brought up by his father in the traditional manner. The latter belonged to the ranks of the impoverished in the small community, eking out a meager living for the support of his family as a *Schulklopfer* (synagogue door knocker), who made early morning rounds to rouse the faithful to prayer, as a teacher of young children, and as a Torah scribe. Despite the family's straitened circumstances, he taught his son the rudiments of Hebrew and the Bible. When Moses was six, his father sent him to Rabbi David Fränkel, who initiated him into the study of the Talmud and its commentaries. Impressed by the boy's keen intellect, Fränkel also introduced him to texts by the medieval philosopher Moses Maimonides. A close bond arose between the teacher and his pupil, and after Fränkel had accepted an appointment as chief rabbi of Berlin and moved there, only a few months passed until the boy bade his parents farewell and departed on foot for the Prussian capital. Having been granted entry into the city at the Rosenthal Gate, the entrance in the town wall reserved for the Jews, he was able to continue his Talmud studies there with Rabbi Fränkel.

The arrival of the fourteen-year-old Mendelssohn in the Prussian metropolis signaled the origins of a historical development that was to turn Prussia into the cradle of the Haskalah. Significantly, a Jewish Enlightenment did not germinate in England or the Netherlands, even though the Jews there enjoyed greater freedoms under a constitutional regime and thus appeared to be more open to their environment and receptive to its modernizing influences. There is indeed a kernel of paradox in the fact that the "rays of Enlightenment" began to penetrate ever deeper into the ghetto specifically under the regime of Frederick II (1740–1786). Frederick saw himself as a "philosopher king" who wished to demonstrate his openness to the ideas of a new era and felt honored by the presence in Berlin of thinkers like Voltaire and Maupertuis. In his state each subject was to find salvation in his own way. He repudiated the religious fanaticism "that decimates the nations" and, in his "Political Testament" of 1752, stressed the importance of peaceful coexistence among Catholics, Lutherans, Reformed Christians, Jews, and other sects. Yet this enlightened conception of a state not bound to an official state religion stood in marked contradiction with his mistrustful policy of strict supervision and control of the Jews, attested by his Revised General Code, the Jewry Reglement of 1750. This was a harsh code contrary to all notions of humane precepts and tolerance. In accordance with utilitarian principles, it institutionalized a hierarchical structuring of Jewish society, turning the Jews into a pariah collectivity whose members were forced to bear collective responsibility to a centralized regime for the transgressions of individuals and simultaneously to suffer heightened internal ten-

39   Moses Mendelssohn at the "Berlin" Gate in Potsdam 1771.
Copper engraving by M. S. Lowe based on a drawing by
Daniel Chodowiecki

sions within their communities. The rigid governmental regulation accelerated the disintegration of Jewish society and the decline in the authority of rabbis and lay leaders, plunging the communities into a crisis of leadership. However, this very process of disintegration generated space for the emergence of a new intellectual elite. That nascent elite was benefited by a concomitant economic development: the mercantilist policies of Frederick II, inspired by the cameralists, had facilitated the rise of a solid, albeit small group of Jewish entrepreneurs in Prussia. Though it numbered no more than fifteen families, this new stratum was to provide the material support for a group of Jewish intellectuals who almost all stemmed from impoverished backgrounds. For the future achievements of Mendelssohn, too, the existence of this entrepreneurial group constituted a necessary precondition.

When the young Moses arrived in Berlin during the third year of Frederick the Great's reign, he did not belong to those categories of Jews tolerated in the Prussian state according to the prevailing material or occupational criteria. Only thanks to the intervention of his mentor, Rabbi Fränkel—who had persuaded a wealthy protected Jew (*Schutzjude*) to take the penniless Talmud student into his house—was Mendelssohn granted a residence permit thanks to the protected status of his rich benefactor. In 1750, Isaac Bernhard, a prosperous silk manufacturer in Berlin, invited Mendelssohn to become a private tutor for his children, later made him bookkeeper in his business, and finally took him into his silk factory as a partner. Once he was financially on a secure footing, Mendelssohn became free to devote himself to his enlightenment activities. After initial success with his early publications, he requested in a letter to Frederick II to be granted the status of a protected Jew:

> From my childhood, I have been continually resident in Your Majesty's states and wish to be able to settle here permanently. But since I was born abroad and do not possess the requisite assets as required by the [Jewry] Regulation, let me be so bold as to make a most humble request: that Your Majesty grant to me and my descendants Your most gracious protection, along with the freedoms which Your subjects enjoy, bearing in mind that I compensate my lack of wealth by my labors in the sciences, which have the good fortune of enjoying Your Majesty's protection.[1]

In 1763 Frederick granted Mendelssohn the status of an "unprivileged protected Jew" (*ausserordentlicher Schutzjude*)—not that of a "privileged" one (*ordentlicher Schutzjude*), a classification that would have also assured his descendants the right of residence.

Israel Samoscz (1700–1772)—who, as his name suggests, stemmed from the small Jewish community of Samoscz in Poland—arrived in the Prussian capital in 1742. In Berlin, he too owed his financial security to a privileged member of the Jewish upper class, the banker Daniel Itzig (1723–1799). Itzig had welcomed Samoscz into his home, and it was there that he met with the young Mendelssohn and his friend Aaron Gumpertz (1723–1769). Samoscz took advantage of these conversations in the house of Daniel Itzig in order to instruct Mendelssohn and Gumpertz in philosophy, mathematics, and literature from the sources of Spanish Jewry. These encounters proved a crucial stimulus for Mendelssohn's intellectual development in the 1740s and fifties—an experience that helped pave his path to Aufklärung. Samoscz, an outstanding student of the Talmud, preferred science and scholarship to a rabbinical profession. In his *Netsaḥ Yisrael* (The Eternal One of Israel, 1741) he combined knowledge of the Talmud with mathematics and astronomy and he also authored several commentaries on works of medieval Jewish philosophy.

The Jewish economic elite under Frederick II not only offered the maskilim a basis for economic security, but also created a favorable climate for the reception of their ideas. Their entrepreneurial activities brought them into close contact with Prussian officialdom, administrators whose outlook was turning increasingly cameralistic. These officials believed it was the aim of the state to care for the common welfare of the people and to bring the happiness of the individual into harmony with that of the whole community. The Jewish entrepreneurs quickly embraced these principles. Their discourse with the officials, centered principally on obtaining concessions under the best possible terms, was shaped by cameralist concepts and the premises of economic rationality. This entrepreneurial elite tended to be open to the outside world, and that receptivity effected a major change in mentality and customs. It was manifested in their language, their dress, frequent attendance at the theater and visits to coffee houses, as well as in their attitudes toward secular education.

Economic relations with non-Jews in the mercantilist era were no longer exclusively instrumental and were accompanied now by a process of internalizing the values and norms of non-Jewish society. Jewish and Gentile society no longer existed as spheres largely separate and closed, isolated one from the other. They were coming closer together, and this bridging led to an incipient process of acculturation under the reign of Frederick II, carried forward by Jewish merchants. That transformation can be confirmed by a glance into the interior of the house of one of their outstanding representatives, provided us by Friedrich Nicolai (1733–1811) in his description of Berlin:

> Mr. Daniel Itzig (in the Burgstrasse) possesses a choice collection of paintings; among these . . . *Moses Striking the Rock*, by Beschey; a large prospect with many figures, by Canaletto; . . . *Ganymede*, by Rubens; *Hercules and Omphale*, from the school of Rubens; *Eli and Elkana, Bringing His Son Samuel*, by Gerbrand von den Ekhout; a family portrait by Peter Hals.

There were also paintings depicting St. Jerome in the desert and Mary Magdalene, by an unknown artist.[2]

The Itzig collection was a sign of gradual change in mentality and attitude. In earlier centuries it would have been virtually inconceivable in a Jewish home, and most certainly not a varied assortment of paintings intermixing figures and motifs from Jewish and Christian religious history. Yet it would be mistaken to assume that Itzig had abandoned traditional Judaism. In his beautiful building, writes Nicolai, there was a "well-built synagogue" and a hall whose ceiling could be opened up, converting the room into a roofless sukkah (booth erected for the Feast of Sukkot). Magnificence and luxury, together with a "rich collection of good paintings," also typified other homes of the Jewish economic elite. When it came to externals of refinement and artistic taste, they did not wish to seem less cultivated than the Christian upper class, the high-ranking officials, war councillors, diplomatic officers, chamberlains, and state ministers. The disposition of a rising property-owning bourgeoisie was also manifest in the new esteem for books on secular subjects. Nicolai noted that the merchant "Aaron Meyer, who lives on Spandauer Strasse, possesses an impressive library, especially rich in works on recent history and literature, in particular a large number of French translations of classical authors, and the best German, Italian, English, and French writers." The personal library thus became one parameter of the enhanced value accorded secular education and culture in well-to-do Jewish families, such as that of Aaron Gumpertz. In his father's library stood the Bible, Talmud, and volumes of rabbinic literature, flanked by works in diverse languages and fields; these had exercised a fascination on Mendelssohn's friend already at a young age, inducing him to supplement traditional Jewish learning with a secular education.

No matter how critically the maskilim viewed the affluent and privileged class of Jewish entrepreneurs, the upsurge of the Berlin Haskalah was inextricably linked with the emergence of this parvenu social stratum. Both Mendelssohn and his disciples were critical of businessmen who had grown rich in the Seven Years War and whose turn toward Enlightenment was expressed only in external lifestyle, not outlook and inner attitude. That "superficial" adaptation in externals, without any simultaneous intellectual effort, aroused the ire of the maskilim. Mendelssohn even went so far as to denounce as dishonorable the way the privileged accommodated unreflectively to the non-Jewish environment and claimed it was often possible to find "more virtue" among the poor Jews, still rooted in tradition and not yet touched by the new enlightened ideas, than in the Jewish upper class. Nonetheless, the Berlin Haskalah remained indebted in manifold ways to the elite of "generally privileged Jews" (*Generalprivi-ligierte*). They were, after all, a genuine locus of power in Jewish society— men who could be of valuable assistance in translating enlightened theory into practice, introducing educational reforms and assisting with the publication of enlightened books and periodicals. These affluent merchants had ushered in that process of opening up to the outside environment that prepared them, or at least their children, to be receptive to the ideas of the maskilim.

Among the factors surrounding the Haskalah in its formative years was, of course, the rise of Berlin as the residential city of the Prussian monarchy, the hub of a state rapidly restructuring itself as a centralized absolutism. Within a half-century Berlin's population doubled, soaring from some fifty thousand to one hundred thousand inhabitants by 1755. The capital began to eclipse all other German cities. Construction flourished; there was a boom in manufacturing and commerce. Efforts to centralize the state administration favored the formation of a class of officials, the bureaucratic buttress of cameralism, from whose ranks adherents of Aufklärung were recruited. When Frederick the Great assumed the throne in 1740, the sciences experienced a phase of rejuvenation. The old Association for the Sciences became the Royal Academy of Sciences, and Maupertuis its president. Its spectrum ranged widely over the humanities and natural sciences, including physics, mathematics, speculative philosophy, and philology. Thanks to the enlightened policies of

Frederick II, Berlin, with its academy and other accoutrements, had become a magnet for the intellectual elite of Germany and Europe.

The city gradually attracted a number of the celebrated figures of the day in the sciences and arts: philosophers, theologians, poets, and natural scientists. These then formed the basis for a new "sociability" in which the maskilim also participated. In the person of Friedrich Nicolai, publishing found an enterprising figure who combined the spirit of Enlightenment with an astute sense of entrepreneurship. Around him a circle interested in science and literature crystallized, counting Gotthold Ephraim Lessing (1729–1781) and Mendelssohn among its members. Nicolai promoted the publication of books and periodicals whose enlightened spirit had an impact that reverberated far beyond the residential city. The fact that Lessing came to Berlin in 1748, for example, was associated with his work on just such a periodical. He remained in Berlin until 1755 and then returned at intervals, spending the years 1758–1760 and 1765–1767 in the city.

Berlin was now a thriving hub of the fine arts, science, and education; for several decades its cultural aura vied with European cities like London and Paris. The encounter there with the ideas of the Enlightenment spawned new forms of sociability, providing the fertile soil conducive to the germination of the Haskalah in its first phase. Yet there were legal impediments standing in the way of these favorable prerequisites for free thought and untrammeled creativity. Between 1750 and 1800 legislation relating to the status of Jewry in Prussia and other German states stagnated. Even though Joseph II had abolished the rigid policies of absolutism toward the Jews in Austria, that could not induce the Prussian monarch to grant the Jews in his state more liberties. His policies remained rigid, shaped by his bigoted view that his subjects had to be protected from the "harmful" influence of the Jews. Guided by reason and respect for science, the scholars exercised tolerance—while the Prussian king disregarded it in practice. This gaping discrepancy between his attitude and the views of the "republic of intellectuals" was pivotal for the genesis phase of the Jewish Enlightenment. While Mendelssohn and the maskilim felt at a distinct disadvantage under the heel of official state policy, the scholarly arena offered the prospect of social integration; at the same time, new intellectual horizons opened up before them. Even before political equality had become a reality for the Jews, they were able to participate in an evolving bourgeois public sphere. This sphere had interposed itself between the corporate bodies of the state, still structured in terms of the old estates, and formed the soil for hopes of a comprehensive renewal of Jewish and non-Jewish society. The bourgeois public had an intellectual rather than a political focus and had not yet raised political demands as in England, France, and the Netherlands. Yet, in contrast to those countries, here was a public sphere in which Jewish intellectuals could actively take part. To the west, in London, Paris, and Amsterdam, the Jews enjoyed greater civil equality, but in Germany a novum evolved in the second half of the eighteenth century: an interdenominational sociability, that is, a new social openness vis-à-vis individual Jews within a limited range of Gentile society. Its power to shape new realities became amply manifest in the circle of Jewish enlighteners around Mendelssohn.

2. A New Sociability

Already, during his first two decades in Berlin, the Jewish community was for Mendelssohn no longer his sole frame of reference. He continued to participate in its life and never broke with the community; yet, at the same time, he shifted his sights toward the outside world, to a circle of like-minded friends not subject to the community's powers of sanction. It was this social sphere, imbued with a spirit of openness, that motivated Mendelssohn in the 1740s and 1750s to acquire secular education. Thus he added modern and classical European languages to his command of Hebrew and Judeo-German and, after a short time, was able to read the works of the most important philosophers in the original German, French, English, Latin, and Greek. In the free hours that remained to him when he was not engaged in Talmud studies or his duties as a private tutor, he immersed himself in the writings of Locke, Spinoza, Voltaire, Rousseau, Leibniz, and Christian Wolff. By unceasing application, both through self-study and with the aid of like-minded Jewish associates, Mendelssohn penetrated the philosophical world of Enlightenment ideas. Among his circle of friends and acquaintances, along with Israel Samoscz, there were also two young Jewish physicians, Abraham Kisch (1725–1803) from Prague and Aaron Gumpertz, son of a family of court Jews. In a letter to Fromet Gugenheim, his fiancée and future bride, Mendelssohn commented on Gumpertz: "You have the good fortune to have the doctor in your home for a bit longer. He is your friend and a man who, as I know from experience, is never remiss in his instruction. Everything I have profited from in the sciences I owe to him, and him alone."[3]

MOSES MENDELSSOHN.
Dem Könige Friedrich Wilhelm II.
unterthänigst gewidmet
von der Jüdischen Freyschule zu Berlin 1787.

40   Portrait of Mendelssohn. Copper engraving by J. C. Müller
based on a painting by J. C. Frisch

For Mendelssohn, science (*Wissenschaft*) meant above all else philosophy; it was the bridge he used to forge the link with enlightened thought. Perhaps he also emphasized Gumpertz's merit because it was Gumpertz who had introduced him to Lessing—as legend would have it, over a game of chess. The acquaintanceship Mendelssohn struck up with Lessing was the prelude to a lifelong friendship, a bond that enabled Mendelssohn to gain entry to the "republic of intellectuals." His ties with that "republic" accompanied the development of Haskalah from this point on, imbuing the latter with a social aspect along with its intellectual dimension.

Mendelssohn engaged in an intensive dialogue with Lessing on questions of aesthetics, ethics, and language, an exchange that shaped his enlightened worldview. They discussed the close link between language and the faculty of thought, the correlation between a pure, cultivated language, human reason, and education. This was the basis for Mendelssohn's zeal for Hebrew and German, their revitalization and cultivation. The exchange of ideas with Lessing led to a joint publication, "Pope ein Metaphysiker" (Pope, a Metaphysician, 1755), an attempt to defend Leibnizian optimism in the face of its detractors in the Berlin Academy. Mendelssohn also owed the speedy publication of his first work, *Philosophische Gespräche* (Philosophical Conversations, 1755), to his friendship with Lessing. According to Mendelssohn's son Joseph, Lessing gave his Jewish friend a copy of a treatise by Shaftesbury. Shortly thereafter Mendelssohn returned the work and, in response to the question how he had liked it, replied: "Well, quite a lot! But I can write something like that myself." "Is that so?" said Lessing, "then go ahead and do it."[4] Several weeks after that, Mendelssohn handed him a manuscript to read, and a few months later Lessing was able to present his friend with a printed copy of *Philosophische Gespräche*.

Only one or two generations earlier such a friendship between Mendelssohn, the tradition-oriented Jew, and the Christian Lessing would have hardly been conceivable; now it formed the nucleus of a gradually expanding social sphere. Part of that ambit, for example, were the publisher Friedrich Nicolai and the theologian and writer Johann Georg Müchler (1724–1819). The two deserve mention here not principally because of their importance as thinkers but rather because of their entrepreneurship on behalf of Aufklärung, which opened up new publication possibilities for Mendelssohn. Nicolai, the editor of various literary periodicals, engaged Mendelssohn as a regular contributor, ultimately publishing his most important works as well, including the Bible translation. But their ties went deeper, beyond a mere business association, and their acquaintanceship blossomed into friendship in its very first year (1755). Mendelssohn lived fairly close to Nicolai, and they regularly visited each other. The fact that, although Jewish, Mendelssohn was able to live in close proximity to Christians—and not isolated in a Judengasse—facilitated the new sociability. Writing to Lessing, Mendelssohn noted:

> For a while now I've become unfaithful to ponderous metaphysics
> . . . I visit Herr Nicolai very often in his garden (I truly love him,
> my dearest friend! And I believe that our own friendship can only
> gain by this, because I cherish in him your true friend as well.) We
> read poetry, Herr Nicolai recites his own compositions too, and I
> sit on my bench, a critical judge, complimenting, laughing,
> approving, finding fault, until evening comes. Then our thoughts
> turn once more to you and we take leave of one other, satisfied
> with the day's accomplishment. I'm on my way to becoming a *bel
> esprit*. Who knows, I may even try my own hand soon at writing
> verse. May Madame Metaphysic forgive me. She maintains that
> friendship stems from a correspondence of inclinations, and I find
> that, vice versa, a correspondence of inclinations can also stem
> from friendship. Because of your friendship and Nicolai's, I've
> withdrawn a portion of my affection from this venerable matron
> and have bestowed it on literature.[5]

Mendelssohn's activity in the new fields of knowledge thus ran parallel to his new social ties, to which Müchler's initiatives also contributed their share. Müchler was the editor of the moral weekly *Der Chamäleon* (The Chameleon) and had published articles by Mendelssohn. He was also one of the founders of the Gelehrtes Kaffeehaus (Learned Coffeehouse) of 1755, one of the many associations that sprang up like mushrooms in the second half of the eighteenth century. This enlightened society was frequented by Mendelssohn and his friend Gumpertz, together with Lessing, Nicolai, and other like-minded men. As a society of supporters of Enlightenment, it was closely linked with the aim of living a life in accordance with its ideals—via self-education, cultivation of the sciences, and a code of ethics overarching all social distinctions of class and estate. This association was part of a sociocultural phenomenon of the day, an initiative that might first appear as a "learned society," or even as a formal "academy," then take on the form of "moral-patriotic" fraternities, masonic lodges, and reading clubs, and finally manifest itself as well in the creation of political groups. In terms of social background and occupation, the membership represented the rising middle class (*Bürgertum*), including government officials, doctors, theologians, professors, secondary school teachers, and merchants, and even several representatives of the nobility. The goals of such voluntary associations were counterposed to those of the old corporative, hierarchical society of estates. Their principal aspiration was the creation of a free zone, an ambit within which members of different social origins, religions, and professions could meet and interact as friends and equals in an atmosphere of amicable social interchange and scholarly discussion, thus driving forward the process of bourgeois self-definition.

This open interstice between the corporate bodies of the old, estates-based social order offered Christians and Jews the occasion for forging closer contact, though that was sometimes accompanied by resistance. It provided the framework for the expansion of casual, informal friendships, such as had evolved between Mendelssohn and Lessing. Commonality of ideas, enlightened discourse, and utopian schemes were the prerequisite for this new social openness—a sociability in total contradiction with the still widely dominant pariah status of the Jew in the state under absolutist rule.

Mendelssohn was admitted as an equal to the Gelehrtes Kaffeehaus, which had a membership of about one hundred. There he presented a paper on "Probability" that earned him applause and acclaim. This only served to bolster his aspirations as an enlightener to work, by means of intellectual effort and requisite action, toward a reform of Jewish and non-Jewish society. That is also the context in which to view his plan to publish the first Hebrew periodical, *Kohelet Musar* (The Moralist), a project launched together with Tobias Bock, probably in 1755.

Mendelssohn here made use of a new genre that enjoyed exceptional popularity in the eighteenth century, first in England and then in Germany: the so-called moral weekly. The philosophy of the Enlightenment was undoubtedly the source of inspiration, but the journal's intention was not to present philosophical ideas for a select readership of scholars. Rather, it aimed at disseminating enlightened thought more broadly within the rising middle class. The ideas of philosophers and of poets influenced by philosophy, such as Locke, Shaftesbury, Pope, Leibniz, and Wolff, were to be presented to a wider public in a language that was readily understandable. The moral weekly would include everything of possible relevance for the rational, confident human being—expressed in a simple, linguistically appealing form, not in the moralizing tones of the preacher.

With the publication of *Kohelet Musar*, the young Mendelssohn (only twenty-six at the time) burst through the narrow framework of the traditional world of thought and sentiment. The periodical was not a philosophical work in German, but a publishing venture in Hebrew, addressed to a Jewish reading public. The basic themes of the magazine, although cloaked in a popular form, are identical with those of the *Philosophische Gespräche* and his *Briefe über die Empfindungen* (Letters on the Sentiments, 1755). In these writings Mendelssohn praises the contemplation of the beautiful and what is "truly perfect": in Nature, God's handiwork and the works of man—poetry, the plastic arts, architecture. Writing in both German and Hebrew, the former Talmud student became the herald of a new aesthetic theory, drawing inspiration from Christian Wolff's *Rational Thoughts on God, the World, Man's Soul, and All Things* (1720) and Shaftesbury's *The Moralists, a Philosophical Rhapsody* (1709). The influence of Shaftesbury is unmistakable when the elated Mendelssohn expresses his enthusiasm on beholding Nature and the order of the cosmos in his first and fourth contribution to *Kohelet Musar* and in the *Briefe über die Empfindungen*: "The contemplation of the whole is a perennial source of delight for the philosophically minded. It sweetens his solitary hours, filling his soul with the most sublime of sensations."[6] And there are also echoes of Shaftesbury when he writes of trancelike "stunning rapture" on regarding the "perfection of the cosmos."

Mendelssohn's ideas did not mark a turning away from the religious path, an abandonment of fidelity to the laws of the Torah. Yet they did constitute a shift in accent: from the closed, isolated circle of the old, normative patterns of Jewish thought into a new sphere—one the tradition-oriented Jew, consciously or unawares, had ignored until then. Basing his argument on Wolff, Mendelssohn contended that one could find delight in aesthetic perfection. To this end, he called for a learning process that would enable human beings to familiarize themselves with aesthetics and develop the necessary sensibility for its achievements. Only a connoisseur of architecture, he argued, knew how to properly evaluate an architectonic creation. Only someone in full command of the system of a language and its lexicon was in a position to relish its beauty in poetry and prose. From this theory of aesthetics, the path led on to the cultivation of

Hebrew and German, and, in the 1750s, Mendelssohn devoted especial effort to both languages.

With the publication of *Kohelet Musar* he secularized that language which he still termed "sacred." Mendelssohn translated sections from Edward Young's "The Complaint or Night Thoughts on Life, Death, and Immortality" from English for publication in the magazine, only to prove that the most sublime lyric poetry could also be rendered beautifully and elegantly in the language of the Bible. Hebrew thus served in *Kohelet Musar* as a medium for presenting ideas that lay beyond the perimeter of traditional Jewish scholarship and, in a certain sense, struck off in new directions that led away from it.

The use of Hebrew points up a bond of cultural continuity; at the same time, however, it contains a covert break with Jewish thought patterns of previous centuries. That rupture is signaled not just in the attentive, loving gaze with which Mendelssohn contemplates the beauties of Nature but also in his treatment of fundamental topics such as life and death, good and evil, the relation of man to God and man's place in the hierarchy of creation. All the contributions in *Kohelet Musar* are marked by a new, basically optimistic outlook on life in this mundane world and the survival of the soul in the world to come. There is a clear shift in perspective when one compares the periodical with the literature on ethics (*musar*) of earlier generations. That traditional genre had depicted death and the agonies hell held in store for the sinner in garish, frightening colors, filling the Jew with profound anxiety. In its worldview evil lurked everywhere, in manifold forms and shapes, from the moment of birth—one could scarcely escape its grasp. The books of musar before the age of Enlightenment presented the simple Jew with a dark, bleak world, and the end that awaited him was even grimmer.

Mendelssohn and Bock pursued a different tack. They endeavored to brighten the prospect, following the example of the moral weeklies that struggled against the "vile and despicable pictures of death, imparted to children, that depicted him as a bare skeleton, wreaking havoc with his scythe," the Grim Reaper. This optimistic agenda in the moral weekly was inspired by the philosophy of Leibniz, which posited the "best of all possible worlds," one from which evil had been banished. Mendelssohn repudiated the image of man as an evil, eternally sinful creature. As he stated in *Kohelet Musar*, human transgressions were due to a lack of education and knowledge. For Mendelssohn, the human being was the crowning glory of creation, above all other creatures in the hierarchy crafted by

God. Faith in human reason was the basis for his enlightened optimism, a power able to repel the forces of evil. By contrast, Jewish literature on ethics before Mendelssohn's time had failed to acknowledge this capacity inherent in the faculty of reason.

Another sign of the changing times was the disappearance of the moralizing darshan (preacher). He had felt superior to the common people, and his somber sermons were often threatening, at times full of palpable contempt. That moralizer was now supplanted by the thinker, the writer, who accommodated to the level of his audience, attempting to draw nearer to them and get across his message through empathy, sympathy, and a friendly smile.

Nonetheless, Mendelssohn's highly promising periodical came to an abrupt end. The cause was not some flagging of his literary enthusiasm, but arbitrary intervention from the outside. All statements by contemporaries suggest that the lay leaders of the Jewish community in Berlin were hostile to the unusual venture one of their nonconformist intellectuals had embarked upon. Thus, one of the first non-Jewish biographers of Mendelssohn, commenting on this incident, wrote: "Hardly had three issues of it appeared, when the rabbis—these orthodox clergy of the Jewish church in the fullest sense of the term—began to fume and fulminate. The clamor grew so loud that the modest sage withdrew—and the journal ceased to exist."[8]

What had specifically provoked the ire of the opponents of *Kohelet Musar*? Mendelssohn certainly did not preach with the aim of bringing about a revolutionary and dangerous change. Nor did he express any ideas that questioned the fundamental principles of the Jewish religion or even the obligatory and binding character of the commandments. The reason for the opposition on the part of the community leadership appears to have been Mendelssohn's independent initiative—the fact that he had undertaken to publish a journal without first obtaining the consent of at least some rabbinical authorities. After all, it was still a standing rule in traditional Jewish society to exercise a kind of censorship over all works published in Hebrew. The disregard for this norm intensified the confrontation between the maskilim and the conservative rabbis in the 1780s after Mendelssohn had completed his Bible translation project. *Kohelet Musar* had provoked a first conflict in the early phase of Haskalah, a movement whose development would lead to ever more heated confrontations in the Jewish community.

The new sociability continued to accompany Mendelssohn's creative work as an Enlightenment thinker after the 1750s as well. While reflecting on the meaning and purpose of human existence in this world and the next and developing his views on the immortality of the soul—later to be elaborated in his *Phädon* (1767)—he was engaged in an intensive dialogue with his friend Thomas Abbt (1738–1766). Abbt's interests were vast, encompassing a broad spectrum of culture, ranging from theology and philosophy to history and literature; gifted with a razor-sharp intellect, he was at the same time a sentimental enthusiast. Abbt became for Mendelssohn the most important interlocutor, a kindred spirit with whom to exchange ideas as well as a close friend. They provided one another mutual intellectual support (Abbt translated the *Briefe über die Empfindungen* into French), and confided in each other about joys and sorrows in their personal lives. Yet in their correspondence they also wrestled over their respective differing views of Enlightenment. When Abbt died at the age of twenty-eight, Mendelssohn deeply mourned the passing of his Christian friend, whom he called a "companion on the way to Truth who warned me of false steps."

Down to the 1780s the new rapprochement between Jews and Christians was principally centered on Mendelssohn. He was not only invited to the Gelehrtes Kaffeehaus, but also to the closed, exclusive circle of the scholarly Montagklub (Monday Club), limited to twenty-four members. He would undoubtedly have been pleased to take up this invitation, since Lessing, Nicolai, Abbt, and other friends and enlighteners also belonged. But their get-together, held every Monday evening, was combined with a common meal. So Mendelssohn, faithful to his principle of not cultivating interfaith sociability at the expense of Judaism and its dietary laws, chose to decline membership. In the 1780s, when he had long since persuaded others of his wish to be a philosopher of the Enlightenment while at the same time remaining a champion of Jewish distinctiveness, Mendelssohn was offered membership in the Mittwochgesellschaft (Wednesday Society), which sponsored a periodical, the *Berlinische Monatsschrift*, whose professed aim was to "smash the teeth of the hyena of superstition and intolerance." The society's membership included eminent theologians such as Wilhelm Abraham Teller and Johann Joachim Spalding as well as high-ranking Prussian government officials such as Christian Wilhelm Dohm (1751–1820) and the privy councillor Karl Gottlieb Svarez (1746–1798), men who would later spur on the reform of legislation regarding the Jews. Svarez opted for "the undisturbed exercise of natural freedom" within the association. A palpable spirit of progress reigned at its meetings, and, if Mendelssohn's general health had been better, he would have taken an active part. As it was, he made do with a corresponding membership, submitting papers "Über die Frage: Was heisst Aufklären?" (On the Question: What is Enlightenment?) and "Über die beste Staatsverfassung" (Thoughts on the Best Form of Government).

The new sociability did not mean only formal membership in an association of enlighteners—it also encompassed scholarly conversation and social gatherings in a domestic context. As long as Mendelssohn was alive, his home remained a center for socializing and for enlightened discourse. He was visited by Christian friends and admirers; young Jews from far and wide gathered at his home to discuss issues of enlightenment. In his house the Jewish variant of Aufklärung gained clear shape. Important projects of the Berlin Haskalah, such as the Bible translation and the reform of Jewish education, were debated and first steps taken to make them a reality. The Mendelssohn home became the focus of a fresh intellectual and social openness to the outside world—a secularized sphere, whose frame of reference was both Jewish and Christian society. Until his death Mendelssohn's house remained the locus where the basic lines of a new Jewish worldview were conceived and delineated.

In 1763 and 1764 Mendelssohn's home had also been sought out by the young Zürich theologian Johann Caspar Lavater (1741–1801), while in Berlin visiting the circle of the *Aufklärer*. He recognized Mendelssohn as one of their outstanding intellects. Nonetheless, it was Lavater who, in 1769, issued a rather blunt open challenge to Mendelssohn to convert to Christianity. This was an attack on tolerance that wounded Mendelssohn deeply. Christian friends repudiated Lavater's action but could no longer undo what had transpired. Mendelssohn stood up to the challenge, despite his reluctance to be dragged into a public controversy over questions of religion. He had to respond and defend his Judaism. This was the beginning of the so-called Lavater dispute of the 1770s, which will be discussed in detail below. Mendelssohn was forced to recognize that even within the "republic of intellectuals" old prejudices still lived on. The new sociability had permitted him to come together with Christians on an equal footing, but it was the point of departure for a transformation that came about only very slowly. Again and again, the traditional modes of thinking violated the new rules of the Enlightenment. After Mendelssohn's death Jews continued to seek out the bourgeois public arena, whose contours became ever more distinct and pronounced. Yet they were not spared confrontations—

on the contrary, the clashes became more fierce. The more clearly and obstinately Jews articulated their claims to equality, the more vehement were the reactions of their adversaries. Social discrimination was obstinate; it outlived the Enlightenment and its learned associations, so that ultimately the Jewish enlighteners formed a separate secular sphere. That ambit was not identical with the general bourgeois sociability—yet neither was it the same as the old Jewish community.

Nonetheless, there was no rupture with the community. Mendelssohn and his disciples remained loyal to it. That often spawned conflict situations from which they could have extricated themselves by a drastic move—either baptism or a contrite return as full members to the bosom of the traditional community. Yet, despite these frictions, they insisted on preserving the complex relationship with two very different and often contradictory worlds. They criticized the "old regime" of the community, championed a reform in education, and finally raised demands for a restructuring of religious life as well—yet they did not dissociate themselves from the Jewish community. There was no break. Their revolt against traditional patterns of thought and ways of living was marked by repeated attempts to have an impact on the course of events within Jewish society. Thus the innovative aspect of the Berlin Haskalah consists inter alia in this two-sided social relation, internally and to the outside. It generated tension and ferment, and it also went through diverse crises.

By his consistent involvement in Jewish affairs, coupled with an increasing social and intellectual participation in the life of the republic of intellectuals, Mendelssohn himself pointed the way. Throughout his life he demonstrated his abiding interest in the Jewish world: by publishing *Kohelet Musar* and entire works in Hebrew, and by his readiness on repeated occasions to represent the cause of the Jewish community through intercession with officials and regents—to whom he enjoyed access thanks to the recognition accorded him, especially since publication of the *Phädon*.

In 1769, Mendelssohn interceded on behalf of the Altona community; its lay leaders had solicited his assistance because of allegations that the rabbinical court had condoned the inclusion of hostile statements against Christianity in a Jewish calendar edited by a member of the community. In 1772 Mendelssohn wrote a memorandum to the duke of Mecklenburg, requesting that he support the community of Mecklenburg-Schwerin in the question of "early burial." The duke had demanded that the Jewish dead be buried only after waiting a period of three days so as to eliminate any doubts that a person was being buried while still alive. Although Mendelssohn was of the opinion that rapid burial was a custom sanctioned by tradition, not a regulation required by Halacha nor one that served a beneficent purpose, he supported the Jewish community in their request.

In 1775 Mendelssohn twice came to the aid of Jewish communities: in a letter to Lavater in Zürich—whom he addressed as a "friend of humanity," this despite their bitter controversy five years before—he asked Lavater to intercede in order to ameliorate the lot of the Jews in the Swiss communities of Endingen and Lengnau. He also requested the court Jew Veitel Ephraim to make use of his special connections to the king of Poland in order to prevent an expulsion of the Jews of Warsaw, since a blood libel had been raised against them. In 1777 representatives of the Jews in Königsberg and Dresden solicited Mendelssohn's assistance. These communities were unable to continue to bear the heavy yoke of extraordinary taxes, and their members were under threat of being expelled from the city. Mendelssohn appealed in this matter to one of his non-Jewish admirers, Baron Ferber, adviser to the elector of Saxony, which helped bring the matter to a successful conclusion.

The readiness of the father of the Berlin Haskalah to take up the cause of Jews in nearby and distant communities, and to perform the function of a voluntary advocate, went hand in hand with an active involvement in the life of his own community. In Berlin he did not have a formal office until 1780. Nonetheless, he placed himself at the service of Berlin Jewry. After the Prussian victories at Rossbach and Leuthen (1757), he wrote the German version of sermons prepared by the rabbis David Fränkel and Aaron Mosessohn. When the Seven Years War came to a victorious conclusion in 1763, he drafted the text of the "Sermon of Peace" for the festive service in the synagogue. Here, in one breath, he praised divine providence, peace, and the glorious Prussian monarch Frederick II. A letter to his friend Lessing intimates that he was not completely at ease in performing this patriotic task, but, as so often in the past, it was his desire to stand by the community in the fulfillment of an obligation. After all, he had a more perfect command of German than anyone else in the Jewish community and was gifted with a masterly touch when it came to phrasing and formulation.

His ready and willing assistance on behalf of the Jewish community is doubly significant if one bears in mind that Mendelssohn's activity as enlightener often provoked intense conflict and counterreactions. These extended all the way to the threat of imposing a ban, as in the case of the journal *Kohelet Musar*, and later as negative reaction to his Bible project. Mendelssohn showed himself to be a circumspect, cautious innovator. He never taxed the ties to the community to the point of rupture—just as he always attempted to strike a happy medium in his philosophical and political writings. Herein lies the difference between him and the uncompromising Spinoza. It was a moderation that ultimately spared him the onus of the ban. Mendelssohn's ability to move simultaneously in two circles, two worlds, despite all obstacles, and to cultivate intensive relations with the Jewish community *and* with enlightened society is a characteristic that surely had a decisive impact on the development of the Berlin Haskalah.

3. Enlightenment Philosophy and Jewish Religion

The process of social adaptation to the Christian environment proceeded along with a trend toward greater openness to the intellectual world of the Enlightenment, which helped shape the development of the Berlin Haskalah. With a zeal and fervor previously unparalleled, young Jews began to immerse themselves in the works of non-Jewish philosophers and to rethink their ideas about Jews and Judaism on the basis of the ideas they discovered there. Here, too, Mendelssohn was paradigmatic. Only eleven years after his arrival in Berlin in 1743, he had already acquired a solid grounding in German and European philosophy. The first work he read after an intensive study of Maimonides was Locke's *Essay Concerning Human Understanding*—in Latin. Then, thanks to his friend Aaron Gumpertz, he discovered Leibniz's *Essays on Theodicy* and Wolff's *Rational Thoughts*. These books confronted Mendelssohn with a number of key metaphysical and ethical questions that would occupy him all his life:

> To you, Locke and Wolff! To you, immortal Leibnitz!—I establish in my heart an everlasting monument. Without your help, I would be lost for all eternity. I never knew you personally, and know only your immortal writings—works still unread by the world at large, books I have beseeched in my hours of loneliness, appealing to them for help. They have guided me onto the sure path to true philosophical wisdom, to the knowledge of my inner self and origin.

They have etched into my soul the sacred truths upon which my
happiness is founded; they have been my edification.[9]

Just how formative the influence of the philosophers of Enlightenment
was on Mendelssohn's thinking is evident not only from these remarks,
but from all his early works: *Philosophische Gespräche* (mentioned
above), *Gedanken über die Wahrscheinlichkeit* (Thoughts on Probability,
1756) and *Betrachtungen über die Quellen und die Verbindungen der
schönen Künste und Wissenschaften* (Observations on the Sources of and
Links Between the Fine Arts and the Sciences, 1757).

Mendelssohn adopted the concept of "prestabilized harmony," the necessary expression of an order of monads in space and time. It permitted
him to regard the existing universe as the best of all possible worlds, in
which all substances created by God strive for perfection, even though
this Leibnizian interpretation of the world as theodicy already seemed
passé, beset by serious difficulties. Wolff's system of reason, based on
mathematics and also soon regarded by many as outdated, was another
influence on Mendelssohn in his *Abhandlung über die Evidenz in
Metaphysischen Wissenschaften* (Treatise on Evidence in Metaphysical
Sciences, 1764). This essay was his reply to the long-winded prize question of the Berlin Academy: "Are metaphysical truths in general, and the
first principles of natural theology and ethics in particular, capable of the
same proof as mathematical proofs; if not, what are the nature and degree
of their certainty, and is this degree of certainty sufficient for persuasion?" (1761). Mendelssohn's reply was honored with a prize, yet by
asserting that metaphysical truths, even if they did not possess the same
"comprehensibility," were nonetheless capable of the "same certainty" as
geometric truths,[10] he had placed himself unabashedly in the camp of
Wolffian metaphysics. In so doing, he took a stance opposed to no less a
figure than Maupertuis, president of the academy until 1756, and also put
himself at odds with the French Enlightenment as represented by a
Condillac, Voltaire, or d'Alembert.

In contrast with the French rationalists, Leibniz and Wolff did not
advocate the total rejection of traditional views and tried to integrate
these into their system. The belief in the existence of God, providence, and
the immortality of the soul as truths of natural religion all had a central
role in their scheme. Even revelation was amenable to accommodation in
their metaphysics. For Mendelssohn that was a great source of relief
philosophically, since he believed in the binding power of the Law

revealed at Sinai. His courage in speaking out in favor of the rational truths of natural religion, a position basically similar to Deism, was falsely interpreted by some as a willingness to turn his back on Judaism. But Mendelssohn did not wish this receptivity to the philosophy of Enlightenment to be understood as an abandonment of the ceremonial laws, let alone of the religious truths of Judaism. Rather, he wanted it interpreted as the readiness to embark upon a quest. With the aid of philosophical concepts taken over from the outside, a compromise formula had to be found that expressed the compatibility of Judaism and natural religion. Mendelssohn thus stood in a long line of Jewish tradition, whose most famous representative was Maimonides, a thinker who had sought, in his *Guide of the Perplexed,* to harmonize rationalistic religious conceptions with fidelity to the Law. All of Mendelssohn's major and shorter philosophical works in German, especially his polemical tracts in defense of Judaism, reflected his desire for reconciliation between reason and revealed religion.

Phädon oder über die Unsterblichkeit der Seele (Phaedon, or On the Soul's Immortality, 1767)—a work that enjoyed enormous success and established Mendelssohn's fame and recognition far beyond Prussia's borders—is similar in its form and title to the Platonic dialogues. It does not awaken any specifically Jewish associations. Nonetheless, this work too, the product of profound admiration for Socrates and Greek philosophy, was a contribution to the new Jewish identity Mendelssohn wished to forge. With the aim of reading Plato in the original, he had begun to study Greek in 1757, after he had already acquired a solid foundation in Latin and the modern European languages. The *Phädon* is a defense of natural religion and one of its most fundamental religious truths, the belief in the soul's immortality. Guided solely by reason, Socrates is made to set forth this doctrine. Mendelssohn has him argue as a Leibnizian in the sense of the Enlightenment:

> I feel that I cannot contradict the theory of immortality, nor that of Divine judgment after death, without causing endless difficulties, shattering everything I have ever deemed true and good. If our soul is mortal, then our Reason is a dream sent by Jupiter to deceive us wretched creatures. Then virtue lacks all the splendor that renders it Divine in our eyes; then what is beautiful and exalted, morally and physically, is not an image of Divine perfection (because nothing that is transitory can grasp even the weakest beam of Divine

perfection). . . . Then even the most depraved mortal has the power to escape God's rule, and a dagger can dissolve the bond that ties man to God.[11]

Socrates cites arguments against French materialism and skepticism. The latter deprives human beings of an optimistic prospect for happiness: "How deplorable is the fate of a mortal who, by unfortunate sophistry, has forfeited the consoling expectation of a future life!" Whoever is incapable of believing in the soul's immortality fails to grasp the "loftiest triumph of human wisdom, the most perfect harmony between the system of intentions and that of active causes." The belief in immortality and recognition of a tender, loving God, as well as faith in providence, are closely interlinked. Accordingly, God's intentions and his "participation" extend "to the smallest changes and individual occurrences among the inanimate as well as the animate," which all possess independence, yet at the same time are willed by God—a view Mendelssohn was familiar with from Maimonides. Immortality is ultimately interlinked with the idea of infinite intellectual and ethical progress.

The theory of the soul's immortality stands immutable for Mendelssohn, before any proofs have been mustered in its defense, since it represents the meaning and purpose of human existence in this life and the next, as part of the world created in accordance with God's will and intention. Inspired by Leibnizian metaphysics, Mendelssohn rehabilitates the world of the living in the *Phädon*, liberating the earth, the body and the senses from an earlier defect by the prospect of eternal happiness for every human soul. He dispels the fear of approaching death and dread of the world beyond the grave. The writing of the *Phädon* was prompted in part by a dispute with his friend Thomas Abbt, in which Mendelssohn spoke out in favor of a leading luminary of Enlightenment theology in Berlin, Johann Joachim Spalding and his work *Observations on the Destiny of Man* (1754). But it was also influenced by Mendelssohn's own conviction that it was possible to reconcile the natural religion of Enlightenment theologians with premodern Jewish metaphysics.

In contrast with the *Phädon, Jerusalem oder über religiöse Macht und Judenthum* (Jerusalem, or On Religious Power and Judaism, 1783) arose out of a Christian-Jewish clash. An anonymous pamphlet, entitled *Das Forschen nach Licht und Recht* (The Search for Light and Justice)[12] provided the immediate impetus for this work, which appeared three years before Mendelssohn's death. Coming years after the Lavater dispute, the pamphlet threw down a similar gauntlet: Mendelssohn should carry his views on Enlightenment and religion to their logical conclusion and convert to Christianity. With Voltaire, bourgeois rationality had embraced the anticlerical slogan *Écrasez l'infâme* and made a substantial contribution in philosophy, theology, political science, literature, and Oriental philology aimed at paving the way for a comprehensive universe of rational discourse. Yet it was an abiding paradox of the Enlightenment that the power of rationality in the educated middle class failed when it came to reducing anti-Jewish prejudices. *Jerusalem* is Mendelssohn's declaration of belief in a rational Judaism, founded on a repudiation of all coercion in matters of faith, a Judaism that enables the devout Jew to become a citizen of the modern state. The work consists of two parts, the first devoted to the general problem of the relation between church and state, the second to the specific Jewish dimension, the reconciling of natural religion and revelation. In the first section Mendelssohn builds on the thinking of non-Jewish theoreticians of natural law, such as Grotius, Hobbes, Locke, and Pufendorf; the second part is based largely on Jewish sources. The treatment of the general problem is antecedent to that specific to the Jews, an approach that indicates a shift in Mendelssohn's self-understanding as a Jew: belonging to the Jewish faith must be justified by principles that are universally valid. There cannot be one yardstick for the Jews and their religion and another for the religion of the dominant majority. Only if there is a universal rationality common to the monotheistic religions can a moral attitude be assured; only such a universal rationality can provide the guarantee that human rights will be protected.

Mendelssohn stresses here that a clear line must be drawn between church and state. He draws on the theory of natural law, according to which persons band together to live in a state based on a social contract that determines the rights and duties of the citizen and also endows the state with the power of coercion. Yet it is precisely this right to coerce that Mendelssohn denies to the church or religion: religion is not based on a contract that entitles ecclesiastical institutions to compel obedience or to punish insubordination. Both social forms, religion and the state, are constituted in order that human beings can "satisfy their needs by mutual assistance" and be brought closer to a condition of happiness. But what the state is permitted—even the use of physical force in order to constrain individuals to take action for the common good—is denied to religion: "It is a moral person; . . . it does not coerce with an iron rod; rather, it guides by the cords of love. . . . Its weapons are arguments and persuasion; . . . the power to ban and the right of expulsion, which the state can occasionally permit itself, are diametrically opposed to the spirit of religion."[13] From this there follows a rejection of the power of the *ḥerem* (the Jewish ban) as well: the universal principles of natural law, based on freedom, must have equal validity for both Christian and Jewish society. Mendelssohn calls courageously for an abandonment of all religious coercion. Familiar with the resistance to such freedom in his own camp due to the pervasive power of tradition, he appeals to reason: "I have confidence in the most illuminated and pious among the rabbis and elders of my nation: they will gladly relinquish such a harmful prerogative, will happily renounce all coercion, religious and synagogal, and permit their brethren to enjoy the same love and toleration for which they themselves have so fervidly pined."[14] On the basis of enlightened thought, Mendelssohn thus argued for relinquishing what was an important component of Jewish tradition. The policies of the absolutist ruler had already contributed to abrogating the right to ban dissidents; in *Jerusalem*, Mendelssohn came out in principled support of such an abrogation, appealing to the universal theory of natural law.

In the second part of his work, where he develops a philosophical interpretation of the essence of Judaism, he also stresses that there is no contradiction between Jewish religion and the universal criteria of reason. Initially, Mendelssohn makes a clear distinction between the eternal verities of the unity of God, divine providence, and the necessity of God's existence, which are accessible to every human being through the power of reason, and the Law revealed at Sinai, which is exclusively binding on the Jewish nation. The eternal truths, familiar to the Jews since the time of the patriarch Abraham, formed the common foundations of faith shared by monotheists and humankind as a whole—a humanity whose earthly vocation is the attainment of happiness. He then stresses: "Judaism does not boast of any *exclusive* revelation of eternal truths indispensable for supreme happiness. . . . The voice that let itself be heard that great day on Sinai did not call out: 'I am the Eternal One, Thy God! The necessary, independent being, omnipotent and omniscient, giving humans their just reward, in accordance with their deeds, in a future life.'"[15] Mendelssohn interprets the revelation of the oral and written law—which cannot be a precondition of natural religion—in a restrictive, particularistic sense: the revelation of the Law, an element that contradicts rational religion, is binding solely on the Jews. At the same time, he is aware that there must be an answer to the question: why cannot the Jews suffice, like the rest of humanity, with a belief in the eternal verities of reason? Over several pages he develops his highly original ideas on signs and symbols in their function as aids for rational human knowledge. Mendelssohn makes a distinction here between sign-symbols and symbolic acts. While sign-symbols are often insufficient to protect human beings from falling prey to idolatry, the laws communicated to the Jews via a supernatural act are meant to preserve a pure religious and ethical knowledge. The symbolic acts prescribed by the ceremonial law have a dual purpose: to aid the Jews in comprehending the rational truths of natural religion and, at the same time, to keep them unified as a nation until this foundation of faith has become the patrimony of the entire human race. The Jews must live according to Mosaic law—not because they are less rational or obligated to observe a state religion that applies force and compulsion in matters of faith (an argument advanced by Spinoza in the seventeenth century)—but because of their special election by God. Divine providence has chosen them "to be a *nation of priests,* that is to say, a nation that, in its institutions and constitution, laws, actions, fate and vicissitudes, always reflects sound, unadulterated concepts of God and his attributes, and—by its very existence, as it were—teaches these unceasingly unto the nations."[16] Mendelssohn stresses that since the destruction of the Second Temple and the loss of political sovereignty, the observance of the ceremonial law has not been based on external penalties but solely on inner faith and conviction.

The publication of *Morgenstunden oder Vorlesungen über das Daseyn Gottes* (Morning Hours, or Lectures on the Existence of God, 1785) on the eve of his death confirmed once again that in his philosophical writings in German for a non-Jewish reading public Mendelssohn only expounded a worldview that he was able to reconcile with his conception of Judaism. Although he wrote in two different languages, his credo as presented to the outside world did not differ essentially from his internal system of belief. *Morgenstunden* is a work distinguished by a clearly defined theme, an original ontological argument to prove the existence of God, and a high degree of systematics.

In seven of the eighteen lectures of the book, Mendelssohn treats "pre-existent knowledge" as a justification for God's existence before moving on to the "scientific theorems for the existence of God." Finally, he goes on to give a concise presentation of natural theology, identical for him with Leibnizian metaphysics. Once again, he writes as an exponent of Leibniz's theodicy and its optimistic view of the universe, according to

Moses Mendelsfohns

Morgenstunden

oder

Vorlesungen

über das Dafeyn Gottes.

Erster Theil.

Veränderte Auflage.

Berlin, 1786.

Bey Christian Friedrich Voß und Sohn.

41 Title page of Mendelssohn's *Morgenstunden,* with a portrait
of Lessing

which God created the world and human beings for the purpose of their happiness. The world is not a dark vale of tears and suffering, not a prison, but a potential paradise, and "God's rule and Providence" can be discerned "in the most minor of events." Consequently, God should be "venerated more in the events of Nature than in miracles."[17] This, he argues, is tantamount to the supreme refinement of human concepts. In his fifteenth lecture Mendelssohn stresses that it is the most exalted way to reflect on God, his rule, and providence.

There were two principal reasons underlying the writing of *Morgenstunden*. Mendelssohn felt a need to initiate his son Joseph, whose instruction in the Bible had also been the occasion for his translation of the Pentateuch, "into the rational knowledge of God at any early age." He thus lectured to his son and two other young pupils on the verities of natural religion and dedicated *Morgenstunden* to them. Another motivation for the book was an allegation that had been raised against his friend Lessing in his final days, charging him with being a "staunch Spinozist." Mendelssohn was shaken, since this came at a time of increasing interest in Spinoza's thought and a concomitant upsurge in unbelief. Mendelssohn therefore felt it necessary to devote three lectures of *Morgenstunden* to an exposition of Spinoza's teachings, concluding that Lessing was a moderate or "purified" Spinozist—not a stalwart exponent of his philosophy.

In his last work, *An die Freunde Lessings* (To Lessing's Friends, 1786), completed shortly before his death, Mendelssohn once more undertook a desperate attempt to clear his friend after death of the charge of being a strict Spinozist and atheist. Once again, Mendelssohn stresses that it was possible for his own Jewish faith, as he lived and practiced it, to coexist with a rational religion, since revelation in Judaism did not contain any dogmas and eternal truths, but only laws for religious worship. Judaism presupposed "natural and rational conviction regarding religious truths," verities that could stand the test of "simple common sense."[18]

Baruch Spinoza, the Jewish philosopher of the seventeenth century, held a special fascination for Mendelssohn, as he had for the older Lessing. Yet his attitude toward him was highly ambivalent. On the one hand, Mendelssohn distanced himself from Spinoza and his "atheism"; on the other, he was influenced by Spinoza's thought, most obviously in *Jerusalem*, when he returns in the second section to the thesis, already mentioned in the Lavater dispute, that Judaism does not lay claim to any exclusive revelation of eternal truths. This passage and the assertion that supernatural, frightening phenomena on Sinai, such as the "voice of thunder" and the "sound of trumpets," could not communicate eternal rational teachings but only a revelation that was limited to laws, are reminiscent of ideas expounded in Spinoza's *Theologico-Political Treatise.* Spinoza asserts there that the voice resounding from Mount Sinai was unable to convince anyone of the existence of God. It could not provide philosophical or mathematical certainty about God's existence; rather, its sole function was to foster obedience to his laws. It was this specific interpretation that Mendelssohn adopted in his *Jerusalem* and that, in debate with his contemporaries, he tried to harmonize with the criteria of natural religion.

An ambivalence toward Spinoza accompanied Mendelssohn from his very first studies of Enlightenment philosophy. He admired Spinoza's towering intellect and even felt complimented when Lessing prophesied that he could "become a second Spinoza." But he did not wish to share the same fate that had befallen Spinoza simply because "by publishing certain writings" he had "excluded himself from the Jewish law." Mendelssohn attempted to rehabilitate Spinoza, since he respected him as an outstanding Jewish philosopher, ranking the sage in a long and honorable series of eminent rationalist thinkers. He also felt that some attacks on Spinoza were unjustified and had been shaped by Christian prejudice—as, for example, in the case of Bayle, who had claimed that in Spinoza's system God forfeited his attribute of perfection, sharing deficiencies and shortcomings with human beings. In the *Philosophische Gespräche* Mendelssohn sought to view Spinoza's rationalist system as a set of teachings compatible with religion. However, as an exponent of Leibniz and Wolff, and a Jew committed to normative Judaism, he was unable to fully endorse the Spinozan system. The thesis that God was the only substance in the universe (and everything else only a modification of that single substance) was unacceptable to Mendelssohn's thinking, as was Spinoza's thesis of the negation of Divine will. Yet he endeavored to prove that the principle formulated in the *Ethics* (1677)—"the order and connection of concepts is identical with the order and connection of things"—had made a major contribution to the "amelioration of our universal insight" before the transition from Descartes to Leibniz and his concept of "prestabilized harmony." Since Mendelssohn wished to include Spinoza in the ranks of the Jewish precursors of Enlightenment philosophy, he regretted all the more that Spinoza had erroneously believed that no universe had ever become a reality external to God, and that the conception of the Leibnizians about the "best of all possible worlds" thus remained an alien notion for Spinoza. So Spinoza had perforce to "fall into the enormous abyss lying between Descartes and Leibniz." But he made a necessary sacrifice for progress in philosophy, and for that reason Mendelssohn stresses his importance: "So let us always admit the fact that a thinker who was not a German and, let me add, not a Christian either—that Spinoza had a large part in the advancement of philosophy."[19] He could not express his attitude to Spinoza any more clearly than this. Mendelssohn considered him to be the first outstanding Jewish philosopher of the modern period, who had made his contribution to the thinking of the Enlightenment.

The second important Jewish thinker after Spinoza was doubtless Mendelssohn himself, separated from his predecessor not just by the span of a century but also by his struggle to find a compromise formula that rendered the principles of natural religion and the revealed Jewish Law reconcilable. Soon Mendelssohn was able to gather around himself the maskilim who agreed with him on his new Jewish self-understanding and supported him in the task of creating a secular sphere of life within Jewish society.

10

The Haskalah as a
Sociocultural Phenomenon

1. The Circle Around Mendelssohn

Mendelssohn had achieved renown as a philosopher of the Enlightenment and gained access to circles of non-Jewish scholars—a formidable accomplishment for a Jew in the era before emancipation; yet that still did not make him the founder of a Jewish movement of *Aufklärung*. The prerequisite for this was a conscious endeavor on his part to promote the acceptance of new ideas within Jewish society. First he had to gather around himself a circle of like-minded thinkers and followers prepared to work together with him to gain recognition for enlightened ideas and make these a formative force in Jewish culture and society. A step in this direction was taken in the 1770s and 1780s when a group of young Jews came together in Berlin, enlighteners for whom the author of the *Phädon* soon became their authority in matters of the intellect and his house a center of attraction, a meeting place for spirited exchange.

Naphtali Herz Wessely (1725–1805), a native of Hamburg, had moved to Berlin from Copenhagen. Thanks to his education, he had certain prerequisites that would prove extremely favorable, perhaps even indispensable for the first phase of the Haskalah. His father, a successful merchant and court purveyor to the Danish king, sought to combine his son's education in the traditional sources of Jewish religion, especially the Talmud (he also studied in the yeshiva of Rabbi Jonathan Eybeschütz), with a good measure of secular knowledge, particularly in European languages.

Wessely later recalled that his father spread out a map one day to teach him some geography about cities and countries. This secular education was meant to aid the young Wessely, whom his father expected to become a merchant, on his future journeys through Europe. No less promising a decision for the young boy's future was the choice of Solomon Hanau (1687–1746), an outstanding scholar of Hebrew, as a private tutor. He initiated the ten-year-old Naphtali into the beauty and systematic character of the language of the Bible. Wessely's love for Hebrew germinated under Hanau's expert guidance, and he would later deepen that knowledge during a stay in Amsterdam, where he came to know the works of Sephardi Hebraists. He soon composed his first philological work, *Ha-Levanon* (Lebanon, 1765–1766), a selection of synonyms for the linguistic understanding of the biblical text. Here, as well as in later works, Wessely proceeded on the assumption that rational, scientific knowledge and Jewish faith can coexist. Alongside his activity as a merchant, an avocation he ultimately had to abandon, Wessely, particularly through self-study, had acquired an education that prepared him to play the role of an innovator in the revitalization of Hebrew language and literature. In Berlin he became a follower of Mendelssohn—not because he had absorbed the philosophical ideas of Wolff and Leibniz but because of his desire to rejuvenate Jewish culture and society. The measured combination of tradition and an open receptivity to secular, scientific education enabled the two men to work together.

Solomon Dubno (1738–1813) and Herz Homberg (1749–1841) also came to Berlin in the 1770s, becoming associates of Mendelssohn and tutors in his home. Without Dubno, the Mendelssohn translation of the Bible and its commentary might never have come to fruition, because it was Dubno who had encouraged Mendelssohn to undertake the difficult project, assisting him as an outstanding expert on masoretic tradition. Dubno had been raised completely in the spirit of traditional Judaism. However, the fact that he had been educated in the Talmud by great scholars in Eastern Europe who could see no contradiction between Talmudic learning and secular scientific knowledge would prove decisive for the direction of his future life. Among these sages was his teacher Rabbi Solomon Chelm (1717–1781), whose rational understanding of Judaism and secular knowledge, combined with a rejection of hasidic mysticism, had opened his pupil's mind, rendering him receptive for enlightened ideas.

Herz Homberg, born in Lieben near Prague, had also acquired a solid grounding in the Talmud. Among other things, he had studied with the

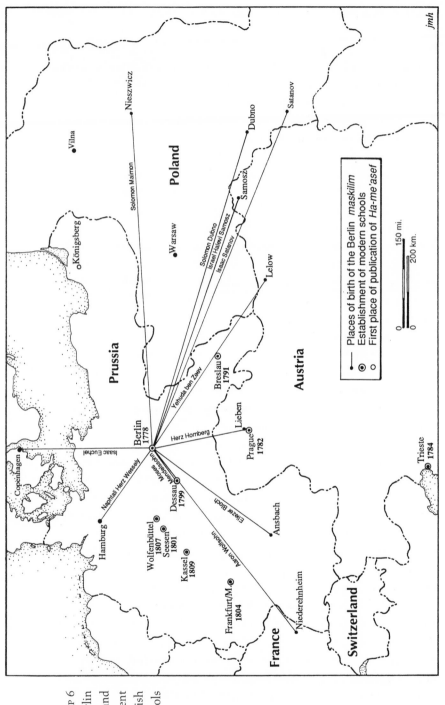

MAP 6
The Berlin
Haskalah and
the Establishment
of Modern Jewish
Schools

Places of birth of the Berlin *maskilim*
Establishment of modern schools
First place of publication of *Ha-me'asef*

150 mi.
200 km.

Vilna

Nieszwicz

Königsberg

Poland

Warsaw

Dubno

Satanov

Samosz

Lelow

Prussia

Solomon Maimon

Solomon Dubno

Israel Halevi Samosz

Isaac Satanov

Breslau
1791

Lieben

Yehuda ben Zeev

Berlin
1778

Herz Homberg

Prague
1782

Austria

Copenhagen

Isaac Euchel

Naphtali Herz Wessely

Moses Mendelssohn

Dessau
1799

Eliezer Bloch

Ansbach

Hamburg

Wolfenbüttel
1807

Seesen
1801

Kassel
1809

Aaron Wolfsohn

Frankfurt/M.
1804

Niederehnheim

France

Switzerland

Trieste
1784

jmh

42   The maskil Herz Homberg

famous Talmud scholar Rabbi Ezekiel Landau. Yet that did not prevent him from also gaining knowledge in secular subjects, such as German, Latin, and mathematics. Inspired by his reading of Rousseau's *Émile*, he became a radical champion of reform in Jewish schools. Like Wessely and several dozen other young Jews who felt keenly attracted by Mendelssohn and his quest for a rationalized Jewish identity, Dubno and Homberg were to a certain extent already predisposed for a new enlightened Judaism when they arrived in Berlin.

The entire inner circle of the Berlin Haskalah, which initiated the important cultural initiatives of the 1770s and 1780s—the Bible project,

editing of a journal, publication of literary works, and the establishment
of new schools—drew on the original sources of Judaism. The maskilim
had absorbed their initial conceptions of Jewish culture in tradition-
oriented homes, had then gone on to Talmud schools, and finally the
yeshiva. Like Mendelssohn, his disciples were also sent as children to
ḥeder to have treatises of the Talmud drummed into their heads even
before they could properly read and understand a sentence from the
Bible. But, also like Mendelssohn, their religious education went beyond this frame: it did not prevent them from assimilating stimulating
new influences from the outside—on the contrary, it even facilitated
their absorption.

Yet a strong background in Jewish knowledge and the attraction
exerted by Mendelssohn and his thought were not a sufficient condition
for joint activity as enlighteners. A material, socioeconomic basis was necessary before their intellectual circle could launch a movement to transform culture and society. As mentioned, such a basis existed in the Jewish
community—in the homes of affluent Jewish merchants. There the former Talmud student turned maskil could earn his keep as a tutor and also
obtain a residence permit in the very center of the Haskalah.

As impoverished servants the Jewish private tutors belonged to a social
group on the fringes of society. The tutor was only granted entry to the
community and the right of temporary residence under the protection of
a privileged Jew; when he had terminated his service he was obliged to
leave the city and then tried his luck in another community. He often
joined the ranks of those poor Jews who wandered from community to
community in search of a place to stay. In his *Autobiography* the philosopher Solomon Maimon (1754–1800), who stemmed from Poland,
describes this itinerant fate. Some three decades after Mendelssohn he
arrived at the Rosenthal Gate in Berlin, which was reserved for Jews, and
requested permission to enter. A gatekeeper, an officer of the Jewish community, refused to let Maimon pass. Until his petition was decided upon,
he was put up in the community poorhouse:

> Since, as is well known, no beggar Jew is tolerated in this residential
> city, the local Jewish community has built a house at the Rosenthal
> Gate for taking care of its needy. The poor are taken in there and
> questioned by the Jewish elders about what it is they seek in Berlin;
> if they are ill or looking for work, after a decision has been reached,
> they are either admitted to the city or sent on their way. So I too was

brought to this house. The place was packed, crowded in part with the sick, but partly with miserable rabble![1]

Mendelssohn had been lucky. Arriving on foot in Berlin as a poor Talmud pupil after a journey from Dessau, without a letter of recommendation in his pocket, his acquaintanceship with the chief rabbi David Fränkel, his former teacher, had saved him from being turned away. Fränkel found him a garret room in the house of the community elder Ḥayim Bamberg, where he also took meals twice a week as a private tutor. Maimon, by contrast, was unable to name even a single acquaintance, and was thus sent on his way. Despite his intellectual gifts, he shared the fate of the beggar Jews and wandered on. Yet, in some places, such as Stettin, they were impressed by the Talmudic training of the Eastern European Jews: "I was received rather nicely here, and invited to Sabbath dinner by the most respected and wealthiest Jew in the town; I went to the synagogue, where I was given the most respected place to sit, and shown all the honors customarily due a rabbi."[2] Solomon Maimon, one of the brilliant intellects of the Berlin Haskalah, and other maskilim as well, led the uncertain, unsettled life of a wandering Jew. Their living conditions only

43   The *Judenherberge* (Jews' Hostel) at the Rosenthal Gate in Berlin. Pen-and-ink drawing by Ludwig Müller, 1807

improved when they managed to find employment with a protected Jew as a tutor for his children.

It is thus all the more remarkable that despite the precarious existence of the Jewish private tutors they managed to become the exponents of the Berlin Haskalah. It was a sign of the new and changing times: education and the desire for reform were now decisive. These factors made it possible for a lower-status and penniless group to provide the essential impetus sparking a process of intellectual ferment and cultural rejuvenation in Jewish society. Thus, Isaac Euchel (1756–1804) became the initiator of the Hevrat dorshe leshon ever (Society for the Promotion of the Hebrew Language) and the journal *Ha-Me'asef* (The Collector), the most important vehicle for the dissemination of the ideas of the Berlin Haskalah. Euchel, born in Copenhagen and traditionally educated, had been converted in Berlin to the Haskalah and was active as a private tutor in Königsberg.

In the eighteenth century secular education was also a prerequisite among Christians for admission to the intellectual elite within the rising middle class. The men who were the bearers of this sociocultural development did not differ basically from the maskilim in terms of their modest social background. In many instances they stemmed from the families of Protestant clergymen. Such pastors were on the bottom rung of the corporate society, led a life of Spartan simplicity, but offered their children intellectual stimulation and education. In a similar manner, the traditional education of children in Jewish families had fostered their intellectual capacities and facilitated access for young Jews to the Haskalah.

The quest for knowledge and education was thus a characteristic feature of the new elite, whether Jewish or Christian. But prospects for social advancement differed substantially. Although some non-Jewish Enlightenment figures, such as Herder, Lessing, and Kant, had temporarily worked as private tutors, the path lay open to them to pursue careers in state and municipal service as professors, legal experts, lawyers, and town jurists. As soon as they had acquired an academic education, they were thus able to find security and status as a "state" intelligentsia. But, for the Jew, the route to a career in public service remained closed; universities were slow in opening their doors to Jewish applicants. Down into the nineteenth century they were constrained to seek their livelihood within the orbit of Jewish society. This is the reason why even maskilim who had acquired a high level of general education and also attended universities ultimately found posts as teachers or directors at the new modernized Jewish schools promoted by the Haskalah. One such example was Lazarus Bendavid (1762–1832), born in Berlin and an outstanding student of Kantian philosophy. After studying at various universities, he had as his goal to become a jurist in Prussia; initially, though, he had to make do with a job as a freelance writer in German. He later became editor of the *Spenersche Zeitung*, and, from 1806 on, served as director of the Jüdische Freischule in Berlin.

Isaac Euchel, who had applied for a post at the University of Königsberg, apparently even with the support of Immanuel Kant, had just as little success in his efforts to receive official recognition as Mendelssohn and Maimon, the outstanding thinkers of the Haskalah. In the 1760s Mendelssohn was denied membership in the Royal Prussian Academy after Frederick the Great had personally intervened to cancel a positive decision by the academy to admit him. Maimon, acclaimed as a brilliant intellectual by virtue of his penetrating analysis of Kant's *Critique of Pure Reason* (1781), led an unsettled life, without ever gaining a permanent position and material security.

Thus, faced with the impossibility of upward mobility, the Jewish intelligentsia remained locked in a community of fate with the rest of Jewish society, whose life was still bound by the old structures and values. In marked contrast with the position of the non-Jewish educated middle class at the end of the eighteenth century, this "pariah status" of the maskilim induced them to turn their enlightening energies inward, in order to bring about a restructuring of Jewish society. As private tutors in wealthy Jewish families, they induced a creative intellectual ferment.

Even before the Berlin Haskalah the tutor-servant was a familiar figure in Jewish society in the German-speaking lands. Already prior to the middle of the eighteenth century hundreds of Polish students of Talmud had migrated westward to secure a post in the employ of court Jews or in their milieu. Since the Polish yeshivot had a considerable reputation, nearly all the Talmud students seeking a place were able to find one. Toward the middle of the eighteenth century their ranks were supplemented by numerous students who, in addition to their solid knowledge of Jewish tradition, also could boast an excellent background in secular studies. This linking of Talmudic learning and *ḥochmah* (wisdom, science, secular knowledge), which they sought to impart to others, implanted a receptivity in their pupils for the ideas of the Enlightenment. Most of the young teachers arriving from the East, and from Bohemia, Moravia, and

Hungary as well, initially took a moderate, balanced view of Jewish tradition. One reason for that moderation was the fact that they belonged to a
generation firmly rooted in rabbinic knowledge and, employed as servants in traditionally oriented homes, they were in no position to advocate a radical change in values and norms. Thus it is also not surprising
that the Hebrew language was still central in their teaching and writings.
Nonetheless, by introducing innovations in the content and methods of
education, the private tutors contributed to a shift in mentality.

Mendelssohn's correspondence is instructive in this regard. It is evident from his letters that his plan to organize the home education of his
own children along enlightened lines, beginning with that of his son
Joseph, was what induced him to launch work on his Bible translation and
the accompanying Hebrew commentary *Bi'ur* (Explanation). Only in
response to the urging of Solomon Dubno, who was teaching Joseph
Hebrew, did the idea take shape to transform the translation for his son
into a project for the wider Jewish public.

In many respects, the work of the private tutor provided the laboratory
for the implementation of enlightened ideas in practice—for example, the
introduction of rationalist literature such as Maimonides' *Guide of the
Perplexed* into the curriculum of Jewish education, and an expanded use of
the Hebrew language. The first beginnings of these new educational priorities can be discerned in the framework of home instruction. As educators, the maskilim were intent to include secular knowledge alongside the
traditional subjects (the latter, of course, did not disappear from one day to
the next). The wealthy families in Berlin, Königsberg, Breslau, and other
centers of the Jewish Enlightenment were the first to translate conceptions
of Haskalah into practice in the daily process of educating their children.

At this stage Wessely and Mendelssohn exercised a moderating influence on the maskilim and forestalled any radicalization. In Mendelssohn's
home the observance of the Jewish ceremonial law was a paramount
obligation. He emphasized this priority in a letter to Herz Homberg, the
former private tutor of his son Joseph:

> We don't hold the same views regarding the necessity of the ritual
> laws. Even if their importance as a kind of script or a symbolic lan-
> guage has lost its utility, their necessity as a unifying bond contin-
> ues. In my view this unity [of the Jewish people] will have to be pre-
> served in the plan of Providence for as long as polytheism, anthro-
> pomorphism, and religious usurpation rule the planet.[3]

In the second half of the eighteenth century the Jewish private tutor thus became the exponent of the new enlightened currents. In this era his membership in an ethnic-religious minority determined his fate, binding him to his community, until the process of emancipation and the consolidation of a modern educational system within Jewish society and beyond gradually led to the demise of the institution of private tutor.

Along with private tutors, physicians also belonged to the group of young Jews affected by the allure of the Berlin Haskalah. Their university medical education had confronted them with secular discplines to a greater extent than was true of other Jews. By reason of that background they were ideally predisposed to endorse and champion an enlightened current within Judaism. Among these university graduates were Marcus Eliezer Bloch (1723–1799), a famous zoologist and the family physician of Mendelssohn, and Mordechai Gumpel Schnaber (1729–1797). Schnaber had learned Talmud together with Mendelssohn under Rabbi Fränkel, but then had gone on to study medicine in London. Later he was active as a physician in Hamburg, where he wrote *Yesod ha-torah* (Foundation of the Torah), an enlightened commentary in Hebrew on Maimonides' "Thirteen Articles of Faith." Jonas Jeitteles (1735–1806) was the physician of the Jewish community in Prague; as an admirer of the new ideas emanating from Berlin, he forged the first intellectual bonds with the Haskalah there, becoming the "father" of the Prague Jewish Enlightenment. Marcus Herz (1747–1803) had received a traditional education in the Talmud academy of Veitel Heine Ephraim, studied medicine in Halle, and returned home to Berlin to take up a post as a physician in the Jewish hospital. Along with medicine as a profession and science, to which he devoted an encyclopedic work, *Grundriss aller medicinischen Wissenschaften* (Comprehensive Outline of the Medical Sciences, 1782), he was also deeply interested in Kantian philosophy. In the privacy of his own home Herz lectured to Jews and Christians, among them Baron von Zedlitz (1731–1793), the Prussian minister of justice. Whereas the somewhat older Mendelssohn no longer felt quite equal to the challenge of Kant's *Critique of Pure Reason*, Herz gave lectures both on the natural sciences and on the system of the great Königsberg philosopher. Kant held the sharp intellect of his Jewish commentator in high regard. Indeed, for Herz, and more generally for the generation of the maskilim after Mendelssohn, it was now the philosophy of Kant that held sway and was deemed authoritative, supplanting that of Leibniz and Wolff. Herz made a major contribution to the reception of Kantian conceptions in the Berlin Enlightenment; he may also have facilitated the adoption of the concept of a rational religion as an alternative to normative Judaism.

2. Mendelssohn's Bible Project

The translation of the Pentateuch from Hebrew into German and the simultaneous preparation of a Hebrew commentary, the *Bi'ur*, was Mendelssohn's grand project, the vehicle by which he chose to demonstrate the independent character of Jewish Enlightenment. The entire work bore the title *Netivot ha-shalom* (Paths of Peace). At the beginning of the 1770s, after his philosophical creativity had passed its highpoint and Mendelssohn pondered the need for enlightened thinking to have a deeper impact in the quest to induce his nation to take "a step in the direction of culture," he saw no more appropriate way than to present the venerable and ancient biblical text in a new enlightened form.

Mendelssohn was undoubtedly familiar with Luther's monumental translation of the Bible into German and had studied it carefully. But it would be mistaken to see his project merely as a Jewish variant of Luther's opus. Rather, a comparison much closer to the contemporary sociocultural frame suggests itself: the *Encyclopédie* of the French philosophes. Their aim was to familiarize the broader public in eighteenth-century France with the rational conceptions of Enlightenment, encapsulated in the form of a collectively authored work presented in a popular style. Taking into account its specific genre and distinctive features, the Bible translation and accompanying *Bi'ur* can nonetheless be viewed as a similar experiment to popularize enlightened conceptions. Analogous to the *Encyclopédie*, Mendelssohn's project too was not the work of a single individual, but a group effort—namely, of those maskilim who had gathered around him in the 1770s. The translation was Mendelssohn's, but the *Bi'ur* commentary was a collective work. Without the assistance of several committed disciples, even the ten long years it actually took (1773–1783) would not have been sufficient to complete the project. Solomon Dubno, Naphtali Herz Wessely, Aaron Jaroslav, and Herz Homberg were among the contributors, though Mendelssohn always remained the authority for them, pointing the way. While Dubno wrote the commentary on Genesis (except for chapter 1) and the grammatical aspects of Exodus, Wessely authored the commentary on Leviticus, Jaroslav on Numbers, and Homberg on two-thirds of Deuteronomy.

They all worked in close collaboration with Mendelssohn, who gave *Netivot ha-shalom* its unified character.

Even when Mendelssohn and his associates incorporated new ideas and concepts into the text, they still proceeded with great respect for Jewish tradition. In a number of instances where a modern rationalistic interpretation of the text was in open contradiction with the traditional reading, Mendelssohn gave preference to the latter. Already in the prospectus *Alim li-terufah* (Leaves for Healing, 1778), which Solomon Dubno had prepared in collaboration with Mendelssohn, and in even more detailed form in his introduction to the translation, "Or la-netivah" (Light for the Path, 1782), Mendelssohn was concerned to dispel the doubts of potential orthodox opponents. He wished for all to see the project firmly planted within the continuity of many centuries of rabbinic tradition. Thus he emphasized the unity and inviolability of the Torah text, which he believed stemmed authentically from the age before the ancient Hebrews entered Canaan. In Mendelssohn's eyes there was no doubt that the entire Pentateuch—from the first chapter of Genesis to the last sections of Deuteronomy, including the report of Moses's death—had been inspired by God and written down by Moses himself:

> The entire community of Israel is thus convinced that we hold in our hands today that text of the Bible actually written by Moses ... and that the text has not experienced the fate of those profane books which, over the course of time, have been distorted by scribes and copyists, carelessly or intentionally, through the addition, omission, and alteration of passages.[4]

In his view the sacred language in which the Bible was composed had also been faithfully transmitted. This was the Hebrew in which God had "spoken to Adam, Cain, Noah, and our holy patriarchs, in which He proclaimed the Ten Commandments at Sinai and engraved them on the tablets. It is the language in which He spoke to Moses and the prophets. And that alone endows it with precedence over all other tongues, so that we may call it 'holy.' "[5] In order to underpin his thesis, Mendelssohn mentions a whole series of names and idiomatic expressions for which there are no parallels in German or other languages.

Never once does he doubt the sacredness of the text and its language. Even the vocalization and punctuation of the Bible, which derive from a period after the time of Moses, are for the translator a binding tradition. Precisely for that reason, Mendelssohn chose Solomon Dubno as his first important collaborator. Dubno was a scholar with a formidable knowledge of the masoretic signs that facilitated the faithful reading and exegesis of the biblical text.

Mendelssohn's rationalistic approach required him, both in the translation and the commentary, to give preference to the method of *peshat* (the plain, literal reading) in order to come closer to the true meaning of the text. However, concentrating principally on a scientific knowledge of the Hebrew language, its grammar and syntax, was by no means synonymous for him with Bible criticism, which he rejected. Even when already an enthusiastic advocate of the Enlightenment and the "republic of intellectuals," Mendelssohn was far from the approach that Spinoza had initiated in his *Theologico-Political Treatise* and that was later intensively promoted by Protestant scholars, especially in the German cultural orbit. One of the express aims of his project was to "render the Scriptures, which have become incomprehensible as a result of hypocrisy and clerical cunning, readable and understandable once again."[6] He wished to counterpose a Jewish rational interpretation to the Christian rational reading, one that did not call the continuity of tradition into question.

Even if it appears that the *Bi'ur* was partially intended to displace the classical commentary by Rashi, it should not be forgotten that Mendelssohn repeatedly stressed his indebtedness to the medieval commentators in France and Spain—Rashi above all others—insofar as they maintained the venerable tradition of peshat exegesis. He impressed upon his collaborator Dubno the need to study the commentaries of Rashi and several later authorities thoroughly, extracting what was appropriate for the project, since they had all remained faithful to the principle of a simple, rational interpretation of the text.

Moreover, his decided bent for peshat readings did not prevent Mendelssohn from giving precedence to the method of *derash* (a homiletically extended reading of the text, often allegorical, "handed down by the sages") whenever there appeared to be a contradiction between the peshat and derash interpretations—so as to avoid any strong deviation from the tradition, even at the cost of consistent rationality.

In view of his veneration for rabbinic erudition and the oral and written tradition, there would appear to be no justification whatsoever for the vehement opposition and rejection his Bible project provoked within orthodox circles. However, it was certainly no accident that Mendelssohn had refrained from obtaining the consent of the leading representatives of orthodoxy for his translation and that they subsequently declared open war on the *Netivot ha-shalom* project. The work was obviously too much in keeping with the spirit of the times. In their opposition the rabbis Ezekiel Landau, Raphael Kohen, Pinchas Horovitz, Elazar Fleckeles, and others were not simply influenced by the irrational apprehensions and biases of orthodoxy, fearful of any sort of deviation from custom and the norms of the majority. They also subjected his translation to biting critique because they had a keen sense for what was novel in the work and, lurking behind his nuanced formulations, they perceived elements that posed a threat to the norms and values of orthodoxy. Thus when Mendelssohn translated Leviticus 19:17, "You can rebuke your neighbor," instead of "You shall," and then added "if he has insulted you," Rabbi Pinchas Horovitz thought this reading implied a lessening of the responsibility incumbent on the individual Jew for the religious and moral behavior of his neighbor as demanded by the Talmud. However, in evaluating the broad impact of the Bible project on respect for tradition and its persistence and in trying to assess its significance for a shift in culture, values, and norms, one must pay particular attention to the objection voiced by Ezekiel Landau:

> It is quite possible that it was the author's intent to prevent readers from rushing to consult the Christian Bible. However, we cannot see any improvement in what he has attempted. . . . The translator has penetrated deeply into the language and employed a very difficult German, one that presupposes an exact knowledge of grammar. Children will have difficulty comprehending it, and the teacher will have to spend most of his time explaining German grammar to them. Moreover, the translation does not follow the text word for word, but gives the general meaning. . . . Since it is used to instruct children, it will mislead the latter to waste their time reading non-Jewish books in order to master a refined German and thus to understand the translation. In the process our Torah is degraded into the role of a handmaiden to the German language.[7]

To be sure, Ezekiel Landau was unable to raise any fundamental religious objections to Mendelssohn's Bible translation because there was no prohibition in Judaism against using a Bible translated from Hebrew. Since Ezra's time, when the Bible was first translated into Aramaic for the Jews of Babylon, who had "forgotten the holy tongue," translations had appeared in the various languages of the cultures and peoples the Jews had encountered on their wanderings in the Diaspora: in Greek, Arabic,

Persian, Spanish, and also in Western Yiddish. In the introduction "Or la-netivah" Mendelssohn recounts all these renderings in order to justify his project. Yet Landau, the great Talmudic scholar and chief rabbi of Prague, feared that because of the enormous linguistic demands Mendelssohn's language placed on Jewish readers, his translation would lead to a weakening of the tradition and the creation of a secular culture among Jews. Once such a secular culture had appeared, Landau warned, it would establish and consolidate itself and then expand. In the view of Landau and the rabbis allied with him, combating the work was therefore a duty. Yet not until one examines Mendelssohn's various statements on the theory of language, beginning with his very first publications, is it evident how the Bible project could be regarded as a contribution to the creation of a "secular culture." His position on questions of language, pertaining to both German and Hebrew, was not determined first and foremost by tradition-oriented, religious considerations.

In 1755, at Lessing's suggestion, Mendelssohn had completed a translation of Rousseau's *Discourse on the Origin of Inequality Among Men*. On that occasion, in an open letter to Lessing, he set down his views on the origin of language and the way in which language is determined by the reflective capacity of human beings, questions Rousseau had touched on in this work. He often discussed the "origin of language and Rousseau's views on the matter" with Lessing.[8]

During the 1750s this was not a negligible topic in the debate among intellectuals. The German moral weeklies had devoted space to its discussion, and it also left traces in *Kohelet Musar* where the attentive reader can already recognize a contradiction between Mendelssohn's avowed adherence to the concept of the "holy language" and his proclivity to accord the Hebrew language new, secular functions, as the language of lyric poetry and philosophy. In 1759 the Prussian Academy in Berlin set a prize competition question: "To what extent do a people's ideas influence its language, and vice versa?" The Göttingen Orientalist Johann David Michaelis (1717–1791) was awarded the winning prize, and Mendelssohn praised his paper—this despite the fact that he had locked horns in controversy with Michaelis on numerous occasions because of the latter's biased attitude toward Jews and Judaism. This time, however, they had something in common: their keen interest in the interrelation between language, reason, and culture. The topic occupied academy members such as Maupertuis and Sulzer and, even earlier, philosophers in France and Germany had indicated that they considered it a main issue on the agenda of Enlightenment.

When Mendelssohn first gained entry into the circle of scholars through Lessing's agency, he quickly came to understand that they saw a close link between the intellectual level of a people and its linguistic development: "In general, the language of a people is the best indication of its education, culture, and enlightenment."[9] For that reason, he had delved into many works of the classical and modern period that dealt with theories of language and translation. Mendelssohn also expressed his interest in these questions in a number of articles for the periodical *Bibliothek der schönen Wissenschaften und der freien Künste,* which Friedrich Nicolai had been editing since 1756.

As Mendelssohn saw it, the enlightened attitude was closely associated with the concept of language as a vehicle of human reason, ethics, and aesthetics. Cultivation of language was a precondition for the achievement of Enlightenment objectives: the eradication of prejudice, irrational, immoral attitudes and habits—in brief, a prerequisite for the improvement of humanity. When, some twenty years after his concepts regarding language had crystallized, Mendelssohn launched his translation of the Pentateuch and publication of the *Bi'ur* commentary, he was undoubtedly motivated by a spirit of enlightenment. He endeavored to moderate that spirit by repeated avowal of his loyalty to the "holy language" and the religious tradition of Judaism. But, in a letter to his friend Hennings, he stated quite clearly that he wished to "bring his own nation closer to culture" and considered the Bible project a first step in that direction. Further measures aimed at disseminating the Haskalah would have to follow.

The fact that Mendelssohn selected the Bible as a vehicle to convey enlightened ideas and concepts, while emphasizing his preference for the traditional peshat interpretation of the text, makes it difficult at first glance to recognize the innovative, nontraditional element involved here. Yet that novelty is certainly present, and the orthodox rabbis could not be shaken in their strong opposition to the work. If one gathers together Mendelssohn's statements on the aims of the project and the urgency of fostering a renaissance of Hebrew as a language in which the most sublime poetry and highest ethical ideals and rationality had been expressed, there can be no doubt about his intention: he wished to introduce non-conformist, rationalistic criteria even into the field of Bible study, a segment of Jewish culture hallowed by tradition and revelation (in which he remained a firm believer). An excerpt from one of his many writings, published in 1757 in the *Bibliothek der schönen Wissenschaften* on

Robert Lowth's lectures on the sacred poetry of the Hebrews, can serve as an example of this underlying aesthetic agenda:

> One reads Homer, Virgil, and the other works of the Ancients; one carefully analyzes all the beauties they contain and takes great pains to mold our taste in accordance with their paradigm. Yet only rarely is there any concern about the rules of art by which those Divine poets among the ancient Hebrews awaken in us the most sublime sentiments and are able to find the direct path to our heart. . . . There has thus been a longstanding desire to see the aesthetic rules in the ancient Hebrew poets explicated, the genius of their poesy marked out with its special characteristics. Yet whoever wishes to rise to this task, must know more than Hebrew grammar alone; his knowledge of the language must be combined with a secure philosophical taste, and he must have a capacity to compare, contrast, and distinguish the genius of diverse peoples.[10]

It was of primary concern to uncover the aesthetic values that lay hidden in the prose of the Hebrews, and most especially in the poetry, whose high point was reached in the Psalms (as Herder also had demonstrated). Mendelssohn thus applied himself with particular enthusiasm to a translation of the Psalms as well, published in 1783.

Along with the new aesthetic approach, Mendelssohn and his collaborators likewise endeavored wherever possible to draw on insights from the natural sciences, philosophical notions, and abstract rational concepts, both in the translation of the Pentateuch and in the *Bi'ur*, in an effort to reduce superstition and prejudice. Mendelssohn's choice of the term "the Eternal One" (*der Ewige*) to render the name of God was an innovation in Judaism. Following Baumgarten's metaphysics, the appellation contained three attributes of the Divine Being always mentioned separately in medieval Jewish hermeneutics: his eternity, necessity, and providence. When he came to interpreting the "hardening of Pharoah's heart" (Exodus 7:3), Mendelssohn pointed out the simultaneity and interactive relation of physiological and psychological events and reiterated views already expressed in the *Phädon* about the compatability of movements in the body of a particular person and the conceptions and longings of his soul. Moreover, Mendelssohn interprets the reference to the "face of God" in Exodus 33:23 in the sense of Maimonides, as the human aspiration to come nearer to God by means of rational conceptions, but without ever being able to attain the level of total knowledge. His intention was clearly to avoid any anthropomorphic associations.

How then was Medelssohn's work received? What public welcomed his Bible project, in view of the stiff opposition voiced by rabbinical authorities, who represented the still orthodox majority of Jewry at the time? A list of subscribers to the first printing contains the names of 515 persons who purchased 750 copies of the complete edition (1781–1783). The list includes Jews from all over Europe, from Holland to Polish Russia, but their concentration in Prussia, particularly Berlin, Königsberg, and Breslau, is conspicuous. Support for the Bible project and the concentration of a middle-class enlightened elite in urban communities went hand in hand.

The maskilim after Mendelssohn endeavored to disseminate the complete work *Netivot ha-shalom* as an inseparable part of the cultural impetus emanating from Berlin. Between 1783 and 1888 the Bible translation and *Bi'ur* commentary went through seventeen printings, some initiated by maskilim in Poland and Russia. There were repeated translations and commentaries published, based in part on *Netivot ha-shalom*, such as Euchel's commentary on Proverbs and the translation of the books of Kings and Job by the maskil Aaron Wolfssohn. The Jewish school principals David Fränkel and M. H. Bock finally published the entire Mendelssohn translation in German script in 1815.

Netivot ha-shalom was integrated into the curriculum in the schools of the Haskalah movement. Thus, Simone Luzzatto, the Italian adherent of the Haskalah, recommended to Joseph Perl in Tarnopol (Galicia) in 1813 that he use it in his new school, since he believed there was no more suitable work for Bible instruction. The schools of Central and Eastern Europe that were founded and directed by maskilim followed Wessely's suggestion to be guided by the new spirit of the Mendelssohn translation in Bible studies for Jewish children. Decades after the Berlin Haskalah had lost its dominant position, its message lived on in the new centers, thanks in significant measure to *Netivot ha-shalom*. This is best illustrated by words of the Hebrew writer Micha Josef Berdyczewski on the occasion of a new printing of the *Bi'ur* in Warsaw in 1888:

> The name *Bi'ur* awakens in each of us youthful memories of the magic power of that work in the age of Haskalah. In me it aroused feelings from another world, far removed from the one in which I was born and raised. . . . I noticed that every time I uttered the word

Bi'ur, my father, a strict believer, would contort his face in a gri-
mace—and with good reason. *Netivot ha-shalom* was actually
enormously attractive to me and spurred me on to battle. . . . Those
who collaborated on the commentary were almost all faithful to tradition. Their language was tradition-bound, their style rabbinic. . . .
But just on that account they were able to kindle a fire in the House
of Jacob, bans were imposed, and a powerful intellectual ferment set
in motion.[11]

3. Secularization of the Hebrew Language

After the successful conclusion of the Bible project, the Jewish Enlightenment was no longer centered upon the thinking of one person: it developed into a sociocultural phenomenon that the maskilim continued to
advance after Mendelssohn's death. They seized new initiatives to carry
the message of the Haskalah into Jewish society and to demonstrate the
beauty and manifold applicability of the biblical language. While the Bible
project had been of paramount concern in the 1770s, the following two
decades witnessed a surge of creativity on a broadened front. The maskilim composed satires and poetry, providing an impetus for the genesis of
a modern literature in Hebrew.

Wessely, who regarded the revitalization of the Hebrew language as
his life's work, became an admired master of the art. He wrote an epic on
Moses in several volumes, *Shire tiferet* (Songs of Splendor, 1789–1802,
1829), inspired by Klopstock's *Messiah* and Herder's *Spirit of Hebrew
Poetry*. Herder had called for a literary work that would do proper honor
to the outstanding personality of the ancient Hebrews. Wessely in his epic
utilized a large number of Hebrew texts from the Bible, Mishnah,
Talmud, apocryphal and medieval literature in order to portray the fate of
ancient Israel from Egyptian slavery and the dramatic exodus under
Moses's leadership down to the giving of the Torah on Sinai. The Hebrew
journal *Ha-Me'asef* had enthusiastic praise for the work, stating that
since the completion of the Bible there had been no comparable creation.
Yet the enthusiasm of contemporaries could not hide the fact that there
were numerous deficiencies and obstacles standing in the way of a secular poetry. In his epic Wessely had followed the biblical tale too closely,
taking too few creative liberties, so that his work seemed long-winded and
devoid of imagination. Still, he must be credited with at least one contri-

44 Title page of the first volume of *Ha-Me'asef*, the Hebrew
journal of the Jewish Enlightenment (1784)

bution: he generated a distinct impetus for the literary creativity of the younger generation of maskilim who founded *Ha-Me'asef* with the aim of educating Jews in the sense and spirit of the Haskalah.

The initiators of this Hebrew periodical were maskilim in Königsberg, among them Isaac Euchel, Mendel Bresslau, and two sons of the Friedländer family. Much longer-lived than *Kohelet Musar*—it was published from 1784 to 1790 and again from 1794–1797 and 1809–1811—*Ha-Me'asef* was modeled on the enlightened monthly *Berlinische Monatsschrift*. The ideal of the Haskalah was clearly spelled out in the prospectus for the new journal: its editors wished to enlighten and educate in Hebrew—not in German, and most certainly not in Yiddish, a language they considered backward. Like Mendelssohn before them, they believed that the enhancement of morality and bourgeois ethical values among their coreligionists was dependent on the return to a pure, scientifically cultivated language. *Ha-Me'asef* was to serve this aim. Despite its "decline," Hebrew was still a language widely understood, especially among those who had received Talmudic training. The prospectus outlined the areas that the journal would treat. Special attention was reserved for the profane fields of natural science, philology, history, poetry, and education, though Jewish studies were not excluded. Texts from the Bible, Mishnah, and Talmud would be interpreted literally and rationally, in the sense of peshat exegesis.

In the last two decades of the eighteenth century *Ha-Me'asef* became a point of cohesion for Mendelssohn's disciples. Contributions to the journal came from more than a dozen maskilim—not just from Germany but from Poland, Bohemia, Austria, Italy, France, and Holland as well. They attested to the scope and impact already achieved by the movement whose beginnings lay in Berlin. Most of these maskilim had received a traditional Jewish education, working their way into the intellectual world of the Enlightenment through self-study. Some, however, such as Marcus Herz and Mordechai Gumpel Schnaber, had become receptive to rational thought and the new educational ideals through their study of medicine, and others, like Aaron Wolfssohn (1754–1835), the brothers Baruch (1762–1813) and Judah Jeitteles (1773–1838) in Prague, because their fathers were physicians. What the generation of maskilim after Mendelssohn lacked in philosophical acumen—aside from Solomon Maimon, it possessed no other outstanding thinker, and *Ha-Me'asef* published no contributions of philosophical importance—its members tried to make up for by the intensity of their activity, with the aim of bringing their enlightened message to broader strata of the people.

45 Idealized portrait of the philosopher Solomon Maimon

A perusal of *Ha-Me'asef* demonstrates just how difficult it proved to implement one of the principal goals of the maskilim in practice, namely the reshaping of Hebrew in order to adapt it to new functions. For centuries the language had been used mainly in prayer and study of the Torah; now it was to do justice to profane subjects. The intention was that the reader should find aesthetic pleasure in Hebrew prose and poetry, genres that had declined markedly since their flowering in medieval Spain. This was no easy task. There was a dearth of poetically talented writers, compounded by the absence of an unbroken literary tradition.

The *me'asfim*, as the contributors called themselves, frequently fell back on the language and narrative of the Bible, and this often seemed imitative and devoid of originality. Indeed, their achievement lay more in the fact that they had given expression to their will to reinvigorate language and literary style via the medium of *Ha-Me'asef* rather than in the actual level attained by the journal itself.

Not just the Bible served as their paradigm—the me'asfim also tried to emulate the style and forms of contemporary, non-Jewish literature. Enlightenment writers such as Fontenelle, Montesquieu, Voltaire, Lessing, and Wieland, who regarded the critique of society and its shortcomings as a prerequisite for its improvement, had revitalized the literary genre of satire once popular in classical antiquity. Wit, mockery, and irony are all elements of satire, which employs caricature and moralizing with the aim of galvanizing a process of critical thinking and facilitating a change in customs, values, and norms. Euchel and Wolfssohn, who both served for a time as editors of *Ha-Me'asef*, utilized satire to jar old patterns of thinking and behavior among the Jews.

To that end, Euchel published his "Mikhteve Meshulam ben Uriyah ha-Eshtemo'i" (Letters of Meshullam ben Uriah Ha-eshtemoi) in *Ha-Me'asef*. These were alleged reports by an eighteen-year-old Jew from Aleppo in Syria who had been "sent overseas by his father to become acquainted with the customs and character of the peoples there." The source of inspiration was Montesquieu's *Lettres persanes* (1721), in which two Persians set out to discover the culture of Europe—France, in particular—for themselves, and then evaluate it critically as outsiders. Montesquieu utilized the genre of satire as an artistic tool that enabled him to critique the ancien régime with irony and grotesque imagery, all deftly placed in the mouth of the Persian travelers, and thus to shake up its system of values and norms.

Imitating Montesquieu, Euchel sends Meshullam from the Orient to Europe, but places his hero into a Jewish context. Already, while on the ship, he finds a Marrano companion to serve him as a guide through Spain, where he discovers the way of life of the Marranos—Spanish and Portuguese Jews who had managed to preserve their Judaism despite forced baptism. He also becomes acquainted there with Christianity. Despite Montesquieu's evident influence, the work has features that reflect Euchel's indepedence. His hero tends rather to investigate the laudable aspects of the countries he visits, such as Spain and Italy. He travels through these lands with the eyes of an enlightened Jew, because

Meshullam has already developed a strong attachment to Haskalah. His father had instructed him in *hokhmah*, that is, secular fields of knowledge: logic, astronomy, his own language and that of other peoples, as well as the fine arts, poetry, and music. In other words, he embodied the pedagogical ideal to which the maskilim aspired.

During his trip Meshullam receives a letter from his grandfather. In essence, it amounts to an intellectual testament of the old orthodox Judaism, which makes the dispute between opponents and adherents of the Haskalah appear as a generational conflict. Meshullam's grandfather gives his grandson three pieces of advice for the journey: fear God, never abandon prayer, and devote yourself to the study of the sacred books. He admonishes him to remain faithful to the old cultural and religious ideals and adds a few words of warning about how to behave in everyday life. These allow Euchel to introduce a satirical tone, as when his grandfather writes, "Make sure you wash your hands before meals! Be very careful about this, because whoever eats bread without observing the duty of washing the hands is like a man who sleeps with a prostitute!"[12] Euchel treats the punctilious strict observance of ritual precepts by orthodox Jews with biting irony, intensifying the antagonism between maskilim and their adversaries.

Contrasted with this grandfatherly advice, the remarks in a letter from Meshullam's father to his son sound serious and persuasive. He encourages his son to embrace the ideas of the Enlightenment—reason, tolerance, and the love of humanity. The conflict between the generations is conspicuous. On the one side there is the demand of his grandfather that Meshullam turn away from the cultures and lifestyles of other peoples; on the other, there is the father's call for closer ties with the non-Jewish environment. Meshullam comes to admire the liberal enlightened regime of the Jewish community in Italy and the literary work of Ephraim Luzzatto, the Hebrew writer living there. The contrast is clear: in Europe he seeks and finds a social model, whereas the traditional Judaism of the Orient embodies the ancien régime in crying need of change and reform. Meshullam, the maskil, also proclaims the change in relations between the sexes and the generations as part of a social utopia, linking this with a satirical critique of the shortcomings of the old behavioral norms. Stylistically, the work bears the stamp of Montesquieu's influence. Yet Euchel composed his letters in Hebrew, infusing them with a specifically Jewish content. They thus became part of an awakening Hebrew literature.

In Aaron Wolfssohn's satire, "Sihah be-erets ha-hayim" (Conversation in the Realm of the Dead), published in *Ha-Me'asef* in 1794–1797, the clash between the old and the new, enlightened Judaism is projected into the world of dead souls. This technique makes it easy for Wolfssohn to freely criticize the evils of society. By employing a projective device he was able to press the authority of personalities long since departed into literary service. A nameless Polish rabbi called Ploni ("So-and-So"), a blindly zealous Jew and an avowed opponent of the Enlightenment, meets together with Maimonides and Mendelssohn for an imaginary conversation, an encounter easily arranged in the world beyond. As in satirical writings in French and German eighteenth-century literature, critical enlightened thought is counterposed here to the superstitions and customs of a society doomed to decline.

The Polish rabbi, who meets with Maimonides in the opening scene, embodies the old style of life. His remarks make him appear grotesque and repulsive, provoking Maimonides to a sharp negative reaction:

> I've certainly known people of your origin and background—individuals none could trust, who were ignorant of the rules of proper behavior, had learned no language, and were totally incapable of expressing themselves in a clear and correct manner. I've had plenty of occasion to regret this when I was in their company. Which is why I vowed long ago to stay away from such persons.[13]

Maimonides distances himself from the rabbi because he lacks education and culture, a comprehensive system of thought and an aesthetic sense— all values championed by the medieval Jewish philosopher. Although he lived many centuries earlier, Maimonides here becomes a protagonist of the movement for enlightenment. That is the distinctive advantage of this literary genre: it enables an author to bring together in the world beyond famous personalities from the distant past with representatives of later generations to whom they praise ideas articulated many centuries after their death. When he repudiates the foolishness of the obscurantists, Maimonides does not employ the terminology of Greek and Arab philosophy but of the Wolffian school. These obscurantists "see the fire of the lightning as it ignites the barn and threshing floor, and think it's because of some evil act they have committed." Arguing his point in the sense of Wolff or Mendelssohn, Maimonides claims this is not the case. The cause is not some evil; it is itself only a manifestation of what is "seemingly evil," meant to serve the True and the Good: "God allows Evil to work to our benefit."[14]

In the satirically constructed world beyond, Jews meet with non-Jews; Plato, Socrates, and Lessing converse with Maimonides and Mendelssohn. Their souls all have a right to survival after death, because in this world they strived for the knowledge of God and the highest ethical values, based on philosophical rationality. When representatives of rabbinic orthodoxy express their dismay at such an equating of Jews and Gentiles, Maimonides responds, "What are you talking about? Do you believe that Greek philosophers such as Socrates, Plato, and their disciples are excluded from this place?" Taking the rabbi to task, he admonishes him to change his thinking: "Leave these mistaken views and learn to recognize God in truth."[15] Maimonides functions here as a spokesman for Mendelssohn's conception of the survival of the soul and the possibility for continually enhancing one's knowledge, so that no human being is damned to exclusion from true happiness in this life or the next—neither the orthodox rabbi, who still espouses obscurantist notions, nor Lessing, the Christian poet and Mendelssohn's friend. Eminent authorities such as Maimonides, who already enjoyed a solid place in Jewish memory, are conjured up by the satirist to put a stamp of legitimacy on nonconformist ideas. In the imaginary other world the Berlin Haskalah had already found recognition—while among Jews in this world, where the majority still lived in accordance with certain outmoded traditional Jewish values and norms, that recognition was not yet forthcoming.

The literary creativity of Euchel and Wolfssohn was not limited to their contributions to *Ha-Me'asef*. For them and for other maskilim the journal was only one of several media they mobilized for the diffusion of Enlightenment and education. They also wrote plays, a previously untapped genre, in order to battle against the prevailing mentality in Jewish society. These dramas did not simply extol common values such as sincerity, rational, moral behavior, love of truth, and tolerance—that is, virtues propagated in the allegorical plays of the Enlightenment—and then contrast them with the vices of hypocrisy, maliciousness, stupidity, and idle illusion. Nor did the dramas of the maskilim project ideal images of man in general. Rather they showed Jews in the round of their daily lives, in the framework of the family of the rising middle class, within the social stratum that provided the Haskalah with its socioeconomic basis.

Both Euchel and Wolfssohn dramatized the abstract conflict "pro" and "contra" the Haskalah and its principles in the form of a family comedy, thus making their social criticism touch closer to home. They sought to impart the ideas of the Enlightenment in a new setting, not just as an

agenda for changing the relations of the Jews to the state or community—
but as a challenge to transform habits, customs, and norms within the
intimate environment of the family.

Wolfssohn's comedy—extant both in a Hebrew version, "R' Ḥanokh
ve-rabi Yosefkhe" and as "Leichtsinn und Frömmelei" (Frivolity and
False Piety), a version in Judeo-German—is a fast-paced play that pillo-
ries hypocrisy and false enlightenment and was praised by contemporaries. The small cast of characters includes the paterfamilias Reb
Ḥanokh (Chenoch in Judeo-German), a prosperous, naively religious
Jew, who adheres to the old customs not out of inner conviction but
because of the binding power of tradition. Along with trying to get rich,
he is desperately concerned to prevent his children from becoming
estranged from Judaism.

The era of the Enlightenment was also a time of economic advancement for a small stratum of Jews in the urban centers in Prussia. It was
this rising class that ventured the first steps in the direction of closer contacts with and integration into non-Jewish bourgeois society. In particular, the young generation of "nouveaux riches" was keen on being
accepted as rapidly as possible in Christian circles—by visiting the coffee
houses, salons, and theaters and accommodating to Christian dress, customs, and colloquial language. A change in social norms also made itself
felt, leading to freer relations between the sexes and intermarriage with
Christians. One upshot was that parents forfeited the influence they had
exercised in traditional matchmaking via the institution of the shadchan
(marriage broker) and the arranged marriage (*shidukh*). Both orthodox
Jews and the maskilim viewed this change with trepidation, although for
different reasons. The maskilim repudiated the newfangled ways of
young Jews from merchant families who, in careless abandonment of
their distinctiveness as Jews, preferred superficial accommodation to the
lifestyle of the Gentile middle class over the educational process advo-
cated by the maskilim. In "Leichtsinn und Frömmelei," the "false"
enlightenment of Reb Ḥanokh's daughter is held up to contempt, since all
she looks for is the flattering company of the Prussian officers on the
promenade. Each soldier fills her head with new foolishness, showering
her with compliments that she accepts at face value. Reb Ḥanokh reacts to
the perils threatening his children by resorting to the traditional means
of wealthy pious Jews—the private tutor—taking two of them into his
home. One is Rabbi Josefkhe, a Talmud scholar of the old school who is
soon unmasked as a hypocrite. Marcus, the other teacher, a maskil, proves

himself to be superior to Josefkhe both intellectually and morally. In conversation with the father Josefkhe gives the impression that he is a devout and strictly observant Jew and wins his confidence. Reb Ḥanoch selects him as the teacher for his son and his daughter's future husband. Josefkhe's task is to assist her to abandon her "frivolity" and improper ways. Yet Josefkhe displays his own unrestrained lust in his overtures to the cook Scheindel, until finally his pious hypocrisy is unmasked. Now all his rabbinical sophistry and his knack of accommodating his language and behavior to the dramatic shift of events is of no use. As the agent of time-honored Jewish learning, he has failed in his role as an educator for the new generation. With a heavy heart, Reb Ḥanokh confesses his error and exclaims, "I would a thousand times rather have the modern, new-style Jews. At least they're open about what they do, while the others [the old-fashioned Jews] want to do everything in secret, misleading God and man."[16] Marcus, the exponent of a modern direction in Judaism, one that is intellectually honest and morally uncorrupted, now becomes the educator and son-in-law. In a rapidly unfolding controversy between the old conception of life and the new alternative, in three acts charged with dramatic tension, the Haskalah finally carries the day.

Wolfssohn depicts the crisis in Jewish society in the age of Enlightenment both realistically and with humor. "The hero of the play Rabbi Josefkhe is a Jewish Tartuffe," noted a contemporary critic in praise. "The way the mother is portrayed is especially vivid; she feels highly honored and flattered that her dear little daughter is surrounded by counts, barons, and officers, who heap lavish praise upon her."[17] The playwright also provides a superb characterization in the person of Reb Ḥanokh, who seems an authentic man of the common people in his dialogue, casually mixing Yiddish vernacular with sentences from the Bible, Mishnah, and Talmud. With this drama, and due in part to his inventive use of language, Wolfssohn was able to broaden the spectrum of Hebrew literature in form and in content.

In terms of theme, Euchel's play "R' Henokh, oder vos tut me damit" (Reb Henokh, or What Do You Do About It?) differs little from Wolfssohn's comedy. Once again, traditional Jewish education is contrasted with the new pedagogical ideals of the Haskalah. The clash is portrayed here as a generational conflict, in the form of a family portrait; a large number of characters appear, though they seem sketchy, flat, and stereotypical. Euchel draws an arbitrary line between the "evil" traditionalists and the "good" maskilim. While the enlightened "doctor" speaks pure German, Euchel has the paterfamilias Reb Henokh converse in Judeo-German, exploiting the vernacular for humorous effects.

As dramatists, Wolfssohn and Euchel wished to influence and reshape contemporary Jewish culture. That intention is also reflected in the fact that their dramas were meant to be staged at Purim as a replacement for traditional Purim pieces. In their view the old, extremely naive Purim plays distorted the biblical narrative, and they wanted to supplant them by the popular enlightening theater of the Haskalah. When Wolfssohn calls his hero Marcus, the name is intended to allude to Mordechai of the Book of Esther and the Purim festival. But the task of the modern Mordechai is to wage war against the enemy within, the "obscurantism" of the old orthodox milieu.

The circle that contributed to *Ha-Me'asef* and had an impact on Jewish culture through the publication of books in the spirit of the Haskalah also included a number of maskilim from Eastern Europe. Isaac Satanow (1732–1804) stemmed from a small community in Podolia, the cradle of Hasidism. A gifted student of the Talmud, his thirst for knowledge had driven him to seek out the circle of maskilim in Berlin. There he eked out a living as a tutor of Hebrew, immersing himself at the same time in the philosophy of the Enlightenment and the natural sciences. In the 1788 volume of *Ha-Me'asef* he published a survey of the development of Hebrew entitled "Mi-darkhe ha-lashon ve-ha-melitsah" (On Language and Ornamental Style). This essay was an astute treatise on possibilities for expanding the lexicon so that the language could satisfy modern demands. In a series of works he imitated the style of earlier epochs, both the Spanish Middle Ages and the biblical period. *Mishle Assaf* (Assaf's Proverbs, 1788), for example, was a collection of parables and maxims in which he included folk wisdom from the Talmud and Midrash and imitated the style of the Book of Proverbs. However, as in most of his other works, he concealed the fact of his authorship, attributing the book to an ancient author, the physician Assaf b. Berakhyahu.

The vacillation between the traditions of their childhood and the less tradition-bound milieu of the Enlightenment left its distinct mark upon the maskilim. Their identity conflicts found expression both in their writings and in everyday life, as the example of Isaac Satanow clearly shows. While he helped to shape the new secular Hebrew literature in *Ha-Me'asef*, like the other me'asfim he proved unable to create a new style of language. His linguistic talents only permitted him to achieve a virtually perfect imitation of biblical Hebrew. For him the clash of tradition and renewal was also apparent in his manner of dress: under the caftan of the Polish Jew he was accustomed to wear the suit of a German bourgeois.

In *Imre binah* (Words of Insight, 1784) Satanow sought to bring together philosophy and Kabbala, which he described as twins. What philosophy seeks to elucidate in clear formulations, Kabbala represents through the language of metaphor, symbol, and mysterious allusions. His attempt to mediate between a strictly rationalistic discipline and Jewish mysticism reflects a high degree of original thought, an originality whose value scholars have only recently come to recognize.

Yehudah Ben-Ze'ev (1764–1811) was, like Satanow, also a typical representative of the maskilim from Poland. Married since the age of thirteen, he lived with his father-in-law in Cracow and dedicated himself solely to the study of the Talmud, becoming an outstanding expert on Jewish sources. When he later turned itinerant teacher, he discovered the forbidden books of the Enlightenment, which quickly captured his interest. Fired by a desire for knowledge and culture, he decided to go to Berlin, where he arrived one year after the death of Mendelssohn. Ben-Ze'ev contributed Hebrew poems and fables to *Ha-Me'asef* and was convinced the Hebrew language must move beyond the narrow bounds of religious discourse. To that end, he wrote satirical verse for Purim in the style of the Psalms, along with light love poetry. He regarded the modernization and secularization of the Hebrew language as an urgent priority, a concern expressed in his grammar (*Talmud leshon ivri*, 1796) and a German-Hebrew dictionary (*Otsar ha-shorashim*, 1807–1808). In the grammar Ben-Ze'ev utilized applied philological knowledge useful for Bible studies and the teaching of Hebrew for a broad Jewish public. His wish was to hasten the renaissance of the language. Ben-Ze'ev's grammar enjoyed notable success, going through no less than twenty printings.

With their activities in the 1780s and 1790s the me'asfim helped the ideas originated by Mendelssohn to gain greater influence. Their contributions to *Ha-Me'asef*, their literary works, and their publication of a large number of books devoted to philology, grammar, the natural sciences, and practical instruction extended the concept of Jewish existence far beyond the exclusively religious sphere, even before the establishment of a Verein für Cultur und Wissenschaft der Juden (Association for Culture and the Scientific Study of the Jews) in the nineteenth century. The maskilim aimed at a reform of Jewish culture and society, not its politicization. They were still too obligated to the old corporative structures, which limited the right to think and act politically to an oligarchy

of community lay leaders. This disinterest in politics is the reason why
the momentous events of the day, such as the French Revolution, are
reflected only marginally in the contributions to *Ha-Me'asef*, and even
then only in connection with the emancipation of the Jews by the
National Assembly. The periodical of the Berlin Haskalah did not become
the organ of struggle for civil rights and equality for the Jews in
Germany; rather, its concerns remained focused on the fight for pedagogical reform and the ever more energetic efforts to curb the influence of the
old system and its representatives, the rabbis.

4. Autobiography: On the Self-Understanding of the Maskilim

An insufficiently noticed literary genre came to the fore with the Berlin
Haskalah: the autobiography. Here the individual articulates his reminis-
cences in close association with an image of society, providing insight into
the relation of the maskil to his Jewish and non-Jewish environment.
Precisely by virtue of its subjective vantage, the autobiography provides
a better understanding of the changes in mentality underway, which cannot be grasped solely on the basis of an analysis of philosophical and
polemic writings. In particular, it sheds light on the personal background
of the process of radicalization, which led in the last two decades of the
eighteenth century to the unavoidable confrontation of the maskilim
with opponents both outside and within. A number of such texts, of vary-
ing length and scope, are extant.

The retrospective, reflective manner of self-presentation is not an
invention of the eighteenth century. There are certain precursor forms in
the Renaissance, but the genre did not become a widespread literary phenomenon until the age of Enlightenment and the rise of bourgeois society. As the process of differentiation and individualization in society
intensified, the old, more homogeneous life-world—in which the individual, from the proverbial cradle to the grave, generally belonged to a
milieu largely closed to the outside—was supplanted by various alternat-
ing and quite disparate circles of life. A need now arose to consciously
reflect on the continuity and ruptures in personal life. In the form of the
autobiography exponents of the Berlin Haskalah attempted to forge a
new self-understanding. The old community and its institutions no
longer constituted the sole frame of reference; they found themselves
exposed to dramatic changes, contradictory influences and wrenching

tensions. In the seventeenth century the authors of Jewish autobiographies had still felt totally bound by Jewish tradition; with pride they proclaimed their allegiance to the Torah, its values and laws, the family, the synagogue, the yeshiva—in short, the "sacred" Jewish community. The memoirs of Glückel of Hameln (1646–1724) circle around the collective centers of life: the old community and the family. Both dominate her retrospective glance, because she still adheres steadfastly to the shared values and norms of Judaism. She was motivated to set down what she remembered in order to pass on a moral testament to her children and grandchildren and to impress upon them the need for fidelity to a pious and virtuous way of life. By contrast, among the maskilim the critically reflecting individual was himself at center stage: the spotlight was on his struggle for meaning and cohesion in a fragmented environment. In their autobiographical texts the maskilim dealt principally with themselves, their conflict-ridden intellectual and psychological paths of development. The "ego" provided the fixed point from which to contemplate the traditional world, which had lost its former meaningfulness and attraction. In the autobiographical text there is a discernible shift in emphases and a new attitude toward family, community, synagogue, yeshiva—in short, toward the traditional Jewish world and its way of life.

The memoirs of Aaron Gumpertz, Lazarus Bendavid, and Solomon Maimon illustrate this change. Aaron Gumpertz's autobiography *Megale sod* (Secrets Revealed, 1765) confirms the shift in emphasis from the collective frame and its values to that of the individual struggling for identity and self-understanding within the ambit of the newly gained freedom from the coercive power of the old society. The attitude of Jews toward life begins to alter, analogously to changes taking place in attitudes among non-Jews. Childhood and youth are viewed as distinct separate phases of life, different from adulthood, and these stages must now be assessed with appropriate yardsticks. Gumpertz interrogates the values of tradition cultivated in his parental home, reconstructing the itinerary of his development from childhood to maskil. A special place in Gumpertz's description is accorded his parents' concern for his education and also his father's voluminous library, rich in books of Jewish and general content, which Gumpertz takes as the sign of a certain openness to outside culture.

Gumpertz underscores the role of his private tutor, Israel Samoscz: it was Samoscz who convinced him as a young boy that Jewish tradition and science (*Wissenschaft*) in the broadest sense could coexist. Gumpertz then attempted to make this possibility a reality: along with biblical

Hebrew, he studied classical Greek, Latin, and modern European languages with private tutors. Thanks to Samoscz, he was able to supplement study of the Talmud with the philosophy of Maimonides, mathematics, and natural sciences. Gumpertz evaluates the course of his education—which led to the internalization of a humanistic concept of science, ultimately determining his decision to become a doctor—as the successful expression of a new Jewish identity. However, his choice of a profession, oriented to the ideals of Enlightenment, led to a crisis and conflict in his parental home, since he had decided against the traditional Jewish ideal of education cherished by his mother. By a solemn vow she had determined, even before his birth, that he would study the Talmud and become a rabbi, but she was unable to dim the allure of Enlightenment, and her son rebelled against parental authority.

In the autobiographies of Lazarus Bendavid and Solomon Maimon the self-reflection of the maskil and the sharper focus on childhood and youth are presented even more vividly. Both devote uncommon attention to the early stages of human life and to the development of psychological needs. The description moves back and forth between the relations to family, teachers, and playmates and to the broader social environment, including non-Jews. The crisis in relation to Jewish society and the critique of its values and norms are articulated in these two instances more pointedly than in the case of Gumpertz.

Lazarus Bendavid stemmed from a Berlin entrepreneurial family that belonged to the privileged stratum of Jews under Frederick II. Economic success and the desire to acculturate were closely intertwined. As Bendavid recalls: "My parents had both enjoyed a liberal education. They both wrote very correct Jewish [Yiddish] and German, and spoke French well; my father in particular wrote very lovely commercial essays and was widely read in the French classical authors."[18] The open-minded cultural attitude of his parents was also expressed in their attitude toward Jewish tradition:

> Their concepts of religion had been shaped according to a system unique to them and deviated rather advantageously from those of most Jews at the time. In our home thousands upon thousands [!] of minor ceremonial laws, whose violation is regarded by other Jews as the greatest sin, were hardly even known by name. Never in our house were members of other religions denounced—and, what amounts to more, not even those who had deserted the Jewish faith.

Ghost stories were never told, nor was I ever forbidden to repeat something naughty I'd done with the threat: God will punish you! I was merely encouraged to pursue a moral and orderly way of life, one in which my parents themselves served with unparalleled conscientiousness as models. And the sole religious practices expected of me were the morning and evening prayers .[19]

Although the laws of Judaism were not strictly observed in Bendavid's parental home, this did not preclude a Jewish education. His father arranged for a private tutor from Poland, loyal to tradition. But the teacher was no opponent of rationalism, so that his pupils did not feel there was any contradiction between Jewish learning and enlightened ideas: "Along with Talmud and the Bible, we also learned Hebrew grammar and the logic of Aristotle according to Maimonides, which is very unusual in Jewish schools." Bendavid's teacher also demonstrated a fine sense of pedagogy in dealing with his pupils: "Even on days when there were no classes, he kept us under his supervision by going out on walks with us and participating in our games."[20] Thanks to this education, down to the age of fourteen, Bendavid felt no desire to depart from the straight path of normative Judaism. But unable any longer to close himself off from external influences, he underwent an intense internal struggle and finally embraced a deistic faith. He decided to forego "everything positive," but retained his "belief in God, immortality, and a better future."[21] Gradually, he abandoned the observance of all ceremonial laws, visiting the synagogue only when his parents demanded it. He went so far as to attend Christian churches because he enjoyed listening to the organ music and sermons. With a frankness that betrays the shift in attitude of the maskil, he admits to his deviation from the tradition followed by the Jewish majority.

Bendavid wrote this retrospective look back on his life to the age of forty-three (1805) from the perspective of a dedicated Jewish enlightener. He describes the stages of his development, in the private and social spheres, from the vantage of an exponent of the Berlin Haskalah, one whose thinking was already more radical than that of Mendelssohn. He only considers those elements worthy of remembrance that appear to confirm his ideal of education and society. Over many pages Bendavid describes his path to secular culture, which he initially trod very cautiously, thanks to his parents and the tutors they engaged to teach him. Later, however, studying on his own and fired by an insatiable hunger for knowledge, he was propelled forward ever faster down that route: "As I said, I had read everything I chanced upon, a motley collection: Abulfeda and the Koran, the New Testament and Rousseau's *Émile*, Voltaire's *Pucelle* and *Thèrese philosophe*, the German poets and Wolff's metaphysics, kabbalistic and medical books."[22] He reports with satisfaction on his success in studying mathematics and philosophy, which he finally mastered, although he had not been formally enrolled at any university. Bendavid gained the acclaim of enlightened circles, which, as is evident from his description, was a source of great pride. In Vienna, where he lived in the 1790s, the lectures he delivered in his home on Kantian philosophy, practical reason, the critique of judgment, and aesthetics became an intellectual event that attracted the educated aristocracy. Like his friend Marcus Herz in Berlin, he too had been unable to gain a post as university lecturer.

The last part of his autobiography deals with Bendavid's success as a philosopher and mathematician and his various travels. These wanderings led him on foot from Vienna to Prague, then by coach to Dresden and back to Berlin. He experiences traveling as an aesthete, an observer who takes pleasure in beauty, art, and nature. His text contains no trace of the dramatic political events of the day, in particular the struggle of his coreligionists for a "civil improvement" in their situation. Judaism and the Jewish community are touched on tangentially and then only in connection with the reform of religion and customs, a topic on which Bendavid felt compelled to write a separate work. Passages from Bendavid's adult life are silent on traditional Jewish education. Similarly, in the recollection of his social relations for this period the Jewish component has been displaced. He only mentions non-Jewish enlightened associations: the Friends of Humanity, of which he was a member and then became director in 1797–1798, and the Philomathic Society, which appointed him secretary in 1800. That is surprising, in view of the fact that at the time he wrote his autobiography he had certainly not broken off relations with Jews. He had even taken over the directorship of the Jewish Free School in Berlin and was, as a result, personally involved in efforts of the maskilim to translate their program of education into practice. But the structure of his autobiography betrays the fact that his reorientation toward the culture of his environment had reached an advanced stage—further along than can be surmised on the basis of his daily life, which still moved largely within the confines of a Jewish circle.

A good example of an autobiography that mirrors the change in mentality of the maskil and its complexity is the *Lebensgeschichte* (Autobiography, 1793) of Solomon Maimon. It is also the best-known example of this literary genre, whose special character Maimon himself clearly underscored: "The first task I have taken upon myself in my tales and descriptions is to remain faithful to the truth, be it to the advantage or disadvantage of my own person, family, nation, or other relations."[23] Maimon thus committed himself to recording his memoirs in a nonconformist and critical style, a goal he doubtless achieved. He offers a vivid description of Jewish society, economy, and religion in his native Poland. With a touch of humor, he reports on popular superstitions, customs, and traditions there, though not without biting condemnation of the negative excesses: the methods and content of education, the obscurantism of rabbinical orthodoxy, and the custom of early marriage. The last was also a trauma for Maimon personally, from which he freed himself first by fleeing to the west and then, much later, by obtaining a divorce. Writing with disarming candor, he paints an accurate picture of a culture until then unknown to the outside world, closely associated with his personal fate: "Thus, I do not wish to conceal . . . or gloss over anything human that might have occurred to me in my life as a result of ignorance, defects in education, and the like." He emphasizes: "Frankness is one of my main traits of character," thereby recalling Rousseau's *Confessions*, which represented a new dimension in enlightened thinking.[24] By focusing on his own person, and describing his wanderings through the most diverse circles of society from a highly subjective point of view, he conveys uncommonly clear vistas of continuity and change in the life of the maskilim.

Maimon's memoirs encompass his childhood and youth in Eastern Europe as well as his later fate as a young intellectual who, now in Germany, encounters Mendelssohn and the Haskalah. The writer Karl Philip Moritz had successfully persuaded this "enfant terrible" of the Berlin scholarly circles to set down his life in writing. As a result, seven years before his death a text came into being that, although extremely subjective, was able to afford unusual insight—perhaps precisely because of its highly personal subjectivity—into the inner transformation experienced by a Jewish enlightener. The autobiography is a chronologically structured look backward by a Talmud student who became a Deist. In Germany, where he arrived from Poland, no hardship was spared him. Despite his superior intellect, he was forced to share the fate of the lowest strata of Jewish society. He wandered from community to community with the poor, who, toward the end of the week, might manage to obtain a meal in the poorhouse at the city gate or at the Sabbath table of a Jewish family—until he finally gained entry to Berlin and was given generous support by wealthy maskilim. Yet all his hardships and adversities had not been able to induce him to return contritely to the old Jewish society in Poland he had left. "That a man of my sort, who had already been in Germany for several years and who had happily broken free from the fetters of superstition and religious prejudice, had cast off his rude customs and former way of life, and greatly expanded his knowledge, should voluntarily return to his previous barbaric and miserable condition, that he should divest himself of all advantages gained and expose himself to rabbinical rage at the slightest deviation from the ceremonial law and the utterance of a free thought"—all that, to Maimon, was simply inconceivable.[25]

Two factors that reinforced one another had a decisive influence on Maimon's development, making a return to the old Jewish community impossible: the philosophy of the Enlightenment and the circle of the maskilim. Self-taught, Maimon soon acquired an exceptional knowledge of the writings of Wolff, Spinoza, Locke, Hume, Leibniz, and, above all, Immanuel Kant. He became an intellectual discussion partner much sought after by both Jewish and non-Jewish enlighteners, contributed essays to periodicals, and wrote a number of books. Only a few years after he had begun the study of rationalist philosophy, he proved himself a penetrating analyst of the *Critique of Pure Reason* with the publication of his *Versuch über die Tranzendental-philosophie* (Essay on Transcendental Philosophy, 1790), to which Kant himself accorded highest recognition. It was the Königsberg philosopher who contributed to the final individualization and rationalization of Maimon's belief, so that he rejected all external compulsion in questions of religion, whether by the church or the synagogue. In looking back on his intellectual development, however, Maimon accords primacy to the Jewish philosopher Maimonides. His works, in particular the *Guide of the Perplexed*, exerted the decisive influence on the development of Maimon's attitude toward religion. "The melancholic and emotionalistic religion [learned as a child] was gradually transformed into a rational one; slavish religious worship was supplanted by the free development of the faculty of cognition and by morality."[26] Thanks to Maimonides, Maimon had, as a young man, developed a critical view of popular superstition and the abuse of religion by a conservative rabbinism. All his life he felt a special "respect for this great teacher" of rational faith. His admiration went so far that he revered Maimonides as the "ideal of a perfect human being" and his conception of Judaism as the sole one that did justice to the original natural religion of the Jews, a faith commensurate with reason. The fact that he consciously borrowed the name of the medieval philosopher for himself and the lengthy extrapolation on the *Guide of the Perplexed* contained in his autobiography confirm the key importance of Maimonides for young Jews' intellectual reception of the Enlightenment.

Maimon endeavored to struggle against a stereotypical image of Judaism. Although he rejected old conventions and values, and very often criticized the abuses in Jewish society with caustic irony, he did not engage in any reductive black-and-white descriptions. He also found words of respect for traditional Jewish society, from which his path as an adherent of Enlightenment had taken him further and further afield since his arrival in Germany: "I would have to write an entire book if I wished to cite all the splendid teachings of rabbinic ethics. The influence of these teachings in practical life is also unmistakable. The Polish Jews . . . earn their livelihood honestly and honorably. Their charity and welfare for the poor . . . are sufficiently well-known."[27] Maimon is also convinced that the Talmud has positive facets, since it contains appeals to ethical behavior—and certainly none of those absurdities that Johann Andreas Eisenmenger "unmasked" when he vilified the Talmud at the end of the seventeenth century.

Maimon's picturesque image of his experiences alongside the frank portrayal of his own intellectual development enabled later generations to gain some insight into the inner conflicts of a maskil in his extremely difficult situation, torn between two worlds. Living in poverty and with no prospects for a proper profession, Maimon considered baptism. He spoke with a Lutheran minister about the matter—again with his accustomed candor. In an extremely undiplomatic manner, he contrasted Christianity and Judaism. Even if Maimon conceded Christianity a certain moral superiority, he nonetheless ranked it below Judaism, a faith that "is closer to reason than the Christian religion." He also criticized the element of mystery intrinsic to Christianity. The upshot of his exposition was that Maimon was rejected as a candidate for admission to the Lutheran Church. He had assimilated the ideas of Enlightenment and wished to be accepted into the circles of the educated middle class. He had enormous enthusiasm for the science, philosophy, and literature of Germany and Europe yet was ultimately incapable of pursuing an immediate integration that would effect a total break with the Jewish world from whence he had come. Pushed to the periphery of two diverse societies, Maimon remained a lone figure. That is also reflected in the circumstances of his interment in 1800: when he was brought for burial in the Jewish community of Glogau, as a "heretic" he was laid to rest outside the Jewish cemetery—an unusual end for an unusual personality. In Maimon's case, perhaps more than in any other, the autobiography clearly conveys the extreme complexity inherent in traveling from within the boundaries of traditional Judaism outward to the Haskalah.

11

Confrontation as a Transformative Force

1. Acceptance and Rejection

The Berlin Haskalah developed under the impact of contradictory forces, in a process of bridging whereby the maskilim moved intellectually and socially ever closer to the non-Jewish world. The allure of the new ideas and the vista of participation in new forms of sociability made entry into the non-Jewish world appear an attractive goal. On the other hand, the maskilim were pushed back by an opposing force, encumbering their accommodation to Gentile society. Their path was obstructed by a double barrier: not just the policies of Frederick II, which continued to make the Jews a pariah minority in German society, but lingering deep-seated anti-Jewish bias, both among the common people and the higher social strata—indeed, even within the circle of the Christian enlighteners. A change in public opinion was not in the immediate offing. The adherents of Enlightenment who were fully prepared to judge the Jews in the light of reason and humanity and to cast aside traditional biases could be counted on the fingers of one hand. Rarely did anyone from the educated class in Germany—those who championed reason and morality in scholarly associations and at the universities—raise their voice in support of the Jews. Only two men stand out as striking exceptions: Gotthold Ephraim Lessing and Christian Wilhelm Dohm, both sons of Christian pastors, thinkers who called publicly for the translation of *Aufklärung* ideas into a new and enlightened attitude toward the Jews.

In 1749, even before his friendship with Mendelssohn, the young Lessing (then only twenty) had written his first play, a one-act comedy entitled *Die Juden* (The Jews). Not published until 1754, *Die Juden* does not rank as one of Lessing's great dramatic works, but its message was unequivocal: the ideas of enlightenment and tolerance demand a change in heart toward the Jews. The playwright does not mock the Jews in this piece, as might be erroneously assumed from the title; instead, he reserves his derision for the bigoted Christians. The main protagonist is a Jew, a "traveler," who, disproving all prejudices, behaves in a selfless manner: with courage and magnanimity, he saves the life of a Christian, a baron and his daughter set upon by highway robbers. The nameless traveler speaks the language of tolerance: "To tell you the truth: I don't much like generalizations about entire peoples. Don't be offended if I take the liberty to speak. There are, I imagine, good and bad souls in any people." By contrast, the Christians—the baron and the representative of the common "rabble"—articulate their unvarnished prejudices with no inhibitions whatever: they revile the Jews as "cheats, thieves, highwaymen." Lessing has the baron remark that "you can read the deviousness, lack of scruples, selfishness, deceit, and perjury very clearly in their eyes"[1]—but then goes on to give his words the lie, revealing to the baron the Jewish identity of the noble traveler who saved his life. The playwright has unmasked the patent prejudice of the Christian baron, who now takes refuge in an argument often advanced by persons who harbor a dislike for Jews: "O how admirable the Jews would be if they were only all like you!" The traveler's repartee: "And how kind the Christians, if they just had all your qualities!"[2] Finally, the whole scene dissolves into farce, making the anti-Jewish bias seem all the more absurd.

In a review of the play published in the *Göttingische Gelehrte Anzeigen* (1754), no less a personage than the renowned Göttingen theologian and Orientalist Johann David Michaelis rejected the ideal image of the virtuous Jew depicted in Lessing's play:

> The anonymous stranger is portrayed as a person so totally and completely good, so magnanimous, so concerned that he could do his neighbor an injustice and offend him by unfounded suspicion, that, though not impossible, it is highly improbable such a noble soul could actually exist; that it could come into being on its own within a people with such principles, way of life, and education—a nation that must truly feel great animosity toward the Christians,

or at least cool antipathy, as a result of their nasty behavior toward the Jews.[3]

This counterargument came from a man who was certainly not deaf to the appeal of enlightened ideas. Michaelis can rightfully be regarded as the founder of a tradition of biblical criticism in Germany. His work *Mosaisches Recht* (Mosaic Law) brought him fame and attested to his attachment to rationalism. His interest in the poetic beauty of the Psalms and the great value he placed on language as indicative of a people's level of culture, reason, and aesthetic sense pointed to the possiblity of common ground between him and Mendelssohn. They had good reason for mutual esteem. Michaelis had written a positive review of Mendelssohn's first work, *Letters on the Sentiments* (1755), in the *Göttingische Gelehrte Anzeigen*. In that same periodical he later voiced his support for Mendelssohn in the dispute with Lavater and paid him respect as an orthodox Jew who was faithful to his religion, even though he used the weapon of modern philosophy to defend the cause of the synagogue. Ultimately, however, neither Michaelis's vast learning nor his rationalist outlook prevented him from clearly rejecting the idea that Jews were entitled to civil equality. Two decades later he chose to remain silent on Lessing's much better known play, *Nathan the Wise* (1779).

Completed shortly before his death, Lessing had written this later drama with the aim of placing all his artistic gifts once more in the service of toleration and the love of humanity. Its main protagonist Nathan, a Jew, becomes the herald of a natural religion of humanity based on universal reason. But the representatives of Christianity and Islam, the Patriarch and Saladin, must first come to the realization that none of the monotheistic religions can lay claim to the privilege of being exclusively chosen. The "parable of the rings" (based on a novella from Boccaccio's *Decamerone*) as retold by Nathan forms the core of the play and was meant to illustrate the truth of that insight.

> My advice is that you take the matter completely as it stands. Each of you has the ring from his father, and each then should believe his ring to be the genuine one. . . . Each should emulate his uncorrupted love, free from the taint of prejudice! May each of you strive in competition to reveal the power of the stone in his ring! Assist this power by gentleness of spirit, heartfelt amicability, beneficence, and the most inward and intense devotion to God![4]

Lessing thus denies all three monotheistic religions any exclusive claim to religious truth. Since he himself had strong leanings toward Deism, he emphasized the superiority of a religion of reason. Public opinion responded to his play as a provocation; it was unable to accept the idea that the message of humanity here was proclaimed by a Jew, that Lessing had made Nathan the mouthpiece and herald of his own convictions. By contrast, the maskilim, in particular Lessing's friend Mendelssohn, drew from this fresh hope that a new era of cooperation was dawning for Jews and Christians. Yet only slowly did they come to realize that they would have to struggle hard for it, entering the fray themselves.

In the 1750s Mendelssohn had avoided openly attacking the Göttingen scholar and his critique of Lessing's one-act play *Die Juden*. But in a letter to his Jewish friend Aaron Gumpertz he confided his feelings of deep disappointment:

> And what do you think it is they [the *Göttingische Gelehrte Anzeigen*] have to criticize about the comedy *Die Juden*? That the main character is, as they put it, far too noble and magnanimous! They say that the pleasure we derive from the beauty of such a character is undercut by his improbability, and finally there remains nothing left in our soul but the mere wish that he might exist. I was crimson with shame after reading these thoughts. I cannot find the words to express what feelings they provoked in me. What humiliation for our oppressed nation! What inordinate disdain! The common Christians have always regarded us as the dregs of Nature, as ulcers of human society. But from learned people I always expected a fairer judgment. . . . How wrong I was when I credited every Christian writer with as much sincerity as he demands from others.[5]

Michaelis's critique of the main protagonist of Lessing's comedy touched Mendelssohn deeply, since he had already embraced the ideas of Enlightenment and counted educated Christians among his friends. Had he remained a Talmud student, oriented solely to Jewish society—like the majority of his coreligionists—he most certainly would not have felt the same sharp pain. When Johann Caspar Lavater then called on Mendelssohn to publicly defend his Judaism, he broke his silence on religious matters and responded to the challenge. In 1769 Lavater had published the German version of a book by the Geneva scholar Charles Bonnet (1720–1793), *Recherches philosophiques sur les preuves du Christianisme* (An Investigation Into the Proofs for Christianity), and sent it to Mendelssohn, challenging him to refute Bonnet's arguments or convert to Christianity. Mendelssohn replied by counterposing the religious tolerance of the enlightened Jew to the mystical position of the Protestant pastor Lavater who, fired by millenarian hopes, believed he could bring about the second coming of Christ and the end of days by a conversion of the Jews: "Among my friends I have the good fortune to count many a fine person who is not of my faith. We love one another truly, although we surmise and presume that when it comes to matters of religion, our views are totally different. . . . Never has my heart called out to me: *What a pity for the beautiful soul!*"[6] Mendelssohn's tolerant attitude was not conditioned solely by tactical considerations. Rather, it corresponded with his view of Judaism that, free of any missionizing zeal, prophesies eternal bliss also for those of other faiths insofar as they live according to the laws of nature and reason—namely, that they observe the seven Noachide commandments incumbent on all human beings, which are largely congruent with natural religion or Deism. This was not a completely new view within Judaism; it had been formulated drawing on internal Jewish sources, especially Maimonides, but now it became the guidepost for a new relation between Christians and Jews in the second half of the eighteenth century.

At the beginning of the 1780s a new attitude toward Jews began to emerge among Christians. Two events appeared to augur a change for the better. In September 1781 Christian Wilhelm Dohm's treatise *Über die bürgerliche Verbesserung der Juden* (On the Improvement of the Civil Status of the Jews) argued for granting the Jews civil equality. Shortly thereafter Joseph II proclaimed his first edicts of toleration: in October 1781 for the Jews of Bohemia, in December of that year for the Jews of Austrian Silesia, and in January 1782 for Jews in Vienna and Lower Austria. The edicts brought some improvement in the Habsburg Jews' previously hardpressed legal situation. The immediate impetus for Dohm's work had been the reports on the vicious hate campaign against the Jews in Alsace, which their community leader and shtadlan, Herz Cerfberr, had presented to Mendelssohn. Mendelssohn then turned to his friend Dohm and asked him to write a tract in defense of the Alsatian Jews, arguing for the abolition of oppressive legislation there (such as the body tax). Dohm agreed, and the result was his call for the "improvement of the civil status of the Jews." However, Dohm's initiative did not go unanswered by its opponents.

The son of a parson from Lemgo, Dohm had studied constitutional law, history, and statistics in Leipzig and Göttingen and gone to Berlin in 1773 after appointment as head of pages at the royal court. From 1779 he exercised the double function of archivist in the Secret State Archives and of a "military councillor" in the Foreign Office. Dohm was thus a higher-ranking official in the Prussian civil service, yet he also moved widely in circles of the Berlin enlighteners and was the cofounder of the *Deutsches Museum*, an enlightened periodical that tried to diffuse knowledge on constitutional law, politics, and statistics. His treatise, intended to spark a change in attitudes toward the Jews among the people and in the government, was the direct product of his own enlightened views. He had no knowledge of the edict that Joseph II was preparing at the time in Vienna. Although he admired Frederick II, he criticized his Jewry policy in the name of the natural rights of man:

> I believe that basically I am not mistaken, and all unprejudiced readers will most certainly agree when I assert that the Jews have been endowed by Nature with the same capacity to become happier, better persons, more useful members of society; that only the oppression so unworthy of our age has corrupted them; and that it is congruous with humaneness, justice, and enlightened politics to banish this oppression and to improve the condition of the Jews for their own well-being and for the good of the state.[7]

In the future the Jews were to live without the burden of protection fees, special taxes, and obligatory levies and be educated and brought up like all other citizens. In calling for the status of full citizenship and equality of rights for them, Dohm was not motivated by any special love for the Jews but by the anticipated advantages of an enlightened state policy. In Dohm's argumentation the good of the state and the happiness of its citizens have priority. This was the basis for his nine-point program, which envisioned, inter alia, a "productivization" of the Jews: "No type of commerce should be prohibited to the Jews. . . . Rather, by promoting the crafts and agriculture among them, the Jews will be drawn away from commerce." On the one hand, in contrast with Mendelssohn, Dohm opts for retention of the rabbinical power to ban dissidents. On the other, he calls for secular education for the Jews and their admission to Christian schools and universities. Thus "it ought to be the special concern of a wise government to provide for the moral education and enlightenment of the Jews."[9] Nor should they be excluded from government employment and the patriotic duty of military service. Dohm's utopian model was a state in which all lived together in harmony—the nobility and the burghers, peasants and scholars, laity and priests, Catholics, Protestants, and those of other faiths—and where sharp class divisions had been eliminated. This was the perspective of a new type of civil servant, who believed in the "improvement" of human beings and citizens but accorded the rational policies of the sovereign and reforms instituted from above a major importance. Persons should not be excluded from civil society either by reason of birth or because of their ethnic-religious affiliation. By means of judicious laws and acts, a wise ruler could make his subjects happy citizens—and Dohm believed Frederick II was just such a prudent sovereign. Neither the Jews' religion and laws nor their messianic belief would stand in the way of an all-embracing plan of reform that included even them. In the second half of the eighteenth century Dohm was the classic representative of the enlightened officialdom in Prussia seriously committed to the ideals of raison d'état and their realization. He was convinced that the universal validity of these ideals made it obligatory to effect a change in public opinion and policy toward the Jews. In this view Dohm anticipated an important element of the French Revolution, although his own political aims did not go beyond enlightened absolutism.

Dohm's book sparked a vehement polemical debate in which pastors, jurists, and professors participated. Once again, it was Johann David Michaelis who, notwithstanding his enlightened views and erudition, spoke out against civil equality for the Jews: "What more can be granted to them than they have now without a disadvantage accruing to the state (no matter how long that might take) and to the native German burgher, who has a right to the land and defends it and for whom the sovereign is father, guardian, and highest servant?"[10] Michaelis believed an enlightened policy toward the Jews was impossible. He was convinced their mentality could not be changed and considered their religious laws responsible:

> Herr D. believes the Law of Moses is excellent; he doesn't think it contains anything inhumane or that might engender hatred among the Jews for other peoples. . . . Yet allow me to raise another question here: do the laws of Moses contain some element that makes it impossible or more difficult for the Jews to become completely naturalized and merge with other peoples? I rather think they do!

Michaelis continued:

> Their intention is to preserve the Jews as a people separate from the other nations. That intent is so thoroughly interwoven in Jewish

laws, even down to pure and impure foods, that this people, contrary to all that can be observed with regard to other nations, has preserved itself, keeping apart in its dispersion for 1,700 years. And as long as the Jews keep the Mosaic law, as long as they cannot, for example, eat with us, or become close friends over meals or among the simple people in the tavern, they will never (and I am not speaking of individuals, but of the greater majority) merge together with us like Catholics and Lutherans, Germans, Wends, and Frenchmen, who all live in a single state.[11]

Michaelis attributes the "national character" of the Jews to their religious law, deducing from this the impossibility of ever applying to them the principles of an enlightened state policy. Their dietary laws and the sacredness of the Sabbath prevent them from fulfilling their patriotic duty and serving in the military; their messianic hope for a return to Palestine makes it impossible for them to forge a close bond to the state: "A people with such hopes will never become completely native."[12]

Mendelssohn joined in the shrill polemics surrounding Dohm's tractate with the publication of a German translation of Manasseh ben Israel's *Vindiciae Judaeorum* entitled *Rettung der Juden* (Deliverance of the Jews, 1782). The noted Amsterdam rabbi had written his apologetic work in 1656 in an attempt to bring about a revocation of the edict of expulsion from England in 1290 and a return of the Jews there. Mendelssohn's friend Marcus Herz prepared a translation of the "brochure," as he called it, and Mendelssohn wrote a preface setting out the reasons that motivated him to publish a German edition:

> It is remarkable to see how prejudice assumes the familiar shapes of the past in order to oppress us and to place difficulties in the path of our entry into civil society. In those superstitious times it was relics that we maliciously desecrated; crucifixes we perforated and made to bleed . . . Christian blood that we required for Easter; wells we poisoned. . . . Now the times have changed; these slanders no longer produce the desired impact. Now we are accused of superstition and stupidity; a lack of moral sentiment, taste, and refinement; an incapacity for arts, sciences, and a useful trade, and especially for military and state service; an insurmountable predilection for deceit, usury, and lawlessness. These have replaced those cruder allegations and have served to exclude us from the ranks of useful citizens and banish us from the maternal bosom of the state.[13]

Mendelssohn thus pointed to the continuity of anti-Jewish prejudice through the ages, though its external forms had altered. It was no longer religiously motivated, as it had been in the Middle Ages. Now secularized, so to speak, it emphasized the civil inferiority of the Jews. But the aim was always to exclude the Jews from society, and even scholars like Michaelis supported such exclusionary practices. The fact that Mendelssohn spoke out openly for the improvement of the civil status of the Jews—thus commenting not just on questions of religion and philosophy but taking a basic stand on a central political issue—can be explained by the dynamics of the confrontation.

Rejection by Christian society was not the only factor underlying the political writings of the maskilim. On occasion even signs of toleration could provide the impetus. The best-known example of this is Naphtali Herz Wessely's *Divre shalom ve-emet* (Words of Peace and Truth, 1782), a reaction to the edict of toleration of Emperor Joseph II of Austria. During his short reign (1780–1790) the Habsburg emperor had introduced a comprehensive reform in all spheres. His policies, known as "Josephinism," were designed to help Austria expand its economic and military capacity and to enhance the intermeshing of state and society by means of a central, rationally organized administration. Serfdom was abolished and the Catholic Church subordinated to the authority of the state. Joseph was guided by the principle of toleration for the other Christian denominations and for the Jews as well; for them he initially signed, on October 19, 1781, the Ordinance on Better Education and Enlightenment, directed to the Jews of Bohemia. Wishing to better the situation of all strata of the population, he noted in the edict for the Jews of Vienna and Lower Austria (January 2, 1782): "Right from the beginning of our government, one of our principal concerns has been that all our subjects, without distinction as to nation and religion, should, as soon as they have been admitted to and are tolerated in our states, have a share in the public welfare of the same, which we wish to expand by our solicitude."[14] However, this edict, meant only for a small but relatively well-situated segment of Austrian Jewry, certainly did not sweep aside all the restrictions of the past. The edict allowed neither for additional Jewish settlement nor the formation in Vienna of a community with a permanent synagogue building. Yet progress was significant when it came to economic activity and education. The Jews resident in Vienna were granted freedom of education. "Since our goal is to make the Jewish nation more useful to the state, principally by better instruction and enlightenment of their youth and application to sciences, arts, and crafts,"[15] Christian elementary and practical schools, as well as academic secondary schools, should be open to Jews. The freedom to pursue any trade now gave them access to the artisan crafts and agriculture. They were encouraged to invest in manufactories, real estate, and country properties. The "body tax," one of the most humiliating forms of taxation, was also to be abolished. All in all, this was the document of an enlightened monarch who—although he had never regarded himself as a "philosopher-king"—was nonetheless prepared to lend an ear to his enlightenment-oriented officials in the state council. He thus issued edicts that were unparalleled at the time anywhere in German-speaking Europe and did not fail to impress the small coterie of maskilim, in particular Naphtali Herz Wessely. Wessely viewed Joseph's reform plans as the sign of the dawning of a new era and a clarion call to the Jews to do their share in bringing about a transformation of their own society.

In his *Divre shalom ve-emet* Wessely expressed his admiration for the emperor: "Popular opinion has long counted him among the greatest and most courageous of regents. . . . Gifted with the purest intellect, endowed with the most noble sentiments of love for his fellow man, qualities that are constantly engaged in promoting the happiness of all his subjects, he has likewise been mindful of us."[16] This was not some sort of empty but necessary formula, a perfunctory expression of politeness to the monarch. Wessely firmly believed in enlightenment disseminated from above with the help of the "wise" ruler. He was not apprehensive about any Christianizing tendency and was prepared to cooperate with the government. "You will do well to adopt the suggestions of your great emperor," Wessely wrote to his Jewish brethren.

Wessely follows Mendelssohn in bifurcating Judaism into the "universal" and the "particular." The universal, the "human sciences" are the foundation upon which the particular, the law revealed at Sinai, can build. "The Creator originally planted the seed of human knowledge in the human soul" and it is the "work of reason" to make use of it. Universal knowledge is placed at least on the same level here as the particularistic law of Judaism, if not higher. Wessely appeals to the conscience of the Talmud scholar:

The divine laws, as exalted as they may be above all human ones, are nonetheless linked with these; one can even be a useful citizen of

46   The poet and educational reformer Naphtali Herz Wessely

the world without the former, propagating light and order universally through science and insight. . . . To be a human being is one
step higher than to be an Israelite.[18]

Wessely wished to set new priorities for Jewish education and, drawing on
the Midrash, made the following admonitory comparison: a scholar well-
versed in the Talmud but lacking general human knowledge and virtue has
less value than the (forbidden) flesh of a dead animal. This statement pro-

voked a storm of indignation among leading rabbis. Simultaneously, however, it pointed the way forward for the maskilim: henceforth, the Jew and his Judaism were to define themselves on the basis of the combination of the secular and sacred, the universally human and the specifically Jewish.

Although short-lived, Joseph II's policy of toleration thus had a definite impact on the Haskalah. The edict of January 2, 1782, was followed by further edicts: for Moravia's Jews (February 13, 1782), the Jews of Hungary (March 31, 1783), and, finally, in 1789, the edict for the Jews of Galicia, who had come under Austrian rule in 1772 following the first partition of Poland. This last edict was the most far-reaching document; more than its predecessors, it awakened confidence and faith in the power of education guided from above as a means to promote civil equality. Given the new atmosphere, Herz Homberg, who had become a dedicated maskil during his stay in Berlin, decided to return to Austria to place himself at the service of the government in Vienna and to assist in the establishment of German-Jewish schools in Gorizia and Trieste. Later he served as imperial head inspector in Galicia in the struggle against orthodoxy and its "obscurantism." Homberg brought with him to Galicia a staff of twenty-eight Jewish teachers from Bohemia who identified completely with the concept of enlightenment from above. In an empirical survey (1794) conducted for the government in Vienna, Homberg formulated the goals of his work radically by recommending that "the Jews should be brought closer to the Christians, and their esprit de corps eliminated." To this end, the study of Talmud was to be restricted and "the Hebrew language removed from use."

2. The Turn Toward Radical Solutions

In addition to Joseph's policies, another salient element that formed the background to the further development and rapid radicalization of the Berlin Haskalah were the events of 1789 in France. David Friedländer and Lazarus Bendavid rushed to translate into German the petitions that had led to the 1791 resolution of the National Assembly on civil equality for the Jews. Ha-Me'asef reported on the course of the events in Paris and the resolution of 1791. Even earlier, shortly after the death of Frederick II, David Friedländer (1750–1824), Mendelssohn's still faithful disciple (though soon to turn radical), had, as head of the "general deputies" of the Jewish communities in Prussia in the years 1787 to 1792, begun the struggle for expanded civil rights. He proved successful in achieving with-

drawal of the worst legal ordinances, such as the body tax (1787) and collective responsibility (1792). However, the government rejected the
demand for civil equality, justifying its position by reference to Jewish
particularity: as long as the Jewish nation "formed a special state within
the state, so to speak, by dint of its internal constitution and hierarchy,"[19]
there could be no abolition of the restrictive laws. Disappointment in the
face of the faltering reforms prompted Friedländer to a desperate step. In
1799 he wrote an "open letter" to Wilhelm Abraham Teller, provost and
head of the Berlin Consistory of Protestantism, in which he considered
the possibility for himself, and a number of like-minded "family heads,"
of converting to the Protestant Church. Behind this letter stood the
opportunism of a successful merchant, but that does not exhaust its content: Friedländer formulated conditions for conversion here that reflected
his conception of religion. It is evident that he had nonetheless remained
a maskil, building on Mendelssohnian concepts the universal verities of a
religion of reason: the belief in one God, his providence, and the immortality of the soul. These were the only elements of Christian religion
acceptable to Friedländer, not the dogma of the holy Trinity. In his eyes,
the Trinity was just as difficult to reconcile with reason as the objectionable Jewish ceremonial law. What remained was a Deism acceptable neither to a traditional Jew nor a representative of a Christian church, along
with a certain modicum of pride: "If the better Jew, for the purification of
his religion, need but cast off the shell of its ceremonial laws, the better
Christian must subject the basic verities of his own faith to renewed
examination; this latter task demands far more effort and intellectual
capacity."[20] The ceremonial law was no longer able to nourish the pride of
being a "chosen" people, but reference to the patriarchs of Israel and to
Moses could: it was they who were the first to have "concepts of religion
freed from all idolatry and paganism."[21]

The offer of conversion was rejected both by Teller and by the theologian Friedrich Schleiermacher. In anonymously authored letters, the latter wrote:

> You should recall that perceptible throughout is a profound attach-
> ment to the original pristine Abrahamite Judaism and to a Judaism
> that still awaits renewal, that does not yet really exist. And [you
> should recall] that Judaism, properly so, is set in opposition to
> Christianity; moreover, that the author derives the fundamental
> truths of his religion from Judaism—and it is precisely for this rea-

47   Mendelssohn's disciple David Friedländer

son that he has objections to Christianity. . . . You will certainly have
as few doubts as I do about the author's sincere hatred for it.[22]

In Schleiermacher's view, the family heads had brought along a great deal
that was distinctively Jewish, a number of Jewish prejudices and superstitions: "Indeed! a judaizing Christianity, that was the real disease" these
candidates for baptism were conjuring up.[23]

The polemic that raged over Friedländer's open letter to Teller brought to the surface old prejudices that stood in the way of closer social ties between Christian and Jews. Teller and Schleiermacher did not belong to the ranks of the Jews' adversaries. Schleiermacher even frequented the celebrated salon of Henriette and Marcus Herz, which, together with other Jewish salons, enjoyed distinct popularity in Berlin at the time and represented a free sphere for social interaction in an order still based on the old corporate structures and strata. Yet only a very limited number of privileged Jews took part in this mode of salon sociability, which did not generate any particular impetus for the development of the Haskalah. Nor was Jewish salon society in any position to reduce deeply ingrained prejudices. As the reactions to Friedländer's open letter attest, the polemic on Jews and Judaism had lost none of its acerbity and intensity.

The younger enlightened generation was not spared the disappointment of rejection. It drove them to taking refuge in Jewish associations, such as the Berlin Gesellschaft der Freunde (Society of Friends, 1792), described by an early chronicler in these terms: "Israelites not granted entry to any Christian facility, and who were unable to feel comfortable even at any public places of entertainment, where they were treated only with repugnance," found an amicable social circle "where they might forget the cares and woes of everyday life, where there was nothing but mutual goodwill and friendliness, with no distinction as to person."[24] The lack of readiness to accept Jews into Christian associations was what motivated Mendelssohn's son Joseph and the editors of *Ha-Me'asef*, Isaac Euchel and Aaron Wolfssohn, among others, to create this social focus for adherents of an enlightened Judaism. The internal confrontation with the traditionally minded community was another reason for their initiative.

The dispute on "early burial," which had occupied Mendelssohn already back in 1772, flared again after his death. Marcus Herz, responding to a call from several maskilim, had written a treatise presenting arguments based on reason and science against the "foolish custom still dominant among us to bury the dead so quickly."[25] Herz and the maskilim more generally wished to do away with a traditional custom that was, in their view, based on ignorance and superstition and not anchored in a law or halachic precept. Two different value systems collided here: on the one side, the values of strict adherence to the traditions of Judaism; arrayed against them, a set of values founded on the general, rational insights of the bourgeois public sphere. No compromise seemed possible, and so the

maskilim and their supporters chose to give social form to their own liberal views by setting up the Society of Friends.

In the 1790s the confrontation thus heightened both with the outside
world and with the Jewish world within. The maskilim founded associations whose aim was to reform education and promote occupational
restructuring. Increasingly, they played a role in the non-Jewish press,
such as the *Berlinische Monatsschrift*, without abandoning publication of
Ha-Me'asef, which Aaron Wolfssohn and Joel Brill Löwe edited in
Breslau until 1797. But the unbridgeable gap between the maskilim and
their opponents became ever more apparent. Leading maskilim such as
Saul Ascher, Lazarus Bendavid, Solomon Maimon, David Friedländer, and
Aaron Wolfssohn now wrote in German and moved further and further
away from the concept of a normative Judaism. Once the debate on a civil
improvement of the Jews' status intensified, questions were also broached

48   Illustration from title page of Marcus Herz, *Über die frühe*
Beerdigung der Juden (On Early Burial Among the Jews), with the grave of
Mendelssohn (*left*) and a questionably dead person (*right*)

about the nature and essence of Judaism. At the heart of this discussion lay a central problem: could Judaism survive as one religion among others after the dissolution of Jewish autonomy? In his work *Leviathan* (1792), the book dealer Saul Ascher (1767–1822) took Mendelssohn's *Jerusalem* as his point of departure, examining the place of religion in the state as a general fundamental problem. A key question for him in this regard was the binding power of Jewish law, a question also relevant from the Kantian perspective. For Ascher and other maskilim, Kant's *Critique of Pure Reason* and the concept of the autonomous human being who thinks for himself, guided by reason and not by external forces, became authoritative. Taking Kant's definition that Enlightenment was "liberation from self-incurred immaturity," they deduced a specific relevance for the Jews and for the binding nature of their religious laws.

In *Leviathan* Ascher attempted to sketch the outlines of a Judaism that could hold its own in confrontation with the Kantian critique of pure reason and its implications. Although he did not abandon the particularistic Jewish law (the form) alongside the "principle and teaching," that is, the universal rational verities of faith (the essence), he reduced the law's significance. Ascher argued for retaining fourteen articles of faith for the modern Jew, which he had selected from the tradition. These made up an "organon," and included the idea of the One God and messianic redemption, the commandment of circumcision and the observance of Sabbath rest. A residue of formal law was to suffice in order to give symbolic expression to the Jews' attachment to the verities of faith. Though this was not a complete negation of the Mendelssohnian concept, it constituted a clear departure from Mendelssohn in two respects. First, Ascher argued that the law had not sprung from an act of revelation on Sinai. It had arisen closely linked to the "principle and teaching," but in a highly specific historical context, the biblical age, as a necessary component of the religion, in order to facilitate its function as a formative element in state and society. Second, here at loggerheads with Mendelssohn, Ascher regarded religious law as an instrument for the "education of humanity" propagated by Lessing. It was temporally conditioned and served as a crutch, as a means of support for human beings whose power of reason in antiquity had not yet reached the knowledge of eternal principles. Now that the Middle Ages had passed and, with the spread of the Enlightenment, reason had gained in influence, most of these laws had become superfluous. Devoid of revelational character, they were the work of human beings, and thus their abolition did not violate divine omnipotence.

Ascher's views came very close to Friedländer's brand of Deism, which also regarded the binding character of the revealed law of Israel as limited in time. In Friedländer's open letter traces of Lessing's conception are likewise evident. For Friedländer, Moses became an educator who, thanks to his legislation in biblical times, had the merit of having facilitated a deeper and more rapid expansion of monotheistic belief, but whose work must now be reformed in keeping with the modern age. The future-oriented Jewish thinking of the 1790s thus also contained the seeds of a new concept: reform of the Jewish religion. The maskilim Lazarus Bendavid, Saul Berlin, and Aaron Wolfssohn were ready to give these notions of a revamped Judaism radical expression.

In his *Etwas über die Charakteristick der Juden* (On Jewish Characteristics, 1793), Bendavid proceeds on the assumption that the essence and form of religion determine the level of human morality and ethics. He argues that the moral decline of the Jewish people in the medieval period had continued unabated into the modern era, manifesting itself in a disregard for human values, freedom, and brotherly love. For Bendavid, the causes for this deterioration were obvious and lay in an exaggerated adherence to external forms, to the rituals of Judaism. The inordinate emphasis on laws and Talmudic traditions had gone hand in hand with greater superstition and prejudice—in short, with an atrophy of the pure teachings of Moses that had formed the pristine core of the Jewish religion. Bendavid argued that the rabbinical elite bore the blame for the "essential failings of the Jewish nation," its slave mentality, hatred of other religions, and loss of human dignity. It is impossible to avoid the impression that in this harsh indictment there is an echo of the criticism of non-Jews as Michaelis had formulated it—a virtually unavoidable concomitant of the orientation to the external world in the age of the Haskalah. Bendavid applies new yardsticks in assessing Jewish society. As he sees it, that society is divided into four different classes, characterized less by socioeconomic levels and more in terms of their relative degree of liberation from the strictures of normative Judaism. The first group, numerically the largest, adheres faithfully to the "whole jumble of traditions"; it lives cut off from the outside world, exclusively cultivating the study of the Talmud, while neglecting the Bible. Its members show respect solely for the rabbi and, caught up in superstition, remain at a distant remove from enlightenment, culture, and education. In its desire to break free from the law, the second class simultaneously jettisons the rules of moral behavior. The third class has tried somehow to liberate itself from formal Judaism but remains indecisive and thus unable to achieve unequivocal success. Only the fourth group, a minority in which Bendavid includes himself and the radical maskilim, has managed to break out of the constrictive magic circle. By abandoning external forms, it has made its Judaism rational. This self-liberation is tantamount to a "reform," which Bendavid regards as the sine qua non for the entry of Jews as equals into civil society. For Bendavid, the abolition of "senseless ceremonial laws no longer appropriate for the present" and the return to a "religion more worthy of the Father of us all, the pure teachings of Moses" are not ends in themselves but part of a larger endeavor by the maskilim to renew Jewish life.

Saul Berlin (1740–1794), for a time rabbi in Frankfurt an der Oder and son of the chief rabbi Hirschel Lewin in Berlin, was a controversial figure—not only because he was a maskil who also served as a rabbi, but due to the fact that, in his satirical writings, he sketched a blisteringly negative image of rabbinic Judaism—even if he refrained from publishing these ideas during his lifetime. Berlin's *Ketav yosher* (Statement of Sincerity, 1794) condemns the traditional system of education by a satirical description of its representatives—the melamed (traditional teacher) and the rabbi steeped in Talmudic learning. The author stresses the absurdities and outmoded character of rabbinic casuistry. Using exaggerated satirical caricature, Berlin's aim was to achieve more freedom for the autonomous, independently thinking individual—a goal Ascher aspired to utilizing the arguments of religious philosophy. *Ketav yosher* also lashes out at customs that, in Berlin's view, reflected only superstition and backwardness, such as the practice of kapparot (an expiation ritual involving the "transfer of sins" to a "sacrificial" chicken) on the eve of the Day of Atonement or the raucous outbursts when the name *Haman* is spoken at Purim during the synagogue reading of the Book of Esther. Saul Berlin was one of the first to call not only for more dignity and aesthetic sense in religious services, but to express doubts about the very necessity of ceremonial laws, "since in their endless number they represent a burden for the Jew, from the very day of his birth. Each and every act is associated with religious commandments and prohibitions. Even when a Jew winks, he is called to account for the deed."[26] Berlin vehemently contests the already shaken priority of the Oral and Written Torah, which Mendelssohn had attempted to salvage by the formula elaborated in *Jerusalem*. His attacks in *Ha-Me'asef* on judges in the Jewish courts and on rabbis stirred up tensions between the maskilim and the conservative majority. Berlin accused the former of greed, the latter of a double deficiency in education: ignorance of the culture and the language both of their own people and of that in whose midst they dwelt.

Aaron Wolfssohn was no less radical than Bendavid and Berlin. In his work *Jeschurun, oder unparteyische Beleuchtung der dem Judenthume neuerdings gemachten Vorwürfe* (Yeshurun, or An Impartial Examination of Recent Criticisms of Judaism, 1804) he adopted Bendavid's classification of Jewish society. He too utilized attitudes toward religion and the ceremonial law as a benchmark, sketching the ideal image of a rational religion, which, "purged of all ceremonies and customs," would become the purpose and final goal of religious history. That history began with Moses; it then led via the prophets and Maimonides to Mendelssohn and his disciples. Wolfssohn and his radical associates believed the highest stage of the Jewish historical continuum was a faith purified by reason. They did not wish to see this as a total break with tradition but interpreted it as a transformation in keeping with the Jews' new status.

The philosophy of Kant had a decisive influence on the maskilim in this later phase, especially on their attempts to liberate Jewish religion from the externals of a "positive ecclesiastical belief." Bendavid, Maimon, Ascher, and, naturally, Marcus Herz, who had studied in Königsberg, were all Kantians. They scrutinized religion in general and the Jewish religion in particular in the light of Kant's *Religion Within the Bounds of Pure Reason*. Their wish was to practice and live a Judaism that did justice to the postulates expounded by Kant. Since Kant was an authority for the later maskilim and his philosophy their point of orientation, they could hardly be indifferent to his bitter critique of Judaism. Saul Ascher in particular was unwilling to accept in passive silence Kant's formulations, which made a sharp distinction between Judaism and a religion based on reason. Ascher's *Eisenmenger der Zweite* (Eisenmenger the Second, 1794) was directed inter alia against Kant's assertion that Judaism was not even a religion, but rather, in terms of its original configuration, the epitome of a complex of laws that were merely statutory, on which a state constitution had been founded. Kant had concluded from this that, unlike Christianity, Judaism could have no part in the world-historical process of redemption. He even denied the role of Judaism as a spiritual wellspring of Christianity or a preparatory stage on the path to the purportedly objective unity of the true and universal faith. Judaism remained excluded from Kant's vision of a "religion of reason." For a maskil like Ascher, who took active part in the discourse of bourgeois public debate, this was a blow to his need to be treated as an equal. Ascher contended that when Kant wrote critically of Judaism he had betrayed his profession as a philosopher. How was it possible that Christianity had arisen suddenly, without any preparatory stage? Anyone who thought in historical terms would "not see Christianity emerging onto the scene abruptly. On the contrary, he would perforce have to discover the entire spirit of Christianity in the Judaism of that era."[27] Just as Ascher could not accept a caesura in the continuum of the past, he found it impossible to endorse the thesis of a rupture in the present that deprived Judaism of its mission, shutting it out from the course of events that would ultimately usher in the millennium for humanity, the realization of the messianic vision. Yet, in speaking of this future, Ascher employed such formulations as "world religion of reason" and "purified faith and pure morality as a bond among men," which hint at his ongoing desire to link Jewish tradition with Kantian philosophy.

The dialectic of the confrontation thus led to a restructuring of centuries-old conceptions of Judaism. Once the question of the "improvement of the civil status" of the Jews had taken on a new urgency, thanks to Dohm's treatise and the toleration edicts of Joseph II, Mendelssohn's functional formula, which postulated that religious laws guide the inquiring intellect to divine truths, lost its appeal. Nor could that formula suffice once the religious and philosophical questions regarding the essence and role of Judaism had become more closely intertwined with the political question: what is to be the status of the Jewish religion and its followers in the modern state? After Mendelssohn the maskilim saw matters differently: the eternal verities, the essence, were now seen to be more significant than the form, the Law binding exclusively on the Jews. Both parts, analogous to body and soul, continued to remain interlinked, but the eternal truths, as the core of a religion of reason, became the dominant element.

The second generation of the maskilim reinterpreted a central idea of Judaism, future redemption, in such a way that the Jewish enlightener could salvage the "essence" of his religion and was not forced to surrender his pride in Jewish origins. Ascher, who let himself be drawn more than others into the confrontation with representatives of the German educated middle class, went furthest in his attempt to rationalize and universalize the Jewish idea of redemption. Thus the resistance the maskilim encountered among non-Jewish intellectuals and the relevant segment of the rising middle class did not produce a radicalism that cut them off completely from their identity as Jews. They neither sought refuge in baptism nor did they return contritely to the waiting folds of the old tradition. Rather, despite the inherent difficulties, they sought to continue their work on the formation of a newly conceived Jewish sphere that brought them into closer relation with the world around them.

12 | Jewish Enlightenment and Education

1. Pedagogic Thinking

The schools established by the maskilim impinged on one of the most sensitive domains of traditional Judaism. Over the centuries its ideal of education had been a prime element in the internal strength and continuity of Jewish community life. Consequently, there was open resistance by the rabbinical elite when the maskilim, outsiders to that select body and in the clear numerical minority, forged ahead with the practical realization of their educational reforms. Three factors were decisive here for the maskilim: first, they were certain such an initiative would find favor with and gain the complete support of enlightened rulers, such as Joseph II, and government officials like Dohm. Second, the small stratum of privileged protected Jews tended to believe, like the maskilim, that pedagogic reform was linked with prospects for civil improvement; thus they expected and received support from wealthy entrepreneurs, such as Isaac Daniel Itzig and David Friedländer in Berlin. Third, the maskilim looked to the European and German Enlightenment in their basic philosophy and conceptions, particularly when it came to education. Indeed, if one seeks to identify the humanistic core of the Enlightenment that underpinned its optimism, there is no doubt that it lay in the idea of education. This topic had occupied virtually all enlightened thinkers, from philosophers and literati to political theorists, and also influenced the new Jewish educators.

Along with his writings on philosophy, political theory, and religion, John Locke (1632–1704) had also authored a treatise entitled *Thoughts Concerning Education* (1693). His ideal of reason and virtue as well as his faith in the human capacity to learn had led him quite spontaneously to grapple in this work with the question of education from infancy to adulthood. In Locke's conception the child is an independent creature whose characteristics and natural inclinations must be respected in the process of learning and education. Thanks to Locke's intellectual stimuli, the Age of Enlightenment also became an age of pedagogy. Jean Jacques Rousseau's *Émile* (1762), the veritable "bible" of many educators at the time, was likewise a fertile source of inspiration for the maskilim. Much of Rousseau's critique of a society that "always seeks the adult in the child, while failing to ask how and what the child is before the stage of adulthood" was transposed by the maskilim into the Jewish context. His demand that there should be more freedom in childhood and less authoritarianism in the education of children—in order to pave the way for the return to the lost paradise of the pristine virtuous human being—was a message whose utopian character could not fail to impress them. Locke and Rousseau facilitated the discovery of the child, the recognition of childhood as a distinct and special phase in maturation.

Within the geographical orbit of German culture, Johann Bernhard Basedow (1724–1790) had absorbed their ideas. His treatise *Vorstellung an Menschenfreunde und vermögende Männer über Schulen, Studien und ihren Einfluss auf die öffentliche Wohlfahrt* (An Expostulation to Philanthropists and Prosperous Men on Schools, Studies, and Their Influence on Public Welfare, 1768) and his establishment of a model school, Philanthropin, in Dessau (1774) were pioneering in the effort to rejuvenate and reform education. In place of uncomprehended authority, games, competition, independent activity, and closeness to nature were to motivate the child to learn. Subject matter gradated in terms of the unfolding of a child's spiritual and intellectual capacities was to further the free development of the personality. Philanthropinism as a movement—especially espoused by Basedow's successor, Joachim Campe (1746–1818), who was in contact with Mendelssohn—propagated inter alia the establishment and promotion of industrial schools. In addition to elementary subjects like reading, writing, arithmetic, and language, such schools were to offer the possibility of vocational training for crafts and agriculture. This concept of education for productive work was in keeping with the utilitarian aims of cameralism and was also emulated by the maskilim. Indeed, Basedow and his model school awakened keen interest within their ranks. Thus the philosophers and educational thinkers of the German and European Enlightenment generated a powerful impetus for educational reform and its practical implementation.

Although Mendelssohn did not write a work especially devoted to the topic of Jewish education, pedagogic thinking and motives underlay many of his writings, such as the Hebrew periodical *Kohelet Musar* and his Bible project. Mendelssohn was motivated by an abiding wish to assure the ideas of the Enlightenment a deep and profound impact via the agency of education. Thus David Friedländer reports that questions of pedagogic reform played a prominent role in discussions of the maskilim in Mendelssohn's home. Mendelssohn also took part in practical steps such as the preparation of a curriculum for the first Jüdische Freischule (Jewish Free School, 1778) and the creation of a first textbook, the *Lesebuch für jüdische Kinder* (A Reader for Jewish Children, 1779).

Of especial interest are the letters from Mendelssohn's voluminous correspondence where he touches on aspects of Jewish education. In a letter in 1779 to his Christian friend Friedrich Nicolai, for example, he stresses how important he regards the training of Jewish children in the crafts. But the most significant proof of Mendelssohn's enlightened attitude on questions of education are his letters to Herz Homberg. Here he writes of the hopes and disappointments associated with the education of his son Joseph while also spelling out his educational ideal and great tolerance in matters of pedagogy:

> My son Joseph is attending public lectures on physics by Dr. Marcus Herz and on chemistry by Herr Klaproth, without my having yet determined that he should take up academic studies. His reasoning ability is good, but he has his difficulties when it comes to languages. Even in Latin he is still at a low level and has forgotten nearly everything you taught him in Hebrew. I let him go his own way; as you know, I am no friend of coercion. And with his iron character, more easily broken than bent, there is nothing that can be accomplished by compulsion in any case. His good common sense will guide him eventually to some goal.[1]

In the circle of his own family Mendelssohn had put into practice two basic ideas of modern Jewish pedagogy that Naphtali Herz Wessely would later elevate to a systematic program of reform: the linking of traditional Jewish and secular education and the adaptation of the educational pro-

Lesebuch

für

Jüdische Kinder.

Zum Besten der jüdischen Freyschule.

Berlin

in Commißion bey Christian Friedrich Voß und Sohn

1 7 7 9.

49 Title page of the reader of the Jewish Free School in Berlin

gram to the emotional and intellectual development of the child. The innovative element in Wessely is not based on the ideas he develops— rather what is significant is the form in which he presents the program and his call for a revamping of Jewish education.

Wessely was one of a minority of knowledgeable students of the Talmud who never rejected the fundamental values of Jewish tradition, leading a pious life as observant Jews, but who nonetheless seized the initiative at the crucial moment to champion the cause of the new spirit. Of decisive influence for that initiative were Mendelssohn's preeminent authority and the favorable political and cultural ambience of the 1770s and 1780s. These were also reflected in Wessely's call to "the entire Jewish nation" in his *Divre shalom ve-emet* (Words of Peace and Truth), which, like all his writings, was composed in Hebrew.

All the new ideas of the Enlightenment that impacted on the Berlin Haskalah—philosophical, cameralist, and pedagogical—can be found in *Divre shalom ve-emet*. One can identify concepts here articulated earlier by Locke, Rousseau, Dohm, and the adherents of Philanthropinism. Already in Wessely's introductory lines there is evidence, still quite uncommon at the time, of a keen interest in the child, its individuality, and specific qualities. They expound the notion that there is no contradiction between the new pedagogical ideas of the Enlightenment (penetrating from the external world) and the venerable ancient texts of the Bible:

> The teaching of the wisest of our kings: "Train up a child in the way he should go, and even when he is old he will not depart from it" (Proverbs 22:6) must be looked at from two sides. Train up a child: give him instruction in accordance with his ways. Begin teaching at an early age. At a time when the child's head and heart are untainted by corrupting principles, unagitated by passions, they are most capable of absorbing the impressions of truth and virtue. But structure it according to the young boy's particular nature, his psychological and physical abilities. It is well-known that there is an extraordinary diversity in such capacities. One person is quick to grasp, another slower, one retains what has been understood effortlessly, another not even with the greatest exertion, etc. Consideration must be given to these characteristics if instruction is to be effective.[2]

Along with the demand that the psyche of the child be taken into account, Wessely calls for a distinction between general knowledge and specifically Jewish subject matter. Both the secular and religious components are intrinsic elements of the educational process, the sine qua non for the "happiness" of the individual and his integration into the state of the enlightened ruler—in Wessely's eyes embodied by Joseph II.

This distinction, which Mendelssohn formulated for the first time in the Lavater dispute and repeated in an expanded form in *Jerusalem* in the context of "state and religion," is based on a religiophilosophical conception that Wessely then interpreted in connection with his principle of a synthesis of religious and profane elements in the educational process. The "sacred" and specifically Jewish element should coexist side by side with the "profane" and universal human component, just as Jews and Christians should live together in the modern state in peaceful harmony. Ethics and international law, mathematics, history, and natural science must be an integral part of the curriculum of the enlightened school. The dream of civil equality and integration into the modern state thus finds expression in the plan of educational reform. In giving priority to secular knowledge, Wessely shifts curricular emphases in favor of a sphere free from rabbinical authority. This was a courageous stance, given a Jewish society at the time still largely dominated by rabbinic orthodoxy. And there was an immediate, absolutely devastating critical reaction by orthodox rabbis to Wessely's work.

As mentioned earlier, the publication of Mendelssohn's translation of the Pentateuch had also triggered a fierce polemical discussion. Shortly after Wessely mapped out a new set of priorities for Jewish education in *Divre shalom ve-emet*, no less a personality than Ezekiel Landau, chief rabbi of Prague—who had earlier expressed approval of Wessely's commentary *Yen levanon* (Wine of Lebanon, 1775) on the *Sayings of the Fathers*—used the occasion in his sermon delivered on the Great Sabbath preceding Passover 1782 to denounce Wessely:

> So now a pious and merciful king [Joseph II] has come to power, and although we are slaves, he has lifted from us the shame of slavery. . . . And now from among our people an evil man has stood up, with the audacity to say that the Torah has no importance whatsoever, that an animal's carcass has more worth than the scholars of Talmud, and that proper manners [*nimusim*] are more important than Torah. . . . I too very much welcome the knowledge of proper manners and the grammar of the languages of the world's peoples. . . . But give heed, be very careful that you fear the Lord. Because as you acquire the language of the country, you will

50   The Prague chief rabbi Ezekiel Landau

also wish to read books of the type that do not serve the purpose of learning the language but deal rather with investigations into matters of religion. And this, God forbid, may awaken in your hearts an aversion to the faith . . . we have inherited from our holy fathers.[3]

In Landau's reaction a clear distinction is evident between the proposal to introduce secular subjects into instruction for Jewish children and the religiophilosophical argument on which the idea of renewal emanating from Berlin was based. For utilitarian reasons, Landau endorsed the

acquisition of secular knowledge in elementary school, just as he welcomed the Edict of Toleration and even supported the establishment of an
elementary school in Prague. However, Landau staunchly rejected the
ideology of the maskilim, which was indebted to the philosophy of the
Enlightenment and had shaken the traditional system of values. The reaction of other rabbis, such as David Tewele in Lissa, was no less severe.
They were indignant at the initiative of a man who did not belong to the
rabbinical elite: "this scoundrel, who lacks any knowledge of the profound
wisdom of the Talmud ... how does this man, bereft of any erudition, have
the audacity to dictate his curriculum to a people of God and instruct it in
God's paths?"[4] The maskil is denied the right to initiate reforms, based on
the argument that he fails to fulfill the requirements for a spiritual leader
in the traditional community. Thus, the outlines of a conflict emerged
involving not only abstractions and value judgments but also status and
formal authority in the society.

The new tendency, regarded by orthodoxy as revolutionary and a danger to the old moorings of the traditional order, was then intensively
expanded by the maskilim toward the end of the century. The Hebrew
journal *Ha-Me'asef*, and later the German periodical *Sulamith*, contributed substantially to making education and its reform an integral
component of the movement for enlightenment centered in Berlin.

From the first to the very last year of its publication the collaborators
of *Ha-Me'asef* denounced the old ossified ways of education in Jewish
society, often with biting irony, and in an increasingly more pointed form.
Critique of the old forms of Jewish life, the religious leadership elite, and
the social abuses led quite naturally to criticism of the educational ideals
of traditional Jewish society: namely the Talmud scholar and the observant Jew, oriented to the norms and values of a society that had cut itself
off from the outside world.

In his "Sendschreiben an die deutsche [*sic*] Juden" (Open Letter to the
German Jews) published in German with Hebrew characters in *Ha-
Me'asef* in 1788, David Friedländer reiterated all the arguments against
the old order and its intellectual elite. He accused the rabbis of antiquated
ideas that had not changed since the twelfth century, alleging that they
were totally alien to the changing times and environment. In his view,
they constituted the major obstacle to a renewal of Jewish society—and
especially a reform of education. Friedländer severely criticized Talmud
instruction and the cultural decline it had brought about in morality and
particularly in the language of the Jews. The way out of the crisis lay in

education, Friedländer argued, which now was beginning to reorient itself to the universal values of the outside world and was no longer exclusively based on immanent Jewish criteria. That opening up to external stimuli led to a revaluation of the place of the German language in instruction and a concomitant reduction of the central educational role of Hebrew.

Critique of the old order and its system of education was meant to accelerate the process of civil equality for the Jews. If the maskilim were emphatically in favor of training young Jews for artisan vocations, naturally that was for cameralist, social-utilitarian reasons, views the exponents of Philanthropinism had also championed. They sought to translate these conceptions into practice by the founding of industrial-vocational schools. Yet for them, as members of an ethnic-religious minority, there was an additional very special motivation underlying their call for "productivization" of the Jews: they wanted to help eradicate old prejudices standing in the way of an abrogation of discriminatory laws and regulations and of civil equality for Jews in the state. In propagating training in artisanship for Jewish children and the secularization of instruction, the maskilim were responding to the impact of external influences. Yet the practical ways and means they selected and the pace at which they pushed ahead with their designs were dictated by the specific situation the Jews found themselves in as an ethnic and religious minority.

The efforts of the maskilim to achieve an educational renaissance within Jewish society are inconceivable without attention to their recognition of childhood as a distinctive stage and their stress on its special character. Thus they referred again and again in their articles to thinkers such as Locke, Rousseau, Basedow, Campe (and later Pestalozzi) in raising the demand that to bring about renewal in Jewish education it was not enough to set new priorities for knowledge and to give preference to the secular over the sacred. More was needed: it was also imperative to take into account the psychological, intellectual, and physical needs and characteristics of the pupil. The maskilim asserted that only if the pedagogical and didactic postulates of the Enlightenment were heeded would it also be possible to attain the sociopolitical goal of education: to shape the young Jew into a useful member of society. The very first volume of *Ha-Me'asef* (1784) contains an article entitled "Letter on the Necessity to Provide Children with a Good Education." The aim of the future virtuous and useful Jewish citizen is linked here with the call for sympathetic understanding of the child, who must later embody this ideal goal.

The issue of *Ha-Me'asef* for 1786 published a contribution on education by a disciple of Wessely and the Berlin Haskalah from Italy, Elijah Morpurgo (1740–1830). He was a leading light in his community in Gradisca, a businessman who was also well acquainted with Jewish sources. Morpurgo's knowledge of Hebrew, Italian, French, and German, the amalgamation of Jewish and general education, placed him in a long line of Italian Jewish tradition extending back to the Golden Age of Spanish Jewry. The Berlin Haskalah found a reliable comrade-in-arms in Morpurgo. He corresponded with Mendelssohn and Wessely, translated the latter's programmatic work into Italian, and fought in the pages of *Ha-Me'asef* for the idea of educational reform. In response to a call of the governing board of the Jewish Free School in Berlin he formulated a pedagogic concept that called for teaching children the elementary skills of reading and writing not just in Hebrew but in the language of their native country as well. From the third to sixth year of instruction, reading should be taught initially by female teachers, "in accordance with the custom of our brethren in Spain and Italy—women have a gentle heart and understand how to instruct the child patiently and in keeping with his nature." Children from six to nine should then be given instruction in language and grammar, along with Bible classes, the study of ethics and the laws of Judaism—two hours in the morning, two in the afternoon. At the age of nine they should be introduced to Mendelssohn's *Bi'ur* commentary. The commandments pertaining to the observance of rest on the Sabbath and festivals should be taught based on the codification by Maimonides. Between the age of nine and thirteen pupils should work through all the books of the Bible as well as the principles of normative Judaism contained in the codex *Shulḥan Arukh*. This curriculum accorded Bible study a clear preference over the Talmud. The latter, if at all, should be studied only following completion of elementary school, after the age of thirteen, and then optionally, by the most gifted pupils from wealthy families. Yet even at this stage the Talmud was not to be the only subject. The Mishnah and Bible, with the rationalist commentary of the Spanish-Jewish scholar Abraham ibn Ezra (d. 1164), philosophical, and even poetic works, should not be neglected. The meaningful combination of general and specifically Jewish knowledge required the preparation of a special textbook. This textbook should also inculcate the "duties of the individual toward the king, the townsman to his city, the human being toward his neighbor, and the Jew toward his fellow Jew," thus promoting the effort to break free from the traditional system of education.

Morpurgo's article reflects the salience of the external influence of the Enlightenment, which left a significant stamp on the form and content of the proposals advanced by the maskilim. Both their fundamental conceptions and practical suggestions for educational reform confirm this. The most minor methodological details were taken into account. These included motivating pupils by competition and posting the results of exams as well as utilizing games and graphic outdoor instruction in nature. Each day, following the afternoon prayer, teachers and pupils should take a walk together outside of town to strengthen and invigorate body and soul. Between the age of nine and thirteen two hours daily were to be set aside for practical training in crafts. The external appearance of the children was to reduce social differences between them by the wearing of clean, uniform clothing. At the same time, Morpurgo expounded basic ideas regarding the preservation of the dignity and individuality of the Jewish child, a consequence of which would be the elimination of corporal punishment.

Morpurgo's voice, raised at a decisive moment in the debate on Wessely's reform program, had its impact and importance. It demonstrated the common bond between the Berlin Haskalah and the leadership stratum of the northern Italian communities, especially Trieste, Gorizia, Venice, Ferrara, Ancona, and Reggio. Their rabbis welcomed Wessely's initiative by publishing special testimonials that were conceived in significant measure as a kind of counterweight to the harsh condemnations by rabbis of Ashkenazi communities. Thus, in his evaluation, Rabbi Isaac ben Moses Formiggini, head of the rabbinical court of the Trieste community, wrote that the works of Mendelssohn and Wessely deserved praise, even though heads of yeshivot in Germany and Poland had denounced them as heretical.

Already in the 1780s the circle around Mendelssohn also made its influence felt in Prague. At the center of the movement for Enlightenment there were Jonas Jeitteles, his two sons Baruch and Judah, and his grandson Ignatius (1783–1843). Jonas had studied medicine in Halle (1755) and had become receptive to the ideas of Enlightenment. He and his sons maintained contacts with Mendelssohn and his circle and then became the initiators and supporters of the Prague elementary school, opened in 1782. This was one of the first schools in the German cultural area to provide pupils with basic secular knowledge. It is astonishing that the establishment of such a school was possible in this religiously conservative community, and even with the approval of the community lay

JONAS JEITTELES

*Medicinæ Doctor, Philosophiæ Baccalaureus,
Bohemo-judaico chyrurgorum gremio Præses*

*in memoriam patris optimi monumentum hocce erigunt,
gratiejue liberi.*

51 The Prague maskil and physician Jonas Jeitteles

leaders and the chief rabbi, Ezekiel Landau—a man who, as mentioned, was one of the principal adversaries of the Berlin initiatives for enlightenment. This early success had undoubtedly been facilitated by the Edict of Toleration issued by Joseph II for the Jews of Bohemia, which had called for the opening of elementary schools for Jewish children. Landau responded to the progressive demands with the pragmatic argument that Jewish children should acquire the basic general knowledge that would prepare them for a modern vocation. At the same time, however, he called for the strict separation of instruction in "sacred" Jewish subjects, which was to remain outside the secular elementary school and its modernizing influences, a view also supported by Jeitteles and his circle. On the whole, the maskilim of Prague trod a path of prudent moderation, clearly differentiated from the tendencies toward radicalization during the 1790s in Berlin. This restraint also temporarily spared them a confrontation with orthodoxy.

2. The New Schools

Elsewhere, as well, educators took action: they did not restrict themselves to publishing articles in periodicals or programmatic statements calling for educational reform in Jewish society but embarked on concrete pedagogical initiatives. Between 1778 and 1816 no less than ten modernized Jewish schools were established in the German cultural area. These included the Jüdische Freischule in Berlin (1778), the Königliche Wilhelmsschule in Breslau (1791), the Jüdische Haupt- und Freischule named after Duke Franz in Dessau (1799), the Religions- und Industrieschule or Jacobson-Schule in Seesen (1801), the Samson'sche Freischule in Wolfenbüttel (1807)—under the direction of Samuel Meyer Ehrenberg, transformed from a Talmud school of the traditional type into an enlightened modernized institution—the Jüdische Philanthropin in Frankfurt am Main (1804), the Konsistorialschule in Kassel (1809), and schools in Prague, Vienna, and Trieste.

A paradox of the Berlin Haskalah was that the schools it helped found were principally for the education and training of children from poor Jewish families. The children of the wealthy middle class, who logically should have been the main candidates for the new schools, either continued to enjoy preferred instruction by private tutors or opted for non-Jewish schools, especially academic secondary schools (*Gymnasien*). The so-called Freischule was considered a school for the indigent, propagated

52   The Philanthropin in Frankfurt am Main, the first school building of
its own (1813 –1845)

by the philanthropists in order to enable children from impoverished backgrounds to prepare for a vocation. The fact that pupils were able to earn their keep after school by diligence and labor, instead of having to live on charity—possibly falling prey to the evils of idleness—was congruous with the bourgeois ethos adhered to by the initiators of the Jewish free schools.

A letter sent by the board of the Gesellschaft für eine jüdische Freischule (Society for a Jewish Free School) in Dessau to Prince Leopold Friedrich Franz of Anhalt-Dessau shortly after the founding of the school is indicative of certain aspects of this ethos:

> The local Jewish community has still had no opportunity to provide its children with suitable instruction. The unfortunate consequences have been ignorance, boorishness, and a lack of morality. This has prompted several young philanthropists, who are much concerned for the welfare of their fellow citizens, to establish a society. Its membership dues help to maintain an institute where children, particularly from poor families, are instructed free of charge in the most necessary and indispensable sciences.[5]

Since the founders were acting in agreement with the community board members (which was not the case in Breslau or Frankfurt am Main), and proclaimed that the "final aim" was the education of "good, upstanding burghers and loyal subjects," the special royal permit for the school was promptly issued. It is evident from their petition that the initiators were a reform-minded group that had banded together for the first time as a separate association, guided by a wish for concord with the state authorities and the community, not radicalization and opposition.

This aspiration is also evident in the statutes of the Religions- und Industrieschule founded by the financier and court Jew Israel Jacobson in Seesen. In 1801 he informed the duke of Brunswick it was his intention to open a Jewish school for poor children. He secured the financial basis by a fund of one hundred thousand Reichstaler and acquired a site for construction of the school in order, as he wrote, "by means of education and instruction, to implant in its pupils the basic foundations, such that they will later function with dignity in society as upstanding moral persons, citizens practically competent in their various vocations."[6] Along with general education and instruction for proper ethical behavior and discipline in keeping with the bourgeois moral code, vocational training had priority, especially in the crafts and agriculture. In a paternalistic manner Israel Jacobson's aim was to translate the principle of achievement, propagated by the Berlin Haskalah as "productivization" of the Jews, into concrete practice. The focus group initially consisted of children from the lower social classes.

The enlightened schools were marginalized as institutions—not only because they were oriented toward children from impoverished families but also due to opposition from orthodox circles, which prevented them from achieving a major success. In Breslau, for example—a community in the border area on the periphery of Polish Jewry, which was still totally traditional in its orientation—the aversion to such modern trends in orthodox circles, which insisted on retaining the priority of Talmud studies, held back the progress of the Wilhelmschule there for many years.

In addition, problems in financing set practical limits to the expansion of these schools. Over the first decade of its existence, the number of pupils studying in the Berlin Free School averaged some fifty-five annually. That figure remained constant down to 1825, when the school had to be shut down due to a lack of funds. The Wilhelmsschule in Breslau stayed in existence somewhat longer than fifty years but was finally forced to close its doors for financial reasons after the 1848 revolution, since the local community had not shown any readiness to help remedy the school's acute financial crisis. Israel Jacobson's school in Seesen fared better, especially since it succeeded in gaining the support of the government and official recognition as a lower secondary school (*Mittelschule*), where Jewish and non-Jewish pupils studied side by side. This interdenominational character was in keeping with the enlightened, philanthropinistic conception espoused by its founder. It thus was able to survive storms and vicissitudes well down into the twentieth century. The Jüdische Philanthropin in Frankfurt had an analogous development.

The example of the Jewish community in Dessau, the birthplace of both Mendelssohn and his teacher David Fränkel, the later rabbi of Berlin, can serve to point up the prerequisites and difficulties of educational reform. Dessau was a small community whose growth had been shaped by the interaction of various factors: the interests of the ducal government and the Wulff family of court Jews, as well as the town's favorable location, in close proximity to the trade fair center of Leipzig. From several dozen Jewish residents in 1685, the Jewish community there had grown to about a thousand members around 1800. The overwhelming majority were still traditional Jews, living in accordance with normative Jewish orthodoxy: rabbis and lay leaders remained distinctly cool toward the new ideas. Rabbi Michael Speyer did not organize a boycott against the small group of Haskalah enthusiasts but loudly denounced Mendelssohn's Bible translation and Wessely's concepts of education. The simple Jewish population in Dessau was totally unprepared for the reformist ideas from Berlin. They did not read the writings of the innovators. Their libraries contained prayer books, the Bible, and popular ethical literature. The old familiar order of things gave them a sense of security and accorded with the reverence in which they held earlier generations. The Dessau Talmud school, whose establishment and maintenance had been made possible by the benefaction of the court factor Moses Benjamin Wulff, was still the focus of the community. It corresponded with the dominant ideal of education: parents, even the less well-to-do, wished at least for the most gifted of their sons to be be trained as rabbis and Talmud scholars.

That desire also animated Philip Moses and his wife, Rebecca Löb, the parents of Moses Philippson (1775–1814). Philip Moses eked out a modest living as a petty trader. Six days a week he was on the road in the small towns and villages of the Duchy of Anhalt, returning to spend the Sabbath with his family. The religious learning he could not impart to his son on that one day of the week he sought to supplement by engaging a private tutor from Poland. Moses Philippson was not yet twelve when he became a pupil in a yeshiva. His father sent him to Halberstadt, where he devoted himself exclusively to the study of the Talmud and rabbinic literature. Two years later, his path took him on to the yeshiva in Brunswick, maintained by the duke's treasury agent and factor, Jacob

Samson. In 1789, finally, he went to study in the yeshiva in Frankfurt an der Oder.

Educated in the strict tradition of normative Judaism, Moses Philippson nonetheless became a disciple of the Haskalah and was among the cofounders and staff teachers of the Free School in Dessau. At the age of seventeen, his intellectual outlook had begun to change: employed as a private tutor in the home of a wealthy Jewish merchant family in Bayreuth, he discovered Mendelssohn's *Morgenstunden* (Morning Hours). This book led him to metaphysics and its internal Jewish roots, to the philosophical works of the Middle Ages, such as Maimonides' *Guide of the Perplexed* and Bahya ibn Paquda's *Hovot ha-levavot* (Duties of the Heart). Through assiduous application and self-study, Philippson became a maskil. He acquired a broad general knowledge by reading widely in mathematical, philosophical, and literary works. This background enabled him to teach at the Franzschule without having first attended an academic high school and then gone on to a university—the route later followed by his sons Phoebus and Ludwig after completing the Jewish Free School in Dessau.

Moses Philippson's pathway was a slow process of drawing closer to enlightened thought and was by no means marked by any radical rupture with tradition. That was also true for three other maskilim who participated together with Philippson in the planning, establishment, and development of the new school in Dessau: David Fränkel (1779–1865), son of the Dessau rabbi Moses Fränkel (1739–1812) and for many years director of the Franzschule, Joseph Wolf (1762–1826), and Gotthold Salomon (1784–1862), later preacher at the Hamburg Reform Temple. They had received a strict traditional education in their family and community as children and in their youth but had then come under the influence of the thought of the Haskalah by personal contact with the Berlin circle and through self-study. Haskalah ideas provided the impetus for them to champion educational reform in their community.

The small group of maskilim in Dessau contributed to the establishment of the Dessau Free School by founding an educational association that acted in accordance with the paradigm of the maskilim in Berlin and Breslau, aiming at bringing together enlightened persons in a single local organization (it could boast 183 members in 1801). Nonetheless, their *Verein* aspired to achieve modernization with the agreement of—not in opposition to—the conservative segment of the community. In the curriculum of their school for its four grades, half of the total hours (twenty) were set aside for Jewish subjects: Bible, biblical history, Hebrew, religion,

Talmud, and Judeo-German; the remainder was given over to German, French, arithmetic, penmanship, history, geography, and natural science. The goal was inclusive: to include all the children in the community in the new system of education, displacing and eventually supplanting the *ḥeder*, if necessary even with backing from the duke.

In remarks two years before his death, Moses Philippson's son Ludwig (1811–1889), the later founder and longtime editor of the *Allgemeine Zeitung des Judenthums*, reminisced about his native community Dessau and his boyhood there, where he had attended the Free School from the age of three to thirteen (1814–1824). His recollection of the school is "not clouded by anything negative, indeed a happy memory, because it contributed a great deal to the joys and pleasures of my youth."[7] What graduate of a traditional ḥeder at that time could have written similar words? And who in an earlier generation would have been able to claim that a Jewish school had taught him general knowledge as well, providing the foundation for his admission to an academic secondary school?

In 1809 the prince of Anhalt-Dessau, acceding to a request by the Jewish educator David Fränkel, ordered that all children in the community must attend the Franzschule for at least four years. This decree was renewed in 1816; the connection of the school with the government was formalized and its maintenance secured by an annual subsidy. The community of interest between the state and the educators was further revealed in 1825, when the government of the duchy agreed to David Fränkel's request and ordered the merger of the Dessau traditional bet hamidrash with the Franzschule—against the will of the community lay board. Although the pattern of cooperation between the state and maskilim in Dessau worked well until 1848, the school then lasted only for about another twenty years and was ultimately closed in 1869. Its closing underscored the fact that the success of the educational institutions founded by the representatives of the Berlin Haskalah was short-lived, limited mainly to the first half of the nineteenth century—a period of unparalleled discrepancy between efforts for integration and the restricted possibilities of achieving such integration given the formidable legal barriers that still remained.

During this period, however, David Fränkel and his circle developed an array of cultural activities that were lively and intense, whose scope extended well beyond the boundaries of their school. They continued the Mendelssohnian Bible project, published a translation with commentary of the Minor Prophets, and also created teaching materials for new subjects at the Franzschule. Moses Philippson edited a *Lesebuch für die Jugend jüdischer Nation und für jeden Liebhaber der hebräischen Sprache* (A Reader for the Youth of the Jewish Nation and for Every Lover of the Hebrew Language), Joseph Wolf wrote *Reshit limudim* (First Studies), a Hebrew textbook for the natural sciences, and Gotthold Salomon translated Maimonides' ethics (*Shemonah perakim*), adding his own notes. A "catechism," that is, a systematic presentation of the basic tenets of the Jewish religion, was also published in the printing house that Moses Philippson had set up specially for enlightened literature.

It should not be forgotten that in the phase of transition from traditional Jewish society to modern and postemancipatory Jewish society, the schools formed a focal point around which the forces of Jewish Enlightenment, generally without financial means, could crystallize and cooperate. A number of followers of the Berlin Haskalah who were unable to secure positions in the civil service or as teachers at an academic secondary school or university found a framework for action and influence within these schools. This practical base enabled them not only to be active as educators but also to dedicate themselves intensively to publishing enlightened literature. Textbooks for children, scholarly-scientific works, and periodicals contributed to shaping an intellectual and cultural current, born in the mid-eighteenth century in the circle around Mendelssohn in Berlin, into a sociocultural phenomenon whose influence in the Jewish world reached far beyond the final decades of that century and the boundaries of the German cultural area. In their quest to bring about a renaissance in Jewish society, education became for the maskilim the preferred domain for their activity.

The publication of a new Jewish periodical by David Fränkel and his associates, *Sulamith* (1806–1848)—the first in the German language—was part of that project of renewal. Its pages contained a wealth of contributions that dealt with questions of pedagogy. Reflecting the ideas of Rousseau, Basedow, Pestalozzi, and Jean Paul, but also drawing on Jewish sources, the Bible and Midrash, the journal had harsh criticism for the traditional system of education, the lack of appreciation for the child's psyche, the practice of corporal punishment in the schools. The maskilim contributors—whose ranks also included former contributors to *Ha-Me'asef*—contrasted and extolled the advantages and achievements of the new schools in Dessau and other communities in the German-speaking lands. *Sulamith* published annual reports on activities in the free schools of Seesen, Berlin, Breslau, Frankfurt am Main, Wolfenbüttel,

Dessau, even Prague, and sought to illustrate the ongoing process of transformation within Jewish culture. As its subtitle stated, it saw itself as a "periodical for the furtherance of culture and humanity in the Jewish nation." The journal constantly broadened its spectrum of topics: Jewish history, philosophy, philology, and book reviews broke through the narrow frame of purely religious themes. In that respect, it was the continuation of its Hebrew precursor *Ha-Me'asef*. The readership of *Sulamith*, drawn from the rising Jewish professional and propertied middle classes, was thus able to convince itself that educational reform, an aim that had high priority along with the struggle for civil equality and religious reform, was part of an embracing transformation of Jewish society. That change was experienced no less intensely in the microcosm of the small community of Dessau than in the large centers of Berlin, Hamburg, or Frankfurt. It was an evolutionary process that was able to proceed without radical restructuring in the external form of the communities.

What then was the historical importance of these free schools, planned and established by the maskilim with the aid of a small number of representatives of the Jewish economic elite and, in some cases, even with state support? To begin with, they constituted the experimental terrain where it proved possible to translate conceptions of a Jewish Enlightenment into concrete practice. For the first time in modern history secular education was promoted by Jewish institutions on the basis of a curriculum that integrated Jewish and general subjects. But, beyond this, these schools also made it possible for a number of representatives of a generation educated in their enlightened ambience to intervene actively later in their lives on behalf of the transformation of Jewish society in the German cultural area. Although the schools and periodicals of the enlighteners were only a passing phenomenon, their pupils and readers initiated two developments that would be of decisive importance for the subsequent history of German Jewry: practical religious reform and the beginnings of the modern scholarly study of Judaism.

Conclusion

As the nineteenth century began, the first stage of the Jewish Enlightenment had come to an end. More than a decade had passed since the death
of Mendelssohn, the father of the Berlin Haskalah. His place had been
taken by his disciples, who endeavored to spread Enlightenment ideas by
practical actions. They published books and periodicals and established
free schools in order to forge the basis for as broad a reception as possible
of their ideals, the aims of broad culture and education that they shared
with the European Enlightenment. Yet their endeavors achieved only partial success. Initially, the ideas of the Haskalah had a limited impact, finding a favorable reception within only a small circle of Jewish society. The
maskilim were unable to effect palpable change in the thinking and action
of the majority.

In the eighteenth century the geographical boundaries of the Jewish
Enlightenment were narrowly drawn, encompassing only a few urban
communities in the German-speaking lands, while extensive areas, in particular the rural communities, remained untouched. The Haskalah did not
galvanize a revolutionary change; it only generated a ferment in the intellectual and cultural sphere. But its influence cannot be measured in terms
of immediate success. A proper evaluation of the phenomenon necessi-
tates an assessment of the full scope of its impact on the broader process
of transformation molding modern Judaism. Thus it is best examined
from the medium-range and long-term historical vantage of the nineteenth century, an era in which the advancing emancipation of the Jews

injected a new dynamism into their life and where the impulse for renewal generated by the Haskalah could fully unfold.

Just how decisively the Jewish Enlightenment shaped the development of Judaism in the nineteenth century can be illustrated by examining four key aspects. First, its adherents had ventured into a secular sphere in which they were no longer automatically subject to religious law and rabbinical authority, a domain in which they could devote themselves to the study of European and German rationalist philosophy. With its aid, they were able to criticize abuses and struggle against superstition, prejudice, and whatever they perceived as a defect in education—in order to help their conception of truth, pure morality, and purified faith to achieve a breakthrough. The scope of this critical bourgeois public sphere, where Jews could think and act free from the power of sanction of the old community, steadily expanded in the nineteenth century. It existed alongside the religious sphere, now restricted more and more to the orbit of the synagogue.

Second, with the advent of the Berlin Haskalah, a new intellectual elite emerged, one no longer identical with the old religious leadership stratum of the rabbis and Talmud scholars. It was distinguished neither by a formal position in the community hierarchy nor by material wealth. This was an intelligentsia that based its claim to leadership in equal measure on its secular philosophical and scientific learning and its knowledge of Judaism. For the most part, the maskilim of the eighteenth century were autodidacts, but their successors in the nineteenth century—such as the founders of the Wissenschaft des Judentums, for example—were largely university graduates. Both were animated by the idea of a mission inspiring them to work for the furtherance and spread of philosophy and science—that is, for the goal of making rational thought a paramount force among the Jews.

Third, the maskilim were the proponents of a new vision of Judaism, further developed by the Jewish intellectuals of the nineteenth century. The core of this conception was the Kantian idea of a "religion within the bounds of pure reason," in which the law revealed at Sinai no longer represented the essential nucleus but was solely an external form, one that at best could be accorded a symbolic function. The tendency to reduce the religious content of Judaism to the universal verities of reason, particularly pronounced among the disciples of Mendelssohn in the 1790s, was not yet linked with demands for a reform of religious worship. Nonetheless, it created the basis for a reform in Judaism. The Berlin Haskalah

53 Two clocks on the Jewish town hall in Prague symbolize the changing
times in the second half of the eighteenth century.

passed on to its heirs the principle of the division of church and state, the distinction in Judaism between political-national and religious-spiritual components. In so doing, it lent support to attempts by the state to abolish community autonomy and the right to ban dissidents.

Finally, concurrent with circumscription of the concept of religion, the idea of Jewish culture changed from monistic to pluralistic. The functional transformation of the Hebrew language played an especially salient role here. It was expanded from a language serving only sacred purposes to an idiom that could also be used in and for profane domains. From a language of prayer and sacred literature, it was refunctionalized into a medium also suitable for secular knowledge and expression. The beginnings of a modern Hebrew literature in its various genres are discernible in this first stage of Enlightenment with its lyrical poetry, satire, drama, and narrative. The inclusion of secular areas of knowledge and creativity also led to increasing use of the German language.

In these various aspects the Haskalah signified a radical new turn. Yet it remained, for the most part, an intellectual and cultural phenomenon and thus had no immediate, profound impact on daily Jewish life of the masses. The Jewish community still remained of central importance for the overwhelming majority of its members. Virtually untouched by the ideas of the maskilim, they remained faithful to the traditions of normative Judaism.

Nonetheless, Jewish community life was not static. It had been undergoing a continuous process of change since the early modern period, since the movement of return migration into the German-speaking lands and the subsiding of mass expulsions. The rapid decline in community autonomy and the diminished authority of rabbis and lay leaders was not solely the result of the emergence of Mendelssohn and the maskilim around the middle the eighteenth century. This process had begun earlier, and it continued unabated throughout the entire eighteenth century. The old structures were weakened by forces from within and without: pressure from the absolutist regime, which intervened more and more in the election of lay leaders and the appointment of rabbis, along with inner tensions generated by the power abuses of families of court Jews, the oligarchical and nepotistic composition of community boards. Internal struggles between rabbis, waged in the communities with great vehemence and passion, were hardly inclined to bolster the old community system, which went through a process of incremental dissolution. This was manifested inter alia in the fact that increasing numbers of Jews involved in law suits appealed rabbinical decisions to general secular courts, contributing to the undermining and decline of rabbinical legal jurisdiction. Against this crisis-ridden background, the criticism by the maskilim of the community and its traditional leadership had an accelerating effect on the process of the old order's disintegration.

The first signs of acculturation had also emerged before the era of Enlightenment; cultural isolation was no longer hermetic. There had been stirrings of a need for a certain adaptation to the customs, dress, and language of the environment, although these were met by criticism from the rabbis. That tendency became visible in the narrow circle of the court Jews and their families at an earlier juncture than elsewhere in the old communities, due to their role in the mercantilist economic system. But even rabbis showed a more open-minded attitude to the outside world, as can be inferred, for example, from the modifications in their conception of education and learning. A number of rabbis no longer occupied themselves solely with Halacha and Kabbala but delved into the natural sciences and philosophy as well. Thus a great Talmudic authority might now be well-versed also in mathematics, astronomy, physics, the works of Aristotle, and Spanish-Jewish philosophy—yet without espousing support for an ideology of Enlightenment. Especially conspicuous is the fact that representatives of the traditional community faithful to the Torah now also found their way to the university, if only (for the present) to study medicine.

In the eighteenth century, then, a transformation occurred within Jewish society on two different planes, marked by differing rhythms. On one level, at the margins of Jewish society, a small minority of advocates of the Enlightenment came together who sought the legitimation of their thinking and action in secular philosophy and secular sciences. On another plane, at the center of Jewish society, was the Jewish majority, in whose eyes normative Judaism and its institutions still possessed definitive authority. While some of the former strove for radical transformation, even to the point of a break with Halacha, change in the old community proceeded in small steps. That community was slowly moving away from old traditions in the routine of everyday life through gradual accommodation to the outside—yet without any conscious program of enlightenment. Indeed, in the era of the Berlin Haskalah, the old community retained the vitality of traditional study. In the large Jewish communities the yeshivot were still the centers and sanctuaries of rabbinic scholarship. Rabbis such as Ezekiel Landau, Jacob Emden, and Jonathan

Eybeschütz wrote Talmudic commentaries and works of responsa that belong to the classic patrimony of rabbinic scholarship.

On the threshhold of the nineteenth century Jewry in the German cultural area was thus split into two—a predominantly conservative segment and a smaller progressive minority, more oriented toward the outside world. But the sharpness of this split may be deceptive, since both parts of Jewry were drawing closer to the society and culture of their environment; only the tempo of that process differed. Progress in civil equality in the nineteenth century, the acceleration of demographic and economic mobility, and the restructuring of state and society eventually forced the conservative majority to abandon its reserve and to appropriate important elements of the program of renewal and revitalization as their own—an agenda that in the second half of the eighteenth century had only been supported by the maskilim, then a minority of Jews within the geographical orbit of German culture.

Abbreviations

Aronius	Julius Aronius, *Regesten zur Geschichte der Juden im Fränkischen und Deutschen Reiche bis zum Jahre 1273* (Berlin, 1902)
Assaf	Simḥa Assaf, *Mekorot le-toldot ha-ḥinukh be-yisrael,* 2d ed., vol. 4 (Tel Aviv, 1947)
AZJ	*Allgemeine Zeitung des Judentums*
Bacharach	Rabbi Yair Ḥayim Bacharach, *Ḥavat Yair* (Lemberg, 1896 [repr. Jerusalem, 1968])
Baer	Fritz [Yitzhak] Baer, *Das Protokollbuch der Landjudenschaft des Herzogtums Kleve* (Berlin, 1936)
BLBI	*Bulletin des Leo Baeck Instituts*
Cooperman	B. D. Cooperman, ed., *Jewish Thought in the Sixteenth Century* (Cambridge, Mass., 1983)
Freund	Ismar Freund, *Die Emanzipation der Juden in Preussen,* vol. 2 (Berlin, 1912)
Glückel	Beth-Zion Abrahams, trans. and ed., *The Life of Glückel of Hameln, 1646–1724, Written by Herself* (London, 1962)
Grab	Walter Grab, ed., *Deutsche Aufklärung und Judenemanzipation* (Tel Aviv, 1980)
Grözinger	Karl E. Grözinger, ed., *Judentum im deutschen Sprachraum* (Frankfurt am Main, 1991)
Gründer	Karlfried Gründer and Nathan Rotenstreich, eds., *Aufklärung und Haskala in jüdischer und nichtjüdischer Sicht* (Heidelberg, 1990)
GSJ	Moses Mendelssohn, *Gesammelte Schriften. Jubiläumsausgabe* (Berlin, Breslau, 1929–1938 [incomplete]; repr. and cont., Stuttgart-Bad Cannstatt, 1971–)

Hahn	Rabbi Joseph Juspa Hahn, *Yosef omets* (Frankfurt am Main, 1928)
Haverkamp	Alfred Haverkamp, ed., *Zur Geschichte der Juden in Deutschland des späten Mittelalters und der frühen Neuzeit* (Stuttgart, 1981)
HUCA	*Hebrew Union College Annual*
HZ	*Historische Zeitschrift*
JJGL	*Jahrbuch für jüdische Geschichte und Literatur*
JJLG	*Jahrbuch der jüdisch-literarischen Gesellschaft*
Kestenberg	Ruth Kestenberg-Gladstein, *Neuere Geschichte der Juden in den böhmischen Ländern*, part 1 (Tübingen, 1969)
Kossmann	Rabbi Joseph Juspa Kossmann, *Noheg katson Yosef* (Tel Aviv, 1969)
LBIYB	*Leo Baeck Institute Year Book*
MGWJ	*Monatsschrift für Geschichte und Wissenschaft des Judentums*
PAAJR	*Proceedings of the American Academy for Jewish Research*
Schudt	Johann Jacob Schudt, *Jüdische Merckwürdigkeiten* (Frankfurt and Leipzig, 1714)
Shoḥet	Azriel Shoḥet, *Im ḥilufe tekufot* (Jerusalem, 1960)
Stein	Siegfried Stein and Raphael Loewe, eds., *Studies in Jewish Religious and Intellectual History, Presented to Alexander Altmann* (University, Ala., 1979)
Treml	Manfred Treml and Josef Kirmeier, eds., with the assistance of Evamatia Brockhoff, *Geschichte und Kultur der Juden in Bayern. Aufsätze* (Munich, 1988)
Wessely	[N. H. Wessely], *Worte des Friedens an die gesammte jüdische Nation*, trans. David Friedländer (Breslau, 1798)
ZGJD	*Zeitschrift für die Geschichte der Juden in Deutschland*

Notes

Introduction

1. See Heinrich Graetz, *Geschichte der Juden*, 4th ed. (Leipzig, 1909), 5:xvii; cf. idem, "Die Construction der jüdischen Geschichte. Eine Skizze," *Zeitschrift für die religiösen Interessen des Judenthums* 3(1846):361. On this see Haim Hillel Ben-Sasson, "What Is the Jewish Middle Ages?" (Hebr.), in *Retsef u-temurah* (Tel Aviv, 1984), 359–78; Jacob Katz, "The Middle Ages in Jewish History" (Hebr.), in M. Bar-Asher, ed., *Mehkarim be-mada'e ha-yahadut* (Jerusalem, 1986), 209–25; H. Z. Dimitrovsky, "Is There a Jewish Middle Ages?" (Hebr.), in M. Bar-Asher, ed., *Mehkarim be-mada'e ha-yahadut* (Jerusalem, 1986), 257–65. See also A. Sharf, "Jews in Byzantium," in C. Roth, ed., *The Dark Ages: 711–1096* (New Brunswick, N.J., 1966), 49; Michael A. Meyer, "Where Does the Modern Period of Jewish History Begin?" *Judaism* 24(Summer 1975):329–38; Jacob Katz, "The Turning Point of Modern Jewish History: The Eighteenth Century," in Ruth Kozodoy, David Sidorsky, and Kalman Sultanik, eds., *Vision Confronts Reality* (Rutherford, N.J., 1989), 40–55.

2. Yitzhak Baer, "Notes on S. W. Baron's *A Social and Religious History of the Jews*" (Hebr.), *Zion* 3(1938):277–99, esp. 291 f.; S. W. Baron, "The Jewish Factor in Medieval Civilization," PAAJR 12(1942):1–48, esp. 35.

3. Yosef Hayim Yerushalmi, *Zakhor: Jewish History and Jewish Memory* (Seattle, 1982), 31–52.

Prologue

1. Babylonian Talmud, *Pesahim*, 87b.

2. Tosefta, *Sanhedrin*, chap. 13. Although the sentence is not mentioned in the

parallel passage in the Babylonian Talmud, Rashi emphasizes it in his explanation to Babylonian Talmud, *Sanhedrin*, 110b, s.v. "Aval ketane ve-ne rishe umot ha-olam." Maimonides codified the sentence; see Mishneh Torah, *Hilkhot teshuvah*, 3:5.

3. Aronius, 70, no. 168.

4. Abbreviated translation, see A. Neubauer and M. Stern, eds., *Hebräische Berichte über die Judenverfolgungen während der Kreuzzüge* (Berlin, 1892), 82.

5. Ibid., 170.

6. Irving A. Agus, ed., *Responsa of the Tosaphists* (New York, 1954), 238.

7. Aronius, 324, no. 770.

8. Ibid., 220, no. 509.

9. Ignaz von Döllinger, *Die Juden in Europa* (Berlin, 1924 [1881]), 13.

10. Cited in Ludwig Rosenthal, "Süsskind von Trimberg. Der jüdische Spruchdichter aus der Gruppe der deutschen Minnesänger des Mittelalters (13. Jahrhundert)," *Hanauer Geschichtsblätter* 24(1969):6.

11. Elazar from Worms, "Hilkhot atseret," *Sefer ha-roke'aḥ*.

12. J. Freimann, ed., Joseph ben Moshe, *Leket yosher* (Berlin, 1903), part 1, 118–19.

13. Daniel Goldschmidt, ed., *Maḥzor la-yamim ha-nora'im* (Jerusalem, 1970), 2:654.

14. Jehuda Wistinetzki, ed., *Sefer ḥasidim* (Berlin, 1891), no. 234, 80.

15. Rabbi Meir of Rothenburg, *Responsa* (ed. Prague), no. 251; idem, *Responsa* (ed. Lemberg), no. 381.

16. Benzion Dinur, *Yisrael ba-golah*, part 2 (Jerusalem, 1966), 2:606, no. 37.

17. Jakob v. Königshoven, *Elsässische u. Strassburgische Chronik*, 296, cited in Ernst Ludwig Ehrlich, *Geschichte der Juden in Deutschland* (*Geschichtliche Quellenschriften*, Heft 6) (Düsseldorf, 1957), 30.

18. Cited in S. W. Baron, *A Social and Religious History of the Jews* (New York and London, 1965), 9:166.

19. Maharil, "Hilkhot shabbat," *Minhagim*.

20. "Pesakim u-khetavim," *Terumat ha-deshen*, no. 142.

21. Ibid., no. 255.

22. Rabbi Moses Minz, *Responsa*, no. 98.

23. Rabbi Israel Bruna, *Responsa*, no. 71; *Terumat ha-deshen*, no. 61.

24. Guido Kisch, *Erasmus' Stellung zu den Juden und Judentum* (Tübingen, 1969), 7.

25. Ludwig Geiger, ed., *Johann Reuchlins Briefwechsel* (Tübingen, 1875), no. 115, 123.

26. Cited in Heiko A. Oberman, "Three Sixteenth-Century Attitudes to Judaism: Reuchlin, Erasmus and Luther" in Cooperman, 347.

27. See Rabbi Moses Isserles, *Responsa*, no. 95.

28. Josel's words, cited in Haim Hillel Ben-Sasson, "The Reformation in

Contemporary Jewish Eyes," *Proceedings of the Israel Academy of Sciences and Humanities* 4(1971):288, n. 145.

29. See Babylonian Talmud, *Ḥagigah*, 13a.

30. Words of Ḥayim ben Bezalel, cited in Ben-Sasson, "The Reformation," 296 (Hebr. ed., 97–98); Mordechai Breuer, ed., David Gans, *Tsemaḥ David* (Jerusalem, 1983), 165.

31. See Eric Zimmer, *Rabbi Ḥayim ben Betsalel mi-Friedberg* (Jerusalem, 1987), 5–6.

32. Maharal, *Derush al ha-torah* (Piotrkov, 1906), 53–55.

33. Zimmer, *Rabbi Ḥayim ben Bezalel*, 102.

1. The Dawn of Early Modern Times

1. Cited in Israel Rabin, *Die Juden in Zülz* (Zülz, 1926), 7.

2. Hahn, 292.

3. Cited in Moritz Stern, *Salomon Kajjem Kaddisch, der erste kurbranden-burgische Landrabbiner* (Berlin, 1919), 3.

4. Stefi Jersch-Wenzel, *Juden und "Franzosen" in der Wirtschaft des Raumes Berlin/Brandenburg zur Zeit des Merkantilismus* (Berlin, 1978).

2. The Court Jews

1. *Glückel*, 80.

2. Baer, 74, n. 66 (Western Yiddish in the original).

3. Ibid., 22.

4. See *Glückel*, 44 (with change in translation).

5. Louis and Henry Fraenkel, *Forgotten Fragments of the History of an Old Jewish Family* (Copenhagen, 1975), 62.

6. Rabbi Jacob Emden, *Ets avot*, in commentary *Leḥem shamayim on the Sayings of the Fathers* (Amsterdam [Altona!], 1751), folio 73c. The identity of "that man" is unknown.

7. Hahn, 74–77, nos. 355, 357, 361, 368.

3. The Jews in the Age of Mercantilism and Early Absolutism

1. *Glückel*, 15.

2. Kestenberg, 14.

3. *Glückel*, 150.

4. Kossmann, no. 93.

5. K. H. Rengstorf and S. v. Kortzfleisch, eds., *Kirche und Synagoge* (Stuttgart, 1968), 1:461.

6. Schudt, 1:391.

7. Cited in Walter Röll, "Zu den Judeneiden an der Schwelle zur Neuzeit," in Haverkamp, 200–201.

8. Cited in Markus Horovitz, *Frankfurter Rabbinen* (with addenda by Joseph Unna) (Jerusalem, 1969), 183.

9. Cited in Baer, 31.

10. *Glückel*, 128–29, 130.

11. Cited in Max Köhler, *Beiträge zur neueren jüdischen Wirtschaftsgeschichte. Die Juden in Halberstadt und Umgebung bis zur Emanzipation* (Berlin, 1927), 11–12.

12. Cited in Baer, 30.

13. The last two citations are from Hans-Ulrich Wehler, *Deutsche Gesellschaftsgeschichte* (Munich, 1987), 1:159–60.

14. C. F. Koch, *Die Juden im preussischen Staate* (Marienwerder, 1833), 20, cited in F. Blankenfeld, "Jüdisches Gemeinderecht in Altpreussen," diss. (Greifswald, 1918), 9.

4. The Jewish Minority Under Enlightened Absolutism

1. Bacharach, no. 136.

2. Ibid., no. 1.

3. Cited in Shoḥet, 66.

4. Adolf Berliner, ed., *Religionsgespräch gehalten am kurfürstlichen Hofe zu Hannover 1704* (Berlin, 1914).

5. Rabbi Moses Hagiz, "Introduction," *Mishnat ḥakhamim* (Wandsbek, 1633), folio 4a.

6. *Glückel*, 85.

7. Rabbi Menachem Mendel Krochmal, *Resp. Tsemaḥ tsedek*, no. 111.

5. Community, Society and Domestic Life

1. Isidor Kracauer, *Geschichte der Juden in Frankfurt a.M.* (Frankfurt am Main, 1925), 1:405; Kossmann, 127, sec. 3.

2. Pinkas Friedberg in PAAJR 17(1947/48):39, 50.

3. Rabbi Jacob Emden, *Resp. She'ilat Yavets*, vol. 1, no. 9.

4. Rabbi Tsevi Hirsh Koydanover, *Kav ha-yashar* (Frankfurt am Main, 1705), chap. 82.

5. *Glückel*, 175–76; Kossmann, no. 3.

6. Bacharach, no. 70.

7. Schudt, book 6, chap. 35, 316.

8. Kossmann, 156; Schudt, book 6, chap. 34, 284–85.

9. *Goethe's Autobiography. Poetry and Truth from my Life*, trans. R. O. Moon (London 1932), 125.

10. *Sefer minhagim di-kehilatenu* (Fürth, 1767), no. 11.

11. Rabbi Shabbetai Sheftel Horowitz, "Amud ha-torah" (chap. 5), *Vave ha-amudim*, in Rabbi Isaiah Horowitz, *Shene luḥot ha-berit* (Amsterdam, 1653), end of second volume.

12. Cited in Shoḥet, 131–32.

6. The *Landjudenschaften*

1. Josel's diary was published by Isidor Kracauer in *Revue des études juives* 16 (1888). On his election as lay leader: sec. 5, 88.

2. Daniel J. Cohen, "Die Landjudenschaften in Hessen-Darmstadt bis zur Emanzipation als Organe der Selbstverwaltung" in *Neunhundert Jahre Geschichte der Juden in Hessen* (Wiesbaden, 1983), 162.

3. Cited in Kestenberg, 24–25.

4. Sources in Daniel J. Cohen's unpublished dissertation in Hebrew, cited in Robert R. Luft, "Landjudenschaft und Judenlandtage in Kurmainz," in Heinz Duchhardt, ed., *Beiträge zur Geschichte der Mainzer Juden in der Frühneuzeit* (Mainz, 1981), 13, n. 50.

5. Assaf, 79–80.

6. Daniel J. Cohen, "Die Landjudenschaften der brandenburgisch-preussischen Staaten im 17. und 18. Jahrhundert—Ihre Beziehungen untereinander aufgrund neuerschlossener jüdischer Quellen," in Peter Baumgart, ed., *Ständetum und Staatsbildung in Brandenburg-Preussen* (Berlin and New York, 1983), 215–16, 220.

7. Intellectual and Religious Life

1. Heinrich Graetz, *Geschichte der Juden*, 3d ed. (Leipzig, 1897), 10:75.

2. The Hebrew letter from the community is reprinted in *Tsefunot* (Tishri 5751 [1991]):96–97.

3. The source for this is in Simon Schwarzfuchs, "The Conditions for Appointment of the Author of *Sha'agat aryeh* in the Metz Community" (Hebr.), *Moriah* (Av 5746 [1986]):87.

4. The source is in Assaf, 108–09.

5. Moses from Rohatyn, *Sugyot ha-talmud* (Hanau, 1714; with Latin translation entitled Clavis Talmudica).

6. Bacharach, nos. 123, 124, 152.

7. "Meḥkenen ist keine Kunst," cited in B. H. Auerbach, *Geschichte der israelitischen Gemeinde Halberstadt* (Halberstadt, 1866), 66.

8. Rabbi Jacob Emden, *Megilat sefer* (Warsaw, 1896), 125–26.

9. Rabbi Pinchas Katzenellenbogen, *Yesh manḥilin* (Jerusalem, 1986), 180.

10. *Minhagim dek"k wormaysah*, 2 vols. (Jerusalem, 1988–92). The manuscript was only recently published for the first time.

11. His legal opinions were not published until two decades ago, as *Nishal*

David (Jerusalem, 1972–75); Rabbi Samuel ben David Halevi, "Introduction," *Naḥalat Shivah* (Fürth, 1692–98).

12. Kossmann, 41, 215.

8. Toward a New Era

1. *Glückel*, 45–46.

2. The passages cited can be found in German translation in JJGL 11(1916):5–7.

3. Morris M. Faierstein, "The Liebes Brief: A Critique of Jewish Society in Germany (1749)" in LBIYB 27(1982):233–34.

4. Rabbi Jonah Landsofer, *Me'il tsedakah* (Prague, 1757), 81a.

5. Rabbi Jonathan Eybeschütz, *Ya'arot devash* (Ed. Makhon Yerushalayim, 1983), chap. 7, 2:122–23.

6. Rabbi Jacob Emden (*Yavets*), *She'ilat Yavets*, part 1, sec. 41.

7. Ibid., part 2, sec. 65.

8. Idem, *Sidur amude shamayim* (Altona, 1745), 1:31a.

9. *She'ilat Yavets*, part 1, sec. 162.

10. Cited in Markus Horovitz, *Frankfurter Rabbinen* (Jerusalem, 1969), 317.

11. Cited by Menachem Friedman in *Michael* 2(1973; Hebr. section):34.

12. Wilhelm Treue, "Die Juden in der Wirtschaftsgeschichte des rheinischen Raumes 1648 bis 1945," *Monumenta Judaica* (Cologne, 1963), 425.

13. Cited in Shoḥet, 153–54.

14. A. F. Thiele, *Die jüdischen Gauner in Deutschland* (Berlin, 1841), 1:17.

15. Cited in B. Z. Kedar, "Continuity and Change in Jewish Conversion to Christianity" (Hebr.), in *Perakim be-toldot ha-ḥevrah ha-yehudit bi-me ha-benayim u-va-et ha-ḥadashah* (Jerusalem, 1980), 164.

16. Cited in Ludwig Geiger, "Vor hundert Jahren," ZGJD 3(1889):229.

17. Quotations from the *Generalreglement* of 1750, cited in Freund, 53.

18. Rabbi Joseph Statthagen, *Divre zikaron* (Amsterdam, 1705), cited in Shoḥet, 76.

9. Beginnings of the Haskalah

1. Cited in Meyer Kayserling, *Moses Mendelssohn. Sein Leben und Wirken* (Leipzig, 1888), 116.

2. Friedrich Nicolai, *Beschreibung der Königlichen Residenzstädte Berlin und Potsdam* (Berlin, 1786), 2:839–40.

3. GSJ, 11:220.

4. Cited in the biographical introduction by Joseph Mendelssohn in *Moses Mendelssohn's Gesammelte Schriften* (Leipzig, 1843), 1:13.

5. GSJ, 11:55.

6. Ibid., 1:51–52.

7. "Die Matrone" (Hamburg 1728), cited in Meir Gilon, *Kohelet musar le-Mendelssohn al reka tekufato* (Jerusalem, 1979), 120.

8. J. G. Müchler, ed., *Moses Mendelssohns kleine philosophische Schriften. Mit einer Skizze seines Lebens und Charakters von D. Jenisch* (Berlin, 1789), 25.

9. GSJ, 1:64–65.

10. Ibid., 2:272.

11. Ibid., 3/1:79.

12. *Das Forschen nach Licht und Recht in einem Schreiben an Herrn Moses Mendelssohn auf Veranlassung seiner merkwürdigen Vorrede zu Manasseh Ben Israel.*

13. GSJ, 8:140.

14. Already in Mendelssohn's preface to Manasseh Ben Israel, *Rettung der Juden*, ibid., 24.

15. Ibid., 164.

16. Ibid., 183.

17. Ibid., 3/2:129.

18. Ibid., 197.

19. Ibid., 1:14.

10. The Haskalah as a Sociocultural Phenomenon

1. *Salomon Maimon's Lebensgeschichte* (Berlin, 1792), 1:268–69.

2. Ibid., 266–67.

3. Letter of September 22, 1783, in GSJ, 13:134.

4. Ibid. (Hebr.), 14:213.

5. Ibid., 214.

6. Ibid., 13:134.

7. *Ha-Me'asef* 3(1786):143.

8. GSJ, 2:104.

9. Ibid., 6/1:116.

10. Ibid., 4:20–21.

11. Cited in Perez Sandler, *Ha-bi'ur la-torah shel Mendelssohn ve-siyato*, 2d ed. (Jerusalem, 1984), 226.

12. *Ha-Me'asef* 6/1(1790):46.

13. Ibid., 7(1794–97):55

14. Ibid., 122.

15. Ibid., 151.

16. Dan Miron, ed., *Aaron Wolfssohn, Kalut da'at u-tsevi'ut* (Tel Aviv, 1977), 68.

17. *Schlesische Provinzialblätter* (1796), cited by Miron in his introduction, ibid., 29.

18. Lazarus Bendavid, [Autobiography] in M. S. Lowe, ed., *Bildnisse jetztlebender Berliner Gelehrten mit ihren Selbstbiographien* (Berlin, 1806), 6.

19. Ibid., 6–7.
20. Ibid., 15.
21. Ibid., 34.
22. Ibid., 21–22.
23. "Preface," *Salomon Maimon's Lebensgeschichte* (Berlin, 1793), vol. 2.
24. Ibid.
25. Ibid., 246–47.
26. Ibid., 2–3.
27. Ibid., 1:177–78.

11. Confrontation as a Transformative Force

1. Richard Gosche, ed., *Lessing's sämmtliche Werke* (Berlin, 1900), 6th scene, 1:474.
2. Ibid., 22d scene, 499.
3. *Göttingische Anzeigen von gelehrten Sachen*, June 13, 1754, 621.
4. *Lessing's sämmtliche Werke*, vol. 2, 3d act, 7th scene, 321.
5. Letter, end of June 1754, in GSJ, 11:10.
6. Ibid., 7:13.
7. Christian Wilhelm Dohm, *Über die bürgerliche Verbesserung der Juden* (Berlin, 1781/83), 1:130.
8. Ibid., 116.
9. Ibid., 120.
10. "Hr. Ritter Michaelis Beurtheilung Über die bürgerliche Verbesserung der Juden von Christian Wilhelm Dohm," ibid., 2:71.
11. Ibid., 40–41.
12. Ibid., 43.
13. GSJ, 8:6.
14. See text in Joseph Karniel, *Die Toleranzpolitik Kaiser Josephs II* (Gerlingen, 1986), 564.
15. Ibid., 567.
16. Wessely, 16.
17. Ibid., 21.
18. Ibid., 4–7.
19. See text in Freund, 126.
20. [D. Friedländer], *Sendschreiben an Seine Hochwürden, Herrn Oberconsistorialrath und Probst Teller zu Berlin von einigen Hausvätern jüdischer Religion* (Berlin, 1799), 39.
21. Ibid., 21.
22. [Friedrich Schleiermacher], *Briefe bei Gelegenheit der politisch theologischen Aufgabe und des Sendschreibens jüdischer Hausväter* (Berlin, 1799), 24–25.
23. Ibid., 36.

24. Ludwig Lesser, *Chronik der Gesellschaft der Freunde in Berlin* (Berlin, 1842), 29.

25. *Marcus Herz an die Herausgeber des hebräischen Sammlers über die frühe Beerdigung der Juden* (Berlin, 1787), 3.

26. "Ketav yosher," reproduced in Yehuda Friedlander, *Perakim ba-satirah ha-ivrit* (Tel Aviv, 1979), 94.

27. Saul Ascher, *Eisenmenger der Zweite* (Berlin, 1794), 68.

12. Jewish Enlightenment and Education

1. Letter of November 20, 1784, in GSJ, 14:233.

2. Wessely, 3.

3. Ezekiel Landau, *Derushe hatslah* (Warsaw, 1899), folio 53.

4. Text in Louis Lewin, "Aus dem jüdischen Kulturkampfe," JJLG 12(1918):182–83.

5. Text in Ludwig Horwitz, "Ein Bildungsverein am Ausgang des vorigen Jahrhunderts," AZJ 61(1897):440.

6. "Statuten der Jacobsons-Schule zu Seesen" (Brunswick, 1838), 3.

7. Ludwig Philippson, "Aus meiner Knabenzeit," AZJ 51(1887):766.

Bibliographical Essay

1. Prologue: The Jewish Middle Ages

Recent general works: Haim Hillel Ben-Sasson, ed., *A History of the Jewish People*, part 5: "The Middle Ages" (1976); Friedrich Battenberg, *Das Europäische Zeitalter der Juden*, vol. 1: *Von den Anfängen bis 1650* (1990). See also Salo W. Baron, *A Social and Religious History of the Jews*, especially vols. 4–14 (1957–1969). An exact and detailed survey of developments in the local communities is provided by the three volumes of *Germania Judaica* (1917–1994). A valuable comprehensive summary is Alfred Haverkamp, "Lebensbedingungen der Juden im spätmittelalterlichen Deutschland," in D. Blasius and D. Diner, eds., *Zerbrochene Geschichte. Leben und Selbstverständnis der Juden in Deutschland* (1991), 11–31.

There is still lively discussion on the question of the origins of Jewish settlement along the Rhine and Danube at the time of the Carolingian and Ottonian emperors; see Avraham Grossman, "Jewish Immigration to Germany in the Ninth to Eleventh Centuries" (Hebr.), in A. Shinan, ed., *Hagirah ve-hityashvut be-yisrael u-va-amim* (Migration and Settlement Among Jews and Non-Jews, 1982), 109–28; for a contrasting view see Simon Schwarzfuchs, "L'opposition Tsarfat-Provence: La formation du judaïsme du nord de la France," in G. Nahon and C. Touati, eds., *Hommage à Georges Vajda* (1980), 135–50. On legal history, see esp. Guido Kisch, *The Jews in Medieval Germany. A Study of their Legal and Social Status*, 2d ed. (1970); Lea Dasberg, *Untersuchungen über die Entwertung des Judenstatus im 11. Jahrhundert* (1965); Gerhard Dilcher, "Die Stellung der Juden in Recht und Verfassung der mittelalterlichen Stadt," in Grözinger, 17–35; Friedrich Battenberg, "Des Kaisers Kammerknechte. Gedanken zur rechtlich-sozialen Situation der Juden in Spätmittelalter und früher Neuzeit," HZ 245(1987):545–99.

On the relation of Ashkenazi to Palestinian rites see Avraham Grossman, "Contacts between Ashkenazi Jews and Jews in the Land of Israel in the Eleventh Century" (Hebr.), *Shalem* 3(1981):57–92; idem, *Ḥakhme ashkenaz ha-rishonim* (The Early Scholars of Ashkenaz, 1981), 424–35. On the early history of community administration, see also idem, "The Attitude of the Early Scholars in Ashkenaz Toward the Authority of Community Administration" (Hebr.), *Shenaton ha-mishpat ha-ivri* (Yearbook of the Research Center for Hebrew Law) 2(1975):175–99. Especially valuable for the later organization of the community is Simon Goldmann, "Die jüdische Gerichtsverfassung innerhalb der jüdischen Gemeindeorganisation. Ein Beitrag zur Geschichte des Judenbischofs im Mittelalter in seiner Entwicklung von den ältesten Zeiten bis zum 15. Jahrhundert," *Udim* 2(1971):21–67. On the ordinances (*takanot*) in general and those of Rabbenu Gershom in particular see Avraham Grossman, "The Historical Background to the Ordinances on Family Affairs Attributed to Rabbenu Gershom Me'or ha-Golah," in *Jewish History: Essays in Honor of Chimen Abramsky* (1988), 3–23. On violations of law in the communities, see idem, "Law-breakers and Violent Criminals in Early Ashkenazi Jewish Society and Their Influence on Legal Procedures" (Hebr.), *Shenaton ha-mishpat ha-ivri* 8(1981):135–52. Valuable material is also to be found in Irving A. Agus, *Rabbi Meir of Rothenburg*, 2 vols. (1947), and idem, *Urban Civilization in Pre-Crusade Europe*, 2 vols. (1965).

More recent studies on the persecutions at the time of the Crusades include Diethard Aschoff, "Zum Judenbild der Deutschen vor den Kreuzzügen," *Theokratia* 2(1970–72):232–52; Robert Chazan, *European Jewry and the First Crusade* (1987). On Jewish-Christian confrontation, see Peter Herde, "Die Kirche und die Juden im Mittelalter," in Treml, 71–84; Marianne Awerbuch, *Christlich-jüdische Begegnung im Zeitalter der Frühscholastik* (1980); Jeremy Cohen, *The Friars and the Jews: The Evolution of Medieval Anti-Judaism* (1982). On the charges of ritual murder (blood libel) and host desecration, see R. Po-Chia Hsia, *The Myth of Ritual Murder: Jews and Magic in Reformation Germany* (1988); Friedrich Lotter, "Hostienfrevelvorwurf und Blutwunderfälschung bei den Judenverfolgungen von 1298 ('Rintfleisch') und 1336–1338 ('Armleder')," in *Monumenta Germaniae Historica. Schriften*, 33(1988):533–83. On pictorial representations of anti-Jewish stereotypes see Stefan Rohrbacher und Michael Schmidt, *Judenbilder. Kulturgeschichte antijüdischer Mythen und antisemitischer Vorurteile* (1991).

For the economic situation see Joseph Shatzmiller, *Shylock Reconsidered: Jews, Moneylending, and Medieval Society* (1990); Michael Toch, "The German Economy in the Thirteenth and Fourteenth Centuries. The Framework for Economic Activities Among the Jews" (Hebr.), in N. Gross, ed., *Yehudim ba-kalkalah* (Jews in Economic Life, 1985), 87–95; Haym Soloveitchik, *Halakhah, kalkalah ve-dimui-atsmi. Ha-mashkona'ut bi-me ha-benayim* (Jewish Law, Economy and Self-Image. Pawnbroking in the Middle Ages, 1985).

On Ashkenazi intellectual life in the High Middle Ages see Joseph Dan, "Das Entstehen der jüdischen Mystik im mittelalterlichen Deutschland," in Grözinger,

127–72; Mordechai Breuer, "Ausdrucksweisen aschkenasischer Frömmigkeit in Synagoge und Lehrhaus," in Grözinger, 103–16; Ivan G. Marcus, *Piety and Society: The Jewish Pietists of Medieval Germany* (1981).

A comprehensive work on persecutions at the time of the Black Death is Frantisek Graus, *Pest—Geissler—Judenmorde. Das 14. Jahrhundert als Krisenzeit* (1987); and see the basic study by Alfred Haverkamp, "Die Judenverfolgungen zur Zeit des Schwarzen Todes im Gesellschaftsgefüge deutscher Städte," in Haverkamp, 27–93; see also Dietricht Andernacht, "Die Verpfändung der Frankfurter Juden 1349," *Udim* 3(1972):9–25; Mordechai Breuer, "The 'Black Death' and Antisemitism," in Sh. Almog, ed., *Antisemitism Through the Ages* (1988), 139–51.

For more recent studies on the situation of the Jews in the fifteenth century, see Karl Schumm, "Konrad von Weinsberg und die Judensteuer unter Kaiser Sigismund," *Württembergisch Franken* 54, n.s. 44(1970):2–58; Markus J. Wenninger, *Man bedarf keiner Juden mehr. Ursachen und Hintergründe ihrer Vertreibung aus den deutschen Reichsstädten im 15. Jahrhundert* (1981); Michael Toch, "Die soziale und demographische Struktur der jüdischen Gemeinde Nürnbergs im Jahre 1489," *Beiträge zur Wirtschaftsgeschichte*, vol. 8: *Wirtschaftskräfte und Wirtschaftswege* (1981): 79–91; idem, "Siedlungsstruktur der Juden Mitteleuropas im Wandel vom Mittelalter zur Neuzeit," in A. Haverkamp and F-J. Ziwes, eds., *Juden in der christlichen Umwelt während des späten Mittelalters* (1992), 29–39.

Studies on the development of the rabbinate include Eric Zimmer, *Harmony and Discord: An Analysis of the Decline of Jewish Self-Government in Fifteenth-Century Central Europe* (1970); Mordechai Breuer, "Die Stellung des Rabbinats in den rheinischen Judengemeinden des Mittelalters," in J. Bohnke-Kollwitz et al., eds., *Köln und das rheinische Judentum. Festschrift Germania Judaica 1959–1984* (1984), 35–46; Yedidya Alter Dinari, *Ḥakhme ashkenaz be-shilḥe yeme ha-benayim* (The Scholars of Ashkenaz at the End of the Middle Ages, 1984); Israel Yuval, *Ḥakhamim be-doram. Ha-manhigut ha-ruḥanit shel yehude germanya be-shilḥe yeme ha-benayim* (Scholars in Their Time: The Intellectual Leadership of German Jewry at the End of the Middle Ages, 1988).

A valuable survey of Christian Hebraism in the fifteenth and sixteenth century is provided by Jerome Friedman, *The Most Ancient Testimony: Sixteenth-Century Christian Hebraica in the Age of Renaissance Nostalgia* (1983). On Reuchlin see James H. Overfield, "A New Look at the Reuchlin Affair," *Studies in Medieval and Renaissance History* 8(1971):165–207; A. Herzig and J. H. Schoeps, eds., *Reuchlin und die Juden* (1993). On humanism, Luther, the Reformation, and the Jews, see Heiko A. Oberman, *The Roots of Anti-Semitism in the Age of the Renaissance and the Reformation* (1984); Klaus Deppermann, "Judenhass und Judenfreundschaft im frühen Protestantismus," in B. Martin and E. Schulin, eds., *Die Juden als Minderheit in der Geschichte* (1981), 110–30; Haim Hillel Ben-Sasson, "The Reformation in Contemporary Jewish Eyes," *Proceedings of the*

Israel Academy of Sciences and Humanities 4(1971):239–326; Stefan Schreiner, "Jüdische Reaktionen auf die Reformation," *Judaica* 39(1983):150–65.

On converts see Ḥavah Fraenkel-Goldschmidt, "At the Margins of Jewish Society: Jewish Converts to Christianity in Germany During the Reformation" (Hebr.), in R. Bonfil et al., eds., *Tarbut ve-ḥevrah be-toldot yisrael bi-me ha-benayim* (Culture and Society in Medieval Jewry, 1989), 623–54 (including an extensive bibliography); Hans-Martin Kirn, *Das Bild vom Juden im Deutschland des frühen 16. Jahrhunderts. Dargestellt an den Schriften Johannes Pfefferkorns* (1989).

The political history of the Jews in the sixteenth century is explored in Wilhelm Güde, *Die rechtliche Stellung der Juden in den Schriften deutscher Juristen des 16. und 17. Jahrhunderts* (1981); Arye Maimon, "Der Judenvertreibungsversuch Albrechts II. von Mainz und sein Misserfolg (1515/1516)," *Jahrbuch für westdeutsche Landesgeschichte* 4(1978):191–220.

On community and intellectual history of the sixteenth century, see Eric Zimmer, *Jewish Synods in Germany During the Late Middle Ages* (1978); Selma Stern, *Josel of Rosheim, Commander of Jewry in the Holy Roman Empire of the German Nation* (1965); Arye Maimon, "Tagungen von Judenschaften in Westdeutschland im frühen 16. Jahrhundert," *Jahrbuch für westdeutsche Landesgeschichte* 5(1979):71–82; Byron L. Sherwin, *Mystical Theology and Social Dissent. The Life and Works of Judah Loeb of Prague* (1982); Mordechai Breuer, "Modernism and Traditionalism in Sixteenth-Century Jewish Historiography: A Study of David Gans' Tzemah David," in Cooperman, 49–88.

2. The Early Modern Period

General works on early modern German history particularly useful for topics relevant to Jewish history are Hans-Ulrich Wehler, *Deutsche Gesellschaftsgeschichte*, vol. 1 (1987); Volker Press, *Kriege und Krisen. Deutschland 1600–1715* (1991). For a description of views on economic policy during the early modern period in Germany, see also Rudolf Vierhaus, *Germany in the Age of Absolutism (1648–1763)* (1988). Still standard for the history of the Jews in the early modern period is the classic work (now available in a new translation) by Jacob Katz, *Tradition and Crisis: Jewish Society at the End of the Middle Ages*, 2d ed. (1993). Likewise of enduring importance is the pioneering study by Felix Priebatsch, "Die Judenpolitik des fürstlichen Absolutismus im 17. und 18. Jahrhundert," in *Forschungen und Versuche zur Geschichte des Mittelalters und der Neuzeit. Festschrift Dietrich Schäfer* (1915). Valuable recent studies include Jonathan I. Israel, *European Jewry in the Age of Mercantilism, 1550–1750* (1985); R. Po-Chia-Hsia, "Die Juden im Alten Reich," in G. Schmidt, ed., *Stände und Gesellschaft im Alten Reich* (1989), 211–21. A most useful survey of the literature can be found in Joseph M. Davis, "The Cultural and Intellectual History of Ashkenazic Jews, 1500–1750: A Selective Bibliography and Essay," LBIYB 38(1993):343–86.

Important for an understanding of the events in Frankfurt am Main in the first quarter of the seventeenth century are Volker Press, "Kaiser Rudolf II. und der Zusammenschluss der deutschen Judenheit. Die sogenannte Frankfurter Rabbinerverschwörung von 1603 und ihre Folgen," in Haverkamp, 243–93; C. R. Friedrichs, "Politics or Pogrom? The Fettmilch Uprising in German and Jewish History," *Central European History* 19(1986):186–228. On the admission of Jews to Brandenburg-Prussia see Stefi Jersch-Wenzel, *Juden und "Franzosen" in der Wirtschaft des Raumes Berlin/Brandenburg zur Zeit des Merkantilismus* (1978).

Indispensable for the history of court Jewry is the six-volume work by Heinrich Schnee, *Die Hoffinanz und der moderne Staat* (1953–1967). However, it should be noted that this study is marred by certain remarks, generalizations, and phraseology that smack of antisemitism. For a general survey on the topic of court Jews, see Selma Stern, *The Court Jew: A Contribution to the History of the Period of Absolutism in Europe* (1950). On the precursors of court Jewry in Germany, see the essay by Franz Irsigler, "Juden und Lombarden am Niederrhein im 14. Jahrhundert," in Haverkamp, 122–62. The diplomatic activity of the court Jews is also examined by Barouh Mevorah, "The Imperial Court-Jew Wolf Wertheimer as Diplomatic Mediator (During the War of the Austrian Succession)," *Scripta Hierosolymitana* 23(1972):184–213. Bernd Schedlitz, *Leffmann Behrens. Untersuchungen zum Hofjudentum im Zeitalter des Absolutismus* (1984) is an excellent critical study of court Jewry. Among the numerous studies on "Jud Süss" the following are worth special mention: Peter Baumgart, "Joseph Süss Oppenheimer," in K. Müller and K. Wittstadt, eds., *Geschichte und Kultur des Judentums* (1988), 91–110; Barbara Gerber, *Jud Süss. Aufstieg und Fall im frühen 18. Jahrhundert. Ein Beitrag zur historischen Antisemitismus- und Rezeptionsforschung* (1990); the latter monograph also contains comprehensive material on court Jewry in general and public opinion in Germany regarding the hated court Jew Süss Oppenheimer. Hannah Arendt, "Privileged Jews," *Jewish Social Studies* 8(1946):3–30, is a notable attempt to accord the court Jew an exaggerated role in the early history of modern Jewry.

Still valuable for the legal status and political stituation of the Jews is the pioneering study by Max Köhler, *Beiträge zur neueren jüdischen Wirtschaftsgeschichte. Die Juden in Halberstadt und Umgebung bis zur Emanzipation* (1927). Especially useful more recent studies focusing on local history include Guido Kisch, *Rechts- und Sozialgeschichte der Juden in Halle 1686–1730* (1970); Fritz Reuter, *Warmaisa. 1000 Jahre Juden in Worms* (1984); Gerhard Renda, "Fürth, das 'bayerische Jerusalem'," in Treml, 225–36; see also the essays by Günter Böhm and Günter Marwedel in Arno Herzig, ed., *Die Juden in Hamburg 1590 bis 1990* (1991); Hermann Kellenbenz, *Sephardim an der unteren Elbe. Ihre wirtschaftliche und politische Bedeutung vom Ende des 16. bis 18. Jahrhunderts* (1958). The Jews in the Habsburg Empire are treated by Nikolaus Vielmetti, "Vom Beginn der Neuzeit bis zur Toleranz," in *Das österreichische Judentum* (1974), 59–82; William O. McCagg, Jr., *A History of Habsburg Jews, 1670–1918* (1989);

Peter Baumgart, "Die Stellung der jüdischen Minorität im Staat des aufgeklärten Absolutismus. Das friederizianische Preussen und das josephinische Österreich im Vergleich," *Kairos* 22(1980):226–45; Ruth Kestenberg-Gladstein, *Neuere Geschichte der Juden in den böhmischen Ländern*, part 1: *Das Zeitalter der Aufklärung 1780–1830* (1969); Ferdinand Seibt, ed., *Die Juden in den böhmischen Ländern* (1983); Barouh Mevorach, "Die Interventionsbestrebungen in Europa zur Verhinderung der Vertreibung der Juden aus Böhmen und Mähren," *Jahrbuch des Instituts für deutsche Geschichte* (Tel Aviv) 9(1980):15–81.

On Jewish-Christian relations see Karl Heinrich Rengstorf and Siegfried Kortzfleisch, eds., *Kirche und Synagoge. Handbuch zur Geschichte von Christen und Juden* (1968); Koppel S. Pinson, "German Pietism and the Jews," in S. W. Baron, Ernest Nagel, and Koppel S. Pinson, eds., *Freedom and Reason: Studies in Philosophy and Jewish Culture, in Memory of Morris Raphael Cohen* (1951), 397–412; Blu Greenberg, "Rabbi Jacob Emden: The View of an Enlightened Traditionalist on Christianity," *Judaism* 27(1978):351–63; Benjamin Z. Kedar, "Continuity and Change in Jewish Conversions to Christianity in Germany in the Eighteenth Century" (Hebr.), in I. Etkes and J. Salmon, eds., *Perakim be-toldot ha-ḥevrah ha-yehudit bi-me ha-benayim u-va-et ha-ḥadashah* (Studies in the History of Jewish Society in the Middle Ages and in the Modern Period, Presented to Professor Jacob Katz, 1980), 154–70.

On education see Salomon Adler, "Die Entwicklung des Schulwesens der Juden zu Frankfurt am Main bis zur Emanzipation," JJLG 18(1927):143–73; 19(1928):237–78. Markus Horovitz, *Frankfurter Rabbinen. Ein Beitrag zur Geschichte der israelitischen Gemeinde in Frankfurt am Main. Mit Ergänzungen von Josef Unna*, 2d ed. (1972) examines the intellectual leadership in a large community. On associations and charity see Avigdor Unna, *Register of Statutes and Protocols of the "Hevra Kadisha" of Worms, 1716–1837* (1980). Herman Pollack, *Jewish Folkways in Germanic Lands (1648–1806)* (1971) provides a compendium on Jewish life in the community and home; see also Jacob R. Marcus, *Communal Sick-Care in the German Ghetto* (1947).

Still valuable for the *Landjudenschaften* is the pioneering study by Fritz [Yitzhak] Baer, *Das Protokollbuch der Landjudenschaft des Herzogtums Kleve* (1936). Of fundamental importance are the studies by Daniel J. Cohen, esp. "Die Entwicklung der Landrabbinate in den deutschen Territorien bis zur Emanzipation," in Haverkamp, 221–42; idem, "Die Landjudenschaften in Hessen-Darmstadt bis zur Emanzipation als Organe der jüdischen Selbstverwaltung," in *Neunhundert Jahre Geschichte der Juden in Hessen* (1983), 151–214; idem, "Die Landjudenschaften der brandenburgisch-preussischen Staaten im 17. und 18. Jahrhundert. Ihre Beziehungen untereinander aufgrund neuerschlossener jüdischer Quellen," in P. Baumgart, ed., *Ständetum und Staatsbildung in Brandenburg-Preussen* (1983), 208–29. Also very instructive is Robert R. Luft, "Landjudenschaft und Judenlandtage in Kurmainz," in H. Duchhardt, ed., *Beiträge zur Geschichte der Mainzer Juden in der Frühneuzeit* (1981), 7–32.

On the history of Hebrew printing, see Raphael Posner and Israel Ta-Shema, eds., *The Hebrew Book* (1975); Menahem Schmelzer, "Hebrew Printing and Publishing in Germany, 1650–1750," LBIYB 33(1988):369–83, and the bibliography there on individual presses.

Invaluable for intellectual history are Siegfried Stein, "Liebliche Tefilloh. A Judaeo-German Prayerbook Printed in 1709," LBIYB 15(1970):41–72; Havah Turniansky, "The 'Bentscherl' and the Yiddish Tablesongs" (Hebr.), *Ale Sefer* 10(1982):51–92; Karl Erich Grözinger, "Jüdische Wundermänner in Deutschland," in Grözinger, 190–221.

Fundamental for a study of the Sabbatian movement in Germany is the work of Gershom Scholem, esp. his *Major Trends in Jewish Mysticism*, 3d ed. (1971), eighth lecture, and *Sabbatai Ṣevi: The Mystical Messiah* (1973). Scholem first pointed out what he believed was the established connection between Sabbatianism, Haskalah, and Reform Judaism in his article "Mitsvah ha-ba'ah ba-averah: Toward an Understanding of Sabbatianism" (Hebr.) *Keneset* 2(1937):347–92 (English: "Redemption Through Sin," in G. Scholem, *The Messianic Idea in Judaism* [1971], 78–141). For a contrasting view, though only weakening Scholem's thesis in part, see Jacob Katz, "The Possible Connection of Sabbataeanism, Haskalah, and Reform Judaism," in Stein (Hebr. sec.), 83–100.

The social problems of the pre-emancipatory period are treated by Rudolf Glanz, *Geschichte des niederen jüdischen Volkes in Deutschland* (1968); see also Ruth Kestenberg-Gladstein, "The Home as a Pillar of Support for the Feudal-Corporate Character of Jewry Prior to Emancipation" (Hebr.), *Tarbiz* 29(1960):176–90, 282–94; Menachem Friedmann, "Letters of Recommendation for Jewish Beggars: A Commentary on the Problem of Jewish Vagrants in Germany in the Eighteenth Century" (Hebr.), *Michael* 2(1973):34–51; Carsten Küther, *Räuber und Gauner in Deutschland* (1976). On relations between the communities in Germany and the Council of the Four Lands in Poland, see Murray J. Rosman, "The Authority of the Council of the Four Lands Outside Poland" (Hebr.), *Bar-Ilan University Annual* 24–25(1989):11–30.

On the multiplying signs in the eighteenth century of a major change on the horizon, see in particular Azriel Shohet, *Im ḥilufe tekufot. Reshit ha-haskalah be-yahadut germanyah* (Change of Eras. Beginnings of the Haskalah in German Jewry, 1960); but see also the review by Barouh Mevorah in *Kiryat Sefer* 37 (1961–62):150–55; Monika Richarz, *Der Eintritt der Juden in die akademischen Berufe* (1974); Chimen Abramsky, "The Crisis of Authority Within European Jewry in the Eighteenth Century," in Stein, 13–28; Morris M. Faierstein, "The Liebes Brief. A Critique of Jewish Society in Germany (1749)," LBIYB 27(1982):219–41. An overview of the amulet controversy is provided by Bernhard Brilling, "Der Hamburger Rabbinerstreit im 18. Jahrhundert," *Zeitschrift des Vereins für Hamburgische Geschichte* 55(1969):219–44. For a more detailed treatment of Eybeschütz, see Elisheva Carlebach, *The Pursuit of Heresy: Rabbi Moses Hagiz and the Sabbatian Controversies* (1990).

3. The Jewish Enlightenment

The following studies provide an overview of various aspects of the Jewish Enlightenment and its genesis: Jacob Katz, *Out of the Ghetto: The Social Background of Jewish Emancipation, 1770–1870* (1973); Michael A. Meyer, *The Origins of the Modern Jew: Jewish Identity and European Culture in Germany, 1749–1824* (1967); David Sorkin, *The Transformation of German Jewry, 1780–1840* (1987); Heinz M. Graupe, *The Rise of Modern Judaism: An Intellectual History of German Jewry, 1650–1942* (1978); Amos Funkenstein, *Perceptions of Jewish History* (1993); and the collective volumes: Walter Grab, ed., *Deutsche Aufklärung und Judenemanzipation. Beiheft 3 des Jahrbuchs für deutsche Geschichte* (1980); Karlfried Gründer and Nathan Rotensteich, eds., *Aufklärung und Haskala in jüdischer und nichtjüdischer Sicht* (1990).

On Jewish history in the Prussian centers of the Haskalah, see Albert A. Bruer, *Geschichte der Juden in Preussen 1750–1820* (1991). Still invaluable for the historical background in Berlin is Ludwig Geiger, *Geschichte der Juden in Berlin*, 2 vols. (1871). New findings and insights on this topic can be found in Marianne Awerbuch and Stefi Jersch-Wenzel, eds., *Bild und Selbstbild der Juden Berlins zwischen Aufklärung und Romantik* (1992); and Steven M. Lowenstein, *The Berlin Jewish Community: Enlightenment, Family, and Crisis, 1770–1830* (1994). Josef Meisl, ed., *Pinkas Kehillat Berlin 5483–5614* (*Protokollbuch der jüdischen Gemeinde Berlins 1723–1854*) (1962) gives valuable insight into the structure, function, and crises of the community. Important studies on the roots of the Haskalah are Josef Eschelbacher, "Die Anfänge allgemeiner Bildung unter den deutschen Juden vor Mendelssohn," in *Beiträge zur Geschichte der deutschen Juden. Festschrift zum siebzigsten Geburtstage Martin Philippsons* (1916), 168–177; and the aforementioned work by Azriel Shohet, *Im hilufe tekufot. Reshit ha-haskalah be-yahadut germanyah* (1960).

For an exploration of bourgeois sociability in Germany, see esp. Jürgen Habermas, *The Structural Transformation of the Public Sphere* (1989); Richard van Dülmen, *The Society of the Enlightenment: The Rise of the Middle Class and Enlightenment Culture in Germany* (1992); Thomas Nipperdey, "Verein als soziale Struktur in Deutschland," in idem, *Gesellschaft, Kultur, Theorie. Gesammelte Aufsätze zur neueren Geschichte* (1976), 174–205; Hans Hümpel, *Die Entstehung des Vereinswesens in Berlin im 18. Jahrhundert. Bürgertum und Organisation* (1973). Extremely suggestive for an understanding of the changing concept of Bildung is the article by Rudolf Vierhaus, "Bildung," in O. Brunner et al., eds., *Geschichtliche Grundbegriffe. Historisches Lexikon zur politisch-sozialen Sprache in Deutschland*, vol. 1 (1972).

Shmuel Ettinger examines the changing image of the Jew in the Enlightenment in his "The Beginnings of the Change in Attitude of European Society Toward the Jews," *Scripta Hierosolymitana* 7(1961):193–219. The importance of Lessing's concept of education is explored by Michael Graetz, " 'Die Erziehung des

Menschengeschlechts' und jüdisches Selbstbewusstsein im 19. Jahrhundert," *Wolfenbütteler Studien zur Aufklärung* 4(1977):273–95. Barouh Mevorah, "Johann Caspar Lavaters Auseinandersetzungen mit Moses Mendelssohn über die Zukunft des Judentums," *Zwingliana* 14(1977):431–50, analyzes Lavater's millenarian motives.

The first Mendelssohn biography, Isaac Euchel, *Toldot rabenu he-ḥakham Moshe Ben Menaḥem* (1788), was written in Hebrew. An older, still useful work in German is Meyer Kayserling, *Moses Mendelssohn. Sein Leben und Wirken*, 2d ed. (1888). However, Alexander Altmann, *Moses Mendelssohn: A Biographical Study* (1973) is now considered to be the standard biography; it places the life of the founder of the Berlin Haskalah in the historical intellectual context of its time. Hermann M. Z. Meyer, *Moses Mendelssohn Bibliographie* (1965) is a serviceable bibliography. Also useful for an understanding of Mendelssohn's thought are Moshe Pelli, *Mosheh Mendelssohn be-ḥevle masoret* (Mendelssohn in the Bonds of Tradition, 1972); Norbert Hinske, ed., *Ich handle mit Vernunft: M. Mendelssohn und die europäische Aufklärung* (1981). The collection edited by Michael Albrecht, Eva J. Engel, and Norbert Hinske, *Moses Mendelssohn und die Kreise seiner Wirksamkeit* (1994), brings together recent research on Mendelssohn's life and impact. A highly detailed study on Mendelssohn's moral weekly is Meir Gilon, *Kohelet musar shel Mendelssohn* (1979). A basic work on the genesis of the Bible translation project is Perez Sandler, *Habi'ur shel Mosheh Mendelssohn ve-si'ato* (Mendelssohn's Commentary on the Pentateuch, 1940). On the history of its reception, see the important study by Steven M. Lowenstein, "The Readership of Mendelssohn's Bible Translation," HUCA 53(1982):179–213.

Israel Zinberg, *A History of Jewish Literature*, vol. 8 (1976), remains the most comprehensive and thorough literary-historical study of the Haskalah. For the religious aspects of the Haskalah, see the important contribution by Isaac Eisenstein-Barzilay, "The Treatment of the Jewish Religion in the Literature of the Berlin Haskalah," PAAJR 24(1955):39–68. Shmuel Werses, "Isaac Satanow and his 'The Sayings of Assaf' " (Hebr.), *Tarbiz* 33(1963):370–92; Moshe Pelli, *The Age of Haskalah: Studies in Hebrew Literature of the Enlightenment in Germany* (1979); Yehuda Friedländer, "The Beginnings of Satire. The 'Letters of Meshullam ben Uriya Ha-eshtemoi' by Isaac Euchel" (Hebr.), *Moznayim* 44(1977):107–18, provide important knowledge on the contributions of individual maskilim to the renaissance of Hebrew language and literature. On Euchel, see also Shmuel Feiner, "Isaac Euchel: 'Entrepreneur' of the Haskalah in Germany" (Hebr.), *Zion* 52(1987):427–69. Tsemaḥ Tsamriyon, *Ha-me'asef. Ketav ha-et ha-moderni ha-rishon be-ivrit* (*Ha-Me'asef*. The First Modern Periodical in Hebrew, 1988) provides a comprehensive study of the journal *Ha-Me'asef*. Siegfried Stein, "Die Zeitschrift 'Sulamith'," ZGJD 7(1937):193–226, furnishes a profile of the first enlightened Jewish periodical in the German language. Material on the autobiography of Jewish enlighteners can be found in Zwi Batscha, "Die Aufklärungsproblematik in Salomon Maimons Lebensgeschichte," in Grab, 91–115; Jacob Guttmann, "Lazarus Bendavid: Seine Stellung zum Judentum und seine literarische Wirksamkeit," MGWJ 61(1917):26–50, 176–211.

For Dohm and the changing relations between the state and the Jews, see Horst Möller, "Aufklärung, Judenemanzipation und Staat. Ursprung und Wirkung von Dohms Schrift 'Über die bürgerliche Verbesserung der Juden'," in Grab, 119–49. The economic effects of Dohm's demands within the Jewish community are treated by Miriam Bodian, "The Jewish Entrepreneurs in Berlin and the 'Improvement of the Civil Status of the Jews' in the 1780s and 1790s" (Hebr.), Zion 49(1984):159–84. Joseph Karniel, Die Toleranzpolitik Josephs II. (1986), and the already mentioned work by Ruth Kestenberg-Gladstein, Neuere Geschichte der Juden in den böhmischen Ländern (1969), describe the impact of the Josephinian policy of toleration in Austria and Bohemia.

Ludwig Lesser, Chronik der Gesellschaft der Freunde in Berlin (1842), deals with the sociability of the maskilim in the post-Mendelssohnian era; Deborah Hertz, Jewish High Society in Old Regime Berlin (1988), examines the sociability of the Jewish women in this period. On the conflict between the Haskalah and traditional Judaism, see Mordechai Breuer, "Das Bild der Aufklärung bei der deutsch-jüdischen Orthodoxie," in Gründer, 123–30; Moshe Samet, "M. Mendelssohn, N. H. Wessely, and the Rabbis of Their Time" (Hebr.), Meḥkarim be-toldot am yisrael ve-erets yisrael 2 (1970); Jacob Katz, "R. Raphael Kohen, the Antagonist of Moses Mendelssohn" (Hebr.), Tarbiz 56(1987):243–64.

The first systematic treatment of the change in Jewish education is Mordechai Eliav, Ha-ḥinukh ha-yehudi be-germanyah bi-me ha-haskalah ve-ha-emantsipatsyah (Jewish Education in Germany in the Age of Haskalah and the Emancipation, 1960). Ernst Simon, "Pedagogical Philanthropinism and Jewish Education" (Hebr.), in Mordecai Kaplan Jubilee Volume (Hebr. sec., 1953), 149–87, is a valuable contribution on non-Jewish influences shaping the thinking of the maskilim. Simḥa Assaf, ed., Mekorot le-toldot ha-ḥinukh be-yisrael (Sources on the History of Jewish Education, vol. 2, 1930), provides rich documentation within the framework of a comprehensive historical perspective. Lois C. Dubin, "Trieste and Berlin: The Italian Role in the Cultural Politics of the Haskalah," in Jacob Katz, ed., Toward Modernity: The European Jewish Model (1987), 189–224, deals with the special case of the northern Italian communities and their support for Wessely. Ludwig Horwitz, Geschichte der herzoglichen Franzschule in Dessau 1799–1849 (1894); Phoebus Philippson, Biographische Skizzen, 3 vols. (1864–1866); Inge Schlotzhauer, Das Philanthropin, 1804–1942. Die Schule der Israelitischen Gemeinde in Frankfurt am Main (1990) explore the schools and teachers that endeavored to translate the educational program of the maskilim into reality.

Chronology

1420–1421	Massacre and expulsion of the Jews from Vienna
1445	Israel Isserlein is appointed rabbi of Wiener Neustadt
1462	Ghetto established in Frankfurt am Main
1510	Beginning of the debate between Reuchlin and Pfefferkorn
1510	Burning of Jews in Berlin and their temporary expulsion from Brandenburg after the charge of host desecration
1512	Hebrew printing house established in Prague
1523	Martin Luther's early work, *Das Jhesus Christus eyn geborner Jude sey* (That Jesus Christ Was Born a Jew), calls for sympathetic treatment of the Jews
1530	Josel of Rosheim, "Commander of Jewry," opposes anti-Jewish allegations at the Augsburg Reichstag
1543	Luther's pamphlet *Von den Juden und iren Lügen* (Of the Jews and Their Falsehoods) demands measures against the Jews
1592	*Tsemaḥ David* by David Gans, the first Ashkenazi world chronicle
1592	Reception of Rabbi Judah ben Bezalel (Maharal) of Prague for an audience with Emperor Rudolf II
1602	*Ma'ase-Buch*, containing tales from the Talmud and Midrash in Western Yiddish
1603	Provincial assembly of community representatives in Frankfurt, the last of its kind in Germany
1614	Fettmilch riots and temporary expulsion of the Jews from Frankfurt am Main
1619	Thirty Portuguese Jews are among the founders of the Bank of Hamburg
1629	Rabbi Yomtov Lipmann Heller arrested in Vienna
1648	Pogroms in the Ukraine under cossack leader Bogdan Chmielnicki trigger increased Jewish migration to Germany
1666	High point of the Sabbatian movement, which gains widespread support in Germany
1670	Expulsion of the Jews from Vienna
1671	Frederick William I of Prussia permits fifty Jewish families to settle in the Mark Brandenburg
1678	First translation of the Bible into Yiddish by Yekutiel Blitz
1690	Glückel of Hameln begins writing her memoirs
1697	Behrend Lehmann, court Jew of August II (the Strong) of Saxony, becomes Polish agent in Brandenburg
1699	Yair Ḥayim Bacharach publishes the important collection of responsa *Ḥavat Yair*
1700	Eisenmenger's anti-Jewish *Entdecktes Judenthum* (Judaism Unmasked)
1711	Frankfurt Judengasse largely destroyed by fire
1714	First community synagogue dedicated in Berlin

1714	J. J. Schudt publishes his *Jüdische Merckwürdigkeiten* (Jewish Curiosities)
1738	Execution of Joseph Süss Oppenheimer
1744–1745	Temporary expulsion of the Jews from Bohemia and Moravia
1749	Lessing's comedy *Die Juden* presents a noble Jew
1750	The Revised General Code issued by Frederick II of Prussia stiffens Prussian legislation on the Jews by classifying them into six categories
1751	Dispute between Rabbis Jonathan Eybeschütz and Jacob Emden
1754	Ezekiel Landau appointed rabbi of Prague and Bohemia
1755	Mendelssohn's short-lived Hebrew journal *Kohelet Musar*
1767	Mendelssohn's most famous philosophical work *Phaedon*
1778	Jewish Free School founded in Berlin
1779	Lessing's *Nathan der Weise* (Nathan the Wise)
1780	Mendelssohn publishes the first part of his translation of the Pentateuch
1781	Dohm's *Über die bürgerliche Verbesserung der Juden* (On the Improvement of the Civil Status of the Jews)
1781	First edict of toleration issued by Joseph II for the Jews of Bohemia
1782	Naphtali Herz Wessely's *Divre shalom ve-emet* (Words of Peace and Truth)
1783	Mendelssohn's *Jerusalem,* a polemic in defense of Judaism
1784	Disciples of Mendelssohn found the Hebrew journal *Ha-Me'asef*
1787	Abrogation of the body tax in Prussia
1792	Solomon Maimon's *Lebensgeschichte* (Autobiography)
1792	Saul Ascher's *Leviathan*
1799	David Friedländer's *Sendschreiben* (Open Letter) to Provost Teller in Berlin

Sources of Illustrations

Bamberg, Diözesanmuseum (photo: Ingeborg Zimmer) 3
Bamberg, Historischer Verein 35
Berlin, Bildarchiv Preussischer Kulturbesitz 22, 26, 29, 30, 39, 40
Brussels, Bibliotheque Royale Albert 1er 12
Cincinnati, Hebrew Union College Library (photos: Druce Reilly) 6, 17, 18, 19, 20, 31, 33, 36, 41, 42, 44, 48, 49, 51
Darmstadt, Hessische Landes- und Hochschulbibliothek 21
Donaueschingen, Fürstlich Fürstenbergisches Archiv 28
Duisburg, Gidal-Bildarchiv im Steinheim-Institut 43
Frankfurt am Main, Historisches Museum 25
Frankfurt am Main, Jüdisches Musem 24, 37
Hamburg, Staats- und Universitätsbibliothek 15
Hanau, Verlag Werner Dausien 53
Heidelberg, Hochschule für jüdische Studien 34
Heidelberg, Universitätsbibliothek 7
Jerusalem, Jewish National and University Library 46
Jerusalem, privately owned by Paul Mendes-Flohr 47, 50
Koblenz, Landeshauptarchiv 11
Leipzig, Universitätsbibliothek 8
London, British Library 9, 16
Mainz, Stadtarchiv 2
Munich, Staatliche Graphische Sammlung 4
New York, Leo Baeck Institute (photos: Jim Strong) 38, 45, 52
Nuremberg, Germanisches Nationalmuseum 32
Oxford, Bodleian Library, Ms. Opp. 154 folio 12 verso 14

Tel Aviv, Beth Hatefutsoth 23
Vatican, Biblioteca Apostolica 1
Vienna, Historisches Museum der Stadt 27
Wittenberg (photo studio: Wilfried Kirsch) 13
Wolfenbüttel, Herzog August Bibliothek 5
Worms, Stadtarchiv 10

Index